Capital Dames

Capital Dames

The Civil War and the Women of Washington,
1848–1868

COKIE
ROBERTS

HARPER ● PERENNIAL

NEW YORK ● LONDON ● TORONTO ● SYDNEY ● NEW DELHI ● AUCKLAND

HARPER ⬤ PERENNIAL

FIRST HARPER PERENNIAL EDITION PUBLISHED 2016.

Designed by Renato Stanisic

The Library of Congress has catalogued the hardcover edition as follows:

Roberts, Cokie.
Capital dames: the Civil War and the women of Washington, 1848–1868 / Cokie Roberts.—First edition.
pages cm
Includes bibliographical references and index.
ISBN 978-0-06-200276-1 (hardcover : alk. paper)—ISBN 978-0-06-200277-8 (pbk. : alk. paper)—ISBN 978-0-06-219928-7 (ebook) 1. United States—History—Civil War, 1861–1865—Women. 2. Washington (D.C.)—History—Civil War, 1861–1865. 3. United States—History—Civil War, 1861–1865—Biography. 4. Women—Washington (D.C.)—Biography. 5. Politicians' spouses—Washington (D.C.)—Biography. 6. Women—Political activity—United States—History—19th century. 7. United States—History—1815–1861—Biography. 8. Reconstruction (U.S. history, 1865–1877)—Biography. 9. Women—United States—History—19th century.
I. Title. II. Title: Civil War and the women of Washington, 1848–1868.
E628.R629 2015
793.7082—dc23   2015001049

18 19 20   OV/RRD   10 9 8 7 6 5 4 3 2

Because I write about women, I have dedicated
my books to them. But I realize that I wouldn't have been able to
write these books without the men in my life having taken me
seriously first as a girl and then as a woman. So it is those men,
three of whom we lost last year, I thank with this book.

My father, Hale Boggs.

My brother, Tom Boggs.

My brother-in-law Marc Roberts.

My brother-in-law Paul Sigmund.

And, most especially, my husband, Steven Roberts.

Woman was at least fifty years in advance of the normal position which continued peace . . . would have assigned her.

—CLARA BARTON, MEMORIAL DAY ADDRESS, MAY 30, 1888

The war had torn the whole social fabric like an earthquake. . . . Women of education and the finest intellectual gifts are to be found in every department.

—MARY CLEMMER AMES, *TEN YEARS IN WASHINGTON*, 1873

Contents

Capital Dames

A northeast view of the Capitol still under construction, taken in 1863.

Introduction

We all recognize that image of Rosie the Riveter, the symbol of American women who went to work in defense industries during World War II, her head wrapped in a red bandana, her fist thrust upward displaying an impressive bicep with the proud motto: "We can do it!" And do it they did—18 million women workers, comprising one-third of the U.S. labor force, took on all kinds of jobs they had never done before, not just in the munitions and aircraft factories but as shipyard and railroad workers, taxi drivers, newspaper reporters, farmers, scientific researchers, and "government girls" who poured into Washington to staff the federal agencies. Women found they could do the work, they liked it, and they wanted to keep working, according to a survey taken by the Women's Bureau of the Labor Department as the war ended. And more than sixty thousand women took advantage of the GI Bill to enroll in college.

In short, World War II forever changed the place of women in American society—even though many went back to their kitchens after the war, the march was on to where we are today, with females making up more than half of our college graduates and almost half of the labor force. If you look at a chart of mothers in the workforce you see a straight progression from the war years on, with only about 14 percent in paid jobs in 1940, compared to almost 70 percent in 2013. The war also spurred women to push for greater equality. The Equal Pay Act, though not passed until 1963, was first introduced in 1945, after the Women's Bureau had lobbied for it. The women's war effort also shamed the Democratic Party into including the ill-fated Equal Rights Amendment in their platform in 1944, four years after the Republican Party had endorsed it.

OVER THE YEARS I've written a good deal about women's roles in the post–World War II period. And in researching books about the Revolutionary War era, I learned that women were in the thick of those battles, too—key actors in the creation of the country. So as the commemoration of the sesquicentennial of the Civil War began in 2011, I started wondering whether that horrific conflict had had a similar impact on American women's lives. To get a handle on that question, I decided to concentrate on the world I know best: the political world of Washington, D.C. I wanted to know not only how the war affected the city that sat as a bull's-eye between battling armies, but also what it meant for the women of Washington. And I learned that the answer was, as I suspected, dramatic. The sleepy little prewar Capital City went from being a social center for self-described belles to a place where purposeful women assembled to effect change. And it was not just the city that was transformed; it was also the women themselves. The antebellum belles spent their days calling on Cabinet and congressional wives or listening to debates in the Capitol galleries, and their nights at dinners and dances. Deeply political, they promoted their husbands' and fathers' careers and competed with each other for preeminent position in the Capital City's close-knit social circles. "Everyone here is well read and well informed," one of the leading belles' mothers wrote to her husband on a visit to Washington in 1854. Varina Davis was expecting a new baby and her mother was charmed by the city where her daughter lived: "Talent makes the aristocracy *here*—money has its admirers too—but talent outranks it." Women of talent could shine in the social gatherings that were dominated by southerners who seemed to have been in Washington forever. Even many of the congressional newcomers and their wives knew each other because their fathers had been there before them. And some of the women had been schoolmates at the Visitation Convent in Georgetown, which educated girls of all faiths and from all regions.

Then secession forced the southern women to depart, and their friends in the city they left behind were soon grappling with questions of safety and sanitation as the capital was transformed first into a huge army camp bursting with frisky fresh soldiers, and then a massive hospital reeking with wounded young warriors. Women engaged in all kinds of activities—nurses, supply organizers, relief workers, pamphleteers all aided the cause and female journalists covered it. Dorothea Dix and Clara Barton became powerful forces helping the soldiers; Anna Ella Carroll provided the propaganda. And the Civil War boasted its own rendition of Rosie the Riveter, women who did the dangerous work of making munitions at arsenals, many losing their lives in awful accidents. An earlier version of the government girls also were called to the Federal City, women who worked at the Treasury Department taking the place of men who had joined the army just as the agency added the enormous job of printing greenbacks to pay for the war. The Washington Navy Yard broke with tradition as well and hired women to sew canvas bags for gunpowder.

AS ENSLAVED PEOPLE sought refuge behind Union lines and other slaves made their way north, Washington beckoned as the Promised Land for tens of thousands of the so-called contrabands. After emancipation was declared in Washington in 1862 and the numbers of newcomers swelled, African-American women like Elizabeth Keckley joined with their white counterparts to found societies aimed at improving conditions in camps crowded with these displaced persons. And, struggling to establish schools and orphanages to handle the children, many women concluded that changes in public policy were needed in order for any real progress to occur, so they stepped up their lobbying and activism, with suffragists coming to the Capitol to press their case.

The city of Washington would never be the same. The population almost doubled as a result of the war, and the size of the federal government exploded. When I was a little girl the National Mall was marred by ugly "temporary buildings" that were hastily erected during the two world wars and marked the rapid growth of government over the previous few decades. The Civil War had the same impact. The federal budget, which had been $78 million in 1860, grew to almost $377 million in 1867, after spending for the war had ended. Measures spurring on industrial and agricultural production plus new initiatives like the Homestead Act and the creation of land grant colleges required new federal agencies and an influx of bureaucrats to run them. No longer a small southern town where everyone important knew everyone else, Washington bustled with the energy of parvenus who paraded through the halls of the Capitol and rose in the ranks of Congress.

————————

AND WHAT OF the women of Washington who called themselves belles? "The gay and thoughtless belle, the accomplished and beautiful leader of society, awoke at once to a new life," judged a book published soon after the war ended, boldly declaring that the conflict provided "a sphere of life and action, of which, a month before, she would have considered herself incapable." Some of the departed southerners experienced horrible deprivation and danger at worst, displacement and distress at best. The Union loyalists endured most of the war in Washington, evacuating to places farther north from time to time as the enemy approached. Their deep engagement in politics never waned, and they shared their views with friends on the other side. Then the war ended, and they got together again. But instead of vying with each other in the balconies of the Capitol or at balls in the embassies and grand homes, they stood together on suffrage platforms, toiled together to form social service organizations, and wrote books and articles that displayed their literary talents and in some cases allowed them to support themselves. One self-supporting journalist, Varina Davis, whose husband had been president of the Confederacy, later in life became fast friends with Julia Grant, whose husband had commanded the Union army. The women were able to put the bitterness of battle behind them when the men of the South were still draping themselves in the Confederate flag and mourning the "lost cause."

Varina Howell Davis is one of the women I follow in this book, along with her Confederate colleagues Virginia Tunstall Clay and Sara Rice Pryor. All three held places of prominence in Washington before the war and all three wrote extensively about their experiences. And they were friends with women who ended up on the Union side, like Elizabeth Blair Lee, whose letters show her political influence. I track her in these pages as well, along with the indomitable Jessie Benton Frémont and the elusive Adele Cutts Douglas, elusive because all of the others write about her but her own thoughts through letters are hard to find. That's not true of another northern sympathizer, Louisa Rodgers Meigs, who draws vivid pictures of the maneuverings in the Capital City.

Happily for us, those letters survive, many of them never before published. When you add the women's published writings, plus newspaper articles and government records, and a couple of revealing diaries, they allow us to learn the stories of these sometimes fierce, sometimes funny, and almost always formidable women. Here, then, they are.

CHAPTER 1

*Dolley Payne Todd Madison, wife of President James Madison,
and the foremost force in Washington for decades.*

Meet the Women of Washington

1848–1856

Church bells chimed their wake-up call for the Capital City just at first light. From the Navy Yard and the Arsenal, sunrise salutes signaled a historic day ahead for tens of thousands of expectant tourists "not only from the immediate vicinity and adjacent cities, but from opposite and distant parts of the Union." They had crowded into town on special trains ordered up for the momentous occasion, the *National Intelligencer* excitedly reported, and bright sunlight greeted them after a day of drenching rain. It was July 4, 1848, and the gawkers just might get a glimpse not only of President James Knox Polk and other high-ranking officials, but of those two great relics of the founding age—Elizabeth Hamilton and Dolley Madison. The wives of America's first fierce partisans would come together in seats of

honor to preside over the laying of the cornerstone of a monument to
the man their husbands both served: George Washington.

Getting to this day was no easy matter. Ever since Washington's
death almost half a century earlier there had been proposals in Congress to erect a fitting shrine to the Father of the Country. In fact,
even earlier than that, back in 1783, before the Constitution was written
creating the presidency, before a capital had been chosen, Congress resolved to honor General Washington with a statue "at the place where
the residence of Congress shall be established." But so far all attempts
at redeeming that pledge had failed—the organizers could never raise
enough money or interest. This time was going to be different. Public
solicitations plus the formation of an "organization of ladies to aid in
collecting funds," headed by Mrs. James Madison, Mrs. John Quincy
Adams, and Mrs. Alexander Hamilton, had collected about $87,000 and
created enough momentum to choose a site for a marble cornerstone
"weighing twenty-four thousand five hundred pounds"! The Speaker
of the House delivered the oration and alluded to the grandes dames
Hamilton and Madison "touchingly and eloquently."

The distinguished dowagers had been present at the creation
of the country. Seeing them there and hearing tributes to the foremost Founding Father conjured up for the crowd happier days, an
era when the United States shared a common cause—an independent
America—a useful reminder at a time when the nation was threatening to break apart over the increasingly contentious issue of slavery.
The recent military victory over Mexico, with its vast new territory
added to the country, led to an upset in the balance between slave
states and free, and raised the specter of the South's "peculiar institution" spreading as far as California and the Pacific. But on this Independence Day, the *Intelligencer* opined, the parades and pyrotechnics
showed that "in these already dubious days of the republic," a spirit

remained that could again be raised "into national strength and unity." From the beginning, that unity had been challenged by regionalism and partisanship. But for almost fifty years, ever since a sorry little village on the Potomac River had been established as the nation's capital, one person—Dolley Madison—could be counted on year in and year out to bring the factions together to put aside, at least temporarily, the rancor. The July 4 ceremony marked a rare public appearance for the ninety-year-old Eliza Hamilton, but not so the eighty-year-old Dolley Madison. She had stayed on the public stage as a figure of enormous influence throughout the decades. But this event would be one of the last public acts of the former first lady who had done so much to calm quarreling politicians. It would have been hard to imagine on that day in 1848 that Dolley Madison would be dead in a little more than a year and that the laying of the cornerstone of the Washington Monument would mark the last truly unified moment for the country.

In 1801 the young and beautiful Mrs. Madison had blown into the muddy, miserable town newly designated as the seat of government as the effervescent wife of the secretary of state. She played hostess to hundreds, maybe thousands, through James Madison's eight years in the Jefferson administration and then the eight years of his own presidency. Already liked by all (Henry Clay once gushed, "Everybody loves Mrs. Madison"), the first lady rose to the level of national heroine during the War of 1812 when she refused to leave the White House as the British approached; she insisted on "waiting until the large picture of Gen. Washington is secured" before fleeing the invasion. With her return to the burned-out ruins a few days later she took up the cause of securing Washington's place as the Capital City despite its near destruction. "Queen Dolley," as she was universally called, left office to paeans of praise: "Like a summer's sun she rose in our political horizon, gloriously, and she sunk, benignly," proclaimed a newspaper of the opposition party, adding that she had turned Thomas Jefferson's inaugural pronouncement that "we are all federalists, we are all republicans" from a "liberal sentiment to a practice."

For twenty years she chafed in retirement with her husband on his family estate in Virginia, where she constantly pestered friends and family for news of her city before she regally returned as a widow to dominate the social scene for the rest of her life. As long as Dolley Madison was alive, everyone knew who ruled Washington. And in recognition of her role, she accumulated extraordinary honors: a seat of her own in the House of Representatives, the privilege of sending the first personal telegraph, the presentation of a specially cast silver medal in memory of the War of 1812. Heads of state called on her to pay her homage. And her funeral shut down the city. "The President of the United States, the Cabinet Officers, gentlemen of the Army and Navy, the Mayor and City Councils, and many distinguished citizens and strangers" jammed into St. John's Church across the street from her house on Lafayette Square on July 16, 1849. After hearing "an eloquent and just eulogy on the character of the deceased," the funeral procession, "a very large and imposing one," trekked more than four miles in the summer heat to the Congressional Cemetery, where the body of the most famous woman in the land would stay until it could be moved to Montpelier, the Madison estate in Virginia.

IN THE COURSE of her reign, Dolley's city had undergone a steady transformation. In its infancy, when asked what he thought of the place, an ambassador replied that it "would be a city when our grandchildren were grown." But when English author Fanny Trollope, who had little good to say about America, visited in 1830 she was surprised to find herself "delighted with the whole aspect of Washington." The

Capitol building, so badly damaged by British fire sixteen years before, greatly impressed her with its "beauty and majesty." When Dolley had first come to town only a few shops huddled around the congressional boardinghouses on Capitol Hill; thirty years later, Pennsylvania Avenue, the still-famous thoroughfare between the Capitol and the White House, had become "a street of most magnificent width, planted on each side with trees, and ornamented by many splendid shops." Fanny found the White House a "handsome mansion," deemed the town hall "very noble," and called the Patent Office "a curious record of the fertility of the mind of man." All in all, the place that had served as the object of ridicule to foreigners and locals alike reminded Mrs. Trollope of Europe's "fashionable watering places." And that praise came even before work began on the Smithsonian Institution in 1847, causing a newspaper correspondent to conclude, "public opinion has decided that the national metropolis shall be distinguished for cultivation of the mind." (On his trip to the capital several years after Mrs. Trollope, Charles Dickens had far less kind things to say, declaring the city "the head-quarters of tobacco-tinctured saliva.")

As the city grew more sophisticated it attracted more people—the population swelled from a village of 8,000 in 1800 to a metropolis of 52,000 by 1850. Lawmakers started bringing their families to the capital for the winter legislative sessions and the size of the Congress itself increased as a result of gains from the Mexican War. But that very growth created a challenge: as each state joined the Union, battles raged in the city and the country about whether those states would be "slave" or "free." Within sight of the Capitol, where the endless debates droned on, traders crammed human chattel into filthy "slave pens" and dealers marched their shackled merchandise from one market to another in long lines called "slave-coffles." The shocking sight gave urgency to the arguments in Congress, even as the city relied on slave labor. From its inception Washington depended on enslaved workers to help build government offices and help serve government officials. By midcentury Washington's slave population stood at about 3,000 while the number of free blacks grew from fewer than 1,000 in 1800 to more than 10,000.

Through all of this growth and change, Dolley Madison had seemed the one constant. But now she was dead. Now what? The woman who had always been able to bring warring factions together, the person whom presidents as well as their wives sought out for council and advice, the undisputed foremost figure of the federal city was gone. It didn't take long for the women of Washington to begin vying to take her place.

———————

THE COMPETITION PLAYED out in the context of the political conflict consuming the capital. These women were the wives, daughters (often both), and sisters of politicians and just as caught up in the campaigns and concerns of the country as the men were. "Their interest was intense" when they crowded the Capitol "from the gallery to the floor; outside of the railing was a parterre of brilliant palpitating color, a solid phalanx of ladies," remembered one who was there for the debate over the Compromise of 1850. "The rosy faces and waving plumes of ladies made points of color against the senators' black garments" when, in an attempt to stave off the disaster of disunion, Congress patched together a series of bills in one more effort to keep peace between the forces for and against slavery.

The possession of people as property had threatened to tear America apart from the very beginning. A paragraph in the Declaration of Independence condemning the slave trade, ironically written by slave owner Thomas Jefferson, produced the most contentious argument in the Continental Congress as it was drafting the decisive document. To reach consensus, the paragraph was dropped. Then, in the Constitutional Convention, the slavery question again looked as though it would sabotage the entire exercise. Only after hard-fought compromise that counted slaves as three-fifths of a person and authorized Congress to outlaw the slave trade after 1807 could the majority of delegates agree to sign the Constitution. However, after the Louisiana Purchase in 1803, as the vast territory added to the country sorted itself into states, the issue of slavery challenged the ability of the Congress to govern, as members failed to agree on whether new territories would enter the union as slave states or free. That time it was the Missouri Compromise of 1820 that postponed the inevitable battle by admitting Missouri as a slave state, Maine as a free state, and outlawing slavery above latitude 36° 30' in the recently purchased lands. But now yet more land had been added to the country by conquest in the Mexican War and some in Congress were desperately trying again to cut a deal that would appease both the pro- and anti-slavery factions. They temporarily succeeded by passing the Compromise of 1850.

The legislation aimed at appealing to abolitionists by admitting California as a free state and outlawing the slave trade in Washington—so the horrific coffles would no longer offend congressional sensibilities—while also soothing slavery advocates by passing a new Fugitive Slave Act that required officials and citizens even in free states to capture runaway slaves and return them to their owners. The law enraged northern "Free-Soilers" and by signing it President Millard Fillmore lost the support of the antislavery wing of his Whig Party. (Fillmore had become president after Zachary Taylor, elected in 1848, attended a blisteringly hot July 4 celebration at the Washington Monument construction site in 1850 and died five days later.) In the election year of 1852, Harriet Beecher Stowe's phenomenal bestseller, *Uncle Tom's Cabin*—it sold more than 300,000 copies in one year—added abolitionist converts, further splitting the Whigs and making it possible for Democratic candidate Franklin Pierce to win a landslide Electoral College victory.

The election did nothing, however, to diminish the jockeying for first place among the women of Washington. Unlike them, Pierce's wife, Jane, hated politics—something she had determined twenty years earlier when her husband served in Congress. Still, she dutifully prepared to go to Washington as first lady when her only remaining child, twelve-year-old Benjamin, was killed in a train accident. She never really recovered. In later years Jane Pierce's contemporaries remembered how she cast a pall over the presidency: "Her woe-begon face with its sunken dark eyes, and skin like yellowed ivory banished all animation in others," lamented one. Another judged: "The Executive Mansion, shrouded in gloom, could never become a social center." With no active first lady dominating society, it was open season among the women of Washington, constantly competing for first place. "In the fifties American hospitality acquired a reputation," explained one of the competitors years later, "and that of the capital was synonymous with an unceasing, an augmenting round of dinners and dances, receptions and balls. A hundred hostesses renowned for their beauty and wit and vivacity vied with each other in evolving novel social relaxations."

And they used their "social relaxations" to promote their own positions along with the men in their lives. "During the four years that Franklin Pierce presided over the nation so many beautiful women came prominently before the public at the capital that his was called the 'beauty administration,'" declared nineteenth-century social historian Virginia Peacock. But the political women in the capital as Pierce's presidency began in 1853 were not just beautiful, though they did describe themselves as "belles." These women who sparred in society in the years leading up to the Civil War turned out to be tough and tenacious. They were a remarkable group whose stories unfolded in vastly different ways during and after the war.

JESSE BENTON FRÉMONT grew up with a father in the U.S. Senate and then her husband served there as well, a husband she was ready to help push to the presidency. She and her good friend Elizabeth Blair Lee had achieved close to native status, since they were brought to Washington as children. Living directly across the street from the White House, Lizzie worked with her father, Francis Preston Blair, a political boss and newspaperman, to foster the careers of her husband and brothers. She formed a close friendship with Varina Davis, described by one of her contemporaries as "the most brilliant woman of her time." The Mississippi belle had been popular in the city a few years before as a Senate spouse; she now returned to the fray as a lady of the Cabinet. New to town, Virginia Clay, the wife of an Alabama senator, and Sara Pryor, whose husband had been recruited to the capital to help edit a Democratic newspaper, quickly joined the competition. And then there was the teenager with no social standing who still managed to achieve chief belle status: Adele Cutts, marveled Virginia Peacock, "attained while yet a very young woman a pre-eminence by reason of her beauty, the distinction of her bearing, and a genuine loveliness of character."

Without either a powerful husband or father, Adele achieved her place through her own "queenly apparition" and the clout of her female relatives. Her great-aunt on her father's side was Dolley Madison, who had groomed "Addie" for prominence, and her mother's sister, Rose Greenhow, was famous—eventually infamous—for the political salon she presided over. But the women of Washington truly admired Adele for herself. Sara Pryor described her as "beautiful as a pearl, sunny-tempered, unselfish, warm-hearted, unaffected, sincere." Jessie Frémont compared her to Dolley and found Adele equal "in beauty and sweetness of nature, while every charm that polished training and associations can give, she has gathered." And "Addie Cutts," wrote her friend Virginia Clay, "was the admired of all foreigners" because she was a gifted linguist adding, "the effect she had on strangers was invariably one of instant adoration."

Everyone agreed that Adele was a great beauty, which was puzzling to her friend Sara Pryor: "I said to her once: 'You know you are not really handsomer than the rest of us! Why do people say so?' 'Because I never trick myself out in diamonds, or have more than one color in a gown. An artist told me once that all those things spoil a picture,'" came the reply. Don't think for a minute that these women weren't thinking about their appearance while they were plotting their political moves, and they all remembered what they were wearing decades later! When Sara looked back on those years, she marveled: "The belle in the fifties lived in an expansive time." Houses weren't crammed with furniture, streets weren't crowded with people. "Ladies wore enormous hoops, and because their heads looked like small handles to huge bells, they widened the coiffure into broad bandeaux and braids, loaded it with garlands of flowers, and enlarged it by means of a wide head-dress of tulle, lace, and feathers, or crowned it with a coal-scuttle bonnet tied under the chin with wide ribbons. In this guise they sailed fearlessly about." They sailed to the Senate and House chambers to listen to debates, and clustered together to make the dutiful calls on the wives of other officials; they also comforted each other on the inevitable losses of their time. It was at a boardinghouse at Thirteenth and G Streets that Virginia Clay sadly stated, "I bore and buried my only child." Varina Davis too mourned her toddler who "after several weeks of pain and steady decline, died at twenty three months old," and though she found the outpouring of sympathy "gratifying," she missed "sorely the opportunity to mourn in secret."

The Washington population ebbed and flowed with the congressional seasons—as the itinerant representatives flooded into the Capital in December, filling hotels and boardinghouses, and usually left at the end of March, beating a retreat before the oppressive heat of the Washington summer. Though more of the men started bringing their wives and children along in the 1840s, most did not, giving the city a certain masculine aspect and creating great demand for the women who did come to town. And the politicians' wives were expected to perform their own rituals—chief among them the custom of "calling," following a strict protocol of who would visit and who would receive visitors. As a Cabinet wife, Varina Davis felt herself besieged. "Every day I have about 30 calls, and the only way to do is to get in a carriage and ride up and down to avoid them," she griped to her mother. "One week I give a dinner, and a party the next week, and every Tuesday morning a reception, to which about sixty people call, sometimes more, and I must stand until half past four, from 12 in the morning." Though sectionalism seethed in the Capitol and "feeling ran high in the Senate and the House, the surface of social life was smiling and peaceful," according to Virginia Clay; "courtesies were exchanged between the wives of some of the Northern and Southern Senators, and formal calls were paid on Cabinet days, as etiquette demanded, upon ladies of the Cabinet circle." Of course many other women beyond the "belles" who dominated the political parlors found occupation in the Capital City. Then as now, the work of the government attracted purposeful women. Some, like Elizabeth Blair Lee, lived in both worlds. She socialized with people like Varina Davis and

Adele Cutts but she also put in long hours at the Washington City Orphan Asylum, a social service agency first started by Dolley Madison and other Federal City women after the British invasion in 1814. Some women lived just on the periphery of the social whirl. Louisa Rodgers Meigs, a native Washingtonian, was one of those. Her father had been a renowned naval commodore and her husband, Montgomery, was working with Jefferson Davis on the expansion of the Capitol building and the construction of the aqueduct. Though Louisa was acquainted with the prominent women of the city—she once went to the opera with Varina Davis—since her husband wasn't a member of congress or the cabinet, she didn't shine in their social gatherings.

———————

GOVERNMENT JOBS BECKONED women to Washington just as they do now. Clara Barton, a successful teacher who had had trouble landing a position because she was a woman, found work in the Patent Office, where she briefly made the same salary as her male colleagues. The capital also inevitably lured women eager to influence the government, chief among them Dorothea Dix, who spent years lobbying on behalf of ill and impoverished Americans, and Anna Ella Carroll, who published propaganda for her chosen causes and candidates.

When Dorothea Dix arrived in Washington in 1848, she was already famous for her work in both northern and southern states, successfully prodding them to establish hospitals for the mentally ill. But she had a much grander scheme planned for the national legislature. Dix proposed nothing less than that the government put aside five million acres of federal land for the "poor and the helpless." She described the conditions of the poverty-stricken and mentally disabled people she had seen everywhere she worked, concluding, "I ask for the people that which is already the property of the people." Her stature was such that the members of Congress actually allocated an alcove in the Capitol Library as office space for the indomitable advocate and there she daily met with the lawmakers, bent on converting them to the justness of her cause.

When they failed to pass her bill the first time it was introduced, she upped the ante. The following session she asked for 12,250,000 acres of land and supported her demand with constituent letters, newspaper editorials, and church sermons. And she succeeded—in the U.S. Senate, but the House refused to consider what she called "my bill." Undeterred, back she came to the next Congress, this time throwing in an additional request for $100,000 for a hospital in Washington for mentally ill military men and District residents. Dix not only lobbied for the hospital; she persuaded a large landowner to sell her the property for it and there St. Elizabeth's still stands, still serving the mentally ill, a visible monument to Miss Dix's persistence. And she finally convinced both houses of Congress to pass her land bill as well. But after all that time and all that effort, President Pierce vetoed the measure, insisting that the care of the poor should be the responsibility of the states, not the federal government. She couldn't muster the votes to override the veto, so a much-discouraged Dorothea Dix packed up the desk in the Capitol and left town. But she would be back again before long—this time as a formidable force.

Always seeking to be a formidable force, Anna Ella Carroll did most of her lobbying and politicking through her writing. The daughter of a former Maryland governor, the scion of a long-established Maryland family fallen on hard times, Carroll cultivated friendships with politicians, using her access to badger them for jobs for friends and family and to promote herself as a political advisor. When Fillmore was president, she wrote to him touting her political knowledge, arguing that though "it may look unique for an 'American lady' to be so heartily embarked in the interest of the political condition of the country," her education and social position gave her a firm understanding of "our political system." And her sex didn't prevent her from attending the Whig Party convention in Baltimore in 1852 to back Fillmore's reelection. When her candidate lost the nomination, Anna turned her attention to the American Party—derided by their opponents as Know-Nothings—whose political clout was on the rise. Though descended from an iconic Catholic family, Anna Carroll emerged as one of the greatest propagandists supporting the anti-Catholic Know-Nothings, whose virulent anti-immigrant stance gained followers at the same time that the established political parties, the Whigs and the Democrats, fractured over the issue of slavery.

ONE CAUSE THAT fell by the wayside with the current crop of political women: the Washington Monument. After the glorious day laying its cornerstone, the actual erection of the obelisk proved problematic. Funds for the project trickled in as the Washington Monument Society begged schoolchildren for "the monthly contribution of even one cent." Similar appeals went to the Masons, Odd Fellows, Sons of Temperance, and military organizations. But the fund-raisers produced little by way of cash, so to drum up interest, solicitors asked each state to send a stone to line the interior of the monument, and then they approached foreign countries as well. And so arrived "a block of marble sent hither from Rome, a tribute to the memory of Washington by the Pontiff, and intended to become a part of the edifice now erecting to signalize his name and glory." Obligingly, Pope Pius IX, the archvillain to the anti-Catholic Know-Nothings, had sent a piece to the stone-seeking Americans from the ruins of the Temple of Concord, built in ancient times to promote harmony. Anything but harmony followed. In March 1854, in the middle of the night, a small band stole onto the building site, surrounded the night watchman, wrapped ropes around the block, maneuvered it into a cart, and pitched it into the Potomac River. The Know-Nothings had struck a blow against Catholicism but a bigger blow to the future of the monument. Then the nativist party staged a coup at the Washington Monument Society, placing a know-nothing sympathizer in every office. Catholics refused to have anything more to do with the project and money dried up. A pathetic sight at a mere 153 feet, no one seemed to care about the shrine to the Father of the Country whose children wanted less and less to have anything to do with each other.

Despite the glow provided by new gas lamps installed on the streets in 1853, times were tough in Washington, as Louisa Meigs described them in a letter to her sister: "Provisions of all kinds are very high at this time—alarmingly so. . . . I fear the poor will suffer very much. Vegetables are scarce and not very good . . . the pumps are often dry." The country was experiencing an economic downturn—just the kind of situation calculated to create a political party like the Know-Nothings, looking for someone to blame for hard times and finding scapegoats in the millions of mostly Catholic Irish and German immigrants inundating the country. And while the new political party vented its venom on immigrants, the old ones ratcheted up their quarrels over slavery and whether the newly organized territories of Kansas and Nebraska would come into the Union as slave states or free.

Attempting to answer that question, Illinois U.S. Senator Stephen Douglas pushed through legislation that ironically had the effect of creating the Republican Party in 1854, a party that eventually ruined him politically. Douglas's doctrine of "popular sovereignty" allowed people in Kansas and Nebraska to decide on slavery for themselves, instead of the federal government making that determination. The

Kansas-Nebraska Act broke the previous covenant covering the spread of enslavement—the Missouri Compromise of 1820—and called into question whether the Compromise of 1850 could be abrogated as well. Bloody battles between proslavery settlers who rushed into Kansas and the abolitionists who followed them provoked political combat in the rest of the country. Those wars ended up destroying the Whig Party, with the Republicans rising to take in the northern Whigs opposed to slavery while most of the southern Whigs fled to the Democrats. The shaky stage was set for the presidential election of 1856.

LEFT: *Harriet Lane, niece of bachelor president James Buchanan, acted as his de facto First Lady during the difficult 1850s.* RIGHT: *Jessie Benton Frémont, once the most famous woman in America, was thought of as the real politician in her marriage to John C. Frémont.*

Jessie Runs for President but Harriet Takes the White House and Mary Jane Reports

1856–1858

Anna Carroll had been pestering Former President Millard Fillmore for months, audaciously advising him that with her help he could be the candidate of the Know-Nothings: "I can have very much to do with your nomination by that party." Having taken the high-minded name of the American Party, the nativists had scored significant victories in congressional and state legislative elections in 1854, emerging with real hope for the presidency. In February 1856 party stalwarts met in Philadelphia and did what Anna had been hoping for—nominated Millard Fillmore. Acting as the unofficial head of the media effort, she published propaganda pamphlets followed by something of a Know-Nothing bible, *The Great American Battle*, advertised as "the contest between Christianity and Political Romanism, with Portraits" and selling for $1.25. Writing under her own name, Miss Carroll produced more pamphlets and yet another book as she trumpeted to Fillmore, "For the first time in our *history* a woman has ventured openly and without disguise to espouse the cause of her Country." But for all of her public pronouncements about politics, Anna Carroll was not the most well-known woman campaigning in 1856. That honor went to Jessie Benton Frémont.

Jessie had grown up surrounded by politics. The daughter of Thomas Hart Benton, who served as senator from Missouri for three decades, the young girl spent much of her childhood at the home of her best friend, Elizabeth Blair, whose father, the publisher of the leading Democratic newspaper, occupied a choice position in Andrew Jackson's "kitchen" Cabinet. As children, both Lizzie Blair and Jessie Benton were great favorites of President Jackson, who gave them the run of the White House and even bestowed his beloved late wife Rachel's wedding ring on Lizzie. Both girls developed strong interests in politics as they grew up, with Lizzie Blair doing a good bit of her father's secretarial work and adding her own thoughts to his correspondence, and Jessie spending much of her time in the Capitol learning about public policy. Neither the Blairs nor the Bentons approved of their daughters' marriages, Lizzie to Samuel Phillips Lee, a navy man, and Jessie to John Charles Frémont, an army man and swashbuckling explorer. Nicknamed "the Pathfinder," Frémont was elected to the Senate from the new state of California in 1850, the same year that Thomas Benton was defeated after thirty years in office because of his opposition to slavery. The Blairs soon accepted

Phil Lee, who was off at sea most of the time, but though Benton for a time reconciled with the hot-tempered Frémont, in 1856 family friction ignited over politics.

The fact that President Pierce had signed the Kansas-Nebraska Act—and that he didn't take Blair and Benton into his inner circle—made him anathema to many Democrats like them who opposed the spread of slavery into the new territories. When the newly formed Republican Party made an impressive showing in the 1854 off-year election, Blair switched allegiances. Despite the fact that he was a slave owner and the Democrats derided the new party as "Black Republicans" for its stand on slavery, Blair became an enthusiastic convert and decided that the famous and handsome John C. Frémont would make the perfect presidential candidate. Benton disagreed about the choice of his somewhat unreliable son-in-law as Republican standard-bearer, causing his relationship to sour not only with his daughter but with his old friend Preston Blair as well. When Frémont established his Washington base at the Blair country house in Maryland, Lizzie Lee did her best to try to keep peace between the erstwhile allies but peace was hard to come by in the politics of 1856.

Politics consumed the capital as the Congress debated what would happen in Kansas and Nebraska. And the women of Washington spent a great deal of time in the galleries of the House and Senate following every legislative maneuver. In among their numbers, generally excluded from the official press gallery, were several female correspondents. Newspaper writing was considered respectable employment for women needing to support themselves; then as now Congress could be counted on for good copy. And it was not just the speeches on the floor but the scene among the spectators that filled the dispatches of women reporters like Mary Jane Windle:

"Groups of gentlemen might be seen clustered around ladies . . . while behind mosaic columns were others '*tête-à-tête*' in a quiet flirtation. Reader, there are secrets in the keeping of those cosy galleries, secrets which might incite the most flagging goose-quill to flowing." Miss Windle's quill flowed freely with a telling eye and taut humor as she wrote for newspapers and journals, mainly in Charleston, South Carolina. "The change produced in the tone of an ordinary man by the letters *Hon.* preceding his name is unmistakable," she chortled about members of Congress. "*Here* he is a *public man!* and everybody is his most obedient servant." The delightful dispatches must have provided welcome relief for her readers from the regular Washington fare, which was filled with foreboding about the crumbling consensus in Congress.

As pro- and anti-slavery settlers waged all-out war in Kansas, with murders and assassinations common occurrences, the rising death toll caused abolitionists like the fiery senator from Massachusetts, Charles Sumner, to proclaim that "Bleeding Kansas" demonstrated the evils wrought by the Kansas-Nebraska Act. With what Lizzie Lee described as "intense excitement in the city about Kansas matters," everyone knew Sumner was preparing a broadside on the subject. The following Monday would be a "big Senatorial day," Lizzie wrote to her husband on May 14, when Sumner would " 'draw the sword and throw away the scabbard,' to attack Butler." For two days Sumner railed against the 1854 law and its authors, Stephen Douglas and Andrew Butler. Famously, his diatribe wreaked the revenge of Butler's cousin Preston Brooks of South Carolina, a member of the House of Representatives who stormed into the Senate chamber a few days later and brutally beat Sumner with his gold-tipped cane. Lizzie and her father galloped into Washington from the family's country house when they heard the news about the attack in the Capitol and then they brought the bloodied and badly injured Sumner home to be nursed by the Blair women, and ironically, the family slaves. The beating turned each lawmaker into a hero in his own region—Brooks received dozens of canes from sympathetic southerners—but in Washington the South Carolina congressman fell into disfavor "after his historic assault on Mr. Sumner," according to fellow southerner Virginia Clay. Sumner's "martyrdom"—the rallying cry of "bleeding Sumner" joined with "Bleeding Kansas"—provided momentum for the new Republican Party when it met in Philadelphia in June to nominate its first presidential candidate.

Jessie Benton Frémont did not doubt that her husband would be chosen. The couple had moved to New York and their home off Fifth Avenue was "a meeting ground for conspirators," she joked that spring when she also found herself "quite the fashion." Jessie boasted to her friend Lizzie Lee, "5th Avenue asks itself, 'Have we a Presidentess among us'—and as I wear fine lace and purple I am in their eyes capable of filling the place." Though ill, Preston Blair, accompanied by Lizzie, traveled to the Musical Fund Hall in Philadelphia to push for Frémont's nomination. Since it was considered unseemly for the candidates to attend their political conventions, Jessie had begged Lizzie to come from Philadelphia to New York "to triumph with us I hope." After the popular "Pathfinder" won on the first official ballot, all of New York seemed ready to share in the triumph when a torchlight parade followed Frémont home from a rally and stood outside his house shouting, "let us see Jessie, let us see Jessie," guaranteeing that for the first time the candidate's wife would play a major role in a presidential campaign, not just behind the scenes but on the public stage.

IT'S EASY TO see why Jessie Frémont captured the public's fascination. The somewhat scandalous tale of the seventeen-year-old daughter of powerful Senator Benton defying his orders by running off with the exciting explorer fifteen years earlier was interesting enough, but Jessie's married life also provided adventuresome fodder. After the elopement, Benton eventually reconciled with his wayward daughter and helped Frémont land a job exploring the Rocky Mountains in 1842. When John returned to Washington just before the birth of their baby girl, Jessie worked with him crafting the report of his travels, giving it the flourishes of her sprightly style. Newspapers published excerpts, John's fame grew, and soon he was tapped for another western trip, this one taking him all the way to California and, with the 1845 publication of an account of that feat, written again with Jessie's help, genuine celebrity status. "As for your report, its popularity astonished even me, your most confirmed & oldest worshipper," Jessie rejoiced to John, who had once again headed west. The outbreak of the Mexican War found Frémont still in California, where he marched from settlement to settlement planting the American flag, making him a conquering hero in the eyes of his countrymen. He finally went home to his wife and baby after more than two years away, marked by some bruising bureaucratic battles resulting in a court-martial—an altercation with authorities that only increased Frémont's popularity. Then, in 1848, the wanderer decided to settle in California; Jessie would have to leave the home she loved and the father who depended on her and make her way to a distant place "cut loose from everything that had made my previous life."

John would go by land in the winter, Jessie by sea the following spring, but first she decided to travel as far as the frontier with her husband. Bringing along five-year-old Lily and her new baby boy, the family reached St. Louis in October, then sailed up the Missouri River to the frontier town of Westport, Missouri. Ten-week-old Benton Frémont died on the boat, leaving his mother disconsolate and depressed to say goodbye to John and sadly take her little girl back to Washington. Jessie feared she "was to be launched literally on an unknown sea, travel to an unknown country, everything absolutely new and strange about me, and undefined for the future."

She wasn't exaggerating about the unknown sea. It was to be an unbelievably difficult journey, down the Atlantic coast from New York, through the jungles of the Isthmus of Panama, then up the Pacific Coast to San Francisco. As Jessie was preparing for the ordeal, the big news broke: gold, tons and tons of gold, lay under the soil of California. Americans by the thousands looking to get rich quick abandoned their farms and shops, grabbed picks and shovels, and set out to seek their fortunes. Gold diggers crammed onto the ship Jessie boarded in the spring of 1849 with six-year-old Lily plus a brother-in-law as chaperone. After her father and sisters said their farewells and went ashore, there was barely another woman to be found. When they arrived in Panama several days later, the ship's captain tried to convince the intrepid young woman to turn back, "telling me that I had no idea of what I was to go through," but Jessie pressed on despite the loss of her male protector—her brother-in-law was too sick to keep going. She too came down with a terrible fever during her almost two months in Panama waiting for transport to San Francisco. (Ships kept losing their crews in California as sailors jumped overboard to join the gold rush.) Though Jessie, as a prominent personage, was well taken care of by the aunt of the Panamanian ambassador to the United States, she still found herself in odd circumstances—served a baked monkey for breakfast one day, the astounded guest declared that it looked like "a little child that had been burned to death." After she had spent almost two months stranded in this exotic outpost, the ship scheduled to carry Jessie Frémont to San Francisco arrived in the Panama City port.

Designed for cargo, not people, the *Panama* packed more than four hundred itching-for-gold passengers into every possible space as it pushed up the Pacific coast for almost three weeks. Finally, on June 4, 1849, two and a half months after leaving New York, Jessie and Lily sailed into San Francisco Bay and the primitive settlement on its shore. "There were then some three or four regularly built houses," as Jessie remembered it; "the rest were canvas and blanket tents." No one wanted to stop looking for gold long enough to build a house; and "the whole force of San Francisco society" numbered sixteen women. Jessie didn't last long in the damp air by the bay, and soon the family moved on to Monterey—"quite a town, with many good houses."

John Frémont had come to California as an explorer but, like everyone else, he had staked a claim on the land. The Spanish had given the huge tract he bought near Yosemite the charming name Las Mariposas, for the butterflies swarming the area. But Frémont found that his property contained something far heavier—gold. Lots of gold. So it was suddenly as people of wealth that the Frémonts greeted the men who assembled in Monterey for the state constitutional convention in September 1849. The issue confronting the gathering? The same as the one being debated on the other side of the continent: slavery. Emphatically insisting to amazed delegates that she would never "own or use a slave," as Jessie remembered it later, "my pretty rooms were the headquarters of the antislavery party, and myself the example of happiness and hospitality without servants." It was a story that would be embellished over the years as it served her husband's political purposes, and those political purposes became paramount a few months later when the new legislature elected John C. Frémont as the first U.S. senator from California. The couple would return to Washington in triumph.

Back in the thick of it, Jessie couldn't have been happier. She returned to her father's house a changed woman, "I had done so many things that I had never done before that a new sense of power had come to me." And she was pregnant again. But her happy stay soon ended because John had to get reelected. In order to stagger the terms of the new state's two senators, one would have to run again in the next election, and Frémont drew the short stick. So back across the country they trekked to find California even wilder than they had left it, filled with more gold seekers who had no romantic notions about the Pathfinder. A hopelessly deadlocked state legislature left John in limbo, so he decided to pursue his commercial interests, protesting that politics was "too costly an amusement in this country just now." Jessie would not be returning to the life she loved anytime soon. Still, she had a new baby boy named Charley and plenty of money, for a while. But Frémont proved a terrible businessman. After a series of missteps and embarrassments almost wiped him out, and a family sojourn in Europe failed to raise money for his enterprises, he went looking again for exploration jobs. With his connections in Washington, a job search there would be more likely to succeed. Home again with a new baby girl in 1853, Jessie quickly attracted the notice of prominent politicians. New York senator William Seward told his wife that Jessie "is a noble-spirited woman," and then added, "She is very outspoken." Mrs. Frémont was making her mark.

Her old friends the Blairs served as a second family—Lizzie and her husband were little Charley's godparents and when Jessie's five-month-old baby girl got sick and died, Lizzie was with her, offering comfort. Another baby, a boy, was born in 1855 and promptly named after Lizzie's father, Francis Preston Blair, and it was to Blair that Jessie turned asking for "advice and friendly counsel" when John was approached as a possible Republican candidate for president. Blair's enthusiastic response jump-started the bandwagon for John C. Frémont.

Once her husband won the nomination, Jessie, like so many candidates' wives after her, served as something of a character witness. When opponents unearthed the fact that her husband was the illegitimate child of a French father, Jessie rushed to Virginia to consult with John's mother's family so she could put her spin on the campaign biography. And she emphatically pronounced that her husband was an Episcopalian and all of her children had been christened in the Episcopal Church when the Know-Nothings spawned rumors that Frémont was a Catholic. She also burnished his antislavery credentials with the widely read novelist and ardent abolitionist Lydia Maria Child. Jessie repeated the story about rejecting slavery in California: "You are quite right in supposing the report true that I refused to buy a slave," Jessie informed the influential author. The tale was taken up, added to, and used repeatedly in pro-Frémont speeches and editorials. The thrust: Jessie Benton Frémont kept California from becoming a slave state.

Her political acumen also garnered kudos in newspapers that touted her support for the Republican Speaker of the House and her ability to explain "the Republican Platform as simple, perspicuous and right—'so plain and easily comprehended that a wayfaring man need not err therein.'" An Ohio newspaper swooned: "Beautiful, graceful, intellectual and enthusiastic, she will make more proselytes to the Rocky Mountain platform in fifteen minutes than five stump orators can win over in a month." Republicans glorifying Frémont's time exploring the Rockies nicknamed their platform as a reminder of those rugged days. He was a hero, she was a wonder. Jessie was so glorified in the Republican press that one Democratic newspaper rejoined, "Inasmuch as black Republicans are making desperate efforts to elect Fremont upon the strength of his wife's—Jessie Benton's—virtues, abilities, patriotism and popularity, we modestly suggest the following as an appropriate design for their ticket:

FOR PRESIDENT

john c. fremont, husband of

JESSIE BENTON

But snide articles did nothing to detract from Jessie's popularity. Women copied her hairstyle, wore her favorite color—violet—and named their babies Jessie Ann. Campaign ditties sang of her: *The choice made by Jessie is ours; / We want the brave man she did wed. / He crowned her with gay bridal flowers / And she is a crown to his head.* For a time she was by far the best-known woman in America.

———————

WHILE JESSIE BENTON Frémont campaigned passionately and publicly for her husband, her father, Thomas Hart Benton, was equally enthusiastic for Frémont's opponent. Benton had refused to join his friend Blair in switching to the Republicans, rejecting the upstarts as nothing more than a northern regional party. Democrats meeting at Smith & Nixon's Hall in Cincinnati in early June definitely attracted broader regional representation, but those diverse delegates had a great deal of difficulty uniting behind a candidate. The incumbent president, Franklin Pierce, had earned the enmity of the North by signing the Kansas-Nebraska Act, but he and the author of the act, Stephen Douglas, both got enough votes in roll call after roll call along with a third candidate, James Buchanan, to keep the convention deadlocked. After sixteen rounds, with defeat likely, Douglas pulled out, giving the nomination to Buchanan on the next ballot.

As secretary of state under President Polk, Buchanan assumed the role of an above-the-fray statesman. He had been lucky enough to be serving abroad as ambassador to Great Britain during the debates over the Kansas-Nebraska Act, so he was conveniently removed from the controversy. If northern Democrats thought the Pennsylvanian would be sympathetic to their opposition to slavery, the party platform endorsing the concept of popular sovereignty and explicitly supporting the Kansas-Nebraska Act quickly dispelled their hopes. But to Thomas Hart Benton, Buchanan represented "the safest chance for preserving the peace of the country." The campaign itself did little to promote peace. The bachelor Buchanan was a homosexual, one round of rumors had it; another whispered that he held his head in an odd way because he had tried to hang himself. But in the end "Old Buck" prevailed.

Benton proved correct in his view that the Republicans at the time represented a regional party. In what was basically a three-way race, Frémont won eleven states in the North, but Buchanan held on to four others plus the solid South. The Know-Nothing candidate Fillmore won only Anna Carroll's home state of Maryland, for which she took full credit, claiming: "my friends say I've been more than a Jessie Fremont to the Fillmore cause." James Buchanan would be the next president. Jessie Frémont admitted to her friend Elizabeth Blair Lee, "We are subsiding into former habits, not without some of the giddy feelings one has after having been a long while on ship board. Things hardly have their natural value and attraction after the engrossing excitement of the one idea we have had in our heads for so many months." Though she found it hard after the headiness of the campaign, for a time Jessie Frémont stepped off the public stage.

———————

THE ARRIVAL OF a new president no longer caused much excitement in Washington—Buchanan was the fourth in eight years—but a wedding soon after the election set the town abuzz. Adele Cutts met Stephen Douglas as he was campaigning for the Democratic nomination for president. Adele's parents' announcement that their not-quite-twenty-one-year-old daughter would marry a widower twice her age with two small boys caused quite a stir in the capital. As one newspaper reported, the engagement was "the absorbing theme of conversation in fashionable and political circles." And some of that conversation was definitely less than admiring of the match. Varina Davis, who couldn't stand Douglas, thought the Cutts family's impecunious position drove her friend's unfortunate decision. "The dirty speculator and party trickster, broken in health by drink, with his first wife's money, buys an elegant, well-bred woman because she is poor and her father is proud," Varina fumed to her parents, then added snarkily that a new water system would soon be coming to Washington, so "sparing his wife's olfactories Douglas may wash a little oftener. If he don't his acquaintance will build larger rooms with more perfect ventilation. However this wedding has put me out of patience."

Varina wasn't kidding about the water situation. As secretary of war, her husband had worked closely with Montgomery Meigs, the man building the aqueduct that would finally bring water into Washington homes, where "all the water for washing cooking and bathing has to be brought from the street pump," Meigs's own wife had complained. The election of Buchanan meant Davis would no longer serve in the Cabinet; instead he would retake his seat as senator from Mississippi. The family, consisting of a newborn baby boy, toddler daughter, and Varina's younger sister and brother, would move from their big house at the corner of Fourteenth and F Streets into a smaller place where they would not have to entertain on so grand a scale. Still recovering from puerperal fever that almost killed her after the birth of the baby, Varina groaned to her father wearily, "I have my large house to break up, a small one to fit up—four dinners, and a reception to give, and return my visits in the space of eighteen days."

Many political families took the much easier route of living in a "mess," as the groups in boardinghouses or hotels were called. Brown's Hotel on Pennsylvania Avenue served as a southern redoubt. "We keep Free-Soilers, Black Republicans and Bloomers on the other side of the street," Virginia Clay, wife of Senator Clement Claiborne Clay of Alabama, wrote to her father-in-law, a former senator himself. The southerners wanted nothing to do with the new political parties or with the women's rights advocates who were showing up in bloomers—ballooning pants—under their skirts as a protest against the unwieldy hoop, to them a symbol of women's oppression. In late 1856, Virginia joked, "Bloomers are most as plenty as blackberries." Though there to make a political statement about women's equality, at that point the bloomers were simply a humorous distraction from the increasingly tense politics of slavery. "Everything is excitement and confusion," Virginia exclaimed to her father-in-law on Christmas Night in 1856. "I expect any day to hear of bloodshed and death, and would not be surprised at any time to witness (repeated here) the Civil War of Kansas!"

For Virginia Clay, the disruption in the Capital City was most unwelcome. One historian has dubbed her the "chief social arbiter" of the time and asserted that the group of southern politicians gathered at Brown's Hotel was called the Clay mess not just because the Alabama senator held power in Congress but also "to give credit to the resolute, lively, accomplished, and clever wife." Of all the "brilliant and beautiful women" who adorned Washington society at the time, Sara Pryor wrote years later, "the wittiest and brightest of them all was Mrs. Clay, the wife of the Senator from Alabama. She was extremely clever, the soul of every company."

The closest company was in the boardinghouse itself and Virginia remembered her "mess mates" fondly when she described them decades later. If there was no big dinner to attend, the boarders all ate together, and they would sometimes all go out to a concert by Jenny Lind or enjoy the farce *Pochahantas*, with its made-for-the-audience lines:

What's all this noise? Be done! Be done!
D'you think you are in Washington?

On the day reserved every week for calling on the wives of Cabinet members, the ladies of the mess made the rounds as a group so they would only have to hire one carriage. "As my parlours were the only ones that boasted a pier-glass," Virginia reminisced, "it became a custom for the women composing our circle to come to my rooms before going out, in order to see how their dresses hung." It was all cozy and companionable among the women, who also went on outings together, like the one to the Naval Observatory when the superintendent showed them the stars and then announced that he had a bill before Congress, "'and if you ladies don't influence your husbands to vote for it, I intend *to publish the ages of each and every one of you to the whole of Washington!*'"

It was a joke but it was one that revealed the power the women held and didn't hesitate to use. Virginia Clay recounted a story of her intervention with the secretary of the Navy on behalf of a pregnant friend whose husband was deployed to Italy. The Cabinet officer agreed to Virginia's appeal to reunite the couple, and when the baby was born he was named after Clay, as a statement of gratitude to the senator's meddling wife.

Now that she too was married to a prominent personage, Adele Cutts Douglas received all sorts of appeals. Anna Cora Ritchie, then a famous actress and author, asked Adele to promote her pupil, a young actress named Avonia Jones, because "your influence, and the prestige of your patronage can do much to contribute to her success." (Avonia Jones went on to become a well-known actress.) Letters begging Adele to intercede with Douglas for jobs for their husbands came from distressed women like Margaret Hertford, who tried to play on their shared Catholicism, claiming that her daughter "offered prayers this day as Child of Sacred Heart that you may be the means of obtaining for her dear Father a Situation." Requests to introduce young visitors to Washington society and to patronize the author's products also arrived on Adele's doorstep, attesting to her perceived power. The beautiful young woman beloved by all was now a force to be courted.

With her husband's money, the new Mrs. Douglas turned the house on New Jersey Avenue into a showplace of hospitality and set the style for the rest of the city, where Adele "soon was regarded as the uncrowned queen of Capitol society," according to a Douglas biographer. The "social arbiter" Virginia Clay, who had always liked "Addie"

Cutts, thought that her friend's marriage allowed her to hold "a remarkable sway for years." But a "crowned queen" would be coming to town and Adele Douglas faced a problem as the Buchanan administration took office. The incoming president still smarted over those sixteen ballots at the Democratic convention before he was nominated, and he lost no love for the Douglas family. Though she had been a younger schoolmate at the Visitation Convent, Adele would not enjoy a friendship with the woman who would serve as the new first lady, Buchanan's niece, Harriet Lane. The accomplished twenty-six-year-old and her bachelor uncle would see to it that a night at the White House would rank as a coveted invitation.

They set the tone immediately at the Inaugural Ball. "All the male population is in a ferment, preparing for the 'Inaugural Ball,'" writer Mary Jane Windle informed "Distant Reader" as she referred to her South Carolina subscribers; "indeed the 'Inaugural Ball' is the engrossing subject of discourse." It had been eight years since the Capital City had enjoyed such an expensive spectacle, with massive amounts of food and drink provided, including 1,200 quarts of ice cream and a three-thousand-dollar bill for the wine. On March 3, 1857, the day before the big event, the *Evening Star* announced that tickets (at ten dollars each) would be for sale at the city's hotels and that "the Ladies Invitations are now ready." Merchants maneuvered to capitalize on the huge crowds expected. "For the Inauguration, anticipating a large increase in our sales, we have employed an extra force of Shuckers and are now prepared to fill the largest orders for our celebrated HERRING BAY OYSTERS," crowed the shop of Schwarz & Drury. Also advertised: "a few fine terrapins." Newspapers around the country rhapsodized about the ball staged in a huge tent erected on Pennsylvania Avenue between the White House and the Capitol, lauding it as "undoubtedly the grandest affair of the kind that has ever been witnessed in this country." According to the *Baltimore American* correspondent, "There appeared to be among the ladies a very general effort to eclipse each other in the display of jewelry and the magnificence and costliness of their apparel," but one shone out: "the lady of Senator Douglas was evidently the star of the evening. Her fine stature gave her the advantage over all competitors as she could be easily discerned in any part of the room." Adele Douglas reigned as the beauty but she did not go unrivaled that heralded night. A new contender had entered the competition: "the niece of President Buchanan, Miss Lane, attracted much attention and was evidently the favorite of the evening." When at nine thirty President Buchanan arrived to the strains of "Hail to the Chief," followed immediately by his tall, striking niece, she commanded the crowd. "Miss Lane who is to do the honors of the White House was present and made a very favorable impression," observed a writer for the *Nashville Union and American*. "She gives much promise of performing the duties of the White House with much grace and dignity."

Harriet Lane was certainly prepared for the job. At her own request, she had been brought up by her politician-uncle since she was orphaned at age eleven. As a senator from Pennsylvania and then secretary of state in the Polk administration, Buchanan educated the girl in the ways of government and society. When he was in the Cabinet she boarded at Visitation Convent in Georgetown and spent one Sunday a month with her uncle and his allies, absorbing the political plots of the moment. After a few years back in Pennsylvania when Polk left office, Buchanan surfaced again as Pierce's ambassador to the Court of St. James's, bringing his beautiful young niece to spend more than a year with him as his official hostess. By then twenty-five years old, Harriet created something of a sensation in London, especially among the members of the royal family, when Queen Victoria bestowed on her the title "Honorary Ambassadress." One of Harriet's friends advised her to marry one of the host of Englishmen pursuing her: "your nature is a very ambitious one & your position in this country *might be* very different from that you now hold."

But Harriet chose to return to the United States as a single woman, with the admonition from her uncle, "Take good care not to display any foreign airs & graces in society at home. . . . I shall be happy on my return to learn that it has been thus said of you, '—she has not been a bit spoiled by her visit to England.'" Buchanan didn't need a snooty niece causing a problem in the upcoming presidential campaign. On election night in 1856, when a torchlight parade marched to their house in Pennsylvania to celebrate the victory, Harriet Lane was with her uncle. And she would be with him throughout one of the worst times in the history of the country and its Capital City. Only two days after the inaugural festivities, whatever temporary coming together of the Congress that the celebration of a new presidency inspired was shattered by the third branch of government when the Supreme Court handed down the *Dred Scott* decision.

DRED SCOTT HAD been enslaved in Missouri when his owners moved to Minnesota and Illinois, where slavery was outlawed. The family then returned to Missouri and sold the slave, moving Scott to sue for his freedom, arguing that his sojourn in free territory meant that he could no longer be held in bondage. Lower courts had decided both for and against the black man, who appealed to the Supreme Court, where he was represented by Montgomery Blair, the prominent lawyer son of Francis Preston Blair and brother of Elizabeth Blair Lee. Much to the horror of the antislavery forces in Congress and around the country, the Court not only ruled that Scott's freedom would be denied, but added that as a noncitizen, he didn't even have the right to sue. Then the justices went even further. The Fifth Amendment to the Constitution, judged Chief Justice Roger B. Taney, prohibited the taking of property. When Congress outlawed slavery in some states, he posited, it in effect destroyed the property of slaveholders moving there. So the Missouri Compromise of 1820—the law determining which states would be slave and which would be free—was unconstitutional and the Fugitive Slave Act should be strictly enforced. Buchanan supported the decision—in fact he privately lobbied the justices to decide the way they did—and hoped that a court ruling on the question of slavery would settle the matter. If the contentious issue could be removed from Congress, the president reasoned, it might mean an end to the debate. And the threat to the Union would be avoided. Instead, just the opposite happened. Northern states vowed to ignore the Court entirely as southern states rejoiced. The forgers of compromise, like Stephen Douglas, looked for ways around the ruling even as he endorsed it, and all the while settlers' bloody battles continued in Kansas. Partly because they feared similar civil unrest in other new territories as a result of the *Dred Scott* decision, depositors staged a run on the banks. That economic calamity came at the same time that northern manufacturers found their supplies had outpaced demand for their goods. The Panic of 1857 ensued, further engulfing the Buchanan presidency.

Harriet Lane managed the increasingly disputatious politicians as well as anyone could, while subtly making some statements about her own views. She let slaveholders know that she disapproved of their "peculiar institution" by firing the staff at the White House, which was largely made up of slaves hired out by their owners. Then she installed German and Irish immigrants in their place. By serving wine at official functions and drinking it herself, she let the women who had started temperance societies, like the suffragists Susan B. Anthony and Elizabeth Cady Stanton, know she disagreed with them. But she mainly tried to keep discord at bay as she carefully seated northerners at one end of the room, southerners at the other. "Miss Lane's entrance into life at the American capital at a trying time, served to keep the surface of society in Washington serene and smiling, though the fires of a volcano raged in the under-political world, and the vibrations of Congressional strife spread to the furthermost ends of the country the knowledge that the Government was tottering," explained Virginia Clay, who heaped praise on the "elegance" of White House functions in Buchanan's time. (But the southern belle didn't endear herself to the first lady by telling her that "she was like a poet's ideal of an English dairymaid, who fed upon blush roses and the milk of her charges.") And newspaperwoman Mary Jane Windle let her readers know "we think Mr. Buchanan most fortunate in having so interesting a relative to do the honors of the Executive mansion. . . . Her manners are self possessed enough to command admiration, even if her position were less distinguished."

Virginia Clay's friend Sara Pryor was less kind in her assessment. Though she found Harriet "very handsome, a fair, blue-eyed, self contained young woman," who was "universally admired," Sara divulged that the White House hostess was not popular. "She lacked magnetism. She followed a prescribed rule of manner from which she never deviated, no matter with whom she was thrown." But Sara admitted that Harriet's containment was probably wise: "she made no enemies, was betrayed into no entangling alliances, and was involved in no contretemps of any kind." Not easy in the Washington of the day, especially for the single niece of a wealthy president. She had to fend off suitors as well as senators—often one and the same—without offending them.

Harriet did manage to offend her uncle's idea of good housekeeping, even though he had entrusted her to undertake a full-scale redecoration of the White House; she was even charged with handling the congressional appropriation for the project. One night the cook served a Virginia ham that Sara Pryor had sent to the first family, along with the recipe. When the meat appeared on the table as a gelatinous mess, the president "looked at it helplessly, and called out—'Take it away! Take it away! Oh, Miss Harriet! You are a poor housekeeper! Not even a Virginia lady can teach you,'" Sara recounted somewhat smugly. (Sara seems to have made her presentation of a Virginia ham with her recipe a signature item. Adele Douglas also received one with the instructions: "Unless you boil your hams in champagne as they always do in New Orleans, the following is the best way. Soak it all night; & put it into a pot of cold water at 10-o'clock for dinner at 6. It must simmer, rather than boil until it is done, then bread crumbs thickly stewed over it & browned in an oven. If you follow these directions your Virginia ham will be perfect.")

Despite the debacle of the ham, Harriet Lane's tenure in the White House won the approval of most of the Washington matrons. The mistress of the Executive Mansion inaugurated concert nights and lobbied for a national gallery of art. "There has been an 'Art Association' recently formed here . . . to establish a 'National Gallery of the Fine Arts,'" Mary Jane Windle was able to tell her readers that spring. And Harriet Lane turned out to be a trendsetter in fashion. Reporting on an evening at "the President's," Varina Davis knew her mother would want to know exactly what she wore: "the old gold coloured silk with a width of black velvet let in the sides, and black lace each side, also a black bertha of lace and lemon colored bows." Harriet had introduced the "bertha"—a strip of sheer fabric covering the top of the bosom—as a nod to modesty, since her necklines were cut low enough to cause comment. Other women might have clucked at Harriet's boldness but they followed her lead, according to Virginia Clay: "Low necks and lace berthas, made fashionable because of their adoption by Miss Lane, were worn almost universally, either with open sleeves revealing inner ones of filmy lace, or sleeves of the shortest possible form, allowing the rounded length of a pretty arm to be seen in its perfection." But pretty arms could not make up for the ugliness that was happening in the Capitol day after day and all sides knew that the election of 1858 could make or break the new, antislavery Republican Party.

———————

THE FATE OF Kansas continued to dominate debate. Stephen Douglas's concept of popular sovereignty was challenged when the territory held a corrupt referendum on a proslavery constitution boycotted by its opponents. Though a subsequent vote in Kansas rejected the so-called Lecompton Constitution, President Buchanan submitted it to Congress anyway as the basis for Kansas's entry into the Union as a slave state. "The 'Lecompton Constitution,' with the Message of the President, was sent into both Houses in the beginning of this week," Mary Jane Windle alerted her readers in January, "and since that time wrangling and anarchy have been as much a national pastime as in the days of the Goths and Vandals." To the shock of his colleagues, Douglas turned against the president of his own party to oppose the constitution. After all, it was Douglas who had managed to pass the Compromise of 1850, with its Fugitive Slave Act, Douglas who had authored the Kansas-Nebraska Law, Douglas who had supported the *Dred Scott* decision, and now it was Douglas breaking with his party's leader over the issue of slavery? The Illinois senator contended that the people of the territory had not approved the constitution and therefore popular sovereignty had been abrogated. As a result, he became the temporary darling of the Republicans but the permanent enemy of President Buchanan.

The animus between the men extended to the women as well and Adele Douglas was cut from the guest list to the Harriet Lane White House. The senator, whose presidential ambitions had never abated, was positioning himself with the northern wing of the Democratic Party by his break with Buchanan but he miscalculated how thoroughly his stance would alienate the southerners. And southerners were feeling particularly powerful in 1858. The Panic of 1857 had barely affected their region, where the economy depended on the production of cotton, not manufactured goods. When the Crimean War ended in Europe, the demand for cotton grew and prices shot up, making slave laborers ever more valuable to the livelihoods of the southern elite. And Dixie lawmakers were convinced that the primacy of cotton gave them such an economic advantage that the South could easily exist as an independent nation if the North persisted in its attacks against slavery. Defending the Lecompton Constitution, Jefferson Davis "poured forth a torrent of withering sarcasm and crushing invective," Miss Windle reported with some shock. The ladies' galleries at the Capitol filled as emboldened southerners carried the day in the Senate—voting to admit Kansas as a slave state under the Lecompton Constitution. Then the House of Representatives defeated it—but only after a literal floor fight was cut off when a member's wig was pulled off—and teed it up as a major issue in the coming election.

In the midst of all of this turmoil, one Washington hostess decided to take a page from Dolley Madison's book and throw a big party to try to bring warring factions together. Just a week after the House voted to reject the Kansas constitution, with passions still at their peak, "Mrs. Gwin's Ball" did indeed briefly distract the debaters and attract all sides, who wrote about the event for years to come. "A portion of our fashionable world have been for the last month excited to the highest pitch of eagerness in preparation for Mrs. Gwin's 'fancy ball,'" Miss Windle gibed. When the big night came, the *New York Times* reported that a dozen senators "cordially fraternized, and appeared to be ignorant that such a place as Kansas existed," as they gathered in the study of Senator William Gwin of California, "Guelphs and Ghibelines—radicals and fire-eaters—fraternized cosily, and seemed to forget that they had recently been shivering lances on each other's reputations in the Senatorial arena." It was a costume ball where the women worked for weeks to perfect their characters, and the newspaper described in detail the "universally admired" Mrs. Douglas's "Aurora," the "vivacity and *esprit*" of Mrs. Davis's "Madame de Staël," and the show stealer, Mrs. Clay, who kept a "crowd around her throughout the evening" as "Dame Partington." Fifty years later Virginia Clay still relished her success: "If I dwell on that evening with particular satisfaction, the onus of such egotism must be laid at the door of my flattering friends."

But the friendliness of the evening was fleeting. Another vote on Kansas was coming up and the whole city seemed to converge on the Capitol. "In the Senate chamber every cranny of the ladies' gallery was entirely filled. . . . In one direction might be seen the lovely face of the lady of the young Senator from Alabama." Virginia Clay's beauty helped Mary Jane Windle find the scene in the gallery "picturesque," not so the floor below: "the dignified assembly, which calls itself a great deliberative body, was considerably out of order . . . we could not but be struck with the bitterness expressed in the angry and menacing look cast from one side of the chamber to the other." Congress decided to send the Lecompton Constitution back to Kansas for another vote and the contentious session started to wrap up. Finally adjournment day brought "a large number of spectators to the galleries," where

Miss Windle enjoyed watching the pandemonium as members packed up their desks. One searched frantically through heaps of papers until he found what he was looking for: "it was a lady's hand-writing . . . the sight of this seemed to inspire reverie, for he sat several moments, with a vague and abstracted dreaminess of eye . . . it is not necessary to tell our readers that this 'Hon,' is a *bachelor member*." Nearby a married member unsentimentally collected "a pile of letters from his absent wife . . . for him the sentiment and romance of life is ended." With the coming of summer the Washington "season" closed down: "The gay season is over; parties are over; Gautier lays no more suppers." Blessedly, the first session of Congress ended as well and then it was time to see how the debates of the past year would play out in the election.

One senator facing a particularly tough campaign was Stephen Douglas. Though his views on the Kansas constitution made him the fleeting darling of abolitionist editorialists like the *New York Tribune*'s Horace Greeley, the Illinois Democrat faced a serious Republican challenger and President Buchanan tried to sabotage his fellow Democrat. Abraham Lincoln served one term in the House years earlier and had been defeated in a recent bid for the Senate, chosen by the state legislature. Now he was trying again and taking his campaign to the people in the hopes that they would elect a legislature that would send him to Washington. When the Springfield lawyer famously challenged the much better known and financed Douglas to a series of debates, the incumbent surprisingly accepted and the Lincoln-Douglas debates commanded the attention of the whole country, partly because Douglas was a probable presidential candidate, partly because arguments over slavery were raging in many American households. Joining her husband on the campaign trail was his young bride, Adele Cutts Douglas.

It seems that at first she was reluctant to make the trip. On a visit to Chicago the year before, Adele wrote to her mother complaining about "how terribly ugly and dirty this city is." But when a cousin who lived there heard that the senator's wife would not travel to Illinois that summer, he scolded her: "I will not attempt to designate the many ways in which you can be of service to your husband by being here." The cousin insisted that Adele's presence would have a great deal of influence; "the encouragements that presence will give to his friends—& the restraint it will be upon his enemies" would make a contribution to his success. And, as usual, the merchants were eager for her business: "It would give us pleasure to furnish you with your 'confectionery' during your stay in this city," a hustling sweet shop owner informed her, reminding the native Washingtonian that he used to have a store at Ninth and F in Washington, D.C.

There wasn't much time for bonbons as Adele moved around the state with her husband and struck up a friendship with his amiable opponent. The six-foot-four storyteller versus the five-foot-four senator attracted huge crowds eager to hear the jostling between the candidates, which could last for hours. Unfailingly elegant even as she traveled the state by train, Adele always graced a ladies' reception at the debate site, impressing those she met so much that a Douglas biographer claimed the editor of a St. Louis newspaper switched his endorsement from Lincoln to Douglas after meeting the senator's wife. Unlike in Douglas's contest with Buchanan, the combatants remained cordial, with Abe and Adele once even enjoying a train ride together on the way from one debate to the next, where they would meet up with Douglas, who had already arrived. The close election resulted in Republicans carrying the popular vote statewide but Democrats prevailing in the legislature. Stephen Douglas returned to Washington but Abraham Lincoln would not be far behind.

Though the Democrat Douglas won in Illinois, the breakthrough election of 1858 gave the Republican Party control of the House of Representatives. Not only were many Democrats defeated—the American Party was routed. And with the collapse of the party came the collapse of Know-Nothing control over the Washington Monument Society. The abandoned stump of the obelisk stood as a bleak reminder of the nation's unfinished business.

LEFT: *Adele Cutts Douglas, called a "popular icon," reigned as a Washington, DC, beauty, able to intercede successfully for her friends with politicians of all parties.* RIGHT: *Varina Davis, the tart-tongued and politically astute First Lady of the Confederate States of America, caused controversy with her unorthodox views.*

Varina Leads and Leaves as Abby Drops By

1859–1861

W e talked of art and artists, galleries in Europe, shops in Paris,—anything except what we were all thinking about." Sara Pryor bemoaned the state of society in early 1859, as Washington tried to go about its business while preparing for the changes the newly elected Congress would bring. Just what those changes might be wouldn't be known for months. The difficulty of traveling long distances, plus the absence of a uniform election day in the states, dictated a peculiar arrangement where the old Congress still met until the spring of odd-numbered years and then the new Congress convened in December, a full year after the election. "Unconsciously, all tentative subjects were avoided by the well-bred of both sections," Varina Davis remembered. Sara Pryor added: "The art of conversation suffered under such circumstances. But some interesting books were just out in England, and everybody was discussing them." Sara and her friends especially enjoyed Thackeray's *The Virginians* and Tennyson's *Elaine*, along with "a new star rising—George Eliot." But an old standby was out of favor: "Dickens, we were, at the moment, cordially hating because of his 'American Notes.'" Still Sara fretted, "We were forced to ignore subjects that possessed us with absorbing interest and to confine ourselves to trivialities."

South and North did come together to host an elaborate farewell ball for the British ambassador, Lord Napier, and his wife. "All that Washington now holds of gay, gallant and distinguished, thronged Willard's Hotel tonight, and partook of an intolerably bad supper, intolerably ill served," chronicled the *New York Times*, whose correspondent was kinder to the women partygoers than to Willard's. One in particular he singled out for praise: "Here we have a brilliant specimen, for instance, of strong emotional power in Mrs. Clay, of Alabama. The beauteous sentimentality of the South finds form in this charming woman, and utters itself in eloquent words, in sympathetic flashes of the eye, in vehemence and passion of expression. The utmost energy seems blended in her with the greatest geniality, an active mind with a loving heart." On the other hand, Stephen Douglas was "a rather unwelcome guest since his errand is to announce the absence of his accomplished wife." Even the newspaper reporter liked Adele better than her husband.

Sara Pryor remained wide-eyed about the Napier ball decades later. The floor was covered with colored sand, representing St. George and the Dragon; portraits of Queen Victoria and George Washington hung from the walls; and Charles Gautier, the most sought-after caterer of the time, "had excelled himself. There were glittering hay-stacks of spun sugar; wonderful Roman chariots, drawn by swans, and driven by Cupids; pyramids of costly bonbons; dolphins in a sea of rock candy; and ices in every form from a pair of turtle doves to a pillared temple." In later years the ball would be remembered as the last big Washington bash before the war.

———————

NO PRICEY BALLS or polite conversation, however, could mask the fact that the country was on the brink of disaster. On Washington's Birthday, Congress did manage to pass one of the few measures members could agree on—a bill incorporating the Washington Monument Society, giving the organization a charter to protect it from any more takeovers and putting it in a position where it might possibly raise enough money to build the obelisk. Then, a few days later it was a murder that totally consumed the Capital. New York Congressman Dan Sickles shot and killed his wife's lover in broad daylight within sight of the White House. District Attorney Philip Barton Key, son of the "Star-Spangled Banner" lyricist, was a well-liked widower deemed by Virginia Clay the "handsomest man in all Washington society." His "death at the hands of Daniel E. Sickles in February, 1859 stirred Washington to its centre." These were men the women all knew, and they knew whose side they were on: the dead man's. A notorious philanderer, Sickles had not only been scandalously linked in the New York press with a well-known prostitute; he even had the temerity to bring her with him to London when he served under Buchanan in the U.S. embassy there, only dispatching her back to New York before the arrival of his wife, Teresa, and their baby daughter. The ambassador and his niece Harriet Lane took a particular liking to the lively eighteen-year-old Teresa Sickles while they were all in London, and when Buchanan became president, the young woman remained a favorite. As a newly minted congressional wife, Mrs. Sickles donned a long-talked-about bonnet decorated with jonquils to occupy a place of honor next to Harriet Lane in the gallery of the House of Representatives the day Buchanan took his oath of office. That night Teresa met Key at the Inaugural Ball.

Sickles might not have noticed his wife's affair—he was having a fairly public one of his own with a woman in Baltimore—had it not been for an informant who wrote him an anonymous letter revealing the trysts, and the servants who subsequently confirmed it. Feeling he had to defend his somewhat besmirched honor, the congressman ambushed Key just as much of Washington was preparing to go to St. John's Church, right across Lafayette Square. "A horrible, horrible thing has happened Virginia," shouted Senator Clay as he burst into the room where his wife was dressing. "Sickles, who for a year or more has forced his wife into Barton's company, has killed Key, killed him most brutally, while he was unarmed!" Just a few days before, along with about a hundred other people, Virginia had called on Teresa, who was performing the political wife's duty of receiving guests "at home" at the Sickles' rented mansion. "She was so young and fair," Virginia recollected, still able to detail exactly what the "girl hostess" was wearing ("a painted muslin gown, filmy and graceful, on which the outlines of the crocus might be traced"), "and so naïve, that none of the party of which I was one was willing to harbor a belief in the rumours which were then in circulation." After the shooting, Teresa, "the unfortunate cause of the tragedy," was bundled off to her parents in New York and never seen in Washington again. As for Sickles, Jessie Frémont had nothing good to say about him when she heard the news in California. The murder of her friend Key capped "an accumulation of heartless cruelties that show a character to justify his wife's looking elsewhere for something to love." But that's not the way the jury saw it. Sickles got off scot-free when his lead lawyer, Edwin Stanton, cooked up a whole new legal defense: "temporary insanity."

It worked. Virginia Clay suspected a political motive in the acquittal—after all, Sickles was a good friend of the president: "So strenuous were the political needs of the time, and so tragic and compelling the demands of national strife now centred in Washington, that the horrible calamity entailed no punishment upon its author." But a report canvassing the jurors concluded it wasn't politics that swayed them, it was adultery. Key got what was coming to him—that was all there was to it. The fact that Sickles, too, had strayed made no difference, his wife had betrayed him and Key had to pay the price. In disgustedly summing up the whole sordid story for her mother, Varina Davis had but two words: "filth, filth."

VARINA HAD BIGGER worries that winter than the Sickles case. She was expecting another baby and was afraid she might die, as she almost had in her last childbirth. Though her house in Washington bustled with activity—with her young sister and brother and her two toddlers "stirring around like mad"—Varina felt alone as her due date approached. Her husband had left town because rising floodwaters threatened to destroy his Mississippi plantation, and she knew he would not be back in time for the birth; she had grown used to separation in her somewhat difficult fourteen-year marriage. From the very beginning, when the first stop on their honeymoon had been at the grave of Davis's first wife, it had been a strained relationship between the nineteen-year-old Varina Howell and the thirty-six-year-old widower. But then the newlyweds went on to a glamorous stay at the St. Charles Hotel in New Orleans, before they moved to Brierfield, his lonely plantation in the Mississippi countryside. The young bride desperately missed her big boisterous family in Natchez and chafed under her husband's idea of the perfect wife. When she had first met Jefferson Davis two years earlier, the Whig-raised Varina told her mother that "he is refined and cultivated and yet he is a Democrat!" (For his part, Davis saw that Varina was "beautiful and she has a fine mind.") Varina soon learned that her somewhat stern husband brooked no disagreement about politics or anything else. Still, the strong-willed and well-educated young woman could not help but declare her independence from time to time, often causing conflict in the marriage. They rattled around in the plantation house without children, and when her mother proffered a "comfortable" dress as a subtle way of asking if she was pregnant, Varina replied: "I do not need a 'comfortable' dress, and I think I shall probably never *require* one." It's hard to know exactly what she meant by that—a rupture in the relationship, a revelation she didn't know before the wedding? But later that year the question of children moved to the background as Davis took a seat in the House of Representatives and his still-teenaged wife took her place among the political women in Washington.

It was an exciting time for the eager-to-learn bride. The National Exposition of 1845, the equivalent of a world's fair, had come to town and was showcasing new inventions like the sewing machine, which fascinated Varina. She watched as a "needle with an eccentric motion played laterally through the cloth and sewed a pretty good seam," but she was dubious about the telegraph: "I think it is a trick but paid my two bits to get a message that it was a fine day." The young woman helped her husband with his speeches and correspondence and enjoyed time in the galleries at the Capitol listening to debate. She was thrilled when former president John Quincy Adams, who was still serving in the House, paid attention to the newly elected Davis: "When

Mr. Adams listened to my husband I was a proud young creature, and knew he must be doing something well; but found, afterward, that to every new member he listened attentively once, and never again, unless pleased." As to the man who was then president? Polk "was not an impressive man at first" until he won over a "person honored with his attention." This first pleasant sojourn in the nation's capital was cut short by Polk's war against Mexico and Davis's recruitment to lead Mississippi's soldiers. Strongly objecting to her husband's decision to join the military, Varina miserably waited out the war at Brierfield, fighting with her domineering brother-in-law on a nearby plantation.

Jefferson Davis emerged from the Mexican War covered with glory. Badly injured in the Battle of Buena Vista, he refused to leave the fray until the enemy was defeated and his heroics earned him a victor's welcome as he arrived in New Orleans and then triumphantly sailed up the Mississippi River to home. There he found another battle scene, which he blamed squarely on the unhappy Varina for her strong-headedness in taking on his older brother. Davis refused to bring his wife to Washington when he was appointed to the Senate in 1847, coldly stating: "I cannot expose myself to conduct such as yours when with me here." He demanded a subservient little woman and meant to have one; otherwise he would find it "impossible for us ever to live together." Varina was ready to swallow her pride if it meant she could go back to the Capital City, so, as she would do many times after that, she tried to stifle her feelings. Still, she couldn't help but comment when she read about one of her husband's particularly inflammatory speeches: "I saw your very forcible little speech in partial answer to Mr. Hale's vituperations against slavery. It was a little too violent, more so than I would have liked to hear you be, however well-deserved the censure might be." But she then quickly assured Jefferson that she was making an honest attempt to be the wife he wanted, reading Mrs. Ellis's *Guide to Social Happiness*, with its treacly meditations on "the poetry of life," and calling herself his "thoughtless, dependent wife." He relented. Varina was invited back to Washington, a city she greatly enjoyed.

The great lions of the Senate—Henry Clay, Daniel Webster, and Varina's friend John Calhoun—were still alive. And they let Varina pull up a stool on the floor of the Senate as they debated the Compromise of 1850. Once again she spent much of her time helping her often ill husband with his work, but she also enjoyed her place in society, made easier by the fact that the couple lived in a "mess" with other political families, so Varina was not forced into hostess duties. Since her husband Jefferson's first wife had been the daughter of President Zachary Taylor, the second wife anticipated her initial visit to the White House with trepidation, but she soon came to be a regular there, beloved by the first couple, and she sat by Taylor's bed as he died. That special connection broke when Vice President Millard Fillmore moved into the Executive Mansion and Davis ran for governor of Mississippi, lost, and then settled with Varina into life at Brierfield for the first time in a long while. With the cotton business booming and the unpaid labor of more than one hundred enslaved workers contributing to its success, the plantation prospered. Then finally, after seven years of marriage, the couple became parents in 1852 with the birth of Samuel Emory Davis. It wasn't long before the baby's father was on the road campaigning for his old friend Franklin Pierce for president.

Once elected, Pierce begged Davis to leave the thriving plantation and return to Washington as a member of his Cabinet. Secretary of War Jefferson Davis would need to live in a substantial house—gone were the days of the relatively carefree congressional "mess"—and his wife would take on the obligations of official entertaining.

With her grieving friend Jane Pierce out of the social picture, Varina moved into position as the foremost hostess in Washington. She made sure to invite the sixty-two senators and 234 members of the House every session, allowing her to argue convincingly that "the wives of Mr. Pierce's Cabinet officers labored in their sphere as well as their husbands." Breakfast meetings, for instance, could be used for lobbying, to offer a "personal explanation" to someone who was "dissatisfied with the Administration." Varina actually enjoyed evenings when she could bring scientists, writers, and artists to her table. Life was good until two-year-old Samuel came down with measles and died. It was a devastating blow not only to his parents but also to Jane and Franklin Pierce, who had grown quite fond of the little boy and had seen their own sons die. Poor Varina had no way to escape the public outpouring of sympathy to retreat into her own grief.

The following year another baby, Margaret Howell Davis, named for Varina's mother, helped soothe their sorrow. President Pierce once again took a delighted interest in the baby and years later told her parents a charming story about their daughter. According to Pierce, he had watched as the family dog snapped at eighteen-month-old Maggie and then seen her plot her revenge. The little girl stretched out next to the offending canine, pretending to be loving until the dog went to sleep "and then biting him on the nose in retribution." After waiting so long to have one baby, now Varina was having them almost yearly. Jefferson Davis Jr. came along in the midst of a paralyzing snowstorm shortly before his father's Cabinet term ended in 1857. The childbirth left Varina deathly ill but the nurse couldn't get through the snow until New York Senator William Seward came riding to the rescue; he "had his own fine horses harnessed to a sleigh" and delivered the nurse.

Seward and Davis could not have been more different in their political views, and when the southerner moved from the Cabinet to the Senate, he and the New Yorker regularly did battle. But even then, at one point Davis himself became horribly sick and Seward kindly visited him daily "to tell all the 'passing show' of the Senate and House of Representatives." Many years later, after the war and Seward's service in Lincoln's Cabinet, the wife of the president of the Confederacy would say of Seward: "He was thoroughly sympathetic with human suffering, and would do the most unexpected kindnesses to those who would have anticipated the opposite only."

The Buchanan White House welcomed the Davises as a like-minded political family but Varina also forged firm friendships with those unsympathetic to the southern cause. Much to the disapproval of their fellow Mississippians, the family even chose a Maine camping trip for a vacation in the summer of 1858. On the way back to Washington, Davis had been invited to speak at Faneuil Hall in Boston, and when they arrived at the city's Tremont House, Varina again needed to depend on the kindness of a Yankee stranger. Little Jeff Jr. seemed on the brink of death: "At the darkest hour when we feared the worst, and a foggy night was setting in upon the evening of a raw day, a large, gentle-looking lady knocked at the door in a house dress. She introduced herself as Mrs. Harrison Gray Otis, with whose name we were of course familiar, and said she had come to spend the night and help me to nurse." Here was the foremost woman of a famous and historic Boston family offering her services to southerners she didn't know. Saying that her house had been freshly painted or else she would take the baby home with her, Mrs. Otis stayed the night diffusing "a sense of relief and confidence about her." It was a trip Varina would always cherish: "These reminiscences of Boston to this day soften all the asperities developed by our bloody war."

When they returned to Washington, Davis threw himself into

work, traveling to campaign for fellow Democrats or staying at the Senate into the early hours of the morning. Varina was left to deal with the family and the social obligations of the Capital City. Though she doted on her children and proudly relayed anecdotes about their cute sayings and doings to her parents and to her husband when he was away, still she lamented to her mother, "Oh, how I would like to be free of care for a few days if only to know how it would feel, if I should not have to lose the objects of those cares." It was a fantasy, Varina knew, but she nonetheless sighed to her father, "It would be lovely sometimes to cut duty, and go on a *bust*." It's something many exhausted mothers have thought in moments of honesty, though it was highly unusual for a woman of her place and time actually to say it. But Varina was an unusual woman. At one point when Davis complained about her spending money she figured out how to earn some of her own by publishing an article for a fifty-dollar fee, using a pseudonym to hide what would have been considered outrageous behavior.

By the fall of 1858, with another baby on the way, and given the experience with her last childbirth, Varina thought she might die. Even so, she tried to keep her own and everyone else's spirits up. Instead of staying shut in at home, as many pregnant women did, she went with her little brother to hear the actress Fanny Kemble read Shakespeare and looked forward to the summer, when she would be staying in a house promised her by Mrs. Montgomery Blair, wife of the lawyer for the slave Dred Scott. Varina was close to the whole Blair family, and though her husband weakly protested against her choice of Republican friends, this time he was willing to give in to her wishes. Jokingly referring to the Republican slogan of "Free Soil, Free Men," Jeff wisecracked to his mother-in-law: "Varina having strong 'free sail' proclivities, as you know, seemed disposed to go out to the neighborhood of Mr. Blair. He had a house which he offered to her at a nominal rent. What guarantee he offered for keeping peace with me I did not learn." Though she from time to time wore the uncomfortable mantle of obedient wife, Davis acknowledged, at least to her mother, that Varina had a will of her own. In any case, Jeff wasn't even in town while Varina was making her summer plans. He was at his plantation in Mississippi trying to stave off disaster from severe flooding. Knowing what he was dealing with, his wife tried to protect him from her own fears: "Don't feel uneasy about me. I am pretty well and quite hopeful." In fact, she was preparing for the worst—getting everything in order, making sure the accounts were up to date, leaving instructions for what needed to be done in the garden in the fall, sewing full wardrobes for all the children, and helping her husband's political career by mailing out two thousand copies of his speeches and preparing government-stamped envelopes for many more. All the while she lived in terror that she would die and that little Jeff Jr., her two-year-old boy, would not remember her; she prayed "every day to rear him."

The baby, another boy, arrived on April 18, 1859, and, much to Varina's relief, all went well. But when the family went to Oakland, Maryland, to spend the summer with the Blairs, Varina's health took a dangerous turn. Luckily for her, the Blair women served as her devoted nurses, little knowing they would soon be on the other side of battle lines. When his wife started having convulsions, Jeff dashed to the Blairs' vacation cottage, where Montgomery's daughter immediately came to his aid; the fact that the president of the Confederacy credited a Blair with saving Varina's life that night would have political implications in the years to come.

As the vacation went on, some of the nursing fell to Varina's friend Elizabeth Blair Lee, Montgomery Blair's sister, who wrote to her father that she had spent the night "watching by Mrs. Davis' bedside.

She is here and out of danger and seems to rally rapidly, she has been fearfully ill & in intense suffering & tis almost a physical sense of relief to me to see her out of pain once again." Once again, Varina believed that she would die, but she recovered enough that her husband felt free to go off campaigning for his allies, leaving his family in the care of the political opposition. While he was gone, in an especially affectionate letter Varina charged him to "remember that you are a part of a powerful party and therefore can be spared, but you are all to your wife and babes." At the end of the summer Lizzie Lee was sorry to see Varina go: "All of my Washington acquaintances leave here on Monday evening & today Mrs. Davis is parting for Washington & all of its comforts and pleasures."

———————

BY 1859 THE comforts and pleasures of Washington were much improved. In January, the water in Montgomery Meigs's elegantly engineered system started flowing into reservoirs and mains that brought running water into private homes. That year too the commissioner of public buildings crowed that over the previous ten years "the city has . . . opened and made more than fifty miles of avenues and streets, at a cost of about one million and a half dollars. It may safely be affirmed that no city, in proportion to its population and wealth, has done more for itself than Washington, notwithstanding nearly one half of the property within its limits belongs to the government, and is not subject to taxation." The Washington *Star* burst with unabashed boosterism: "Persons of wealth and taste . . . are coming more and more to appreciate the advantages and pleasures of having a home among the public men of America while the latter are assembled together. . . . In the northern cities what is termed fashionable society is intensely exclusive, the key to admission to it being a golden one. Here, the lock is off and the door stands wide open for any to enter who may be so intelligent, entertaining and well-behaved as to prove agreeable acquaintances." But, adds a Capital City historian: "No decade of Washington's history presents sharper contrasts than the 1850's. Poverty, squalor, prejudice, and violence were as abundantly evident as the 'wealth and taste' to which the *Star* drew attention." Though the elite private schools, especially the Visitation Convent and Georgetown, offered excellent education, the overcrowded public schools took in so few pupils that only about half of the white school-aged children were enrolled. And there were no public schools for the 18 percent of the population that was black. Still, Catholic nuns and priests and some other enterprising individuals—notably Myrtilla Miner, who opened a high school for girls with the support of prominent abolitionists like Harriet Beecher Stowe—operated private schools that educated more than one thousand African-American children. And Congress appropriated funds for "each deaf, dumb or blind pupil" in the District whose family could not pay for the newly established school headed by educator Edward Gallaudet. Gallaudet University still stands as the nation's beacon of higher education for the deaf.

As the city grew in size and sophistication, arts and culture established a toehold. The Smithsonian Institution became a center for research as well as a museum and gathering place. For most of the 1850s the National Theatre produced shows featuring everything from Shakespeare to Chinese acrobats, but a fire in 1857 closed the decades-old performance hall for several years. One of the most popular novelists of the day, Mrs. E.D.E.N. Southworth (her name was Emma Dorothy Eliza Nevitte, but she used her initials as her byline, or simply signed herself Mrs. Southworth), churned out her serialized melodramas from a large house in Georgetown, which the single mother of two—she had left an unhappy marriage—was able to buy with her own earnings as a writer. In 1859, her hugely successful *Hidden Hand* captured readers with the story of a starving and frightened abandoned little girl who disguises herself as a boy because "while all the ragged boys I knew could get little jobs to earn bread, I, because I was a girl, was not allowed to carry a gentleman's parcel or black his boots, or shovel the snow off a shopkeeper's pavement, or put in coal, or do anything that I could do just as well as they. And so because I was a girl there seemed to be nothing but starvation or beggary before me!" Mrs. Southworth hadn't yet joined forces with the women who had met at Seneca Falls, New York, in 1848, but she found other ways to make the point!

Another sign of progress: the major expansion of the Capitol building, under the direction of Montgomery Meigs with the combined support of strange bedfellows Jefferson Davis and William Seward. Large new chambers for both the House of Representatives and the Senate were ready for occupancy by 1859 and work on the massive new unifying dome was under way. But that symbol of unity belied the reality of what was happening inside the building. The Supreme Court upheld the constitutionality of the Fugitive Slave Act in March 1859, causing abolitionists to press their case against slavery louder and more insistently. And they got some ammunition from a white southerner named Hinton Helper, who published the book *The Impending Crisis* in an attempt to rally the nonslaveholders of the South to the abolitionist cause, calling on them to rise up against the slaveholding class. The Republicans reproduced an abridged version of the tract as a piece of political propaganda, and sixty-eight congressmen signed an advertisement for the pamphlet. On the other side, Varina Davis quoted President Buchanan: "No book could be better calculated for the purpose of intensifying the mutual hatred between North and South." And then John Brown staged his raid on Harpers Ferry.

Three years earlier the fanatical abolitionist had terrorized the proslavery forces in Kansas when he and four of his twenty children kidnapped five men and split their skulls. Brown deemed it a retaliatory attack after some Free Soilers had been killed, and he got away with the murders in the tumult of the Kansas civil war. On October 16, 1859, Brown struck again. Believing he was commissioned by God, the fiery-eyed zealot led a gang of eighteen men, including three of his sons, as he stormed the federal arsenal at Harpers Ferry, Virginia, in an attempt to foment an armed slave rebellion. After seizing the lightly guarded building, Brown sent his followers into the countryside to grab hostages while he waited for what he was convinced would be an outpouring of slaves ready to join him. Undeterred when no outpouring occurred, Brown and his men holed up in a firehouse with the hostages. Along with the citizens of Harpers Ferry, alarmed militia men from Maryland and Virginia tried to roust the raiders out of their fortress without harming the hostages; it didn't take long before they called in the Marines. Led by Colonel Robert E. Lee, the troops succeeded in capturing Brown and his band, killing two of them in the skirmish.

At first the whole country was horrified at the idea that John Brown planned to arm slaves and move through the South promoting violence. But antislavery sentiment shifted to Brown's side as his trial and subsequent hanging turned him first into a sympathetic figure, then into a martyr, and finally into a saint—provoking outrage in the South. Varina Davis later enlisted President Buchanan's postwar book to bolster the argument that it was not the raid by the "pestilent, forceful man" itself that "made a deeper impression on the Southern mind against the Union than all former events," but rather that "on the day of Brown's execution bells were tolled in many places, cannon fired, and prayers offered up for him as if he were a martyr . . . and churches were draped in mourning." John Brown was hanged on De-cember 2, 1859. The new Congress convened five days later.

THE CONGRESS MET when "the whole country was in ferment of the execution of John Brown," fretted Sara Pryor. "It was evident from the first hour that the atmosphere was heavily charged." Sara's hus-band had left his newspaper job and been newly elected as a Demo-crat to what became the infamous Thirty-Sixth Congress. Though for the first time the Republicans held the most seats, the party's choice for Speaker of the House was blocked by Democrats joining with members from smaller parties. During the almost two months of balloting, "everything was said that could be said to fan the flame," Sara protested. "Hot disputes were accentuated by bitter personal re-marks. One day a pistol accidentally fell from the pocket of a member from New York, and, thinking it had been drawn with the intention of using it, some of the members were wild with passion . . . turning the House into a pandemonium." One of the newcomers from the Re-publican ranks was also alarmed about the weaponry: "the other side all go armed and put their hands into their breasts upon the slightest provocation," Abigail Brooks Adams wrote home to her son Henry, arguing, "I believe the Republicans would like a free fight, though they profess to be cool." She added for good measure, "if there is a free fight I should like to punch a head or two, & kick & bite too." The pugilistic Mrs. Adams was married to Charles Francis Adams, the son and grandson of presidents, and like the women in his family before her, she had strong views about politics and everything else. And she was eager to express them.

Though new to Congress, the Adams family was neither new to politics nor to Washington. Charles Francis had served in the

Massachusetts legislature and run for vice president on the Free Soil ticket in 1848 before he briefly withdrew from the fray and, with his wife's help, edited a successful book of his grandmother Abigail Adams's letters. This Abigail Adams—called Abby—had spent a good bit of time in the Capital City; in fact that's where the couple met in 1826 when John Quincy Adams was president. As a nineteen-year-old visiting her sister who was married to Massachusetts Congressman Edward Everett, Abby was invited to the White House, where she was introduced to the president's son, who promptly fell in love with her. In later years she made regular trips to help take care of her mother-in-law, former first lady Louisa Catherine Adams, who had become such a venerated figure that both houses of Congress adjourned in respect and declared a day of silence when she died in 1852. During her frequent visits Abby earned a place as a popular visitor in Washington parlors, entertained by presidents and enlightened by politicians like her friend Charles Sumner. So when the Adams' officially joined the capital circle the couple were already A-list guests, even at the home of Rose Greenhow, a southern sympathizer who was a friend and advisor to President Buchanan.

An alluring widow sought after by many suitors, Rose never stopped inviting politicians of all stripes to her home as a way of garnering information and gaining influence. And her influence was great, not only in the private rooms of the White House but also in the public square. Giving her the pseudonym Veritas, the *New York Herald*'s publication of her letters from Washington meant that Abby and Charles knew exactly the sentiments of their hostess when they sat down at Mrs. Greenhow's dinner table, but that didn't stop Mrs. Adams from wading right into the hottest political topic of the day, declaring John Brown a "holy saint and martyr." Rose instantly shot back: "He was a traitor, and met a traitor's doom." The other guests, including New

York abolitionist William Seward, shifted uncomfortably in their seats and tried to change the subject but the face-off between the two women made for juicy gossip in society's sitting rooms—Buchanan told Rose that he had heard about it from "five or six persons, who all greatly commended your spirit and independence. And you have my most hearty approval."

Abby knew she was treading in dangerous waters with her outspoken views, which were even more frank in her letters to her son Henry. She referred to fellow Massachusetts Republican Anson Burlingame as a "pig" and was horrified when her husband brought him home for dinner. "I was obliged to be polite, but cool. . . . Dear me I should be killed if these remarks leaked out. It is dreadful to hold my tongue." Congressman Adams's grandmother, the first Abigail, had written almost the same words to her husband, John, many years before. And if she had harsh words for the members of Congress, Abby's pen also mercilessly skewered their wives: "Most of the Republicans are dowdies & I don't wonder the party wanted us here, for if we are not much, we are better than that. I wish our party was a little more upper crust." Dowdy wives, however, were the least of the party's problems. Republicans pushed John Sherman of Ohio for Speaker; the Democrats rejected him outright because he had signed the endorsement of the Hinton Helper book earlier that year. An astonished Sara Pryor reported that Sherman professed total naïveté about the political situation, saying: " 'When I came here I did not believe that the slavery question would come up; and but for the unfortunate affair of Brown at Harper's Ferry I do not believe that there would have been any feeling on the subject.' " He couldn't have been more mistaken—there was a great deal of feeling and there was no other subject.

The Republicans kept Sherman's name before the House for thirty-nine ballots, and at times he came tantalizingly close. Anna

Carroll, who was trying to effect a merger between what was left of the Know-Nothings and the Republicans, backed Sherman through much of the battle, but by late January, when she knew he'd never be elected, she declared to one of his political patrons: "I intend to tell him the whole truth as I know it and as no man . . . would ever tell him." Anna might be ready to tell the truth; it took Sherman's party a few more days to work up the same kind of courage. The Ohio Congressman had to go; New Jersey's William Pennington would be the compromise candidate. Despite her husband's objections, Abby Adams insisted on going to the House for the vote: "It meets at twelve, at ½ past ten the immense galleries were packed . . . & oh the excitement of all." It was quite a moment of surprise for the Democrats when all the Republicans switched to Pennington. However, Abby observed, "Now the question is, what can they do with him . . . this is all private, strictly, but they feel they have a heavy load to carry. He made a dozen mistakes in half an hour & will be a laughing stock I know, mainly from ignorance."

The election of a Speaker did little to calm the roiled relationships in Washington. Both the House and Senate launched investigations of the John Brown raid, questioning whether it was backed by a conspiracy and keeping it alive as topic number one. Politics took precedence over politeness: "Our social lines were now strictly drawn between North and South. Names were dropped from visiting lists, occasions avoided on which we might expect to meet members of the party antagonistic to our own," Sara Pryor sadly attested. "My friend Mrs. Douglas espoused all her husband's quarrels and distinctly 'cut' his opponents." Senator Douglas's chief opponent was the president of the United States, and that intraparty rift meant that "Mrs. Douglas never appeared at Miss Lane's receptions in the winter of 1859–1860." Adele had other reasons to stay away from the social scene through most of the fall, when she was pregnant and then almost died after her short-lived daughter's birth. But in the election year 1860, with Stephen Douglas running hard for president, his wife was back at his side.

Adele wasn't missing much by being shut out of the White House. President Buchanan only occasionally hosted the large receptions that had been such a fixture of early Washington when Louisa and John Quincy Adams occupied the Executive Mansion. And when Abby Adams went to one of the rare affairs in early February, she thought it didn't hold a candle to the ones she remembered, which "were stately & elegant & all appeared in their best. At that time, they were held once a week the season through & it was the mode of seeing & paying respect to the Chief Magistrate. But things are changed & Miss Lane does things which would have overturned the government then."

For all her criticism of the ways of current Washington, Mrs. Adams had to admit she too had "made one great blunder." President Buchanan had been roundly criticized for never inviting the opposition party to his dinners, but then when he sought to right the wrong, the Republicans rejected his peace offerings: "the 'house' last year declined his invitations, all but one man & many of the Senate." But the well-brought-up Charles Adams would of course say yes in a display of good manners and "accept any civilities he offered." When the presidential dinner invitation did come, the Adams had another engagement and Abby determinedly ignored the dictum that White House invitations take precedence. Buchanan took umbrage and, in Abby's words, the "old Pig, had not dignity enough to hold his tongue, but discussed it at dinner, expressed his mortification & hinted that the excuse was made up, for that we must know Etiquette." Of course the slight became the talk of the town and Abigail was forced to apologize at the next reception, which rankled her mightily, but she took satisfaction in telling Henry, "Our friends who positively hate him, are tickled beyond measure, not that we were wrong, but that *he* was mortified." So much for "paying respect to the Chief Magistrate."

The president was hardly alone in preferring to entertain only members of his own party, as Abby reported: "All I meet of the other side are polite enough & at receptions we cross each other, but they never invite any of us to dinners . . . this has been going on for years, but has been increased by the growth of our party & the John Brown affair & the 'Helper Book' nonsense." The distance between and within the parties would only increase as the presidential campaign heated up.

———————

THE CAPITAL CITY did stop bickering for a day on George Washington's Birthday. Though the monument so grandly dedicated twelve years earlier stood forlornly abandoned at 153 feet high, another tribute to the first president had been completed—an equestrian statue of General Washington was ready for an unveiling ceremony. American sculptor Clark Mills, who had dazzled the city a few years earlier with his replica of Andrew Jackson on horseback, received a commission from Congress to cast the commander in chief as he looked in the Revolutionary War. (Since most of the work going on at the Capitol was in the hands of European artists, the lawmakers were determined to reward a fellow countryman even though Mills's critics claimed that the only way he had managed to balance Jackson's horse on his hind legs was by filling its tail with cannonballs.)

As the day of the unveiling arrived, it seemed doomed to disappoint, clucked the Raleigh, North Carolina, *Weekly Standard.* "The inclement weather and seeming indifference of our people in regard to the celebration of the day, until the very last moment, kept numbers away who imagined that the display would be poor and unworthy of such an occasion." The city clearly wasn't in a mood to celebrate anything that Ash Wednesday, and the event was "wretchedly managed in all its details." But by afternoon the clouds cleared and crowds spilled onto the streets, where "every window and available stand-point on the route was occupied by fair ladies." At the site, after the president spoke "and the covering fell from the statue disclosing the revered Washington on his charger, the shout that burst from thousands of patriotic hearts was deafening." The cheers sounded for a somewhat scaled-down statue: "the appropriation by Congress was insufficient to carry out the original design." The fleeting celebratory moment brought regions and parties together for the last time before the war.

As the partisan divisions deepened, they extended beyond Congress to courtship. Abby and Charles Adams brought the two youngest of their surviving six children with them to Washington, but others of their offspring visited from time to time. When their son Charles came in March and started keeping company with the daughter of Democratic senator James A. Bayard Jr. of Delaware, his mother was none too pleased. The girl's mother might be "a fine woman" but "her father's character is not first class & a slave holder." That rankled Congressman Adams as well: "He thought it would be a bad thing for all, this mixture of slave & free. . . . I should rejoice in a good honest love match. It is worth all the money in the world, indeed makes money, for it is an incentive to a man to work." Though Abby was sorry to see Charles leave, she was glad he was getting out of town before becoming too entangled.

She wished she could leave as well. All the calling and partying and late-night dinners were wearing her out. (Most of the women voiced similar complaints. Virginia Clay could often only rally for the evening with the help of a "shocking box," which apparently sent some sort of electrical charge through her!) But Mrs. Adams did finally accept a dinner invitation at the White House, where there were "thirty six of us, Mr. Speaker Pennington & wife, members of Congress, of both parties, & a few strangers. The Speaker is a funny old man & it appears to me, silly. She is a motherly old lady. The President took her into dinner & I, as the oldest guest, sat to his left & I never intend doing it again. He is a heavy old toad." Abby's litany of must-attend events—a post–White House reception at the Sewards', a late dinner at Rose Greenhow's—would exhaust anyone. "This life kills me, but I go, as the Party seem to expect it & I am treated like a queen, only with more kindness." Because of their position as presidential descendants, the Adams enjoyed a unique place in polarized Washington, where Abby found "all acknowledge me on the other side politely, some much more." That was far from the norm: "We see nothing of each other excepting in morning visits, when we are strictly polite & amicable. It cannot be otherwise while this terrible struggle lasts & the excitement is so great. . . . As to Sumner, he neither speaks to, nor is spoke to, by a Southern person. His situation is very painful here. . . . Seward is *the great man* here, but not a Democrat have I ever seen at his receptions, although I believe he has one or two to dine." Abby found the partisan behavior disturbing if not downright offensive. She described running into Senator James Murray Mason of Virginia at someone's house: "To me, he never spoke, avoided me with great ease & when he could not do it civilly did it rudely." It would not be long before Mason and Adams faced off against each other in London representing the two sides of the American conflict to the British government.

Abby was used to political dissension. After all, her own family and friends usually disagreed with her husband, but, she advised her son, "they treated papa with the greatest respect. Had they ever by word or look done otherwise, I would have fought like a tiger with every one of them, & they know it." Still, his wife implied there were times when Charles Adams's views could be a trial: "As long as I respect my husband it is all easy enough, the agony would be to feel ashamed of him, as some women must." On the other hand, the not-so-long-suffering Abby concluded: "I would advise any young woman who wishes to have an easy, quiet life, not to marry an Adams. They are headstrong, willful, fighting ever, but honest & brave & straight-forward." Her husband's mother and grandmother had often felt the same way.

Most of the time Mrs. Adams found herself in pleasant company. Senator Seward took her to Silver Spring, Maryland, to spend time with the Blair family, and there she "met several nice people." It amused her that the patriarch, Preston Blair, had been "the bitterest opponent Grandpapa ever had. Now he is one of our warm Republicans. They are old fashioned, hospitable people, & have been very polite to us. They are the people who took Sumner home & nursed him so tenderly when he was injured." Abby also found that women of both parties, "even Mrs. Jeff Davis sit most amicably at my receptions." For her part, Mrs. Davis was finding it harder to socialize with the opposition as the congressional debates turned more personal. And one day when Lizzie Lee went to call on her old friend from Mississippi, she heard Varina tell a servant "that's the Blairs' carriage. Don't let any of them in but Mrs. Lee." This was the family that had lovingly nursed Varina the previous summer! Addie Douglas, on the other hand, seemed willing to call on anyone outside the White House, working the social circuit as hard as she could for her husband's candidacy, even showing up repeatedly at the home of the Seward stalwart Abby Adams: "as to

Mrs. Douglas, she returns my visits quite too fast, for my taste. I stick to the Seward colors, & don't wish to be mixed up with that beast." Another woman clearly not charmed by "the beast" Stephen Douglas, making Adele's politicking all the more important.

With the party conventions fast approaching, the women of Washington assessed the odds of each candidate—and Abby worried about what would happen if the Democrats picked the Illinois senator: "if that brute Douglas is nominated, it rejects Seward's nomination," because the Republicans would need to nominate someone with more appeal to the West than the New York senator. And, as his friend, Abby fretted about that outcome: "Seward is heart and soul in it, & I don't know how he will bear defeat." Even so, she entertained a man who might have been just the person to best Seward, another anti-slavery Republican who showed up in Washington that spring, clearly courting his party's politicians for the nomination. Ohio governor Salmon P. Chase knew the city well; he had been there as a young man studying law and returned as senator a decade earlier, when he had fought against the Kansas-Nebraska Act. Now he was back as "the rebel candidate for the presidency," in the view of Mrs. Adams. She threw a small dinner for him one night and he joined her and a lively group at the Blairs' another night, along with his nineteen-year-old daughter. It would not be long before Kate Chase would make her mark as one of the leading ladies of Washington.

———————

THE DEMOCRATS COULD not have called their convention in a less promising place for Stephen Douglas. Charleston, South Carolina, might have been a reasonable choice four years earlier, when the party was still able to come together to unite behind a candidate, but by the time the delegates assembled on April 23, 1860, the usually charming southern city was known as the "hotbed of disunion." Northerners expecting to enjoy the famous South Carolina graciousness were cut off and chagrined, according to Sara Pryor: "Charleston turned a cold shoulder to its guests from the North. All hearts, however, and all homes were opened to the Southerners. They dined with the aristocrats, drove with richly dressed ladies in gay equipages, and were entertained generally with lavish hospitality. All this tended to widen the breach between the sections." When the men went to sessions in the South Carolina Institute Hall, the women repaired to St. Michael's Episcopal Church to pray daily for the success of the southern proslavery platform, opposed by Douglas. And Buchanan's henchmen were doing everything they could to derail the president's sworn enemy.

Still, at first it looked like the Illinois senator could prevail. One of his backers from Boston, F. O. Prince, wrote to Adele with the good news that though he didn't "reckon the number of chickens until the same are fully hatched—I feel assured that the day is ours. Our colors are nailed to the mast . . . we are resolved 'never to say die.'" As to Charleston? He was impressed by the "beauty and fashion" and pleased to learn "that Washington does not hold all the loveliness & grace & wit of the Union—although *lately* I have had some suspicions to the contrary." His big complaint was the price of everything and he joked to Adele, "If Mr. Douglas is not nominated pretty soon, I shall become a *pauper* . . . to avert this catastrophe, you better come here and electioneer." But no amount of electioneering could have secured the nomination for Douglas, who had infuriated the southern delegates by his rejection of Kansas as a slave state. When the North managed to win the fight over the party platform, balking at the South's adamant insistence on a federal slave code proposed by Jefferson Davis, southern states walked out. The voting for president proceeded anyway, but with a requirement that a candidate receive the votes of two-thirds of the delegates, no one got enough for the nomination. After fifty-seven ballots the party decided to call it quits and try again in a few weeks, this time in Baltimore. But first the Republicans would meet in Chicago.

The Seward backer, Abby Adams, didn't know what the opposition's debacle would mean for her candidate. "The Democratic Convention, you will see in the papers. It complicates things as much for us, as for them." The Republicans had planned to pick their nominee after the other party's choice was clear, so they could counterbalance it. She expected Douglas to win in Baltimore in June, but, she said, "We feel ticklish. There is one hope ever uppermost, that the breach in the Democratic party can't be healed, the hatred of the Southern men to Douglas is terrible, intense, & many of them openly say they should prefer Mr. Seward as president to Mr. Douglas. To be sure they are fire-eaters, & seceders & wish to make that an excuse, for dissolving our blessed Union." Abby had that right. But it's not surprising she knew the score, since "there is of course nothing but politics talked of here, by men and women." She clearly relished the political conversation and planned to take in Jefferson Davis's speech defending his platform position in a couple of days: "Visits are falling off, so I hope to be able to be at the Capitol more."

Though she protested against those visits, plus the endless round of receptions and dinners, Mrs. Charles Francis Adams understood she must do her part for the embattled Republican Party, and she became quite cross with those who refused to pull their weight—especially her old friend Charles Sumner. "I gave him a piece of my mind yesterday," she indignantly told her son. "That he expected us all to go out & show ourselves, & entertain, & work all the time for the cause & he did nothing, not a thing." Still, she kept up her end both hosting dinners and attending them, including one at the home of that "silly old goose" Speaker Pennington, who was "weak as water, I think & I snub him terribly, but his wife & daughter are nice good people. He is a trial to his party, & the worse that they can't say so." Mrs. Adams, on the other hand, said so without hesitancy.

FOR ALL THE political clouds hanging over Washington, "never was a spring more delightful than that of 1860. The Marine Band played every Saturday in the President's grounds, and thither the whole world repaired," Sara Pryor recalled happily. "Easy compliments to the ladies fell from the lips of the men who could apply to each other in debate abuse too painful to remember." Abby Adams also enjoyed the "warm & lovely" spring, with "the trees & grass superb" and music on the White House lawn. And she had to admit that the city offered other diversions as well. The "famous juggler" at the theater was "very wonderful" and the auctions amazed her. "The ladies all go here to auctions & bid themselves quite as much as the gentlemen & it is considered a regular entertainment. You meet all your friends & chat & gossip, & laugh & spend money." When friends came to visit Abby, she took them on tours of the expanded Capitol building, which she deemed "superb." Then there were trips to Mount Vernon, the nearby Virginia home of George and Martha Washington, which a determined group of women had managed to buy from the first president's heirs and were trying to save. "The whole thing is a disgraceful ruin," Abby reported with disgust. She had done some fund-raising for the Mount Vernon Ladies Association back home in Quincy, Massachusetts, but the "ladies" faced a daunting task: "They estimate it will cost twenty thousand dollars to put it in repairs, & two thousand yearly to keep it so." (With a great deal of difficulty, the women succeeded. Without any government money, they restored and preserved the mansion and grounds and eventually built the impressive museums and libraries that are on the site now.)

Conversation about what would happen at the Republican convention when it met in Chicago on May 18 took a brief breath when all of Washington stopped to stare in wonder at the first ever visiting delegation from Japan. "We had much curiosity about the Japanese," Sara Pryor said by way of understatement, "and were delighted with the prospect of receiving the embassy from the new land." There would be a series of events, including one at the White House "to witness the presentation of credentials and the reception of the President." Sara and a friend were in the Senate gallery when a member rose to propose adjourning "to meet and welcome the Japanese." Even so simple a proposal as that could not go unchallenged in 1860, when another senator huffed that he hoped "the Senate of the United States of America will not adjourn for every show that comes along." But the city was mesmerized by the "show." When the ship carrying the strangers pulled into the Navy Yard, "half the town repaired to the barracks to witness the debarkation of the strange and gorgeously appareled voyagers from the gaily decorated vessel," Virginia Clay excitedly recollected, "as they descended the flag-bedecked gangplanks and passed out through a corridor formed of eager people, crowding curiously to gaze at them." Abby Adams picked up the story from there: "we walked down to the steamer where many servants & others were left in charge of affairs & saw several of them, some sat for their photographs & were very funny." At the White House the next day, "Mr. Buchanan would have done well to select his guests with regard to their slimness," Sara quipped; it was so crowded that no one could see anything and "the ceremony was long. The murmured voices were low. One might have imagined oneself at a funeral." With a somewhat better view, Abby saw the box with the treaty presented and thought that the Japanese visitors were "dignified"; not so was the president, who was "all inelegant."

———————

BUT MRS. ADAMS was much more concerned about the next president than the current one and feared for her friend Seward: "If he is not nominated it will be a cruel blow to him." A few days earlier a group of moderate former Whigs had met in Baltimore and nominated their own candidates—John Bell of Tennessee, who had held many offices, including Speaker of the House, and Edward Everett of Massachusetts, who happened to be Abby's brother-in-law. Officially called the Constitutional Union Party, its elderly members immediately earned it the nickname of the "old gentleman's" party and Abby was astonished that at age 67 Everett would "stoop to such tricks," as she feared he would take votes away from her party in Massachusetts.

The Republican gathering in a "Wigwam" built for the occasion in Chicago was far less contentious than the Democratic convention in Charleston but hardly less infused with intrigue. Though party insiders genuinely worried about the New Yorker Seward's appeal in the West and saw him as a single-issue antislavery candidate, more than a few shenanigans helped deny him the nomination. Illinois's favorite son, Abraham Lincoln, the dark horse candidate, had tremendous support from the Chicago crowd of some ten thousand people who crammed the unsteady building and many counterfeit tickets issued to Lincoln backers allowed them to block Seward supporters trying to take their seats. Convention organizers also placed the New York senator's delegates at a distance from any pivotal state, making persuasive conversations difficult. William Seward's shaky lead on the first two ballots collapsed, the Illinois men wheeled and dealed so furiously their candidate made it over the top on the third go-round. One deal:

a pledge to the Ohio delegation that favorite son Salmon Chase could have anything he wanted from Lincoln. The delegates then picked Hannibal Hamlin of Maine for vice president. Though the platform took a stand against the spread of slavery, it also condemned John Brown's raid and pledged to protect the "peculiar institution" in the southern states where it existed. Other proposals, such as the building of a transcontinental railroad, the creation of a Homestead Act, and a higher tariff to protect northern manufacturers, moved the party away from a straight antislavery stance. But that did nothing to placate the South, where Lincoln's nomination "represented nothing but the embodiment of the enmity of his party," lamented Varina Davis.

Back in Washington, Abby Adams admired Seward's acceptance of his defeat: "No whining, complaint, or boasting. He has behaved splendidly & don't seem to care, & is really a *man*." But as for herself, "it was a bitter disappointment." And her sons "were heart & soul for Seward and don't care a pin for Lincoln." Seward tried to convince them otherwise, arguing "he has known him well & that he is an honest true man." She just hoped that Congress would wrap things up so she could go home. The House had already voted to adjourn on June 18, but "the Senate behave like children and silly ones at that." The problem? "Jeff Davis & Douglas make speeches & quarrel, all the time, & don't care whether they adjourn or not, they & their family both live here." That's been the complaint of congressional families wanting to get out of town to this day. And in 1860 they still had a Democratic convention to get through.

The second attempt to unify the party proved no more successful than the first. The "Old Gentlemen's" party had already split away and, hoping to defuse the slavery grenades exploding around them, adopted a platform that simply endorsed the Constitution and Union. When the remainder of the Democrats showed up at the Front

Street Theatre in Baltimore on June 18, nothing had been resolved. This time Stephen Douglas was able to secure the nomination, with Georgian Herschel V. Johnson as his running mate, but the southerners, still insisting on their proslavery plank, once again walked out. A few days later they assembled their own Baltimore convention at the Maryland Institute Hall. With Buchanan's vice president, John Breckinridge, as their candidate and Joseph Lane of Oregon in the number-two slot, the four-way race was on. The only thing all the candidates could agree on: a railroad to cross the fracturing nation all the way to the Pacific Ocean.

———

CONGRESS FINALLY ADJOURNED in late June. Many of the members were out of town that October when the eighteen-year-old Prince of Wales paid a visit to his mother the queen's old friend Harriet Lane, and Harriet's uncle, the president. The Prince's entourage took up so much space in the White House that Buchanan and Harriet had to sleep in the hallway, but Queen Victoria's affable young son cordially greeted the thousands of guests at the state dinner held in his honor and then accompanied Harriet on a sightseeing tour of the city. It included a stop at Mrs. Smith's Institute for young ladies, where his hostess bested the prince at tenpins in a shocking display of a woman playing sports. He was then brought back to the White House for another dinner and a soggy fireworks display. Harriet Lane had become quite popular with the American public. A picture of her printed on cards became something people collected like baseball cards and a copy of it filled a full page in *Frank Leslie's Illustrated Newspaper*, along with a flattering article that referred to her as the "first lady in the land." This made her the first inhabitant of the White House to be referred to by that title in public print.

The day after the prince's defeat at tenpins the party boarded the cutter named for the first lady, the *Harriet Lane*, and to the strains of the Marine Band's music sailed down the Potomac River to Mount Vernon. Here was Prince Edward, the great-grandson of George III, honoring the man, George Washington, who had defeated the British king. Once at the estate, they were "conducted with an absurd formality to the house," scorned the *New York Times*. The prince was shown the prize object, the key to the Bastille, but he "seemed more interested in the fascinations of Miss Lane than in the terrible reminiscences of the key." More formal entertainments in Washington followed and then the prince planned to "take the cars for Richmond, at which place they hope to arrive in time to see a great slave sale which takes place in the afternoon." It's so startling now to see those words in print—but it was startling even then. The visit to the South had been highly controversial and in the end Edward went only to church and the state capitol, staying clear of the slavery controversy. Years later, in 1902, when he was crowned King Edward VII, the monarch invited Harriet Lane to his coronation.

The Congress was still out of town when the results of the election came in. With less than 40 percent of the vote, Abraham Lincoln would be the first Republican president. Stephen Douglas had waged a vigorous campaign, barnstorming the country with Adele at his side and breaking with all tradition that dictated a candidate stays decorously at home while surrogates hit the trail. When Douglas realized that Lincoln would win, he turned his tour into a call for preserving the Union. But few were listening in the cacophony of voices raised during the race, which completely divided the regions of the country. In the states surrounding the disenfranchised District of Columbia, barely anyone had voted for the new president—less than 3 percent in Maryland, less than 2 percent in Virginia.

No one knew what the results would mean for the city and the country, but a diary entry from Elizabeth Lomax, a widow from Virginia living in Washington, summed up the speculation: "The papers speak of the dissolution of the Union as an accomplished fact." The heated partisanship of the first session of Congress infected rowdies in the streets as roving drunken gangs turned the Capital City into "the centre of violence and disorder," moaned one usually upbeat newspaper correspondent. "It has a monument that will never be finished; a Capitol that is to have a dome," and "the reputation of Sodom." No one could think about anything but the "danger of dissolution of the Union . . . everything else is forgotten . . . crime goes unpunished," a distressed Louisa Meigs told her husband. Such was the atmosphere as the politicians returned.

"WHEN BELLES MET they no longer discussed furbelows and flounces, but talked of forts and fusillades," in Virginia Clay's telling. "Women went daily to the Senate gallery to listen to the angry debates on the floor below." Her friend Sara Pryor shared the memory: "Thoroughly alarmed, the women of Washington thronged the galleries of the House and the Senate Chamber. From morning until the hour of adjournment we would sit, spell-bound, as one after another drew the lurid picture of disunion and war." The alarms of the southern women were sounded as well by their northern sisters. Louisa Meigs informed her husband, Montgomery, who was in Florida, "There is not doubt I suppose that Carolina will go out of the Union. . . . If none of the Southern States shall follow her lead she will find in a short time—that '*spunk* however justified is not a *paying* institution.'" That was the northern hope—that any separation would be short-lived. And separation seemed more and more inevitable. Elizabeth Lomax's diary tracks the buildup to the actual break: "Dec. 2, 'The papers are teeming with secession.' Dec. 3, 'The South seems determined on disunion. God forbid!' Dec. 5, 'Many persons have gone to the Capitol to hear the debate in Congress. Much excitement expected. One retires at night with the feeling anything may happen tomorrow.' Dec. 8, 'The general opinion seems to be that there is little hope of preserving the Union.' Dec. 14, 'There are very few parties, though usually Washington is gay at this season—everyone is too anxious over the political situation to indulge in light hearted gaiety.' Dec. 18, 'I am, after much thought and deliberation, *definitely for the Union with some amendments to the Constitution.*' Dec. 20, 'South Carolina has seceded—God defend us from civil war.'"

President Buchanan was at a wedding reception when he heard the news. After the ceremony, guests had spread out around the bride's parents' house but the president stayed in his chair receiving well-wishers. To be polite, Sara Pryor kept him company, until the noise in the hallway reached such a pitch that Buchanan wanted to know if the house was on fire. She went to investigate and found a congressman from South Carolina ecstatically clutching a telegram with the bulletin that his state had seceded. It was then left to Mrs. Pryor to inform the President of the United States that his country was coming apart. "Falling back and grasping the arms of his chair, he whispered, 'Madam, might I beg you to have my carriage called?'" After she saw the sad and shaken Buchanan safely off, Sara and Roger Pryor also left the wedding and life as they knew it: "This was the tremendous event which was to change all our lives—to give us poverty for riches, mutilation and wounds for strength and health, obscurity and degradation for honor and distinction, exile and loneliness for inherited homes and friends, pain and death for happiness and life."

Washington initially reacted to the news of secession with a show of patriotic fervor. "My heart swells with emotion at the sound of the Star Spangled banner and unfurling of our national flag," Louisa Meigs exulted, though she claimed to have "no sectional feeling." Lizzie Lee, on the other hand, sided firmly with the North: "The Union Flag streams from nearly every house top," she ballyhooed to her husband, but she added that her father, Preston Blair, "& all thinking men are sure that peaceable secession is a fallacy." That specter of impending war made for a somber Christmas season: "People look gloomy and talk despondently of our condition," a saddened Louisa Meigs wrote; "it would seem to be a defiance of public feeling and sentiment to give any entertainment at this time." Even New Year's was subdued. "This is usually a gala day in Washington," Elizabeth Lomax recorded on January 1, 1861, "but this day is oh, so different. No social calling, everyone looks harassed and anxious—the state of our beloved country the cause."

Harriet Lane was on hand to receive at the annual New Year's open house at the White House, and Adele Douglas threw a counter-reception where "the North and South mingled fraternally," including the secessionist firebrand Roger Pryor. Roger's wife, however, admitted that no one pretended all was normal: "The season which was always ushered in on New Year's Day resolved itself literally this year into a residence in the galleries of the Senate Chamber and the House of Representatives." In the Capitol the antagonists and onlookers like Virginia Clay kept watch around the clock, uncertain of what the future would bring. "For weeks, men would not leave their seats by day or by night, lest they might lose their votes on the vital questions of the times. At the elbows of Senators, drowsy with long vigils, pages stood, ready to waken them at the calling of the roll." And the women cared just as passionately about the politics as the men. When Louisa Meigs went to visit Varina Davis she was shocked by her friend: "her face and eyes were pregnant with storm and cloud. . . . Mrs. D has done and is no doubt doing all that she can to urge her husband by all the influence she possesses to the most determined uncompromising measures."

Compromise had long since been abandoned. When Senator Seward of New York made a much-anticipated speech on January 12, it disappointed Elizabeth Lomax because it "was not considered conciliatory. Political events breathe defiance to the Federal Government." By then Mississippi, Florida, and Alabama had joined South Carolina in withdrawing from the Union and militias from those states had seized the U.S. Navy Yard in Pensacola, Florida. The southern woman who was purser at the yard eventually made her way to Washington, where she "amused us by telling of the manner in which she *sassed* the Secessionist officials—she has a woman's tongue and knows how to use it," Louisa Meigs jested to her husband; "if she had been a man I suppose they would have tried to blow her brains out." But it was no laughing matter on January 21 when the senators from those states said their farewells in the United States Capitol. Calling it "the saddest day of my life," Virginia Clay described the scene: "The galleries of the Senate, which hold, it is estimated, one thousand people, were packed densely, principally with women, who, trembling with excitement, awaited the denouement of the day." As one by one the senators stood and announced their departure from the chamber and from the country, "women grew hysterical and waved their handkerchiefs. . . . Men wept and embraced each other mournfully. . . . Scarcely a member of that Senatorial body but was pale with the terrible significance of the hour . . . nor was there a patriot on either side who did not deplore and whiten before the evil that brooded so low over the nation."

The last of the southerners to speak on "Secession Day," as it came to be called, was Jefferson Davis. "Mr. Davis told me that he had great difficulty in reaching his seat, as the ladies, of course, could not be crowded, and each one feared that the other would encroach on her scanty bit of room," his wife reported. She wondered if the crowd "saw beyond the cold exterior of the orator—his deep depression, his desire for reconciliation, and his overweening love for the Union in whose cause he had bled, and to maintain which he was ready to sacrifice all but liberty and equality." But then Varina realized: "Not his wife alone, but all who sat spellbound before him knew how genuine was his grief, and entered into the spirit of his loving appeal." A tearful "final adieu" and then "inexpressibly sad he left the chamber, with but faint hope; and that night I heard the often reiterated prayer, 'May God have us in His holy keeping, and grant that before it is too late peaceful councils may prevail.'" But peaceful councils had been trying and failing to avert disunion and war since the Congress had convened. And by the second of February 1861, Georgia, Louisiana, and Texas would join the list of seceding states.

"From the hour of this exodus of Senators from the official body, all of Washington seemed to change," Virginia Clay remembered. "Each step preparatory to our departure was a pang. Carriages and messengers dashed through the streets excitedly. Farewells were to be spoken, and many, we knew, would be final." That finality struck Varina Davis as well: "To wrench oneself from the ties of fifteen years is a most distressing effort. Our friends had entered into our joys and sorrows with unfailing sympathy. We had shared their anxieties and seen their children grow from infancy to adolescence." One of those friends, Lizzie Lee, was equally sad: "Mrs. Jeff. asked me if I was going down south to fight her—I told her no. I would kiss & hug her too tight to break any *bonds* between us." But there was nothing to be done: "We left Washington 'exceeding sorrowful' and took our three little children with us." Varina had tried to take the family seamstress with them as well, but Elizabeth Keckley, a former slave, decided it was wiser not to go south. The *New York Herald* later surmised, "To none of these ladies was the thought pleasant of secession from the Union and consequent giving up whatever of social dominion she had acquired."

"The poor old gentleman who presides at the White House thinks it's best for the preservation of his own health and reason that he should not give himself entirely over to grief at the condition of affairs to which he finds his country is brought." Thus did Louisa Meigs divulge the attitude toward hapless President Buchanan, who seemed to do nothing as the United States disintegrated. "He is said to have no friend either North or South—He has utterly failed to please either section of the Country." Ironically, just at this time the state that had been such a cause of conflict, Kansas, came peaceably into the Union as a free state on January 29. And various peace committees kept trying to hold what was left of the country together, focusing on the slave states that had not yet left the Union. In one of them, Maryland, Anna Carroll worked with Governor Thomas Hicks to keep the secessionists at bay. He welcomed her letters to the newspapers in support of him, and her Republican politician friends were heartened by Hicks's letters to Anna assuring her that he was a solid Union man. In early February, just as the seceded states were meeting in Montgomery, Alabama, to form a government, one more "Peace Convention" convened in a blinding snowstorm in Washington. Making another effort at gaiety, Adele Douglas hosted a party for the putative peacemakers, but Elizabeth Lomax probably summed up the mood of most when she tersely noted, "Declined: we do not feel in a party mood."

Union sympathizers tried to put the best face on what was happening. "The arrival of 1000 U.S. troops & the departure of the

Secessionists has rendered the City very gay—a party every night," Lizzie Lee regaled her husband with all the news, including her hope that war could be averted because she believed that the newly elected president of the Confederacy, Jefferson Davis, was a moderate and "*in private* antisecession," and that "Mrs. Davis is a warm personal friend—of Anderson," meaning Robert Anderson, the U.S. Army major holding South Carolina's Fort Sumter for the Union. Personal friendships could always be counted on before to smooth over differences, and so many women in Washington had friendships on both sides—in these tense days Elizabeth Lomax entertained both Custis Lee and Robert Lincoln, the sons of the two men who would soon be mournfully pitted against each other. But everyone knew it would take more than friendships to prevent the coming catastrophe and the Capital City cowered in terror. That's why troops were coming in by the thousands—for fear of riots. No one knew what violence might erupt on February 13, the day when the Electoral College votes were to be counted, or February 23, when President-elect Lincoln was expected to arrive in town, or, most especially, on March 4—Inauguration Day.

Anna Carroll sought assurances from Maryland's Governor Hicks that she would be safe as the only border state woman in her boardinghouse. She didn't want to set a bad example, concerned that her departure "would be the immediate signal of every Northern lady's leaving—supposing it be done from apprehension of danger." Lizzie Lee, as a trustee of the orphan asylum, didn't think she had a choice but to send "some of our children out to the far west today—I felt reluctant about it—but the hard times makes me cautious about keeping them when we can make any other sure provision for them." As the inauguration approached, "we were advised to send our women and children out of the city," Sara Pryor regretfully recalled. Though her hotheaded husband had been pushing their home state of Virginia to secede, the state stayed in the Union and Roger Pryor stayed in Washington. But Sara "hastily" packed up and with her little boys sailed down the Potomac, "standing on deck as long as I could to see the dome of the Capitol." It was the end of the Washington she knew and loved: "We must bid adieu to the bright days—the balls, the merry hair-dresser, the round of visits, the levees, the charming 'at homes.' The setting sun of such a day should pillow itself on golden clouds, bright harbingers of a morning of beauty and happiness. Alas, alas! 'whom the gods destroy they first infatuate.'"

CHAPTER 4

LEFT: *Dorothea Dix, whose advocacy for the mentally ill made her a prominent personage internationally, was appointed Superintendent of Army Nurses by the Union Army.* RIGHT: *Rose O'Neal Greenhow, a Washington, D.C., hostess to the politically powerful, spied for the Confederacy and landed in jail with her daughter, "Little Rose."*

Rose Goes to Jail, Jessie Goes to the White House, Dorothea Goes to Work

1861

I felt rather anxious as this was the day for counting the president's votes and trouble was threatened. However, it passed off quietly," Elizabeth Lomax sighed with relief on February 13, 1861, Ash Wednesday. The Joint Session of Congress called to preside over the official count of Abraham Lincoln's electoral landslide had gone off without a hitch after weeks of rumors that the southern states were planning to invade Washington and make it the Confederate capital. Secessionist sympathizers proudly sported their blue cockades as they promoted their case, causing cautious congressmen to post guards at the Capitol and conduct searches for explosives. So it was only a select group who could attend the proclamation of the vote for the new president. Acting in his role as president of the Senate, Vice President Breckinridge, who had been defeated by Lincoln, announced the tally, lending an air of drama to the occasion.

The expectation of invasion had reached such a level of credibility that the old general in chief Winfield Scott had imported a few companies of troops from other parts of the country. "The city has assumed a very military appearance," Louisa Meigs complained. "The sound of the bugle is heard and soldiers are seen at every point. The Southern people are very indignant at such a display by Gen[era]l Scott of Federal troops. They think it aggravating to the people and totally unnecessary." Even so, on Washington's Birthday Scott staged a grand military parade, defying the peace commissioners who were still meeting in a final attempt to avoid war. Praying that the conflict could be avoided, sixty-four-year old Ann Green, a widow living on a farm inside the district limits, wrote to her daughter in Virginia that the family thought it "the grandest parade that ever was in Washington." And Elizabeth Lomax, who went with her household to "see the regulars marching by, wonderful looking men and well drilled," still hoped that the anniversary of the first president's birth the following year would "find us a united and happy people." But that prospect grew more remote with each passing day.

Events of the very next day underlined how very disunited and unhappy the people were. "The President is to arrive here today. The reception will be a very quiet one," Mrs. Lomax jotted in her diary, then, apparently later, added: "Have just heard that President Lincoln arrived in the six o'clock train—Mrs. Lincoln and son came in the afternoon." The president's protectors had picked up reports that there was a plot to kill him as he traveled through the hostile city of

Baltimore. Death threats had followed Lincoln all along the way of his whistle-stop tour from Illinois, but the one in Maryland seemed believable. It was a slave state and, though it had not seceded, was considered particularly antagonistic toward Republican rule. Plus the warning came from a prominent man—the head of the Philadelphia, Wilmington and Baltimore Railroad, Samuel Felton. His source? The well-known social reformer Dorothea Dix, who, in her travels to inspect mental institutions throughout the South, heard of an "extensive and organized conspiracy" to seize Washington and take the president-elect's life.

So, against his better judgment, Lincoln allowed his advisors to bundle him surreptitiously onto an early morning train and steal him into the Capital City in disguise. "The president-elect was to have arrived this afternoon and measures were taken to receive him." Ann Green attested. "To everybody's surprise he reached the Willard Hotel at six this morning—many think because he did not wish to pass through Baltimore with the knowledge of the people." And from the White House, Harriet Lane apprised a friend of her impressions of events: "I suppose you have heard of Lincoln's sudden & unexpected arrival yesterday morning—it will no doubt create a profound sensation. He was here at before 11. The glimpse I caught of him was the image of Burns—our awkward bus man who waits on the door. Burns is the best looking, but I only had a side view. They say Mrs. L. is awfully western, loud and unrefined."

Harriet's political sensibilities were well-attuned—the ignominious arrival did cause a sensation, becoming the stuff of endless political jokes and cartoons that Lincoln regretted for the rest of his life. Up until that point, as Lizzie Lee correctly noted, the Lincolns' progression by train from Illinois was "in triumph all the way." Cheering crowds had greeted them all along the route as opposition politicians made their peace with the next president and a reception held by Mary Lincoln in New York met with press approval. The pro-Republican *New York Times* declared the event augured well "for the social qualities of the future mistress of the National Mansion, promising to Mrs. [*sic*] Harriet Lane a worthy successor." Now all of that goodwill could be wiped away by the ludicrous image of a panicky president sneaking into town in Scotch cap and cloak. Still, even if they were the butt of jokes, the Lincolns would now occupy the chief seat of power in Washington. And the ladies were eager to size up the newcomers.

A meeting with President Buchanan and his Cabinet, followed by a session with the peace commissioners at his hotel, took up much of the day. "Mr. Lincoln was then notified that the ante-rooms and main parlors of the hotel were filled with ladies who desired to pay their respects, to which the president elect very promptly consented," reported a friendly Pennsylvania newspaper; "the ladies, who thought he was awkward at first sight, changed their opinion and now declare him 'a very pleasant, sociable gentleman, and not bad looking by any means.'" If the president-elect met with some initial approval from "the ladies," Mary Lincoln was not so lucky. The first-lady-to-be wisely surrounded herself with a bevy of female relatives for her debut in the Capital City, where the matrons of society—most of them southerners—snickered behind their hands at her. They saw Mrs. Lincoln as nothing more than a country bumpkin, with the unpolished manners of the unsophisticated West.

———————

MANNERS WERE THE least of the administration's concerns as March 4—Inauguration Day—approached. While Lincoln carefully constructed what would be his war Cabinet, made up mostly of men who had opposed him in the political campaign, General Scott placed squads of soldiers at strategic spots around the city in preparation for disaster. Some of those soldiers, West Point men, visited at Virginian Elizabeth Lomax's house on February 28 along with "Bob Lincoln (son of President Lincoln)." It was one of the last times that a gathering like that would occur. The young men Mrs. Lomax entertained that night ended up on opposite sides in the war—a war she knew would soon come. For the moment, she simply recorded: "The city thronged with strangers." But no longer with members of the peace commission, who had failed to produce a plan acceptable to anyone and packed up in time to make way for the merrymakers celebrating the inauguration.

"Mr. Lincoln will without doubt be inaugurated and safely installed in the White House, but what must be his feelings at taking the reins of such a government into his hand," Louisa's daughter Mary Meigs wrote to her brother at West Point; "he is hated by half the people he means to protect with a hatred which cannot be described." Not everyone shared the young woman's certainty that the transfer of power would go off as planned. "This day Mr. Lincoln has been inaugurated amidst the fears and apprehension of many people that had anticipated mobs and riots of devious descriptions," Ann Green noted to her daughter with relief, but "everything went off peacefully—the military were placed in various positions throughout the city ready to act should any occasion make it necessary." Elizabeth Lomax echoed the sentiment: "This dreaded day has at last arrived. Thank Heaven all is peaceful and quiet." Her son Lindsay had "commanded the escort for President Lincoln," whose inaugural address her household read aloud when they received their Washington *Star* that evening. Her conclusion: "I thought there was no doubt of its sanity and its excellence."

That was not the first time that day that someone other than the president read the speech out loud. Early that morning Lincoln had enlisted his son Robert to deliver it, so the soon-to-be president could hear what it sounded like. The predawn reading of the address started a busy day in the Capital City, where, the *New York Times* reported, "From early daylight the streets were thronged with people, some still carrying carpet-bags in hand, having found no quarters in which to stop." It was close to noon when President Buchanan left the White House to collect President-elect Lincoln at Willard's Hotel. As the pair proceeded tensely down Pennsylvania Avenue toward the Capitol, "troops lined the avenue and at every corner there was a mounted orderly," leaving young Julia Taft wide-eyed. "The usual applause was lacking as the President's carriage, surrounded by a close guard of cavalry, passed and an ugly murmur punctuated by some abusive remarks followed it down the avenue." This was the sixteen-year-old's first view of the man who no one was sure would survive the day: "One of the ladies near us said, 'There goes that Illinois ape, the cursed Abolitionist. But he will never come back alive.'"

For the first time tight security surrounded the Senate chamber, where, explained the *New York Times*, "only the favored few were admitted upon the floor, while the galleries were reserved for and occupied by a select number of ladies." After Vice President Hannibal Hamlin took his oath, the outgoing and incoming presidents entered the room "arm in arm" before they emerged out on the ceremonial platform erected in front of the still-under-construction dome. Before crowds of onlookers, including "the entire Diplomatic Corps, dressed in gorgeous attire," and "fair ladies by the score," Abraham Lincoln moved many to tears as he concluded with his heart-wrenching plea that the "mystic chords of memory" might yet "swell the chorus of the Union, when again touched, as surely they will be by the better angels of our nature." Excited by the events of the day, government worker Clara Barton described it to a friend: "we have a *live Republican* President, and, what is perhaps singular, during the whole day we saw no one who appeared to manifest the least dislike to his living."

With the relief of an unmarred ceremony behind him, the president faced an exhausting day. He received hundreds of strangers and kissed thirty-four little girls representing all of the states, including those that had seceded, before heading off to the Inaugural Ball, which would serve as a coming-out party for Mary Todd Lincoln. Reports from that night vary markedly depending on the political persuasion of the newspaper covering it. "The ball is a decided success," heralded the *New York Times*, whose founder, Henry Raymond, was also a prominent Republican politician; "toilettes of ladies are noticeable, with but few exceptions, for elegance and good taste." At 10:45, when the guests of honor made their entrance into a hall built for the occasion and "tastefully decorated with shields and flags," the vice president and the president's friend Senator Edward Baker of Oregon escorted Lincoln while Mrs. Lincoln held the arm of Senator Douglas, who had wooed and lost the young Mary Todd decades earlier. "Miss Edwards, niece of Mrs. Lincoln, is acknowledged to be the belle of the evening," the *Times* reporter emphatically declared.

While the rival *New York Herald* agreed that the ball presented "a beautiful spectacle," its "monster chandeliers" and "numerous jets of gas" producing a "brilliant effect," on closer examination "considering the day, the occasion and the gorgeous array of distinguished celebrities which have figured at our preceding inauguration balls, the present one exhibited a decidedly meager collection of lions of any description." Though Mary Lincoln came in for some condescending praise for adapting herself "to the exalted station to which she has been so strangely advanced, from the simple social life of the little inland capital of Illinois," all in all, the reporter found it a "melancholy affair, abounding in fears and forebodings of coming evil." The partygoers seemed unable to put aside the cares of the times and enjoy the evening: "The Southern element of vitality was missing. . . . It was a Northern and Northwestern assemblage. The women were extensively the representatives of the maids and matrons of the rural districts of the North and the great West; the nasal twang of the strong-willed Puritan was heard on every side." No Mrs. Clay, Mrs. Davis, or Mrs. Pryor to liven up the evening, or the parlors of Washington, from there on out.

Many of the women who remained in the Capital City turned cold shoulders to the new first lady, choosing not to call on her at Willard's Hotel before the inauguration, as protocol expected. "The capital had buzzed for weeks with stories of the uncouth manners of the President-elect and his wife," remembered Julia Taft, who came to be a welcome and regular guest of the Lincolns. "Elegant Washington ladies raised holy hands of horror at the thought of such a rustic pair following the polished Buchanan and his accomplished niece, Miss Lane in the White House." The ladies had their opportunity to get a look at how Mrs. Lincoln would perform a few nights after the inauguration when she nervously introduced her White House receptions. A huge crush of people pushed into the Blue Room, where a Washington reporter marveled that Mrs. Lincoln, dressed in magenta silk, "bore the fatigue of the two and a half hour siege with great patience."

What the reporter couldn't know was how her lack of patience had almost prevented Mrs. Lincoln from attending her own event. Mary had hired Varina Davis's dressmaker, Elizabeth Keckley, for that very important evening, but Mrs. Keckley had not yet arrived with her creation when Mrs. Lincoln was ready to get dressed. When the seamstress did show up she found the ladies of the household pleading with a petulant Mary Lincoln, who insisted: "I have no time now to dress, and, what is more, I will not dress, and go down-stairs." With some effort, Mary was finally coaxed into letting Mrs. Keckley help her into her gown, and so began a complicated but important friendship between the first lady and the former slave.

If she made a friend the night of that first huge reception, which ended with no one being able to find their wraps, Mary Lincoln also realized that she had entertained an enemy. The beautiful, brilliant, and haughty Kate Chase, the twenty-one-year-old daughter of the secretary of the Treasury, former Ohio Governor Salmon Chase, thought Mary had usurped her place. She, Kate, standing tall and statuesque, all in white, should be the first lady of the land, not the somewhat dumpy forty-two-year-old wife of the gawky man who had, in the young woman's view, stolen the presidency from her father. Miss Chase shone at the center of her own circle at Mary's reception and again starred a few weeks later when the Lincolns hosted their first dinner in the State Dining Room, to honor the Cabinet. But the president had a great deal more on his mind that April night than a possible feud between his wife and the daughter of his Treasury secretary. When the men adjourned to the Red Room after dinner, he told his Cabinet about the dire situation at Fort Sumter.

———————

STANDING ON A tiny island in the middle of Charleston Harbor, the unfinished fort served as the only garrison in the area still occupied by federal troops—South Carolina had seized the others after secession. In early January, President Buchanan's meager attempt to deliver fresh men and supplies had been turned back when the ship came under fire by military cadets, and now Major Robert Anderson was unsure how long he could hold out without more food. When Jefferson Davis sent negotiators to Washington to discuss a handover of the fort to the Confederacy, Lincoln refused to meet with them if it meant recognizing their claim to represent a sovereign power. Now one group of his advisors, including General Scott, counseled him to evacuate the fort, and another, led by now Postmaster General Montgomery Blair, insisted on holding firm. Parsing through his entire inaugural address and not just reflecting on its stirring ending, Lincoln's advisors found it difficult to divine his intentions. Did his pledge to "hold, occupy and possess the property and places belonging to the government" include doing so by force? When Lincoln's erstwhile opponent Stephen Douglas was asked for a reaction to the speech in the same way members of Congress are pressed to do today, he first replied, "He does not mean coercion; he says nothing about retaking the forts or Federal property," but when asked by someone else, Douglas admitted: "I hardly know what he means. Every point in the address is susceptible of a double construction." And that was the way the president wanted it for the moment.

Virginia was still in the Union, and that key state's decision about secession would influence the other states of the upper South—North Carolina, Tennessee, Kentucky, and Maryland. If Maryland and Virginia both joined the Confederacy and surrounded Washington with enemy territory, the fate of the Capital City would be bleak. On the flip side, holding the breakaway states to the seven that had so far seceded could make for a short-lived rebellion. Maryland's pro-Union governor, his backbone stiffened by Anna Carroll, simply refused to call the legislature into session, so members couldn't take a vote on secession. And so far, the Unionists had prevailed in the March convention in Virginia, choosing on April 4 to reject secession. But a forcible move on Fort Sumter could easily swing the state in the opposite direction by rallying opinion against the federal government.

That was just what southern hotheads—chief among them Sara Pryor's husband, Roger—were counting on. Lizzie Lee still held out hope that the friendship between the commander at Fort Sumter, Robert Anderson, and the new president of the Confederacy would keep the agitators from acting: "South Carolina is trying to *precipitate* War—as she did secession—but to that Jeff Davis is opposed and will do his utmost to avert an attack upon Anderson." Sadly, she was wrong.

With food running out on the isolated island, on April 8 Lincoln sent word to the governor of South Carolina that he planned to replenish the provisions—no troops, no weapons, no ammunition—just food, unless the fort came under attack. But the Confederacy saw resupply as capitulation and instead on April 11 Davis instructed General P. G. T. Beauregard to order Anderson to surrender. Anderson refused while informing them he would soon have to evacuate or starve, but he tried to stall the southerners by making the date of his evacuation April 15, in the hopes that the flotilla of resupply ships, led by the revenue cutter *Harriet Lane*, would have arrived by then. Beauregard saw through the delay and played into Lincoln's hands by ordering an attack. Now the South would be the aggressor in the eyes of the world. Thirty-four hours and three thousand shots later, Major Robert Anderson surrendered Fort Sumter. The Civil War had begun. Washington feared for its future.

"Sumter has surrendered—we are in great trouble," Elizabeth Lomax lamented the next day when President Lincoln called on the states still in the Union to supply 75,000 militiamen to fight for their country. "A number of troops ordered here." Her son Lindsay had been assigned to a company that had just come in from Texas; "they are to be quartered in the south wing of the Treasury Building." And then a couple of days later, after first hearing a false rumor, the dread truth: "Virginia *has* seceded!! Heaven help us!" The outbreak of a hot war caused the Commonwealth of Virginia to take sides with fellow southerners and Robert E. Lee to resign his commission with the U.S. Army in order to defend his state.

On April 18, three days after President Lincoln had sent out his call for 75,000 volunteers, Lee rode his horse over the bridge from Arlington to the home of Preston Blair, across the street from the White House. There the old political operative had the proxy of President Lincoln to offer Lee the job of general in chief of the U.S. Army. Lee declined to answer, continued on to see his friend and mentor General Winfield Scott, where he was officially offered the job, and then rode back across the bridge. The next time he would be in Washington would be under very different circumstances. A couple of days later he joined the Army of Virginia. Elizabeth Lomax's son Lindsay soon followed suit. Calling his decision "heartrending," his mother tried to understand it by quoting his letter to a fellow West Pointer: "My state is out of the Union and when she calls for my services I feel that I must go. I regret it very much, realizing that the whole thing is suicidal." If he didn't know how true those words would be, his mother certainly seemed to, mourning as her newly minted Confederate soldier headed South. (By the end of the war, Lunsford Lindsay Lomax would have risen to the rank of general fighting William Tecumseh Sherman to the end.) "God only knows when I shall see him again."

———

THE SIGHT OF the American flag under attack at Fort Sumter caused the North, which had been somewhat indifferent up to this point, to rally. Men rushed to join their militias as tens of thousands of troops were summoned to defend the vastly vulnerable nation's capital. The Richmond *Enquirer* had been sounding a drumbeat for months: "Can there not be found men bold and brave enough in Maryland to unite with Virginians in seizing the Capital?" Now the newspaper's call to action appeared all too likely as Confederates destroyed the U.S. naval base in Norfolk, Virginia, and took the federal arsenal at Harpers Ferry, where the defending officer had escaped after destroying most of the weapons to keep them from falling into enemy hands. General Scott feared that the city was surrounded. The "military appearance" that Louisa Meigs had complained of was really only about six hundred U.S. Army regulars who had come in from Texas plus 1,500 ill-trained local troops guarding government buildings, nowhere near enough to protect the city against a full-scale attack even if all the soldiers could be counted on to fight.

That was far from certain—no one could be sure where the men's sympathies lay now that nearby Virginia was out of the Union and Maryland seemed to be teetering on the edge of secession. Imminent invasion appeared inevitable. As the city waited anxiously for reinforcements to arrive, some prominent men in town feebly tried to ward off total destruction by raising small militias, but those units represented little more than bravado as they bivouacked in the East Room of the White House. Men over forty formed their own "Fossil Guards," men over sixty the "Silver Grays." But none of them could mount a true defense. If the South marched on Washington, as most of the men in power thought likely, the city would fall, the war would be over, and the Union would be dismantled. The British ambassador warned his government that there was urgent apprehension "for this city." The secretary of state received a letter from a businessman in New York informing him that a cocky Varina Davis had written her friends there to invite them to her White House reception on May 1. The office-seekers who had been swarming over government buildings pressing for jobs dispersed from the overcrowded hotels. Women and children fled along with any men who could. They staged a run on the banks as they demanded hard currency. Those who stayed hoarded food and supplies; the price of flour jumped from $6 a barrel to $15.20. "The papers report our condition to be very critical— immediate danger of bombardment and thousands of other rumors," Louisa Meigs anguished in a letter to her mother. "Many persons in the city have been subject with a panic and have taken flight with their families." She planned to stay put for the time being, but "Heaven only knows what a few days may disclose to us."

Billboards posted to summon soldiers warned of an anticipated attack on Washington, and young men rushed to defend their capital. But it took some time to assemble the troops and get them in place, and the question was whether the Union soldiers would reach the city before the Confederates, who were rumored to be on the move, with the southern newspapers ballyhooing their advance. Three days after Lincoln's call went out for volunteers, the first fresh troops arrived—the First Pennsylvania and Company F of the Fourth U.S. Artillery, but they arrived beaten and bloodied by a mob of southern sympathizers in Baltimore who had set upon them as they transferred from one train station to another. The soldiers made camp in the chamber of the House of Representatives, the only place big enough to hold them, and government worker Clara Barton and her sister arrived to tend to the wounded. By the next day, many more men would need attention.

This time, instead of a somewhat spontaneous demonstration by Baltimore rowdies, the anti-Union forces in the Maryland city were ready. When the Sixth Massachusetts pulled into the station on the north side of town, the soldiers had prepared for harassment. But the size of the force meeting them made it almost impossible for them to reach the next station. With every manner of missile hurled at them, the troops opened fire. By the time they reached the next train the body count stood at four soldiers and at least nine civilians, with many more injured. But the toll was much higher in terms of its effect on Washington—as the Sixth Massachusetts made their wounded way to the Senate chamber, the city feared attack would come that night from both Virginia and Maryland. "Our hitherto peaceful town and city presents a fearful spectacle," Ann Green shivered with trepidation; "a drawn sword keeping sentinel meets you at almost every square—while the squads of men at the corners and the collected mob along the streets show you that fearful apprehensions rule the hour."

And the next day, April 20, the city awakened to the news that Governor Hicks of Maryland, prodded by the mayor of Baltimore, who claimed he could not control the mobs, had burned the bridges connecting the rail lines to the North. Washington was completely cut off from the loyal states. No troops, no supplies, no food, no mail, no newspapers could relieve the besieged bastion. "A beautiful bright day—but the inhabitants in terror and confusion at the hourly rumors of the coming foe—the greater part turn out false—but there is enough of truth to startle the reflecting mind," Ann Green trembled. "There is a report today that martial law will be proclaimed in Washington tomorrow but no one knows what to believe." No one included the president of the United States, who a year later described these days as a "condition of siege." The only preparation for that siege seemed to be the stockpiling of thousands of barrels of flour seized by the military from the Georgetown mills and ships in the harbor and an attempt to protect the treasures of the Capitol. "About the entrance and between the pillars were barricades of iron plates, intended for the dome," Julia Taft later remembered in amazement. "All the statuary in the rotunda had been boxed and the pictures covered by rough boards."

With the rail lines mangled, the troops moving south from New York and Massachusetts were forced to go by boat to Annapolis, Maryland, much against the wishes of Governor Hicks, who feared civil unrest. His old supporter Anna Carroll was outraged: "You cannot deny the right of transit to the Northern troops through the territory of Maryland, called by the President to defend their capital and your own," she lectured. With or without Hicks's approval, the soldiers pushed on, managing to make their way from Annapolis even though the tracks had been destroyed. First they repaired an old steam engine and then they patched together tracks to take them to Annapolis Junction, where they could hook up with the undamaged Baltimore and Ohio Railroad. While they worked, rumors spread among the troops that the Rebels had taken the Capital City; rumors spread around Washington that the troops had been killed along the way. With the telegraph lines down and no communication, anything could be true. "The rumor of invasion and battle was startling," Ann Green confessed.

But then at last, after five days without information, as food supplies dwindled and terror of annihilation escalated, the train filled with the exhausted, hungry, but triumphant men of the long-awaited New York Seventh chugged into the B&O station to the great rejoicing and relief of the country's capital. "The city was in commotion with all sorts of rumors. The far famed Seventh Regiment arrived and was submitted to the President's inspection," Ann Green advised her daughter in Virginia. "There are several other regiments in Annapolis which will continue to arrive." Soon soldiers from Rhode Island and Massachusetts filled government buildings, including the White House: "Troops occupy the Capitol, the East room at the Presidents and there is a large company at Silver Spring to make Mr. Blair safe. Indeed the times are worse than anyone at the distance could imagine. What it will all end in God alone knows." But relieved residents of Washington did finally know that if attacked, the city could fight back.

As Mrs. Green reported, more troops did keep arriving. "There is something grand and sublime in the unanimity with which the whole North has responded to the call for the defense of the Capital," Louisa Meigs cheered to her son at West Point. "I think this unanimity of feeling on men of all classes and all parties—of all ages will astound and appall the South when it is fully understood." The most eye-catching of the recruits were the rambunctious "Fire Zouaves" from New York, with their colorful baggy pants and their choleric boastful personalities. Troops around the world had taken to copying the somewhat outlandish costumes of particularly fierce Berber soldiers in North Africa, called Zouaves. Twenty-four-year-old Elmer Ellsworth, who had worked with the president's secretaries and become something of a surrogate son to Abe and Mary Lincoln, adopted the attire for the boisterous young volunteer firemen he brought in from New York. Before leading them merrily to their campground in the Capitol building he proudly paraded them by the White House, where Willie and Tad, the Lincoln boys, watched with such excitement that they insisted on having their own outfits made and dubbed themselves Mrs. Lincoln's Zouaves.

With all of the troops swarming the city, Washington was relatively safe, and since the president had essentially declared martial law along the railroad line to Philadelphia, supplies were coming in, but the citizens now had another complaint: all those soldiers made for a rowdy bunch. Some of their antics were harmless, like the mock congressional sessions they held in the halls of the House and Senate, but there were thousands of men sleeping under desks and in hallways, wreaking destruction in the government buildings, which soon smelled like latrines: "You would not know this God-forsaken city, our beautiful capital, with all its artistic wealth, desecrated, disgraced with Lincoln's low soldiery," a friend of Virginia Clay raged in a letter to her departed fellow secessionist. And one of the architects of the Capitol divulged to his wife in disgust: "The building is like one grand water closet—every hole and corner is defiled." Even staunch Unionist Louisa Meigs looked with dismay on the Capitol as campground: "The frescoed walls are lined with *flour barrels*—the corridors resound with the tramp of armed men and the click of the rifle and the clatter of arms is heard all over that great building which was constructed for the purpose of peaceful legislation." Still, Louisa was at first impressed by the demeanor of the soldiers: "It is said that there are over 20,000 soldiers in Washington—The avenue swarms with them—but in all the other streets an unusual quiet and stillness appears which is actually painful—it seems like the dead calm which often precedes the storm." That didn't last long; soon boredom set in and the soldiers' restless escapades unnerved the somewhat somnambulant city.

Also, a good many residents remained either supporters of the Confederacy or at least sympathetic to their family members in the South and the Yankee soldiers frightened them. "The whole district is filled with spies, every word is caught up and reported to the powers that be, and individuals are marked for vengeance. It is a complete reign of terror," Ann Green recounted angrily, describing "a man shot in his own door by a troop of four or five men, for expressing secession sentiments." Ann was desperately trying to keep her own children from voicing their views; she felt that their insistence on "the right of independence of speech" was dangerously unwise: "I only ask the common sense of silence." But the troops were edgy as Maryland's loyalty remained uncertain, and southern members of the U.S. military followed their states out of the Union. "Every officer at the Navy Yard here sent in his resignation the same day," Louisa Meigs told her son with sadness. "Being Southerners they all resigned. It was a hard struggle for them. Many of them shed tears on handing in their resignation. A sense of duty and honor which we think mistaken has impelled them to this sacrifice." It was not just military men who headed south; so did civilian public servants. All told about four hundred left to take positions in the Rebel Army and Confederate government. And as more southerners left, more northerners kept coming. "Troops are still pouring in, and affairs continue worse and worse," Ann Green moaned. Georgetown College had been completely surprised, she noted, when New York's Sixty-Ninth Regiment, the so-called Irish Brigade, was dispatched to the campus where Father John Early, the college president, "had no choice in the matter, and was allowed but two hours and a half to vacate one of his buildings, for the purpose of receiving fourteen hundred and fifteen soldiers." A student at the college, young Stephen Douglas Jr., wrote to his stepmother, Adele Cutts Douglas, who was with his father in Chicago, about "the troops that are quartered here" and the false rumor, typical of the time, that "Virginia troops had attacked Washington."

To defend against any such attack, federal soldiers soon surrounded the city, building impressive fortifications and setting up camp in every spare space. Massachusetts masons installed huge ovens in the basement of the Capitol that worked day and night baking up hundreds of loaves of bread. For meat, a herd of cows was set to graze on the unfamiliar grounds of the Washington Monument, where several of them fell into the nearby canal. Provisions of all types— food, clothes, guns, ammunition—appeared by the carload to supply the ill-prepared platoons as Montgomery Meigs took on the job of quartermaster, but the sheer size of the military presence was overwhelming. "There are 30,000 troops here. Think of it! They go about the avenue insulting women and taking property without paying for it," Virginia Clay's southern friend furiously related. "I heard these Blairs are at the bottom of all this war policy. Old Blair's country place was threatened and his family, including the fanatical Mrs. Lee, had to fly into the city." In Maryland, home to the Blairs' country house, the legislature finally met and rejected secession. Union troops moved into rebellious Baltimore in mid-May, quelling any further uprisings there. Washington would still have to guard against Virginia but the city would not be surrounded by states pledged to the enemy.

The Lincolns tried to restore some sense of normalcy to the city. Ann Green and her family went to the White House toward the end of May and found that "the music was fine and the scene gay. Mr. Lincoln leant against the pillar of the portico, apparently oblivious of the sight before him, talking and laughing with a young man. There was nothing to adorn his face except a very nice set of teeth which he showed very often." The president might be smiling, but war was never far from anyone's mind. Hostile Virginia sat right across the Potomac and a tavern in Alexandria proudly flew a Confederate flag large enough to be seen from Washington. "It is rumored that an attack on Alexandria is expected within the next few days," Elizabeth Lomax fretted on May 1. Her family had been urging her to leave town because "as Southerners we would not be safe," but she was determined to stay, insisting, "We have so many old friends in the army that I feel sure we would be in no danger." As the daughter of a Revolutionary War hero and the widow of an officer who had fought in the Seminole Wars, Mrs. Lomax could not imagine that any member of the American armed forces would harm her.

She tried to make the best of the tense situation, going to visit the

New York Seventh Regiment camp: "They have a charming military band and are a wonderful looking body of men. We stayed to see them drill, but oh, to think they are drilling to kill—and to kill my own people." As the pressure on her built to leave home, Mrs. Lomax was truly in distress: "The country riven with dissensions, obliged to forsake my home, to scatter my children, some here, some there, to know that my darling son is in constant danger, to endure poverty, to see armed men everywhere knowing that they are the enemies of my own people, and never knowing the outcome of this frightful war. I feel *desolated.*" Left to raise six small children on an army widow's paltry pension, supplemented by taking in copying work for the government and giving piano lessons, Elizabeth Lomax had managed remarkably well for herself and her family over the years. She loved her "sweet home" and she opposed this "fratricidal conflict," having declared herself only a few months before "definitely for the Union." Now her son had signed with the Confederate army and she was forced to abandon the life she had put together with pluck and perseverance. She left Washington on May 13 "with a sad heart" and crossed the river to stay with relatives in Virginia. Ten days later a referendum ratified Virginia's choice to join the Confederacy.

In the middle of that night, Union troops crossed the Potomac River to strike against the newly declared enemy. Louisa Meigs kept vigil into the night to see the soldiers pass: "It was a magnificent yet painful sight, and filled me with emotion. I never thought to behold such a spectacle in our peaceful happy Country. As column after column appeared in sight and passed away, the knowledge that many of them would never return in all human probability, young & active and vigorous as they were, depressed & saddened me, while the gleam of their arms and the rattling of their saber and the clang of their weapons stirred and excited me." Men on foot and on horseback crossed the bridges and took Arlington, a high spot that could be used to launch balloons for tracking enemy troop movements. Young Elmer Ellsworth led his Fire Zouaves on boats that crossed over to Alexandria, with its offending Confederate flag flying atop the Marshall House hotel. Landing shortly before dawn, the Union forces demanded surrender of the town filled with women and children and the Rebel officer complied. But Ellsworth couldn't resist the urge to tear down that flag, knowing he would win the praise of his patrons in the White House. He marched to the hotel, climbed to the roof, and yanked down the banner. As he started down the steps, the proud southern innkeeper—James Jackson—shot Ellsworth point blank and then one of the Zouaves shot Jackson.

Thousands of mourners paid tribute to the young soldier when his body came back to Washington. Then the chief mourner, the President of the United States, moved Elmer Ellsworth's remains to the East Room of the White House to lie in state before his solemn military funeral. "The bell tolled all day," Ann Green wrote, describing the grief-stricken scene, with the hearse "drawn by four magnificent white horses" and the various regiments in front, "then followed all the different Zouave companies headed by his own with the secession flag which he pulled down. . . . Then came the President's carriage and heads of departments, his horse covered with a black pall was led by the side of the procession by a field officer on horseback." All of this for one very young colonel, but a colonel loved by President Lincoln and his family. "It was the most impressive military funeral I have seen, the times & the circumstances conspired to make it so," Louisa Meigs described it to her mother. "The Zouaves followed the hearse, looking dull and depressed. Many persons saw them wiping away their tears." The cannon salute to the young soldier confused and terrified the edgy city; many thought the Virginians had counterattacked and soldiers rushed to cross the bridges in "one moving mass of glittering bayonets." Ann Green somewhat breathlessly relayed before finishing: "All a false alarm, I am happy to say."

––––––––––

BUT THERE WAS no letting down of the guard; the city fully understood the danger still looming: "Oh how happily I thought I should spend this month with my children and grandchildren all around me at Rosedale," moaned Ann Green as the month of June came to the capital, "but what a changed scene—in the midst of civil war—our own neighborhood the field of action (for a speedy battle is expected between here and Manassas Gap)." And bad news just kept coming. On June 8, Tennessee joined the Confederacy, following Arkansas and North Carolina, bringing the total to eleven states in rebellion. Then word came from Chicago that Stephen Douglas, who had traveled west rallying support for the Union, had died at the age of forty-eight, as Adele held his hand. The *New York Times* declared the death a "national calamity," mourning that "his influence in favor of the right, can, in these perilous times, be illy spared by the nation." The White House, occupied by the man who had run against Douglas twice, was draped in black. Testimonials addressed to Adele streamed in from across the nation hailing the son of Illinois as she attended to business there. By the end of June she was back home in Washington and in the hands of dressmaker Elizabeth Keckley, who outfitted the widow "in deep mourning, with excellent taste," the seamstress admiringly attested, "and several of the leading ladies of Washington society were extremely jealous of her superior attractions."

Mrs. Keckley also made "fifteen or sixteen" dresses for the woman who was becoming her fast friend, Mary Todd Lincoln. Though she could count few friends in her new home—"the women kind are giving Mrs. Lincoln the cold shoulder in the City," Lizzie Lee confided to her husband—the first lady doggedly continued to entertain through the "perilous times." On June 4, thirty-four members of the diplomatic corps convened in the State Dining Room for an evening the Washington *Star* declared "the most brilliant affair of the sort that has ever taken place in the Executive Mansion," giving full credit to "the good taste of Mrs. Lincoln." If the women of Washington were cool to the new mistress of the White House, at least for the time being she was enjoying some good press. The evening was calculated to woo the diplomats into sticking with the Union, even as the Confederates sought recognition from the European nations their cotton merchants had done business with for years. "I cannot think England will take any part in this war," Elizabeth Blair Lee judged hopefully at the beginning of June. She knew the new ambassador to the Court of St. James's since Charles Francis Adams and his wife, Abigail, had been to dinner at Silver Spring several times while they were in Washington. And the Union was counting on Adams to convince the British not to build blockade-breaking privateers in their shipyards.

Soon after the surrender of Fort Sumter, Lincoln had thrown up a blockade of southern ports; Lizzie's husband, Captain Samuel Phillips Lee, a cousin of Robert E. Lee, commanded a Navy vessel enforcing the sanction and Lizzie and their little boy Blair traveled to Philadelphia to visit the renowned social reformer Rebecca Gratz, a distant relative. (Lizzie's aunt was married to Rebecca's brother.) It was mainly a social visit to "Aunt Becky" but also an opportunity to check out the living arrangements in Pennsylvania if the Blair family determined that Lizzie should evacuate from Washington or the Maryland country house, Silver Spring. For now, she felt safe. "We are never at night with less than 4 or eight soldiers sleeping in the house," she assured her husband; "our horses are fast—& our neighbors reliable." Back at home a few days later, Lizzie Lee entertained a friend who had just returned from the South and a visit with Varina Davis. "Mrs. D talks all the time of Washington & of her friends with unaltered feelings. She is one of the victims of this war," came the report; "how sincerely I wish her no ill—& yet how fervently I pray that our Government may go through the trials now beset it & come out—greater & better than ever." Her country and her friend in rebellion against the country both mattered to Lizzie. But the war was young. As it festered on, friendships frayed.

More and more troops marched into the city, many with the "vivandieres," the women in uniform who provided supplies for the soldiers, marching alongside them. Now Washington was ready for war and wondering why it wasn't happening. Mary Lincoln went regularly to visit the soldiers in their camps, often bringing her little boys with her. After one of those visits to the New York Twenty-Fifth Regiment, "the tongue of the carriage suddenly broke, and the horses started off at a rapid rate . . . but for the timely assistance of several members of the twenty-fifth, serious consequences might have ensued." Lucky for Mrs. Lincoln, who was quite shaken by the near calamity, the soldiers had ready reflexes, all the more reason to question why General Scott wasn't mustering his men and taking on the Confederate States Army in what the capital was convinced would be a single decisive battle.

———

IN THE SAME way that the South had pressed for a march on Washington, now the North demanded a raid of Richmond, the new Confederate capital. "On to Richmond," Horace Greeley's *New York Tribune* shouted. But days, then weeks passed with no real action. The vaunted New York Seventh had signed up for only a month so they had already headed home, having collected $103 for the Washington Monument fund as a parting gesture. "There are now 75 thousand men in front of—& in the City of Washington & one universal grumble at Gen[era]l Scott's do nothing policy with such immense means," Lizzie Lee divulged to Phil. "Some think him too old & others that his heart is averse to an attack upon Virginia—but all this is speculation. I only know he says he is not ready yet & that horses & cannon & men & wagons are now pouring in to the city." The soldiers were beginning to get on everyone's nerves as they foraged for food. "Six of the soldiers came and flourished about the place, and helped themselves to cherries," Ann Green complained. "I went out and told them gently that if they did not want anything that they had better go, and they were quite civil and went off, giving the good advice 'not to make a fuss for a few cherries.' Poor creatures—I pitied them very much. They have a hard time of it." She might pity the soldiers but Mrs. Green had no sympathy for the politicians: "At the bottom of all this wretched war may be traced pride, ambition and personal feud. I pray God it may speedily be brought to a close." The politicians were coming back to town. President Lincoln had called a special session of Congress. "I do hope for some good result."

Lincoln chose the symbolic date of July 4 for Congress to convene. Just two nights earlier a huge comet lit up the skies of the city, "far exceeding in splendor any which the present generation have ever witnessed and probably outshining the great comet of 1758," marveled the *National Republican*. The astronomical phenomenon came as a complete surprise and many saw it as an ominous portent as the lawmakers reassembled. The halls and walls of the Capitol had been scrubbed and painted to try to clean up the mess left by the soldiers who had camped there. But the warm aromas from the bakeries below still wafted into the chambers where members met, reminding them of the war at hand. Also reminding them were the empty seats of the departed southerners, and the silent voices of southern men. Though Kentucky uneasily remained in the Union, one of its senators, former Vice President John Breckinridge, stood on the edge of revolt, accusing President Lincoln of unconstitutional "executive usurpation" of power. On July 17, Lizzie Lee and some female friends went to hear Breckinridge's speech. "All he said was easily answered—but I held my tongue and endured his specious pleading," Lizzie reported, clearly considering herself an equal in debate.

Anna Ella Carroll did not hold her tongue or her pen. She wrote a pamphlet answering Breckinridge's every point, earning praise from Lincoln supporters like Secretary of the Interior Caleb Smith: "I trust this reply may have an extended circulation at the present time, as I am sure its perusal by the people will do much to aid the cause of the Constitution and the Union." Ignoring Breckinridge, who soon joined the Confederate army, the Congress accepted Lincoln's assumption of war powers and retroactively approved his call up of troops, upping the ante by authorizing up to a million more. But why, members pressed the president, weren't the current crop of soldiers fighting? Why wasn't Scott moving on the enemy assembling at Manassas, Virginia? The press, the politicians, and the public demanded that the Union army advance.

In mid-July, the soldiers who had been gathering in and around Washington finally received their marching orders. "Overwhelming forces are making their way to the scene of action today," Ann Green reported with trepidation on July 16. Friends had gone to Arlington and seen the men breaking camp; "they saw seven regiments and three hundred wagons go." As the troops moved deeper into Virginia, some of their friends went with them as far as Fairfax Courthouse, where one told Ann what he had witnessed: "The soldiers were destroying everything that they could lay their hands on. He saw beautiful pianos smashed to pieces with all other kinds of furniture—law libraries thrown into the gutters, and four houses on the edge of town set fire to and quietly allowed to burn down. All sorts of barbarous acts." Finally, this war was real.

Even so, as troops advanced on Manassas, Virginia, they were accompanied by hundreds of civilians who thought the whole thing was a lark. Expecting an easy victory, they brought picnic baskets for a day in the country, where they watched the action through opera glasses as if it were a play. The soundtrack of the performance could be heard in the city, thirty miles away from the battle along the shores of Bull Run Creek: "the morning guns seem very loud to me," Lizzie Lee shuddered on that fateful July 21 as she went for a walk, "hoping the woods would stop the *roar* in my ears." Ann Green also heard the "booming of cannon" and trembled at the sound: "It is in vain to attempt to describe the feeling produced by every report. The conviction that each sound brought death and destruction to our countrymen—either on one side or the other . . . I still cling to the idea that they are all my fellow citizens but it is very unlikely that bloodshed will restore or perpetuate the Union that we have heretofore enjoyed." At first reports reached the capital that the Union was winning: "when last news at 5 o'clock came in our side were victorious, 3 batteries taken—the Confederate lines broken—& they retreating to their entrenchment at the Junction," Lizzie Lee reported, "but at 8 o'clock—as I was rocking our boy to sleep I heard that dreadful roar still."

By the time the battle finally ended the North had been firmly trounced; defeated Union soldiers retreated to Washington along with the frightened congressmen and their friends who kept getting in the soldiers' way. The makeshift hospitals were quickly overwhelmed with the wounded. Louisa Meigs waited all night for news of her young son, until "a horseman came galloping to the door. It was John, black with dust & smoke." He personally delivered news of the debacle to his father, now the Quartermaster of the Union army: "Father, the army is completely routed." Ann Green echoed that account: "Every face betrayed the horrors of the preceding day. Soldiers were coming in, in every direction, some in wagons wounded, some still able to sit their horses but man and beast bleeding—others rushing in for self-preservation, with such tales of carnage and bloodshed and final flight that one's blood ran cold to hear." She was fearful "that all who sympathized with the southern victory were to be arrested." As someone with relatives in the South and an opponent of the war, Mrs. Green lived in suspicion of people she considered Union spies. "I have heard and read much of the reign of terror—but never expected to live under it in this our boasted free country. But here no one ventures to express their sentiments."

———

As IT TURNED out, the Union was right to worry about southern spies—one southern spy in particular, who had been largely responsible for the Rebel victory at Bull Run: Rose Greenhow. Rose was not doing her usual round of entertaining that spring and summer because her daughter Gertrude had just died, marking the loss of the fifth of her eight children. She didn't think much of the society in town those days anyway: "the refinement and grace which had once constituted the charm of Washington life had long since departed, and like its former freedom, was now alas! A tradition only." And she was angry with her niece, Adele Cutts Douglas, for what she considered fraternizing with the enemy—Abe and Mary Lincoln. Still, Rose was doing a good bit of fraternizing of her own, much of it late at night with the shades drawn. She saw enough of Massachusetts senator Henry Wilson, the chairman of the Military Affairs Committee, and government functionaries from department clerks to Secretary of State Seward that she was able to keep abreast of Union plans.

So when Confederate spymaster Captain Thomas Jordan came to ask her to do some espionage work, she was in an excellent position to help him out. He gave her an elementary code for encrypting her messages and she assembled a network of southern spies, even as she entertained northern congressmen and lobbied for a position for her son-in-law in the Union army. She hit the jackpot with her intelligence gathering when she learned the date of the Yankees' advance on Manassas. Rose summoned one of her team, the very beautiful Bettie Duvall, and arranged for her to carry the critical information to the southern command. Disguised as a simple farm girl, Bettie drove her cart past Union sentries until she reached a friendly home in Virginia, where she changed into riding gear and traveled on to Fairfax Courthouse. There she unpinned her glossy brown hair, letting it cascade down her back as she reached under it for a tiny purse with the message for General Beauregard, the commander of the Rebel forces at Manassas. The surprise attack planned by the North was thwarted, Rebel reinforcements sent for, and another messenger dispatched to Rose for more information.

On July 16 she sent back word that more than fifty thousand troops "would positively commence that day to advance from Arlington Heights and Alexandria on to Manassas, via Fairfax Court House and Centerville." By then "the tramp of armed men was heard on every side—martial music filled the air; in short, a mighty host was marshalling, with all the 'pomp and circumstance of glorious war.' 'On to Richmond!' was the war-cry," Rose remembered a few years later, proudly taking credit for stopping that march to the Confederate capital. The word came from Captain Jordan in Manassas: "Yours was received at eight o'clock at night. Let them come: we are ready for them." Then yet another piece of essential information arrived from the alluring widow in Washington: the Union planned to cut the railroad line leading into Manassas. Forewarned, the South could prepare its defenses.

A story in the *New York Times* a few days after the battle quotes a British man who went to watch the excitement with a senator, got lost in the confusion of retreat, and ended up briefly as a prisoner in camp with the southern officers. There Jordan "boasted that he had received, before the attack at Bull Run, a cipher dispatch from some well-informed person within our lines, giving full details of movement, including the particulars of the plan of battle, the time at which operations would commence, and the number of our troops." And Rose Greenhow, that "well-informed person," received her due from the captain when the victory in that first major battle of the Civil War went to the Confederates: "Our President and Our General direct me to thank you. We rely upon you for further information. The Confederacy owes you a debt."

Exultant, Rose rushed to the Capitol to consult with her unwitting accomplices. Several senators assured her "that it was their individual exertions alone which had prevented the entire 'Grand Army' from precipitating itself pell-mell into the Potomac." As humorous as she found their exaggerated accounts, the city was becoming a dangerous place for her: "the fanatical feeling was now at its height. Maddened by defeat, they sought a safe means of venting their pent-up wrath. The streets were filled with armed and unarmed ruffians; women were afraid to go singly into the streets for fear of insult; curses and blasphemy rent the air, and no one would have been surprised at any hour at a general massacre of the peaceful inhabitants." Rose was urged to leave town. Lizzie Lee did leave. So did Louisa Meigs. But, flush with pride from her accomplishment, Mrs. Greenhow "resolved to remain, conscious of the great service I could render my country, my position giving me remarkable facilities for obtaining information." Her oldest living daughter, far off in Nevada, warned her mother: "They say some ladies have been taken up as spies. I so dread to hear of some of my friends. Dear mama, please keep as clear of all secessionists as you possibly can. I so much fear everything to you all alone there." But Rose, with her cadre of co-conspirators, was hardly alone.

Now that the Yankees had been soundly defeated, Washington was even more concerned about attack, convinced that General Beauregard would follow the retreating Yankees right to the Capitol. "A strong guard was stationed around all the public buildings." Rose mockingly reported, "Everything about the national Capitol betokened the panic of the administration. Preparations were made for the expected attack, and signals arranged to give the alarm." Excited to repeat her triumph, the spy "took advantage of the situation. The alarm-guns of the Yankees were the rallying cry of a devoted band whose hearts beat high with hope." If the Rebels advanced on the city, Rose had organized her sympathizers in the shadows to assist them. But that's not what happened. Here's what happened: Rose Greenhow was arrested.

Sixteen-year-old Julia Taft had advance warning: "To our house came one day a bland gentleman with distinguished black whiskers to make inquiries about Mrs. Rose Greenhow. Mrs. Greenhow and her little daughter Rose often came to our house and we liked them both." Julia could not imagine why the strange man, who turned out to be secret service agent Allan Pinkerton, would be asking about the "dashing, beautiful woman . . . a brilliant conversationalist, dressed in the mode, and a leader in Washington society." But, in answer to his questions, the family admitted: "Yes, she did seem glad to meet officers who visited our house. Yes she had asked Bud and Holly and me about our visits to the White House and what Mr. Lincoln said. My father remembered that she had asked him questions about the regiments that had arrived." Then Pinkerton took Taft aside, whispered something, and cautioned the children not to say anything about the mysterious visit.

Tad Lincoln solved the mystery with his announcement that "Mrs. Greenhow had been arrested as a dangerous spy." The little boy shouted with glee, "'they'll probably shoot her at sunrise tomorrow.'" That turned out not to be true, but the rest of his report was accurate: Rose Greenhow had secretly been put under house arrest along with other spies who had come to her home to exchange information. They had walked into a trap. "Various persons called at her residence and were taken in custody and held until evidence was shown that they were loyal," explained the *New York Times*. "It was little Rose who at last gave the alarm and perhaps prevented the capture of other Confederate agents," Julia revealed. Everyone else in the house was watched constantly but the eight-year-old daughter was allowed to go outside to play. She climbed a tree near the garden wall and screamed so all could hear: "'Mother has been arrested. Mother has been arrested.'"

Rose was not surprised. One of her spies had passed along the information that arrest was imminent. When it happened, detectives searched her house for days, going through all of her papers, but Rose managed, right under the noses of her captors, to spirit out the documents that would be most damaging to the Confederate cause. As the juicy content of her letters and diary spread through the town there was more than one embarrassed member of the Lincoln administration and Congress. And Rose kept finding ways to receive and reveal important information even while confined to her home prison. Eventually the government turned her house into a jail for other suspected female spies and the establishment was quickly dubbed "Fort Greenhow" by the Washington wags.

The guards allowed members of the press to roam around in the makeshift prison, hoping to humiliate their charges. Accounts about the house and its occupants even appeared in the European papers. One curious correspondent took in Rose's first floor: "The two parlors were divided by a red gauze, and in the backroom stood a handsome rosewood piano, with pearl keys . . . the walls of the room were hung with portraits. . . . The Sixteenth-street gaol has been an object of considerable interest for months past, to citizens as well as visitors." Rose managed to get her own side of the story out by leaking a letter to her friend Secretary Seward describing her rude and rough treatment—"whenever necessity forced me to seek my chamber, a detective stood sentinel at the open door." This aroused so much sympathy for the still-admired figure that her pro-Union family finally relented and came to visit her. Her niece, Adele Douglas, brought Christmas presents for the eight-year-old child, but then, the *New York Times* reported, Rose "received a cake from some friend of hers, unknown to the guard." When he examined it he "found embedded therein a note informing the lady that arrangements had been made for her escape and conveyance to Richmond." A follow-up story described Rose's reaction: "When Mrs. Greenhow lost her cake, containing her plan of escape, she was furious, not desisting from ringing her bell until the guard threatened to shut her in the garret and feed her on bread and water. . . . She has been cut off from her allowance of a quart of wine a day." Mrs. Greenhow's captors decided to move her to the more secure and far less comfortable Old Capitol Prison.

ONCE A BOARDINGHOUSE that had been home to such notables as John C. Calhoun and to Rose Greenhow herself, the prison boasted a distinguished past. After the British burned the Capitol in the War of 1812, the government hurriedly erected a structure across the street from the ruin as a place for Congress to meet while it was restored. Abandoned as an official building when the new Capitol opened, private owners started a school in what came to be called The Old Capitol and then took in boarders until the government bought the site again, this time as a holding pen for Confederate spies and prisoners of war. When the first of those prisoners arrived after the Battle of Bull Run, "they were pelted with stones and other missiles, which seriously wounded a number. In order to prevent the prisoners from being actually torn to pieces, a company of U.S. regulars had to be called out to protect them to their quarters, the old Capitol prison," Rose Greenhow indignantly recounted, never dreaming she would eventually end up there herself. The secessionist spy wasn't the only one outraged by the mob. Ann Green too was horrified: "the Southern prisoners were attacked by some infuriated soldiers yesterday as they were being brought into Washington and would have been killed but that a Company of Cavalry charged on and dispersed them."

Rumors ran rampant that the Rebels, who had captured many more prisoners than the Yankees, were treating their captives badly. And those were just some of the stories Mrs. Green heard spreading through the city after the massive Union defeat: "All sorts of reports have been floating about today. One was that a boat had been kept steamed all night in readiness for Lincoln and his Cabinet to desert the premises." For days the city churned chaotically: "Soldiers lying all on the cellar doors and pavement—some sleeping and some drunk, but in inconceivable numbers," clucked Mrs. Green. "They are completely demoralized and are still coming in." Blame, of course, had to be assigned and General Irvin McDowell, who led the charge, came in for most of it, along with General Daniel Tyler: "Great censure is cast on the commanding officers—and persons did not hesitate to say today that both McDowell and Tyler were drunk," Ann Green confided the whispered charges. "The government is making great exertions to reorganize the Army—it is not supposed they can succeed before three months." That was one report Mrs. Green had right.

As far as the president's advisor Francis Preston Blair was concerned, the silver lining in the defeat would be reorganization of the army. He informed his daughter Lizzie Lee, who had taken refuge in Philadelphia and was desperate for news, "I think we have gained more than we have lost by the late battle—It is the opinion of everybody that we have gained a good general for the fold & probably are released from several bad ones." General George B. McClellan rode in from the west to replace McDowell, but even as he rounded up soldiers off the streets and cellar doors and herded them into camps where they drilled day and night, the city huddled once again in terror of imminent attack. The Blair family was so sure that it would come that Preston Blair sent a telegraph to Lizzie in Philadelphia ordering her to " 'stay till you hear from me.' " And a subsequent letter informed her that "defences were being thrown up all around the City to the north—even 'around Silver Spring vicinity.' "

For families who had no choice but to stay in Washington, the situation was both frightening and infuriating. "We have had a day of commotion—two or three thousand troops with numerous wagons went up the road. There was nothing but shouting and shooting. Two balls came near the house . . . one seemed to go over my head and lodge in the garden," fussed Ann Green, who was trying to eke out a living for her family on the farm while ducking bullets and dodging begging from the soldiers. And still more soldiers came: "More artillery passed up today. There are now about fifteen thousand troops about Tennallytown," a section of the District very close by and where the officer in command assured a neighbor "the Southerners were confidently expected to make an attack on Washington immediately." Visiting a neighbor, Mrs. Green learned that just a few hours earlier "a musket shot passed through her clothes, just grazing the knee, and fell at her feet. I looked at the shot hole, made through five garments and the pieces of each, laying with the ball which she had preserved." Close calls for these women, from the men who were supposed to be protecting them.

The soldiers were not just careless, they were crass, helping themselves to pretty much anything they wanted. One friend had "not less than fifty soldiers lolling and moving around her doors . . . everything about her was destroyed, the cornfield cut down and every particle of poultry gone." Mrs. Green's orchard was also there for the picking: "All our peaches that were capable of being shaken off were taken today." Every day soldiers would show up foraging for food; "one of the days we counted forty-two . . . they have finished on the fruit and begun on the vegetables," food planted to feed Mrs. Green's large family. But then, as a welcome reminder that life goes on despite danger and deprivation, on August 6 Mrs. Green's daughter-in-law, Mimi, gave birth to a "dear little boy." That baby became the family's salvation during those long months fearing for their lives. "What a difference the baby's arrival has made, it seems as if everybody had someone and the same thing to love," Ann smilingly related when the baby was twelve days old, but this new grandchild also reminded her of the others, the children of her two daughters in Virginia: "How much I would enjoy my other grandchildren that I have not seen in so long!"

Not only could she not see her family, she couldn't even hear from them. When the U.S. Post Office cut off mail to Dixie at the beginning of June, families straddling both sides of the lines had to rely on travelers between the warring regions to deliver personal information.

And then it could be agonizing. If someone brought her word of a sick grandchild, Ann had no way of knowing whether the child had gotten better or died, as so many did. "Oh the separation with all its restrictions is dreadful!" she sighed, and she was totally in the dark about what to expect. As the fall approached Mrs. Green, like many in Washington, waited for the next shoe to drop: "About the war we know nothing—everything is kept still."

Even those close to the president knew very little. "My argument is that McClellan can embody against them 100,000 men & that he is active & able & knows how to handle them," Preston Blair confidently told his daughter Lizzie in late August, guessing about the Rebels, "If they do not take Washington in ten days they will never do it." All the same, he continued to advise her to stay put in Pennsylvania. And since her boy Blair, who had just turned five, was with her, she readily acquiesced: "I shall not come home when the Army at Wash[ington] are daily reported to have slept on their arms." Though she was an ardent Unionist, Lizzie worried about her friend Varina Davis. In early September a false report hit the newspapers that Jefferson Davis was dead: "I have thought a great deal of Mrs. Jeff Davis. If she has lost her husband it is really one of those cases where death has been deliverer from a more bitter sorrow. For I cannot believe in the eventual success of this wicked conspiracy." Little did Lizzie know that Varina too had trouble believing in secessionist success. Soon after she arrived in Richmond, the much-hailed first lady of the Confederacy confided to her mother, "Amidst all this enthusiasm however comes over me the deep horror of our not being ready & armed. *Their* hordes are very near & their bitterness is very great. *They* have manufactures of arms—we have none." But still, she had "made up my mind to come here & be happy no matter what danger there was." And her friend Lizzie Lee knew Varina would not be happy if anything had happened to her husband: "She will be a heart broken woman for tho' in some awe of her husband she was devotedly in love with him." A few days later Lizzie reported a different story: "we hear Mrs. Jeff. has another Baby & old Jeff is still alive." In fact the baby wasn't born for another three months, but the President of the Confederacy was still very much alive, with a war to wage against the men in Lizzie's family.

The Blairs were pleased with McClellan's appointment as commander of the Army of the Potomac, and they helped manipulate the selection of their old comrade in politics John C. Frémont as head of the Western Department, headquartered in St. Louis, Missouri. Congressman Frank Blair, Lizzie's brother and Preston's son, had schemed against the secessionist governor there to keep the state in the Union and his success allowed him to wield considerable clout in Washington, along with his father the presidential advisor and his brother Montgomery the Cabinet member. "The point which Father has been laboring for is at last attained—McClellan has the eastern division & Fremont the West," Lizzie announced with satisfaction, "for nearly two months this has been labored for by our *set*—to get the work out of *lukewarm hands heads & hearts*." But Frémont had ideas of his own about how to manage the Rebels making trouble in Missouri, and President Lincoln was far from pleased with the general's orders. To make his case, John C. Frémont sent his wife to Washington.

JESSIE BENTON FRÉMONT, once the most recognizable woman in the capital, had only been to Washington briefly in the five years since her husband's presidential defeat in 1856. She and her father, Thomas Hart Benton, had reached an uneasy rapprochement after the bitterness of the campaign. And in 1858, following a grand tour of Europe hailed as an American celebrity, Jessie went to comfort Benton while he was dying. But then her husband summoned her back to their home in California to help him run Las Mariposas, so with the four children she once again crossed the country for hard work in the far west. Life improved for the now thirty-four-year-old matron when the family moved from the remote Mariposa settlement into San Francisco, where Jessie established a must-visit salon for literary and political sojourners. But when the war broke out the passionately antislavery Frémonts saw an opportunity to relive their glory days and to contribute to the Union cause.

Once John received his command, thanks to lobbying by the Blair family, Jessie and the children packed up to join him in Missouri, a place she knew well. The state that sent her father to Congress for so many decades was now represented in the House by Elizabeth Blair Lee's younger brother Frank. Jessie had kept up her correspondence with the Blairs, especially with her girlhood companion Lizzie, over the years and when Jessie announced to them her intention to relocate to St. Louis with the army, the scion of the family, Preston Blair, advised her instead to come to Washington. The general's wife wouldn't hear of it—she would be with John. For headquarters the couple rented a mansion belonging to a relative of Jessie, where officers could live and work together and where she could keep closely involved with everything going on. And there was a great deal going on.

Though Missouri was officially in the Union, the secessionist governor refused to supply troops to the Army and turned a blind-eye to Confederate sympathizers staging attacks across the state. Jessie spent the summer militating for more men and matériel. Griping to Lizzie that General Frémont was forced to cope with "an arsenal without arms or ammunition—troops on paper" because western soldiers had been diverted to protect Washington, she wanted to make the case for more troops and arms to President Lincoln herself. "I have begged Mr. Fremont to let me go on & tell him how things are here." Since she had just made the long trip through Panama to New York and then on to Missouri, her husband thought the journey would exhaust her, so she stayed in St. Louis. But she kept up her barrage of badgering letters.

To Lizzie's brother, Postmaster General Montgomery Blair, Jessie complained: "I don't like this neglect & I look to you & to the President to see that it has not a fatal effect. Just now the Potomac is so interesting that I do not blame every care for it but don't expect miracles on the Mississippi." Bureaucratic red tape kept getting in the way of sending the money and munitions needed even as the Confederate army closed in from both the south and north. Frémont went north and staved off that advance; General Nathaniel Lyon went south with too few soldiers and lost his life. As southwest Missouri fell to the enemy, Jessie's letters became more agitated: "By dint of begging and bullying some guns & money are being gotten in, but every useful thing is being concentrated around Washington." The hounding missives didn't stop at the Cabinet level. Jessie went right to the top, protesting to President Lincoln: "The State is being occupied by the Home Guards & the occupation would have been complete but for the absolute want of arms." The fact that Frémont had found men to fill the "Home Guards"—many of them German immigrants—to secure Union rule convinced the Blairs that their man could do the job. "Fremont has stirred up things in St. Louis & given new life there," Lizzie Lee rejoiced to her husband; "if he & Frank can't take care of Missouri I am mistaken in the men."

But when Frank Blair went back to Missouri after the congressional session, he heard grumblings not just *from* the Frémonts, but *about* them as well. John was said to be aloof, refusing to see anyone, including his officers. Jessie was said to be running the show, protecting her husband from information he needed. Behind her back she was derisively called "General Jessie." And she had in fact organized everything—including the hospitals where she enlisted the newly named Superintendent of Army nurses Dorothea Dix. Frank, who had originally been one of Frémont's staunchest supporters, now advised his brother Montgomery of mass irregularities in the Western Division: Frémont's suspicious dealings with contractors, his excessive spending, and his disorganization. The state was in danger of falling entirely into enemy hands.

Just as Blair's private communication reached Washington, General Frémont dropped his bombshell. He declared martial law, emancipated the slaves of the thousands of Missouri men in revolt against the Union, and instituted a "bureau of abolition." Lincoln learned about it from the newspapers. Convinced that the move would drive Kentucky right out of the Union and that Missouri and Maryland would follow, the president privately asked his general to change the order to coincide with the law passed by Congress that only freed the slaves being used for Rebel military purposes. Frémont refused. His emancipation order made him an abolitionist icon, hailed as a hero by the antislavery press. He had intended to rally the abolitionist forces into action and he did. He also made himself their champion and guaranteed a conflict with the President of the United States. This time John agreed that his wife should go to Washington to explain his position.

"I see Jessie is at Washington but I have not had a line from there for *near* a week & I expect Fremont is in a peck of trouble about his proclamation—I *do not know* it, only *infer* from *signs*," Lizzie Lee accurately reported that September. After a three-day train ride, sitting up the whole way, Jessie Benton Frémont checked into the familiar Willard's Hotel, where she had arranged for some influential friends from New York to meet her and accompany her to the White House. She immediately sent a message to President Lincoln saying she had brought a letter and some "verbal communications" from General Frémont: "If it suits the President's convenience will he name a time this evening to receive them—or at some early hour tomorrow." According to Jessie, the messenger soon returned with a card "on which was written, 'A. Lincoln. Now.'" From there on out the story changes depending on who is telling it.

John Hay, Lincoln's secretary and biographer, wrote that "Mrs. Fremont took the opportunity, in her interview with Mr. Lincoln, to justify General Fremont in all he had done, and to denounce his accusers with impetuous earnestness." Describing Frémont's action as a purely political move that Hay thought was calculated to raise the general "to the position of new party leader," the secretary printed a memorandum of a conversation Lincoln had in his office a few years later when the president recalled the meeting with Jessie: "She sought an audience with me at midnight, and taxed me so violently with many things that I had to exercise all the awkward tact I have to avoid quarreling with her." He even implied that Jessie had threatened him. When she read the account, Mrs. Frémont quickly penned one of her own.

She had just arrived, she said, dusty and exhausted at the hotel and met her friends from New York when the president summoned her for their interview: "All my life I had been at home in the President's House—as well received there as in the family circle, and with the old confidence of the past I went forward now," said this former pet of Andrew Jackson. But this time would be starkly different. "The President did not speak, only bowed slightly. . . . I gave him the letter, telling him General Fremont felt the subject to be of so much importance, that he had sent me to answer any points on which the President might want more information. At this he smiled with an expression that was not agreeable." When Lincoln informed her that he had written to Frémont stating what he wanted done, Jessie retorted that her husband thought arms alone would not win the war, "that there must be other considerations to get us the support of foreign countries." She then proceeded to make the argument for emancipation. "The President said, 'You are quite a female politician.' I felt the sneering tone and saw there was a foregone decision against all listening."

Then, Jessie claimed, Lincoln got mad: "'The General should never have dragged the negro into the war. It is a war for a great national object and the negro has nothing to do with it,'" she reports Lincoln saying. And, for good measure: "'he never would have done it if he had consulted Frank Blair.'" Stunned, Mrs. Frémont took her leave, asking when she might have a reply for Frémont from the president. He answered curtly, "tomorrow or the day after." Reflecting back on this remarkable scene, Jessie later concluded: "When a man expresses a conviction fearlessly, he is reported as having made a trenchant and forceful statement, but when a woman speaks thus earnestly, she is reported as a lady who has lost her temper."

If Jessie had lost her temper, she wasn't the only one. The next day a livid Preston Blair, whom she had loved so much that she named a child after him, came to call at Willard's. As Jessie told the story, her old friend shouted: "'Look what Fremont has done; made the President his enemy,'" and he castigated her for not heeding him in his advice to come to Washington: "'it is not fit for a woman to go with an army. If you had stayed here in Washington you could have had anything you wanted.'" Of course, Blair was worried that Lincoln would blame his family for their protégé's actions and he berated the woman he had raised like his own child, reminding her of all the Blairs had done for Frémont—to promote him, protect his property, "to elevate him in the public eye." Then, Preston recounted to his daughter

Lizzie, Jessie "bridled up at this & put on a very *high* look." In the three hours he spent at Willard's venting his frustration, Preston Blair let slip the fact that Frank had written about Frémont's incompetence and arrogance, and he revealed to Jessie that the president had just dispatched Montgomery Blair and the Quartermaster General of the Army, Montgomery Meigs, to St. Louis to inspect the situation.

Jessie shot off a telegram to John, warning him of the impending investigation—and then probably leaked it to the *New York Times*, which printed the missive along with the fact that she was in Washington. She then sent off a message to the president demanding to see Frank's letter "and any other communications, if any, which in your judgment have made that investigation necessary." She followed up with a second note, when she wanted to know from the president if she would have an answer to her husband's letter. Lincoln dismissively notified her that he had replied directly to Frémont by mail and would not show her "copies of letters in my possession without the consent of the writer," but, he assured her, "no impression has been made on my mind against the honor or integrity of Gen. Fremont; and I now enter my protest against being understood as acting in any hostility towards him." Just as Frémont had done, President Lincoln announced publicly that he had ordered the general to rescind his emancipation proclamation, and the story hit the newspapers before Lincoln's letter reached Missouri. And with that, Jessie Benton Frémont returned to St. Louis. The *New York Times* reported rumblings that Frémont would be replaced by Meigs but then added in an editorial note that a telegram had arrived from Washington advising "that Mrs. Fremont left there yesterday morning for St. Louis with assurances that the General should not be interfered with." That was far from the end of the story, however.

When John Frémont read about Frank Blair's letter he slammed his former ally behind bars, arresting him for "conduct unbecoming an officer and a gentleman," in his criticism of the commander. The long relationship between the Blairs and the Frémonts had come to an end. "I had been astonished by reading the telegraph on Frank's arrest. Jessie carried a *high head.*" Lizzie was astonished that her best friend of decades had crossed the family: "the day of the arrest with pride precedes a fall & when down they come this time let them stay." But the Frémonts weren't falling anywhere fast, despite the efforts of the Blairs to depose them. "All the members of the Cabinet are or seemed to be impressed with the necessity of removing Fremont," Preston Blair fretted to his daughter, but the general kept his command. "One of the leading members told me that it is Seward's jealousy of the Blairs."

President Lincoln hesitated before removing the popular Frémont while the story played out in the press, with the Blairs leaking their letters and Jessie's communications with the president, and the Frémont forces wooing reporters with interviews and access to the Army encampment in Jefferson City, where "the General and his Body Guard proceeded to the depot and received Mrs. Fremont on her arrival from Washington." That was enough information for Louisa Meigs. Her husband might be filing reports critical of Frémont, but as far as she was concerned, "Whatever his conduct as a General may be, there is no doubt that he is a very gallant & devoted husband. His reception of Mrs. F at the Camp was a proof of his attention to that lady which every military man will do well to consider." Louisa was miserable about her exile from Washington for safety's sake, and wanted her husband to want her at home. Lizzie Lee, of course, had a more sarcastic take on the Frémont pair: "He travels with a grand cuisine & his fine traveling carriage—Jessie went off to Jefferson in a special train."

But Lizzie was none too happy with her own family, either: "I have just read Fremont's charges against Frank," she bristled to her husband, blaming her father and brother Montgomery "for the want of the right reserve." The men in her family had gone overboard: "Father was most incautious in his talk with Jessie." And Montgomery Blair was convinced it was Preston's confrontation with Jessie that caused his brother's arrest: "That was . . . 'Genl' Jessie's doing altogether," he contended. "I understand now that spies are set upon Frank by Jessie to see if she can't get hold of some talk to eke out the prosecution. . . . She is perfectly unscrupulous you know." Montgomery Blair managed to calm Frémont down enough to get Frank out of jail but Lizzie sadly concluded, "Jessie's part in this matter has disappointed me sorely. Things which I had learnt to believe about her husband made me think him unreliable—but only added to my pity & affection for her. I am now convinced that in countenancing & covering his sins she has shared & been degraded by them—& yet I can see in her efforts to elevate him & excite his ambition a struggle to win him from his groveling nature." Lizzie kept trying to hold on to something to save her female friendships.

Jessie was doing her best to save her husband's job, defending his handling of the war to anyone who would listen, accusing other generals of trying to sabotage John: "If anyone had the power to put this truth clearly before Mr. Lincoln so that he would recognize it as the simple truth it would be a benefit rendered to the country. He is too prejudiced against me, I can't do it." Jessie thought she knew someone who could get to the president—Dorothea Dix. "I can but think that if the President had one interview with Mr. Fremont there never would have grown up this state of injury to the public service," she insisted to the influential woman. It was all the Blairs' fault that the general was in trouble: "the same good brain & bad heart that made the President so unjust and deaf to me has influenced not only the President but the newspapers." Her pleading in the end was to no avail. Frémont's incompetent leadership continued to take its toll in Missouri. President Lincoln relieved General John C. Frémont of his command. The couple moved to New York, where abolitionists celebrated John's stance against slavery and Jessie put the best spin on their situation that she could: "It is nobler, & one can but feel it so, even after having had the charm of power, to work without visible reward. And good work we are doing. Perhaps serving to point the evils of this tenderness toward slavery."

THOUGH LINCOLN WAS trying to frame the war as a struggle to preserve the Union, the issue of slavery could not be avoided. Even with the Deep South out of the counsels of government, the subject still divided the politicians and the people. The president's own Cabinet included Montgomery Blair from a slaveholding family and Salmon Chase, an ardent abolitionist. The Congress met in a Capitol built by enslaved workers, took taxis driven by hired-out slaves, and headed to restaurants or barbershops where they were likely to be waited on by slaves. The whole city where the war was being orchestrated depended on slave labor. To the locals, it was nothing remarkable. "We were accustomed to the convenience of having Negro servants and a good many Northern people, like my parents, hired such servants from their masters, though they would have been horrified at the idea of actually owning slaves," the Lincolns' friend Julia Taft remembered years later. To the abolitionists it was an outrage and their voices were growing louder, arguing for both moral and practical reasons that the president should declare publicly and proudly what everyone knew— that this war was about slavery, despite the congressional resolution passed in July explicitly disavowing the abolition of slavery as a war aim. Yes, the North wanted to preserve the Union, but the Union had shattered because the South seceded. And yes, the South seceded to defend states' rights, but the right the secessionists cared about was the right to own people as property.

Abolitionists contended that European countries toying with recognizing the Confederacy would not be able to do so if the war were defined as a crusade against slavery, because public opinion in England and France would then demand support for the Union. And they fervently believed the moral force of the issue would inspire northern men to enlist for the fight. Still President Lincoln temporized. He had promised in his inaugural address that he would not interfere with slavery where it already existed. And it existed in Missouri, Kentucky, and Maryland—states he had to hold on to. They presented a far bigger concern at the moment than Britain or France. But regardless of what the president proclaimed, many enslaved people believed the war would set them free. And they found ways to make it so.

As Union forces occupied parts of Virginia, African Americans there started to show up in the army camps, assuming they were crossing into safety. When a few men arrived at General Benjamin Butler's garrison, he put them to work rather than return them to their owners, who were no longer protected by the Fugitive Slave Act, in his view, because they claimed to hail from a foreign country, the Confederate States of America. Word spread, and more men came and told their stories to a newspaper reporter: "'We had heard it . . . . since last Fall, that if Lincoln was elected, you would come down and set us free . . . the colored people have talked it all over; we heard that if we could get in here we should be free, or, at any rate, we should be among friends.'" With no official guidance from Washington to tell him what to do, Butler decided that the men were contraband property and could be removed from their enemy owners in the same way that horses or ammunition could be. When the word went out,

more escaped slaves, including whole families, arrived at his fort daily.
The reporter disclosed, "I understand that the General has decided
to retain all the negroes who have come." The floodgates opened. Between May and July, close to one thousand slaves found refuge with
Butler at Fort Monroe near Norfolk. And many of the so-called contrabands made their way to Washington, adding to the already over-
burdened capital teeming with soldiers still expecting an attack.

Lizzie Lee, accustomed to being useful, battled boredom in Philadelphia that fall as her plugged-in father insisted she stay there because any day the siege could begin. General Meigs too had exiled his
restive wife, Louisa, to points north, telling her that in Washington
people "think every artillery drill the beginning of a battle." For Ann
Green, still trying to farm her fields well inside the District lines, every
few days brought new alarms: "Everybody seems to expect that some
important war event will take place in a day or two, which keeps me
very anxious." Abraham Lincoln kept thinking that an important war
event *should* take place. But his cocky young general George McClellan
seemed curiously hesitant to take action even as he amassed thousands
of troops in and around Washington—reaching some 200,000 strong.

So many young men concentrated in the area in turn attracted all
kinds of unsavory characters, and Congress tried to exert some control by making it illegal to sell alcohol to the soldiers. Wildly popular
with his troops, McClellan had managed to instill discipline and dignity but camps crammed with men in close quarters bred something
neither the Congress nor the commanders could control—disease.
Epidemics coursed through the campgrounds, sending hundreds of
sick and dying men to the hospitals set up in government buildings,
hotels, schools, and churches all over the city. And hundreds of dedicated women came in to care for them under the direction of Superintendent of the Female Nurses of the Army Dorothea Dix.

WHEN PRESIDENT LINCOLN called up the troops in response to the attack on Fort Sumter, Dorothea Dix answered the call. Arriving in Baltimore the same day as the Massachusetts regiment was attacked, Dorothea quietly made her way across town and into Washington, where she immediately volunteered her services to the Surgeon General and the War Department. The Secretary of War accepted with alacrity: "she will give aid in organizing Military Hospitals . . . aiding the Chief Surgeon by supplying nurses . . . she is fully authorized to receive, control and disburse special supplies bestowed by individuals or associations for the comfort of their friends . . . also . . . to draw from the army stores." Miss Dix continued to be well-known in Washington, where she had kept up her connections after the failure of her bill to set aside public lands for the poor. The indefatigable advocate had spent the last few years traveling Europe and the United States investigating the conditions of the mentally ill, establishing hospitals where there were none and inspecting the hospitals born out of her efforts. She was so admired that she was given free passes for her transportation and had access to the powerful the world over, including the pope.

Now she would use that influence to create a corps of female nurses, something that had never happened before; formal nursing had never been women's work. But women were eager to play a part in the war effort and when thousands applied for the nursing jobs, Dorothea Dix immediately ruled out whole categories of them. No Catholic nuns; no young, good-looking women need apply. First priority would be given to "matronly persons of experience, good conduct or superior education and serious disposition." They would be required to "dress plain, (colors brown, grey, or black) and while connected with the service without ornaments of any sort." All applicants must be between the ages of thirty-five and fifty, though she herself was almost sixty.

The Lincolns' young friend Julia Taft was rejected because she was too young but she volunteered to read to the soldiers and write letters for them at the hospital run by her half brother. "My brother would not have any women nurses in his hospital," she noted, reflecting the resistance of many military doctors. "Doctor Mary Walker wanted to be taken on his staff but he had a horror of her because she wore men's clothes." Mary Walker was the first female surgeon in America and only the second woman to have graduated from medical school. As an ardent supporter of women's rights, she always wore men's clothes, something that caused her to be arrested from time to time. Because she was a woman, the military brass would not hire her at the beginning of the war, so she donated her services as assistant surgeon at the hospital set up in the Patent Office. Later in the conflict, she received a salary under military contract to work in field hospitals. She was captured by the Confederates and held prisoner under horrific conditions, until released in a prisoner of war exchange. When the war was over she received the Medal of Honor—still the only woman to have ever been awarded with the highest distinction the country confers.

Dorothea Dix turned to the first woman in the United States to graduate from medical school, Elizabeth Blackwell, as she looked for someone to train her nurses. Dr. Blackwell wisely replied that the training should take place in a different hospital "so the male surgeons may take the credit." Women in the wards was going to be a tough enough sell—better to have them trained by men. Dr. Blackwell was involved in a war effort of her own in New York, trying to organize the outpouring of supplies coming from relatives of the soldiers. Seeing that donations arrived in a completely haphazard fashion, often never reaching the men they were meant for, Elizabeth convoked a huge assembly that resulted in the formation of the Women's Central Association of Relief "to organize the whole benevolence of women of the country into a general and central association."

The WCAR appointed a board of twelve women and twelve men, and some of the men then traveled to Washington to meet with the War Department. On the way, they came up with the idea of a civilian sanitary commission, similar to one that operated in Britain during the Crimean War, to promote cleanliness in military camps and hospitals. When they reached the capital, they met with Dorothea Dix and with President Lincoln and, after some bureaucratic hassles, were able to form the United States Sanitary Commission. In addition to its duties in the field, the commission would work with aid societies around the country soliciting and delivering food and clothes for the troops, plus overseeing the training of nurses. The women's association took on those tasks and organized enormous fairs to support the cause, eventually bringing in a billion dollars for the war effort.

As the war began the medical situation was disorganized and disorderly. No one was really in charge and the biggest army hospital was in Kansas, hundreds of miles away from the action. When combat came at Bull Run, and two thousand killed or wounded soldiers were carried to Washington, the city was totally unprepared. But Dorothea Dix was everywhere—setting up hospitals anywhere she could, using part of her own creation, the Government Hospital for the Insane, for the worst cases, and tapping her contacts around the country to hasten the delivery of medical supplies and food to the capital. Though most male doctors resented Dorothea and her army of female nurses, it was clear they couldn't function without them. Miss Dix made it easy to resent her. She was used to getting her way by staring down state legislators and she made it patently clear that she had no patience for men blocking her path. Always having operated as a sole practitioner,

Dorothea Dix showed no talent working within an organization. One of the original board members of the Sanitary Commission, Harvard's Dr. Samuel Gridley Howe, offered one of the kinder descriptions of this whirlwind of a woman: "Miss Dix, who is the terror of all mere formalists, idlers, and evildoers . . . goes everywhere to prevent and remedy abuses and shortcomings."

Howe saw Dorothea Dix in action when he and his wife, Julia Ward Howe, traveled to Washington in the fall of 1861. "The enemy's troops was then stationed in the near neighborhood of Washington, and the capture of the national capital would have been a great strategic advantage to their cause," the famous poet wrote later as she remembered the wartime city. Still fresh in her mind was the startling advertisement she saw from her window at Willard's for "an agency for embalming and forwarding the bodies of those who had fallen in the fight or who had perished by fever." On a visit to the camps outside the city, she heard soldiers repeatedly singing one song they particularly liked: "John Brown's body lays a mouldering in the ground, / His soul is marching on." Urged by a friend to write " 'some good words for that stirring tune,' " she replied that she had wanted to but the words hadn't come to her. The next day as she awoke at Willard's "in the morning twilight . . . the long lines of the desired poem began to twine themselves in my mind." Worried that she might forget what had come to her, she jumped up, dashed down the words, and then went back to sleep, "saying to myself, 'I like this better than most things that I have written.' " And thus was born "The Battle Hymn of the Republic," which became the clarion call of the federal army.

During their visit the Howes called on President Lincoln, who "was laboring at this time under a terrible pressure of doubt and anxiety." With General McClellan dragging his feet about taking his troops into battle, the country wondered why the president wasn't

taking charge. "Few people praised or trusted him," Mrs. Howe recalled with amazement later. The public wanted to know, "'Why did
he not do this, or that, or the other? He a President, indeed! Look at
this war, dragging on so slowly!'" The best thing anyone said about
Abraham Lincoln at that point: "he meant well."

PRESIDENT LINCOLN TOO wondered why the war was dragging
on so slowly but he couldn't get his general to act. At McClellan's insistence, he had pushed old General Scott out and named the younger
man general in chief of the whole army while he also kept his command at the head of the Army of the Potomac. The nightly call "all
quiet along the Potomac," once a source of comfort, had turned into a
mocking reminder that nothing was happening in this war. McClellan
kept his troops busy drilling and practicing but with one brief exception, they did not fight and that one battle, at Ball's Bluff on the upper
Potomac, did not go well. Eight hundred federal soldiers were killed,
including Lincoln's dear friend Senator Edward Baker. The Lincolns
had named their little boy who died after Baker, and Abe and Mary
both loved him. So did their boys. That affection made it even worse
that the battle did nothing to dislodge the Dixie forces from their
redoubt in nearby Virginia. As Ann Green summed up the situation:
"The character of the war now assumes the appearance of lasting a
very long time."

In this period in limbo, the capital took on a somewhat festive
air, despite miserable November weather when a rising Potomac River
carried the bodies of soldiers killed at Ball's Bluff down to the city.
Performances of plays, concerts, and magicians' acts entertained the
throngs coming to work in the war effort or to make money off of it.
At the White House, the president and first lady entertained regularly.

They hosted Prince Napoleon, the cousin of the sitting emperor of France, in the summer and were gearing up for the social season that the return of Congress always ushered in. If it weren't for the thousands of soldiers in the town, and the fortifications surrounding it, life almost seemed normal. Schools had closed in the city, however, so "in the fall of 1861, Mrs. Lincoln had a desk and blackboard put into the end of the state dining room and secured a tutor for the boys," Julia Taft recalled. Julia's brothers joined the Lincoln boys as the pupils in that exclusive academy and she herself "was in and out of the White House almost every day."

Both Lincolns seemed to enjoy the teenager's company, though she spent most of her time with Mary Lincoln, who took on something of a mentoring role. But Julia found the first lady a sometimes daunting character, telling a story of the day her parents visited the White House and Mary Lincoln decided she liked Mrs. Taft's bonnet and must have it. When she peremptorily demanded it, her somewhat amazed guest gave it to her, leaving Julia to conclude: "It was an outstanding characteristic of Mary Todd Lincoln that what she wanted she wanted when she wanted it and no substitute! And as far as we know, she always had it, including a President of the United States." Mary Lincoln wanted a White House resplendent with fine furniture, draperies, rugs, and china, and she had it—but at a price that would come back to haunt her. And the New York press corps followed her every purchase. During one shopping spree the sympathetic *Chicago Tribune* chided: "They divided into squads and platoons, part of them alighting upon her milliners, part on her flunkies and part on her hostler. . . . No lady of the White House has ever been so maltreated by the public press."

Mary Lincoln didn't get much credit for her many acts of kindness in visiting the hospitals and army camps. That might be why President Lincoln put out the word that she was responsible for the pardon of a young soldier scheduled for execution. William Scott had fallen asleep on guard duty and been convicted of dereliction of duty after he had volunteered for all-night watch to fill in for a sick friend, and then, after a full day and night awake, drew his own overnight assignment. Both Mrs. Lincoln and her little boy Tad were distressed that the young man had received such a harsh punishment. After first worrying about interfering with military discipline, on the day before the scheduled execution Lincoln told General in Chief McClellan to pardon the soldier at "the request of the 'Lady President.'"

The pardon was a good public relations move for the "Lady President," who barely escaped public humiliation, but not private gossip, over the infamous leaking of the president's State of the Union message. As he prepared for the return of Congress, Lincoln knew he would have to address the louder and louder calls for the abolition of slavery coming from the faction splitting the party—the Radical Republicans. He could not ignore the subject in his message; still he approached it cautiously with the Union in such a precarious position. But before he even delivered to the Capitol the admonition that "the struggle for today, is not altogether for today—it is for a vast future also," the public had already read his words. The *New York Herald* printed the text that morning. Congress suspected it was Mary Lincoln who had provided it to the paper in exchange for favorable coverage, or maybe, members speculated, even an outright bribe to help offset her huge expenditures, or maybe she was having an affair with someone connected to the newspaper. A congressional investigation threatened to embarrass the first family so much that the president personally went to Capitol Hill to beg the senators to "spare him the disgrace." The matter was dropped, but not before testimony from a competitor to the *Herald* telling the investigating committee that he couldn't compete because "the *Herald* had relations with the female members of the Pres[iden]ts. Family & gave that paper an advantage over the rest of us."

Abraham Lincoln didn't need enemies when he had potential leakers in his own household and unhelpful freelancing on the part of Union officers. Not only had he had to deal with John Frémont's impetuous proclamation; now he was faced with the threat of war with Britain as the result of a Union ship captain's unauthorized actions. Acting without orders, Charles Wilkes seized two Confederate envoys to London, James Mason and John Slidell, from the British mail ship the *Trent* and imprisoned them in Boston. The captain basked in a hero's spotlight until the news reached London, where the press excitedly demanded retaliation for the violation of a ship flying the Union Jack.

While he waited to see what the British would do, Lincoln sent his message to Congress on December 3. Again he placed preservation of the Union first and foremost among his priorities and urged against rushing into "radical and extreme actions." He pointed out that the war had already freed many slaves and expressed hope that the slave states still in the Union might voluntarily enact emancipation. Lincoln called on Congress to compensate owners for their enslaved workers if the states chose that course. He also suggested colonization, moving the freed blacks to a "climate congenial to them." The president had at least one supporter, Anna Ella Carroll, who published a defense that December in her book, *The War Powers of the General Government*. But Lincoln's message far from satisfied the Radical Republicans already seething over the course of the war. In a sour mood, the Congress formed a Joint Committee on the Conduct of the War to investigate the failures of the past year and summoned John Frémont to testify. "This is the end of our silence & now will come justice & retribution," crowed Jessie. "Now Fortune turn thy wheel."

As if all of that were not enough for the beleaguered president, on December 19 official word came from Great Britain. Her Majesty's Government demanded the release of the two southern envoys and their return to British protection plus a formal apology from the United States, adding the threat that the British ambassador would be recalled to London in a few days if the Americans had not responded. Lincoln couldn't risk starting another war but he had public opinion to contend with and the public did not want to surrender Mason and Slidell. One of the few northern sympathizers who worried about the imprisoned men was Louisa Meigs: "I cannot help feeling sorry for Mrs. Slidell and the girls." These women had been friends for years and felt for each other across the battle lines.

On Christmas morning the Cabinet met to consider Secretary of State Seward's proposal to free the diplomats using as a fig leaf the fact that a court should have decided the legality of seizing them. Lizzie Lee reflected the skepticism of Seward shared by many, huffing to her husband that he would *back down flat.* The public perception of the Secretary of State who was trying to help the president navigate through the shoals of border state politics, abolitionist demands, and foreign policy predicaments was that he would flounder rather than sail straight. But Lincoln trusted Seward's judgment whether his fellow Cabinet members did or not. When the advisors met, the other Cabinet members resisted the release of the southern envoys. President Lincoln remained undecided. Christmas cheer was in short supply.

Lizzie Lee and her family were invited to the White House for

Christmas dinner, and the Lincoln boys and their friends the Tafts added some merriment to the occasion, but the question of what to do about Slidell and Mason hung heavy. The next day the Cabinet and president decided that it was the better part of wisdom to let the Confederate envoys go. "We are now all in a state of collapse and reaction," Lizzie sighed, and there was the Congress to contend with "the members are in an explosive condition." It was not an auspicious way to begin the New Year.

CHAPTER 5

LEFT: *Clara Barton, the "angel of the battlefield" where she dodged bullets to aid soldiers, and later founded the American Red Cross and convinced the Congress to ratify the Geneva Conventions.* RIGHT: *Kate Chase Sprague visiting troops. She was the daughter of Salmon P. Chase, and considered a conniving political operative trying for years to elect her father president as she acted on the Washington social stage.*

Rose Is Released, Clara Goes to War, Louisa May Briefly Nurses

1862

In 1862 Washington was a third rate Southern city," Mary Clemmer Ames recalled several years later from her perch as a prominent journalist. "All public offices, magnificent in conception, seemed to be in a state of crude incompleteness." Hulks of half-built structures poked up out of the mud—a crane loomed over the Capitol as work on the dome dragged on, a new wing for the Treasury Building crept toward completion, and "the unfinished Washington monument stood the monument to the nation's neglect and shame." Even harsher in his view of the Capital City was British writer Anthony Trollope, who had no hope either for the city itself or for the stub of a monument to its namesake: "No one has a word to say for it. No one thinks that money will ever again be subscribed for its completion." Trollope followed in his mother Fanny's footsteps of thirty years earlier touring America; she had had complimentary things to say about the fledgling Federal City in her *Domestic Manners of the Americans*. Her son chose to make his New World journey during the Civil War, coloring his view of everything he saw. Washington would languish and die, the acerbic Englishman dismissively concluded, as a foolish experiment in creating a capital out of nowhere, constructed as the seat of government, not commerce.

Visiting over New Year's, Trollope complained that society "had been almost destroyed by the loss of the Southern half of the usual sojourners in the city." It just wasn't as much fun without southern gentlemen, "more given to enjoy hospitality than his Northern brother; and this difference is quite as strong with the women as with the men." But the Lincolns tried to liven things up with the annual reception at the newly refurbished and resplendent White House even as the president chafed at his inability to push his army into action. General Mc-Clellan had been ill and uncommunicative. The war stumbled on at a stalemate. And the Congress demanded answers. The Frémonts were in town defending John's actions in Missouri and being well received by the Joint Committee on the Conduct of the War, composed mainly of Republicans itching for an emancipation decree. But Lincoln continued to resist the antislavery agitators, unceremoniously removing Secretary of War Simon Cameron from the Cabinet after he asserted to the committee that it was "clearly a right of the Government to arm slaves" and "employ them in the service against the rebels." Lincoln didn't know the report was coming, and the angry president dispatched Cameron to replace the ambassador to Russia, replacing him in turn with the prickly but upright Edwin Stanton. The political brushfire over the Cabinet shakeup still flared as yet another general's wife came to town to make the case for her husband.

This time it was Mrs. William Tecumseh Sherman who sought a session with the commander in chief. As the Union commander in Kentucky, General Sherman had informed Secretary Cameron that he would need tens of thousands more men to hold his position and 200,000 more to go on the offensive. The Cabinet member thought the general must be unbalanced to make such an impossible request; a newspaper reporter picked up the story and when headlines blared, "General William T. Sherman Insane," his wife decided to intervene. Like Jessie Frémont, Ellen Ewing Sherman was wise in the ways of Washington. Her father, Thomas Ewing, had served in the Senate from Ohio and as a Cabinet member under four presidents; she had lived for years in the capital, attended the Visitation Convent, and married at the Blairs' home with all of official Washington as wedding guests. She had grown up with her future groom, who was adopted by her family after his father died. And now she was back in Washington to defend him, her father in tow. "I hope you do not fear that I will behave ridiculously here," Ellen revealed her nervousness to her embattled husband before seeing Lincoln. But she then reported with relief that she and her father "had a long & most satisfactory interview with the President today." She had mounted a strenuous argument: "I told him you had enemies among your fellow Generals & that the newspaper correspondents were mere tools. . . . I told him that I did not come to ask for anything but to say a word against those who had conspired against you & in vindication of your name. He seemed very anxious that we should believe that he felt kindly toward you." Lucky for Abraham Lincoln that Ellen Sherman was willing to make that trip and save one of the key generals of the Union Army.

AT THE END of January, the war briefly took a backseat to another troublesome topic: the White House guest list. "The Sewards & Mrs. Lincoln have invitations out for Soirees," Lizzie Lee announced, scoring one of the select five hundred invitations to Mary Lincoln's grand reception on February 5. The first lady, who had badly overspent her allotted funds for White House redecoration, decided to do away with the expensive weekly dinners hosted by Harriet Lane, instead reinstituting the regular receptions for the public and adding a few large, lavish events. Mary first broached the idea with her dressmaker and then presented it to the president, who worried about breaking precedent. However, as Elizabeth Keckley related the conversation, Mrs. Lincoln insisted: "Public receptions are more democratic than stupid state dinners—are more in keeping with the spirit of institutions in our country, as you would say if called upon to make a stump speech." Mary Lincoln knew how to get to her husband but one of Lincoln's secretaries, John Nicolay, had his own take on the "Queen": "La Reine has determined to abrogate state dinners." The president's staff lost no love for their boss's imperious wife, often referring to her as a "Hell Cat." But Mary prevailed and when the invitations went out in January, everyone left off the list tried desperately to wangle a way in while a few outraged souls, like Ohio Senator Benjamin Wade, the chairman of the Conduct of the War Committee, huffed that it was unseemly to be holding such festivities while soldiers shivered in their tents just a few miles away.

Rumor had it that some eighty Republicans had defied etiquette and turned the Lincolns down. John and Jessie Frémont planned to be among those sending their regrets but a messenger from the President begged them to come in a show of unity, and since John still sought a military command, the couple agreed. Then, at the last minute the grand event was almost canceled, but not because of the war. The Lincolns' son Willie was running a high fever and the parents, who had already lost one son, feared for his life. A hastily summoned doctor assured them that Willie faced no immediate danger and with the invitations already out the Lincolns made the call—the party must go on. Even though the boy took a turn for the worse the night of the event, the doctor insisted there was no cause for alarm and Elizabeth Keckley promised to keep watch while the president and first lady entertained their guests.

Before taking up her post at Willie's bedside, Mrs. Keckley helped Mary into her low-cut white satin dress, trimmed in black lace with a long train sweeping behind her. When her husband took one look he advised, "'Mother, it is my opinion, if some of that tail was nearer the head, it would be in better style.'" But he didn't deter his wife as she marched to the music of the Marine Band to greet her guests, who would feast on foie gras, oysters, partridge, venison, and all kinds of other delicacies, including a cake shaped like Fort Sumter. Though the hosts had deemed dancing inappropriate, the newspapers headlined the affair as "Mrs. Lincoln's Dancing Party." The reporter for the *Cincinnati Daily Press* described the evening as a display of "fashion, beauty and manliness" and catalogued "the decorations and candy ornaments." Among them: "A representation of a United States steam frigate of forty guns, with all sails set, and the flag of the Union flying at the main . . . A warrior's helmet, supported by cupids . . . The Goddess of Liberty, elevated above a simple but elegant shrine, within which was a life-like fountain of water." And though he conceded that "such a display of elegance, taste and loveliness has perhaps never before been witnessed within the walls of the White House," the correspondent, or perhaps the editors, clucked about the "costly and inappropriate festivity" and topped the story with one about additional congressional appropriations for White House expenditures.

Jessie Frémont judged the evening "a ghastly failure" for her enemies the Lincolns, but for her husband, she boasted, it constituted "a complete success." The president had "made our reception marked" and Secretary of War Stanton had stopped to speak to them. Clearly the Frémonts weren't on the outs and the Lincolns were coming in for a good deal of criticism. A few days after the grand event Kansas's *Emporia News* raged against "the utter unconsciousness of the ruin and misery of the country which prevails in Washington." Ridiculing the Lincolns' staging of acts by magicians and circus performers at the White House, the newspaper castigated the "prevailing gaiety and thoughtlessness in the National Capital . . . all while our soldiers are sick, suffering and dying in the camps, the strength of the army wasting from inaction." Abraham Lincoln needed the army to act.

Then—at last—came the news the president had been waiting for, a string of Union victories. On February 6, aided by the navy's ironclad ships attacking from the Tennessee River, General Ulysses S. Grant took Fort Henry in Tennessee. Two days later the navy captured Roanoke Island in North Carolina, tightening the stranglehold on southern ports, and then the big one—the Rebels acquiesced to Grant's demand for unconditional surrender at Fort Donelson, on the Cumberland River. By capturing that important Rebel redoubt Grant ensured that Kentucky, separated by the federal army from Tennessee, would stay safely in the Union, Nashville would come under Yankee control, and the rivers and railroads of western Tennessee would be closed off to the Confederacy. Newly baptized "Unconditional Surrender" Grant received a promotion and Washington reveled in the victory: "The jubilant feelings of the members of the House of Representatives over the recent victories," exulted Washington's *National Republican*, had not diminished after a night's sleep, and "the House could remain in session only a half hour yesterday, before it had to adjourn, to allow of a season of mutual congratulations." But there was no jubilation at the White House, where Willie Lincoln lay dying of typhoid fever.

The eleven-year-old's condition had steadily worsened the night of the big party. With Elizabeth Keckley on duty, both of his parents slipped away from the festivities from time to time to check on the child, showing the seamstress their great concern. The little boy called for his good friend Bud Taft, his constant playmate of the past year, and Bud's sister Julia later remember "my brother was with him most of the time." The boys and their younger brothers, the only pupils of the White House tutor, had lived in and out of each other's houses as an inseparable band. They had commandeered the attic and the roof of the Executive Mansion for forts, circuses, and theatrical performances. Though visiting Cabinet members and other notables grumbled at the interruptions of the incorrigible foursome, the president enjoyed the boys' antics and Mary only wished to "let the children have a good time."

But now one of the children was dying and his friend stayed by his side. When the president tried to get the little boy to go to bed late one night the staunch playmate protested: " 'If I go he will call for me.' " At noon on February 20, Bud thought his friend was better, but Willie died at five o'clock that evening. Mrs. Keckley washed and dressed the child then stood at the foot of the bed and watched as Abraham Lincoln "buried his head in his hands, and his tall frame was convulsed with emotion. . . . I did not dream that his rugged nature could be so moved." Mary Lincoln told the Taft boys' mother to keep them home the day of the funeral; " 'it makes me feel worse to see them.' " But the president took pity on the stalwart little friend and "sent for Bud to see

Willie before he was put in the casket." It was the last time this daily companion of Willie and Tad Lincoln would be in the White House because Mrs. Lincoln wouldn't allow him to visit. Poor little Tad, who was sick himself, had not only lost his brother, he had also lost his best friends. Mary Lincoln came close to losing her mind.

The first lady took to her bed in spasms of agony. Her older son Robert, home from Harvard, prevailed on his mother's sister to come stay with her, and President Lincoln contacted Dorothea Dix asking her to find a nurse for his younger son. Miss Dix sent the very competent and kind nurse Rebecca Pomroy to minister to Tad. But no one could help Mary. Elizabeth Keckley witnessed a dramatic moment when the President brought his wife to the window and showed her the hospital for the insane in the distance, with the warning: "'Try and control your grief, or it will drive you mad, and we may have to send you there.'" Rebecca Pomroy, who had lost her husband and two sons, counseled both of the Lincolns. And friends like Lizzie Lee tried to help. Not long after Willie died she called at the White House to inquire about Tad and Mary: "Mrs. L sent me a kind message of thanks & sent her sister Mrs. Edwards down to see me . . . she is ten times better looking than Mrs. Lincoln." Poor Mary couldn't catch a break from the constant criticism, even in mourning. And Mrs. Lee could be counted among her friends! Almost a month later, when Lizzie called again, Mary did receive her across-the-street neighbor, "& was tearful but very kind." When she was finally able to rouse herself enough to write a letter, Mary admitted to an old friend, "I am so completely unnerved, that I can scarcely command myself to write."

MARY LINCOLN'S WITHDRAWAL from the social scene provided just the opening Kate Chase needed. She had already been running a rival salon, throwing her own large party the night after the one at the White House, with the added entertainment of the Hutchinson Family singers, a pro-abolitionist ensemble. The whole town had repeated the tale of the young woman's curt remarks to the first lady at the dinner given for the Cabinet soon after Lincoln took office. When Mary tried to be gracious to the much younger woman, assuring her, "I shall be glad to see you any time, Miss Chase," she was met by the arrogant retort: "Mrs. Lincoln, I shall be glad for *you* to call on *me* at any time." There was no mistake about it—the battle lines were drawn. Kate believed *she* should be the hostess in the White House, and that her father should be president; nothing the Lincolns could do or say would erase the animosity.

Even young Julia Taft felt the heat of the competition. One day Mrs. Lincoln sent the girl home from the White House greenhouse with a bouquet intended for Governor William Sprague of Rhode Island. He had accompanied his troops to Washington, where they were assigned to space in the Patent Office building—Julia's father's workplace. The teenager developed something of a crush on "the little governor," as Sprague was called, so to please her young friend, Mary suggested the gift of flowers. "But as I was proudly bearing the bouquet to my father's room in the Patent Office, thinking on the way of a proper speech to go with it, Miss Kate Chase appeared, sweeping along the hall escorted by two officers. Miss Chase was a reigning society belle and, as the daughter of the Secretary of Treasury, very much in the swim." When Kate asked Julia where she was taking the flowers and received the reply, "Mrs. Lincoln gave them to me to take to Governor Sprague," she snatched the bouquet away saying she would deliver it, "'with Mrs. Lincoln's compliments.'" Julia pouted. "She was very handsome, beautifully dressed, and accustomed to have what she wanted. . . . I went back to Mrs. Lincoln in wrath and tears.

'Never mind, Julia,' she said. 'You shall have another just as pretty for the governor when Miss Chase isn't around.' But Miss Chase was always around. In fact she married him."

The petty social snubs were one thing. Far more harmful was the fact that as secretary of the Treasury, Salmon Chase knew what Mary Lincoln was spending to decorate the White House and spread stories of her extravagance. Some members of the "team of rivals" Lincoln put together in his Cabinet, men who had opposed him for the Republican nomination, had come to support the president fully. But Chase, though doing a superb job for the administration at the Treasury Department, still lusted after the top spot and found ways to undermine his boss and Mrs. Lincoln's expenditures gave him fodder. The reports of the first lady's shopping sprees gained such circulation that she was hounded by the press on her trips to New York, with reporters covering her every purchase: "Mrs. Lincoln, who is still sojourning at the Metropolitan Hotel, was engaged nearly all day yesterday in making extensive purchases at Lord & Taylor's and various other places about the city." Even after Mary Lincoln left the White House, journalist Mary Clemmer Ames was still incensed about the spendthrift first lady: "While her sister-women scraped lint, sewed bandages, and put on nurses' caps, and gave their all to country and to death, the wife of its President spent her time in rolling to and fro between Washington and New York, intent on extravagant purchases for herself and the White House. Mrs. Lincoln seemed to have nothing to do but to 'shop,' and the reports of her lavish bargains, in the newspapers, were vulgar and sensational in the extreme." The wounded and dying were being brought to the capital to be ministered to by the women, but "through it all, Mrs. Lincoln 'shopped.'" In fact Mary Lincoln did make her rounds of the hospitals but received little credit for it, and Kate Chase too was making those expensive shopping excursions to New York, threatening her father with bankruptcy. But she wasn't spending public money.

Mary Lincoln drew criticism from Kate even if she acted admirably from the abolitionist Chase's perspective. As emancipation for slaves in the District of Columbia drew near, Mrs. Lincoln asked Rebecca Orville, an African-American teacher, to come to tea. When the visitor was shown to the kitchen entrance, the first lady, embarrassed at the slight to her guest, escorted Miss Orville into the Red Room for a conversation about establishing a school for black children, and then showed her out through the front door. Just at that moment Secretary Chase pulled up with his daughter in the carriage. At the next Cabinet dinner Kate commented that the first lady was "making too much of the Negro." This from the woman who endlessly entertained abolitionists in an effort to replace the president with her father.

From the time she was a small child, Kate Chase had concerned herself with her father's political future. Salmon Chase had bad luck in wives. His first wife had died in childbirth, then his second wife, Kate's mother, died of tuberculosis when Kate was five, and his third wife also succumbed to tuberculosis. So at age eleven Kate became the "woman of the house," taking on her father and baby sister Nettie as her charges. Visitors to Governor Chase's home in Ohio commented on the political acumen of the beautiful young girl, who had every expectation of moving to the White House after the 1860 election. When she found herself in a mansion at Sixth and E Streets instead, Miss Chase used it as campaign headquarters for her father and herself, certain she could convince Washington that she would make a more worthy occupant of the Executive Mansion than the woman living there now. The whole town watched as the competition played out.

The rivals agreed on one thing, however: they both believed General McClellan had to go. "A humbug," was Mary Lincoln's assessment

of the vain little popinjay with his fancy uniforms and elaborate dinners. Kate hosted the men in the Cabinet, like Secretary of War Stanton, who complained: "This army has got to fight or run away, and
while men are striving nobly in the West, the champagne and oyster
suppers on the Potomac must be stopped." McClellan's sumptuous
dinners at his establishment on H Street contrasted markedly with the
Spartan nights in the camps where most of the generals bunked down
with their soldiers.

THE MEN "STRIVING nobly in the West" responded to President
Lincoln's extraordinary General War Order #1 commanding all sea and
land forces to advance on February 22. The politicians would wait for
the military men no longer. In early March a battle at Pea Ridge in
Arkansas gave the Union control over a southern portion of the Mississippi River, and in early April at Shiloh, Tennessee, General Grant won
again, at huge human cost—23,000 casualties—the greatest ever at the
time, serving as a grisly harbinger for the horror ahead. The navy also
scored successes. After the South had refitted the USS *Merrimack* with
iron sides and renamed it the CSS *Virginia*, the fortress of a ship destroyed several federal vessels and threatened to sail up the Potomac to
attack Washington. However, an innovative little ironclad built in New
York, the *Monitor*, scampered down the Atlantic to Hampton Roads,
Virginia, and held the *Merrimack* at bay. Then in mid-April came the
news of the Confederate surrender of Fort Pulaski, near the mouth of
the Savannah River in Georgia. John C. Frémont went west to take over
the Mountain Department in West Virginia. But still nothing from
General McClellan's Army of the Potomac.

The congressional committee investigating the conduct of the war
suspected the Democrat McClellan of disloyalty, particularly after he

refused to cooperate with the inquiry. McClellan, like so many in the Pentagon since his time, claimed he couldn't share his plans because in talkative Washington they would be leaked. The general contended that he couldn't even divulge his strategy to his commander in chief because, he sneered, Lincoln would tell Tad. Always keeping his daughter Kate cognizant of current affairs, Salmon Chase gave her the news: "The President is trying to put life and motion into the inert army," but McClellan "has had no man 'of his counsel'—thoroughly conversant with his plans." The army officer even ignored a direct presidential order to advance on the southern army entrenched in Manassas, where the Rebels provided a defense of the city of Richmond and protected a vital rail line. Now Lincoln wanted them routed so the Union could take the Confederate capital and perhaps end the war. McClellan balked.

Instead of marching overland, the general chose to invade Virginia by the Rappahannock River, landing between Richmond and Manassas. But just as he was about to put that plan in place, Confederate general Joe Johnston, whose scouts had seen Union troops preparing to move, withdrew his ill-prepared men from Manassas and stationed them closer to Richmond, leaving behind or destroying vast stores of food and equipment in the army's wake. So McClellan altered his plan of attack—he would bring his well-trained, well-equipped army more than 120,000 strong to the tip of the peninsula between the James and York Rivers and then with navy power to back up the ground forces they would work their way up to Richmond. On St. Patrick's Day, General George McClellan was finally ready to lead his men into battle.

As the daughter of one of the president's key advisors, Lizzie Lee put total faith in the Army of the Potomac: "It is believed in town that Virginia will be evacuated without a fight." From Silver Spring, she watched as the troops assembled: "The Army below us had orders last night to move & is now dragging its slow length along the streets & roads leading to Washington." First the soldiers went door-to-door paying for the damage they had done to property in the area as a new squad arrived to guard the capital, "thirty thousand troops about Washington and its surrounding forts." From the beginning, the sailor's wife had been certain that the Union would quickly win the war, and she was thrilled with the news of the Rebel retreat from Manassas: "Such retreats must be nearly as disastrous to them as lost battles, it must demoralize the men & as well as diminish their means of war." One of the men off to do battle gave her little boy Blair "a huge Newfoundland dog a noble animal—he seems sorry to part with him but he cannot carry him into Dixie with him."

As the army engaged and hurriedly built breast-high defenses, Lizzie provided a running commentary. On April 10, "McClellan invested Yorktown on Saturday—where they have breastworks extending from the York to the James River seven miles." On April 11, "McClellan has 80,000 troops. . . . He wants more troops." On April 12, "reinforcements were sent to him last night & today 40,000 more troops. . . . I think the Yorktown siege will be slow & long." On April 17: "Father had a very manly letter from McClellan says he knows all the difficulties of his situation . . . we are all in the most anxious condition—New Orleans—& Yorktown are on the lips of all." On April 30, "the siege is not likely to close at Yorktown for ten days. . . . All eyes & hearts are now turned to New Orleans." With McClellan mired in the mud in Virginia, Lizzie was much more concerned about what was happening in New Orleans. That's where her husband was poised to attack. And then on May 7, "Our people are in a frenzy of exultation over New Orleans & it keeps all of McC's doings on the Yorktown line under eclipse." The mighty Mississippi port of New Orleans had fallen to the federal navy.

Samuel Phillips Lee's ship had come under fire but he was unscathed. His brother and sister-in-law, firm supporters of the South, were "both full of joy *for you*—but Nelly's heart is sadly on the other side of the question. . . . I have felt very bitter sometimes of late—They joyed in my joy over your safety & that is the biggest feeling in my heart." It was so unnatural this war between families, and as staunch a Unionist as she was, Lizzie couldn't hate the other side: "I can't for an instant divest myself of the feeling that they are my people my countrymen—mad men as they are my heart aches for them." That was true for everyplace but New Orleans: "There they are my enemies & I feel it but always think of them as Frenchmen & quadroons." The people in Virginia and Kentucky and Missouri were Lizzie's friends and relatives and she was gratified when one of them brought news of Varina Davis: "She said 'Memory overlept the horrid gulf now between us & took her back to that happiest part of her life, that spent at Washington.'" The First Lady of the Confederacy had relayed a message that Lizzie Lee would be "'to me dear unto life's end.'" The captain of a French steamer docked in Washington reported from his trip to Richmond "astonished there so much at the warmth of friendship expressed by individuals separated by this War." But still they killed each other. On May 3, southern troops, having delayed McClellan long enough to receive reinforcements, retrenched to Williamsburg and allowed the federals to take Yorktown. This was no Yorktown surrender like the one in the Revolutionary War—the defense of Richmond grew stronger by the day.

———————

IN WASHINGTON a war of another sort played out that spring. On April 16 President Lincoln signed a bill emancipating the city's slaves. With that signature more than three thousand enslaved men and women in the District of Columbia were immediately set free. "The

legislation of the greatest free Government that ever existed will here-
after be conducted on *free* soil," the Pennsylvania *Raftsman's Journal*
rejoiced in a typical view from northern newspapers; "the apprehension that the slaves who are released from bondage in Washington will
flock to the Northern States is not well founded." No one was sure
where the newly freed people would go or what they would do. In the
only compensated emancipation enacted in this country, the measure
provided up to $1 million to pay owners for their human property and
added another $100,000 to relocate any of newly freed who wanted to
emigrate to Haiti, Liberia, or "such other country beyond the limits
of the United States as the President may determine." The president
was feeling the heat from Radical Republicans pushing for emancipation as they started mounting their campaigns for the 1864 election.
"I hope *somebody* will get tired of Presidential Candidates," Lizzie Lee
sighed a couple of days before Lincoln signed the emancipation bill,
deriding "Miss Kate's father" in his push for abolition.

Lincoln's views on the subject had evolved over time. He had proposed freedom for the slaves in the District of Columbia back when
he was in Congress decades earlier, but only if the majority of city residents agreed. Now he was eager to convince the slaveholding states
still in the Union to go for compensated emancipation, and the Capital City could serve as a laboratory for those states. Lincoln had also
long advocated colonization for African Americans, but most of them
had no interest in leaving their country; instead many of the formerly
enslaved now saw Washington as their Mecca, especially slaves from
Virginia and Maryland, where the Fugitive Slave Act still applied.

The District of Columbia government strenuously opposed the
emancipation law, reflecting the views of many residents and just
before the president signed the bill "several hundred slaves were sent
by their masters to Baltimore and the lower counties of Maryland,"

the *National Republican*, a Lincoln-supporting newspaper in Washington, reported. "We are informed that early yesterday morning several wagon loads of 'chattels' left Washington for Prince George's and St. Mary's counties, Maryland." Not all District slave owners would take emancipation lying down, even with compensation. "This bill has liberated about one thousand blacks & has made about two thousand very miserable—by having them sent away in Maryland, Kentucky & Virginia," Lizzie Lee voiced the sentiments of many conservative Republicans. She insisted that the law would hurt African Americans and that in Baltimore it "renewed the rebellious spirit there & almost everywhere in the Secesh parts of Maryland." Among those objecting to the emancipation were widows like Margaret Barber, who made her living hiring out her slaves and taking a percentage of their income. But the compensation, which was laboriously calculated, provided ready cash.

Though they strongly supported the Union and opposed the *spread* of slavery, the Blairs still owned the people who worked for them. With emancipation, Preston Blair claimed that "his servants always knew they could go when they wished—& they were of course now at liberty to do so." Somewhat to Lizzie's surprise, only one of the now-former slaves chose to leave, because as one who stayed explained, "she knows when she is well off but is evidently delighted that her children are free." Mrs. Lee might have had a great deal of affection for some of the African Americans in her household, and her little boy's nurse clearly loved him, but the Maryland woman was a typical racist of her time and place. At one point in an argument with Kate Chase on the "darky question," Lizzie raged "if Congress did not deliver us of the freed ones we would dispose of them as the Yankees had the Pequots," referring to a massacre of the Pequot Indians in the seventeenth century. Most of these women saw African Americans as inferior at best. And the southern women—Varina Davis, Virginia

Clay, Sara Pryor—at the time of the war strongly defended the institution of slavery, though the Pryors had never owned humans.

Keep in mind that these women were themselves the property of their husbands under the law of couverture, which forbade married women from owning property. So some of them just didn't see slavery as being all that different from marriage. One southern woman, Mary Chesnut, who had been in Washington briefly with her husband, Senator James Chesnut Jr. of South Carolina, went with him to Montgomery, Alabama, where the Confederate government first met. There the plantation mistress witnessed a slave sale and recorded her reaction in her now-famous diary: "South Carolina slave holder as I am my very soul sickened—it is too dreadful. I tried to reason—this is not worse than the willing sale most women make of themselves in marriage—nor can the consequences be worse. The Bible authorizes marriage & slavery—poor women! poor slaves!" Those views for some women would change over time, just as the president's had, but not until after a great deal of blood had been shed.

A FEW WEEKS after the enactment of the emancipation law, a woman who went to her grave still defending the South's "peculiar institution" got out of jail. Rose Greenhow, along with her eight-year-old daughter, had been locked up in the filthy, stinking Old Capitol Prison for more than four months. Confined to their room with a bedbug-infested straw mattress and insulted that they were incarcerated with blacks, the pair remained defiant even as they starved and Little Rose became quite sick. "Rose is subject to the same rigorous restrictions as myself," the proud mother revealed to her journal. "I was fearful at first that she would pine, and said, 'My little darling, you must show yourself superior to these Yankees, and, not pine.' She replied quickly, 'o mamma, never fear; I hate them too much. I intend to dance and sing "Jeff Davis is coming," just to scare them!'" Rose railed against her captors, who fed newspaper reporters regular nuggets about the famous Rebel spy and put her on display for tourists like a circus side-show freak. In April, papers around the country, including the Charlotte *Evening Bulletin*, ran a tidbit about a scene at the prison: "Mrs. Greenhow and another female prisoner having taken possession of a wagon which had been driven into the yard, and driving it around with a Confederate flag displayed and shouting huzzas for 'the Southern wagon.' Since then Mrs. Greenhow had been charged with insanity."

In fact Mrs. Greenhow hadn't been officially charged with any-thing. In March she had been summoned to a hearing before the U.S. Commission Relating to State Prisoners, held in a house that must have been eerily familiar to Rose. The government had confiscated it from southern sympathizers—former California senator William Gwin and his wife. So the prisoner was in the very place where she had shone at Mrs. Gwin's ball four years earlier. And she shone again that day, thrusting and parrying with her interrogators but admitting to nothing as they produced evidence of her treasonous writings. But the commissioners were ready to make a deal—Mrs. Greenhow could get out of jail if she left Washington for good and moved behind Con-federate lines. Rose didn't accept the offer on the spot—after all, there was no official document before her and she didn't trust these men to be telling the truth.

When the story of her refusal appeared in the newspaper, Rose's niece Adele Douglas dashed off a harsh rebuke: "I do believe you have a stern joy in your martyrdom, else you would embrace the opportunity to escape from it." The prisoner had obtained permission for Addie to visit her, but the young widow hadn't been around since Christ-mas and Rose was clearly hurt and angry. "I am to be driven forth from my home by this magnanimous Government, in the midst of the bloodshed and carnage with which they are pursuing all who cherish my own political faith." She heard from her old source Henry Wilson that he had "advised my being immediately sent South," but that Mc-Clellan and Seward "thought differently" and some in the press were calling for her head: "The law fixes the penalty for treason. It is not 'to be sent beyond the lines,' but it is DEATH," raved a Minnesota paper in an article titled "Traitors in Crinoline and in Congress." The outraged correspondent continued: "Mrs. Greenhow refused to reveal to the committee who her secret agents in Washington were; but from other sources they discover the names of several, including two ex-senators, and several members of congress, one of whom, the report says, still retains his seat. If this is true it is past all endurance."

So Rose didn't know what would happen, until suddenly on May 31 the superintendent barged in with the news that Mrs. Greenhow and her daughter would begin their journey south that very day. The War Department sent a lieutenant as her chief escort: "He had six men detailed to accompany him, making quite a military display, dressed in full uniform, with sword and carbine in hand. Outside the prison the whole guard were drawn up under arms, besides a mounted guard also with swords and carbines." Clearly the government feared that this wily woman might somehow escape. For her part, Rose wasn't sure whether to trust her guards, extracting a promise from the lieutenant that he was indeed sending her south and not to a northern prison.

First they traveled to Baltimore, where they would board a ship to take them to Virginia. When they arrived in that conflicted city the Greenhows were held on the train until all the passengers had left the station and then they were escorted under heavy guard to a hotel. But word got out that the famous southern spy was in town and the next day "a large number of persons" offered their congratulations, "and many friends followed to the boat." While Rose and her daughter waited for their official escorts a crowd formed on the wharf: "So far as the eye could reach handkerchiefs were waving, and the tearful eye and hearty 'God bless you!'" cheered Rose in the belief that "the hearts of the people of Maryland . . . beat in unison with their brethren of the South."

They sailed to Fort Monroe, off Norfolk, Virginia, now occupied by federal troops. With McClellan skirmishing on the peninsula, Rose heard false reports that Richmond had fallen, but she determined to proceed to the Confederate capital anyway. Carried by a Union vessel up the James River, she saw the fallout from the fight— the remains of the *Merrimack*, scuttled to keep it out of Union hands, plus the ships the ironclad had destroyed. The *Monitor*, there to back up McClellan, sent out a support ship to collect the party for the trip under a white flag into City Point, a port a few miles outside Richmond: "I was under intense excitement, for, after nearly ten weary months of imprisonment, I was in sight of the promised land." Rose had been allowed the use of a sewing machine in prison, so she had secretly crafted a large Confederate flag and now wrapped it around her shoulders in the folds of her shawl. She was tempted to "unfold it and cast it to the breeze as a parting defiance to the Yankees," but then decided she didn't want to lose it.

On June 4, Rose and Little Rose Greenhow settled in the best hotel in town and immediately the commandant of Richmond paid his respects. It must have been quite a contrast with the last four months in the Old Capitol Prison and even to her imprisonment in her own home. The next day Jefferson Davis came to call: "And his words of greeting, 'But for you there would have been no battle of Bull Run,' repaid me for all that I had endured. . . . And I shall ever remember that as the proudest moment of my life." The President of the Confederacy told his wife that even if Rose was now free, her imprisonment had made its mark: "The Madam looks much changed and has the air of one whose nerves were shaken by mental torture." Even so, before long he would have another assignment for the confirmed Confederate.

GENERAL MCCLELLAN'S REFUSAL to engage the Confederates on the Virginia Peninsula so frustrated President Lincoln that the day after the Rebel withdrawal from Yorktown, he himself went to see what was going on. From the time the Army of the Potomac landed in Virginia almost two months earlier, the President had been pushing McClellan to move. But the general, fearing that the enemy forces were far greater in number than they were (this overestimation of Rebel strength was a constant—twice already in the war what the Yankees thought were Confederate gun batteries turned out to be "Quaker guns," wooden logs designed to deceive), kept planning rather than acting. So on May 6, a ship carrying President Lincoln, Secretary of War Stanton, Secretary of the Treasury Chase, and General Egbert Viele, brigadier general of the United States Volunteers, docked outside Fort Monroe. The three civilians and the one military man mapped out a strategy for capturing Norfolk, Virginia, the base for the formidable *Merrimack*. When they went secretly to investigate what kind of resistance the Union would meet if the army tried to take the town from the rear, they found two women and a dog as the sole inhabitants of that area. The city quickly fell.

"The President ordered the attack on Norfolk & is taking a pretty active part down there," Lizzie Lee delivered the news to her husband. "I am glad of it as it endears him to the country." With the source of its supplies now in Yankee hands, "the *Merrimac* committed suicide,"

Lizzie chortled, "blown up and Secesh surrenders the sea." The crew of the *Merrimack* set the ship aflame and now the North hoped the federal fleet could proceed up the James River to Richmond. But as the ships, led by the *Monitor*, got within seven miles of the capital, Confederates opened fire from the shore, stopping their advance. "Our fleet on the James River has had to retreat," Lizzie despaired; "they encountered a battery two hundred feet high & the river chained— spiked & filled with sunken vessels."

As McClellan finally pushed northward, Mary Custis Lee, the wife of Confederate general Robert E. Lee, was forced to flee from her son's home, called White House. It had belonged to her great-grandmother Martha Custis Washington and was the place where Martha and George Washington had lived when they were first married. Mrs. Lee had already been forced to evacuate her own home, Arlington House, and leave behind her Washington memorabilia. Now as she abandoned another heirloom she left a message for McClellan asking him to preserve the premises in honor of the first president. The general "put a guard there & kept them inviolate," Lizzie proudly reported, though she hated Robert E. Lee, her husband's cousin: "No weak woman in my opinion was ever more easily lured from honor & duty by flattering than was this weak man by the overtures of wily politicians but I'll not wound any who like him by saying so." She knew that General Lee had many admirers on both sides of the divide. Despite McClellan's efforts to save it, the Virginia White House eventually was destroyed in crossfire during what turned out to be a vicious siege on the peninsula.

McClellan's men made it to the outskirts of Richmond, where they could hear church bells ring from the city's steeples. Their success at taking the city seemed so certain that a holiday air pervaded the camp as women in Washington joined in the excitement. "Betty returned from the Headquarters of McClellan today where she & 15 others paid a flying visit on Sunday, within 2½ miles of Richmond," Lizzie Lee breezily reported about her niece and friends. "She says he looks thin but well." Every day, Lizzie kept expecting the news that the Confederate capital had fallen and the Rebels had retreated to the Cotton States. Instead, with the help of teenage spy Belle Boyd, General Stonewall Jackson diverted the troops ready to reinforce McClellan, defeating them at Front Royal, Virginia, and panicking the Union Secretary of War with the possibility of invading Washington: "Mr. Stanton's 'scare' is a street joke," dismissed Lizzie. Blasé Washington viewed this latest threat with a yawn, a far cry from a year before, when everyone feared attack. But it was no joke to McClellan, who had been insisting on reinforcements that Lincoln had been ready to send until the troops were deemed essential for the protection of the capital.

Still, Union hopes remained high until McClellan's army encountered the Rebels at Seven Pines at the end of May, again convincing the general that he was outnumbered, fortifying his fear of movement. Southern General Joe Johnston was wounded in the battle and the command transferred to General Lee, who then led his troops through seven days of relentless attacks that resulted in McClellan's defeat and retreat at the beginning of July. Lizzie Lee mourned for the "carnage of my Country men—for I can not yet feel alien to the Rebels." "The war is at a standstill," Salmon Chase moaned to his daughter Kate. "Heaven save our poor country!"

As if Lincoln weren't having enough problems, that July another angry woman showed up in his office making demands. This time it was for herself, not her husband. Anna Ella Carroll had no husband and the forty-six-year-old "maiden lady" was always in need of cash.

She strongly believed she was owed money for her widely circulated pamphlet answering Kentucky Senator Breckinridge's attacks on Lincoln and for her book *The War Powers of the Federal Government*, defending the president's suspension of habeas corpus, basically imposing martial law. And she continued to churn out the propaganda. In June the *National Republican* reviewed her latest effort, *The Relation of the National Government to the Revolted Citizens*, concluding: "It is written with Miss Carroll's usual vigor, and displays a great mount of legal learning." Anna solicited many endorsements from members of Congress and the War Department to support her claim that she should be paid more than the $1,250 she had already received. In July she took her request, plus a much bigger one, in to the president himself. Telling him that her *War Powers* treatise "was destined to stand, as long as the Declaration of Independence," she not only sought compensation for the work she had already done: Anna proposed to Lincoln that he send her to Europe as a Union public relations agent. The cost? Fifty thousand dollars. For a man whose own salary was $25,000 the request constituted " 'the most outrageous one ever made to any government on earth.' " What the president may or may not have known was that Anna Carroll thought the government owed her for much more than her writings. She took credit for originating the strategy that gave General Grant his great victory in Tennessee and she had planned to bill the United States for that as well, until Lincoln blew up at her. Anna had even written out what she would say: "Now, Mr. President, there is another subject, which I desire to bring to your attention. . . ."

The previous fall the single woman traveled to Chicago and St. Louis to gather material on Union activities as fodder for her propaganda. Knowing that control of the Mississippi was key to Yankee success but also that the Rebel fortifications along the river appeared impregnable, she looked for another approach rather than a head-on assault. So Anna enlisted the help of a riverboat pilot whose wife was staying in her hotel to inquire as to whether Union gunboats could navigate the Tennessee or Cumberland Rivers. Learning that the Tennessee could handle the vessels, she then designed a plan of attack and dispatched it to the attorney general, the assistant secretary of war, and directly to President Lincoln. When she returned to Washington that November she presented the blueprint in detail, maps included, to her friend Thomas Scott, the assistant secretary of war. The following February, when Grant did in fact go by the Tennessee River to capture the southern fortifications, Anna Carroll was certain he was following her directions. Now she wanted to cash in on his success. "If the plan of the Western campaign was based upon the facts, furnished by me, to the Secretary of War," she insisted, "I ought now to have a substantial and liberal recognition of this service."

Anna Ella Carroll would spend the rest of her life trying to persuade the government of the rightness of her cause. And she had many supporters along the way. She collected letters from members of Congress, including the chairman of the Committee on the Conduct of the War, and at various times different committees of the House and Senate voted to compensate her, but the bills never went through both houses of Congress to the president's desk. Women's organizations rallied around her, making her a cause célèbre to suffragists in years to come. And a legend grew up that the empty chair in a famous painting of Lincoln's Cabinet by Francis Bicknell Carpenter signified the seat that should have been occupied by Anna Ella Carroll. While she cultivated the narrative of her genius, Miss Carroll still had a living to make and a cause she could not forsake as the war ground on.

MARY LINCOLN MOVED the family into the relative cool of the
Soldier's Home, a couple of miles away from the White House, that
typically hot Washington summer as her husband conferred with his
Cabinet about his audacious plan to free the slaves in the rebellious
states. In May Lincoln once again had to overrule one of his generals,
as he had Frémont, when David Hunter, commander of the Department of the South, issued his own decree freeing the slaves in South
Carolina, Georgia, and Florida. Once again the president read about a
general's decree in the newspaper and once again he angered the ever-
more-powerful abolitionists by insisting that only he had the right to
issue such an order. Lincoln was determined to do it in his own way
and at his own time. And the president had a more pressing problem
that sultry summer. (Secretary Chase warned his daughter Kate, who
was visiting her grandmother in Ohio, "Don't think about coming
back to Washington. It is hot, hotter, hottest.")

McClellan's defeat had so dispirited the Union, the army found new
recruits hard to attract and desertions hard to stop; the ranks needed
reinforcement. But Lincoln wanted to avoid issuing what would look
like a desperate plea for more soldiers. Lucky for him, Secretary of
State Seward came up with a ruse to solve the problem: he would privately tell the governors to call on Lincoln to ask for volunteers, so it
would look like the call-up wasn't the president's idea. "Gov. Seward
has returned from his visit to the Governors," Salmon Chase confided
to Kate in early July. "It is not settled what will become of McClellan's
army. In my judgment it ought to have been already embarked and on
its way here or somebody should have been put in command who has
resources & energy to retrieve its disasters." The next day President

Lincoln traveled to McClellan's headquarters himself to determine if someone else should take charge. A few days later Chase conveyed the news, "Halleck is, I am told, invited here. I *fear* we're to have a repetition of McClellanism in him. I *hope* better." Lincoln made his move. Henry Halleck would replace George McClellan as general in chief of the army. McClellan would retain his post at the head of the Army of the Potomac.

McClellan still had his strong Democratic supporters in Congress, which divided almost entirely along party lines on any legislation that touched on slavery. But without southern members to block them in the legislature, other major bills sailed through that changed the face of the country: the Homestead Act, giving anyone willing to settle the West 160 acres; the Morrill Act, establishing land grant colleges to provide higher education in agriculture, mechanical skills, and military training; the Pacific Railroad Act, appropriating funds to build a transcontinental railroad; plus two measures designed to pay for the war, the Internal Revenue Act to levy taxes and the Legal Tender Bill to print paper money. But, given the large Republican majority, the more contentious measures also passed, among them emancipation for the District of Columbia, and the Confiscation Act, seizing the property of "traitors," including slaves held as property. The law declared that enslaved people seized by the North "shall be deemed captives of war and shall be forever free." Another bill gave the president the power to enroll in the army "persons of African descent." Lincoln was laying the groundwork for his Emancipation Proclamation. In mid-July he reached out again to the Border States, bringing their representatives to the Executive Mansion in another attempt to bring them around to the concept of compensated emancipation. When they rejected him he determined that an executive order would be the way to go. On July 22 he informed the Cabinet of his thinking. Montgomery Blair warned an Emancipation Proclamation would mean trouble for the Republicans in the fall elections; William Seward counseled that the president wait until he had a Union victory in the field to bolster his case.

To show support for the army and boost morale, Washington held a huge rally at the Capitol with all the government dignitaries seated on a platform erected at the East Front. President Lincoln told the cheering crowd he knew McClellan wished to succeed, adding, "I hope he will." But no success followed. Trying to find a winning strategy, Lincoln ordered McClellan to pull his forces out of the peninsula and he consolidated other commands, including John Frémont's under John Pope as commander of the Army of Virginia. As a result Frémont resigned. In August—once again at Manassas—Pope's troops confronted those of Robert E. Lee, Stonewall Jackson, and James Longstreet. And once again the Rebels dealt the Union army a decisive defeat. Pope was relieved of his command and an emboldened Lee turned his exhausted, hungry, and sick soldiers north. Stonewall Jackson crossed the Potomac into Frederick, Maryland, causing considerable concern in Washington. Lizzie Lee took her little boy to Philadelphia to stay with Rebecca Gratz until the danger passed. From there she followed the action as Robert E. Lee prepared to encounter McClellan's Army of the Potomac in Sharpsburg, Maryland, along Antietam Creek. "I never have endured more anxious feelings," admitted this woman who had always been so sure of victory, "yet I try to be calm & hopeful for I have no right to oppress those around me." Almost as if proving it to herself, Lizzie prayed: "Our cause is righteous and God will bless us."

This time McClellan's men were not going to lose. But they weren't exactly going to win, either. "McClellan is slow oh so slow," Lizzie Lee fretted. "I have a tremor of anxiety about his movements lest he will lose the fruits of this hard won fight by following it up too *slowly*."

Once again the general was convinced he was outnumbered, though in fact he had a considerably larger force than the Confederates. Mc-Clellan missed several opportunities to score a significant victory and once Lee's men pulled back to Virginia, the Union army failed to give chase, much to the commander in chief's disgust. The battle ended in a draw but the Rebel army had been driven out of Union territory and the president was able to claim enough of a victory to move forward with his Emancipation Proclamation. It came at enormous cost. September 17, 1862, still stands as the bloodiest single day in American military history.

ON THE BATTLEFIELD with the troops that dreadful day when 23,000 soldiers were killed or wounded—one casualty for every one and a half seconds of combat—worked a fearless woman. Clara Barton had rushed to the front with wagonloads of supplies to help the surgeons tending the wounded and dying. When she located the bullet-ridden farmhouse serving as a field hospital, the doctor in charge could not believe his eyes: "God has indeed remembered us," he rejoiced. "I have torn up the last sheets we could find in this house, have not a bandage, rag, lint, or string. And all these wounded men bleeding to death." Dr. James Dunn knew this tiny woman would be bringing what he needed—linen for bandages, chloroform, food, water, lanterns. She worked with him for three days without sleep as the battle raged around them, tending to soldiers in the house, in the barn and on the grounds. "A man lying upon the ground asked for drink—I stooped to give it . . . when I felt a sudden twitch of the loose sleeve of my dress—the poor fellow sprang from my hands and fell back quivering in the agonies of death—a ball had passed between my body—and the right arm which supported him." The bullet ripped a hole in her dress, and her face and arms were covered with gunpowder and dirt as she stirred up gruel from cornmeal she found in the farmhouse cellar after her supplies ran out. But that didn't stop Dr. Dunn from telling his wife, "General McClellan, with all his laurels, sinks into insignificance beside the true heroine of the age, *the angel of the battlefield.*" Clara Barton had shown the men that she could work with them at the scene of combat—and not flinch from the bullets and the blood and the bodies.

It wasn't easy to get to that point. For some time, the military authorities had refused to allow her to go to the front. But she had been eager to be of service from the moment the Massachusetts soldiers had arrived in Washington after the melee in Baltimore more than a year earlier. When she went to the train station that April day to greet the soldiers, she was gratified when some of them recognized her as their former schoolteacher from back in Boston. She started tending to those hometown boys as they camped in the capital and never really returned regularly to her job in the Patent Office, though it was highly unusual for a woman to have such a good government job. But nothing seemed unusual to Clara Barton.

Clara (her real name was Clarissa, after the heroine in the popular Samuel Richardson novel) had absorbed the principles of abolition and feminism at the knee of her eccentric mother, Sarah, so much so that she thought she "must have been born believing in the full right of woman to all privileges and positions which nature and justice accord her." But believing in that right and being afforded it turned out to be two very different things in mid-nineteenth-century America. Clara constantly tilted against male rule. As a young schoolteacher in Massachusetts she had turned down a position because she flatly declared, "I shall never do a man's work for less than a man's pay." She got the job at her price. But she was not always so successful, and often found herself battling against women's second-class status. So in 1854 she decided to try her luck in the nation's capital. There she located her cousin Congressman Alexander DeWitt, who represented her family's Massachusetts district and he put her in touch with Commissioner of Patents Charles Mason, who hired the thirty-two-year-old woman. Mason never put her name on the roster of employees sent to Congress—why stir up trouble?—but he did pay Miss Barton just what he paid the men. Then, as so often happens in Washington, Clara lost her protector, when Mason was replaced by a man who was shocked at the "obvious impropriety of mixing two sexes within the walls of a public office." No amount of pressure from Clara's politician friends could change his mind. And she was forced to take work home at a much-reduced salary.

Happily for her, Mason returned after an outcry from the scientific community demanding his patent expertise. Miss Barton was back at her desk and often in the galleries of the House and Senate, listening with fascination to the increasingly heated debates over slavery. A bout of malaria and another change in administrators at work sent her home to Massachusetts and then on to New York for a few unproductive but consciousness-raising years. "The registrar says he has no room for ladies," she erupted after one job interview, expressing the wish that the "gentlemen who *have* the *power* could only know for one twenty-four hours all that oppresses and gnaws at my peace." When she wasn't busy at work this industrious woman often sank into depression, taking to her bed for prolonged periods.

The election of Abraham Lincoln brought Clara Barton bustling back to Washington, back to work in the Patent Office, and back to the boardinghouse she had lived in earlier. She made a point of befriending Massachusetts Senator Henry Wilson, who was sympathetic to women's demands, and she used her increasingly secure position to help other women along the way, deciding, "It does not hurt me to pioneer." Into this pleasant interlude in her life came the startling news of the surrender of Fort Sumter and the alarms of an attack on Washington. When soldiers from her own state were among the first to arrive to protect the capital, she resolved to protect them. The Baltimore mob that pummeled the men of the Massachusetts Sixth also stole their luggage. So Clara not only nursed her self-appointed charges, sending the most severely wounded to recuperate at her sister's house, but she also collected clothes and food for them. She organized delivery of the supplies to the Senate chamber "camp," where she sat in the vice president's chair and read a Massachusetts newspaper to the soldiers, joking that they were paying more attention than was usually the case in that hallowed hall. It was the first of a wartime of such efforts. And when letters home from the troops told of her work, people started sending care packages to Miss Barton. She had to find a bigger place to store everything, so she and her supplies moved into the business district even as the city anticipated an invasion, declaring that "while our soldiers can stand and *fight*, I can stand and feed and nurse them." She bristled with pride and purpose. And that was before the fighting began.

Once Clara Barton saw the lack of preparedness for sick and wounded soldiers after the first big battle at Manassas, she started soliciting supplies from the women of her home state through advertisements in the *Worcester Spy*. She instructed the donors on what to send and how to pack the goods, which came in such profusion that three warehouses were required to store everything. But that wasn't enough for Clara. She wanted to be where the action was—to go to the battlefield herself to minister to the men. Even the bold Miss Barton, however, worried about the propriety of a single woman appearing in a military camp.

It was her father, of all people, who talked her into doing what she wanted to do. When she went back to Massachusetts to be with him as he was dying, Clara raised the question of whether she would be mistaken for a prostitute if she joined the soldiers in the field. No, he assured her, she was a respectable woman and would be treated as such, but, more important, she had a duty to do what she could for her country. So with not just a blessing but a command from her father, Clara Barton had to convince the brass in Washington to let her carry out her mission.

In July 1862 she succeeded. The Army of the Potomac had left the peninsula and set up camp in Fredericksburg, Virginia, not far from the capital. Clara took the opportunity to explain to an officer in the Quartermaster's Office that she was sitting on three warehouses full of supplies, and he agreed to provide her with a travel pass plus wagons to transport the goods to the troops. In early August Miss Barton made her first delivery to soldiers in camp. When she returned to Washington a few days later for more supplies, she learned that fighting had broken out in Culpeper, Virginia, and, with her travel pass still in hand, she headed directly for the field. Going by train, then wagon, she reached the battlefront hospital, where she found grateful medical men eager to accept her supplies and support. At first the human carnage cowed her but there was work to be done. Surgeons operating feverishly to try to save the wounded soldiers had no time to clean the hospitals, where the filth from blood and body parts threatened to spread disease. Clara organized civilians to assist her in cleaning up the begrimed bedsides. She moved from makeshift hospital to hospital, scrubbing floors and distributing supplies, ending in a house crammed with wounded Rebels. She gave them the shirts she had left. But all of this work, as exhausting and rewarding as it was, was just a brief rehearsal for the major battle ahead—the second siege at Manassas, where the Union Army sustained sixteen thousand casualties.

At Fairfax Station, where the train deposited her, Clara Barton was aghast at the sight of hundreds of wounded men screaming in pain, waiting for care. She did her best to give them relief and get them into ambulances to Washington, but the numbers were staggering and the battle was still going on all around them. The Union was retreating in the face of Stonewall Jackson's advance when an officer pulled up and asked if she could ride a horse. When Clara answered yes, he replied that would give her an extra hour to work before the enemy fought their way there; if necessary she could escape on horseback. Luckily she and her coworkers managed to get the last man on the train and board it themselves just as Rebel soldiers rode in and set fire to the station. It had been overwhelming and frightening, but she had done it. And she knew now that the battlefield was where she was meant to be.

Life in Washington seemed frivolous to Clara Barton after what she had seen. But she wouldn't be there for long. The woman who had begged to go to battle now was summoned there. A soldier brought her orders: Harpers Ferry. So she was off and then on to Stone Mountain. As the army moved toward Sharpsburg she realized that her supply wagons were too far in the rear, that she wouldn't be able to get to the field in time to be of help. She spent the night pushing her way past the wagons filled with sleeping soldiers so Clara Barton would be where she needed to be when the sun came up that awful morning of September 17.

———

THOUGH THE BATTLE at Sharpsburg had been inconclusive, it served as a turning point in the war. President Lincoln deemed it a decisive enough victory for him to make his next move. On September 22 he informed his Cabinet that he planned to issue an executive order forever freeing all the slaves in the states in rebellion unless those states rejoined to the Union by January 1. Again Montgomery Blair warned that the measure could drive off the Border States and give the Democrats a major issue in the coming elections. But Lincoln thought he had placated the slave states still in the Union long enough—it was time to act: "we had about played our last card and must change our tactics, or lose the game." The newspapers published the president's Preliminary Emancipation Proclamation, letting the country and the world know that on January 1 he would sign the order. "The President's proclamation took the breath out of me," Lizzie Lee declared her distress; "it seems to me that all that could be done to hurt our cause has been done there." But in fact the announcement helped the cause. Britain and France, countries where slavery was outlawed, could no longer toy with the idea of recognizing the Confederacy. Fears that the troops might not fight for the slaves turned out to be mostly misplaced—the soldiers knew the Rebels were using slave labor to support their army and what the fighting men wanted above all was to defeat the enemy and end the war. If freeing the slaves helped do that—fine. But concern about the effect on the election was justified. Republicans lost gubernatorial races in New York and New Jersey and were defeated in several state legislatures, plus the Democrats added thirty-four seats in the House of Representatives. Still, the Republicans emerged with a majority of twenty-five members in the House and actually added five new senators.

"It is now quite ascertained that the President has a good working majority in the next House of Reps," Lizzie Lee announced, "anything more is hardly desirable—a strong opposition is a healthy condition of things for the country's well being." A strong opposition definitely greeted President Lincoln when the lame-duck Congress came into session in December. In his annual message, the President simply stated: "Fellow-citizens, *we* cannot escape history. . . . We *say* we are for the Union. The world will not forget that we say this. We know how to save the Union. The world knows we do know how to save it. . . . In *giving* freedom to the *slave*, we *assure* freedom to the *free*." A Democratic resolution condemning emancipation as a "high crime against the Constitution" went down in a party-line vote. And the new state of West Virginia would come into the Union only on the condition that slavery there was abolished.

The enslaved African Americans who could do so were already freeing themselves by escaping to the North, especially to Washington, where they crowded into contraband camps that were soon rife with disease. "Poor dusky children of slavery, men and women of my own race," Elizabeth Keckley, a former slave herself, lamented, "you were not prepared for the new life that opened before you, and the great masses of the North learned to look upon your helplessness with indifference— learned to speak of you as an idle, dependent race." Seeing the tremendous need, Mrs. Keckley formed the Contraband Relief Association to collect money and goods for the impoverished blacks. Mary Lincoln gave the first contribution of two hundred dollars and explained the expense to her husband by telling him what Mrs. Keckley had told her: "She says the immense number of Contrabands in W[ashington] are suffering intensely, many without bed covering & having to use any bits of carpeting to cover themselves—Many dying of want."

The plight of the contrabands was beginning to get public attention. The abolitionist editor William Lloyd Garrison sent Harriet Jacobs to report on the situation for his *Liberator* newspaper. Miss Jacobs had become something of a celebrity with the publication a year earlier of her *Incidents in the Life of a Slave Girl*, a harrowing account of her life in slavery and escape from it. Now she was taking on her first journalistic assignment and she was appalled by what she found—people packed together "without any distinction or regard for age or sex." Every day some died and every day more came but there was no one "to administer to the comfort of the sick and dying." Elizabeth Keckley tried to fill that void but with the Emancipation Proclamation in the offing, the need would only increase.

WHILE WASHINGTON DEALT with the effects of the war, the war itself raged in nearby Virginia. "There is great excitement in the city, the battle has opened on Fredericksburg which I heard was in flames this morning," Lizzie Lee reported with alarm in the middle of December. It would be one of the largest, and for the Union one of the most costly battles, signaling the Civil War's first urban combat. The Confederates occupied the abandoned city before the Union army had built pontoon boats to get across the Rappahannock River. Clara Barton watched from the federal camp on the other side, knowing the next day's battle would be brutal. As Yankee soldiers crossed on rickety bridges and slapped-together boats the Rebels fired from inside houses and behind garden walls. A Union surgeon who had set up a hospital in Fredericksburg sent word to the intrepid little woman: "Come to me—your place is here." Against advice from soldiers telling her she'd never survive, Clara made the dangerous crossing with bullets bursting around her and then nursed and fed the soldiers for several days, piling up body parts among the platters and pitchers of the town's fine houses. The surgeon she worked with had been attached to the Massachusetts Twenty-First, which had inducted Clara as a daughter of the regiment on a happier occasion when a dress parade was held in her honor. There would be no parades after "Burnside's Blunder," where nearly 200,000 soldiers skirmished over four days until the Federals conceded defeat with more than 13,000 casualties compared to the Confederates' 4,500. Calling it a folly from beginning to end, Lizzie sputtered that "the enemy could make themselves impregnable except by army able to surround them." She sadly added that Brigadier General George Bayard died from the wounds he sustained at Fredericksburg and was buried the day he had planned to be married: "many is the young heart that is broken by this woeful war."

With the new influx of wounded men, yet more buildings in Washington were requisitioned as hospitals. "Our city is being filled with hospitals, 5 churches are now being fitted into hospitals," Lizzie Lee informed her husband. So far Harriet Lane's Episcopal church had escaped, a friend told her with some relief. "Our church has not been converted into a hospital yet." Georgetown College had to turn over a couple of buildings to the Surgeon General but he did spare one religious institution—the Visitation Convent, Harriet Lane's old school. General Winfield Scott's daughter had joined the Visitation order and was buried on school property. The old general still had enough clout to stop the secretary of war from confiscating the school, so it stayed in operation through the war with both northern and southern nuns and students tensely sharing the dormitories and the duties necessary to keep the place operating. But the convent was one of the few places and the nuns were some of the few women not called into action as the wounded soldiers kept coming.

The women of Washington were urged to help out in the wards: "the gov[ernmen]t exhorts the ladies to attend & keep the menials there from neglecting the soldiers." Lizzie Lee regretted that she couldn't respond to the exhortation. She had always been sickly and her mother wouldn't hear of her risking her health in a hospital, much to Lizzie's regret. "I never coveted robust health more than I might help to serve them for here there's a great want of good nurses." Louisa

Meigs, on the other hand, hoped that the female recruitment meant she could come home: "I am quite a skillful nurse, and I feel that I could make myself exceedingly useful in taking care of the sick & wounded." She was clearly hurt that her husband didn't seem to miss her, but with the Rebels so close in Virginia, Quartermaster Montgomery Meigs simply didn't want to worry about his wife: "I am busy & anxious & I'm relieved from a portion of this anxiety by knowing that my family are far from the center of the great struggle now going on." The struggle, they all knew now, was likely to go on for some time. There would be no quick end to the fighting and dying, all the more reason, from Louisa's standpoint, for her to return to Washington: "If you are contented to have me prolong my absence in Germantown until the *termination* of our *national difficulties,* I shall bend to your decision," she huffed, but she didn't see why she would be in any more danger than anyone else, "The General in Chief who is supposed to have some knowledge on the subject deems it quite safe & proper to bring his wife to that beleaguered city." But Meigs was more concerned about supplying the army than soothing his wife. And now more and more of the men needing supplies were lying in overcrowded make-do hospitals.

"OUR CITY IS hourly receiving the wounded & their number is appalling so I hear," Lizzie Lee lamented. "I would not be surprised if they made requisition of the private houses in a few days—hotels certainly—the last would have been taken before but for their being all so badly ventilated." When the hotels were converted to hospitals, that lack of ventilation posed a health risk much of the country learned about through stories by one of the nurses—a young Massachusetts woman named Louisa May Alcott. She had just turned thirty and felt she "*must* let out my pent up energy in some new way," so the fledgling writer "decided to go to Washington as a nurse if I could find a place." She received word in December of an opening at the old Union Hotel in Georgetown and set off immediately from Boston, leaving behind a few "tales" to be published. A last-minute tinge of fear threatened to derail her: "'Shall I stay, Mother?' as I hugged her close. 'No, go! And the Lord be with you!' answered the Spartan woman," Louisa recorded in her journal, wondering if she would ever "see that dear old face again" and feeling like "the son of the house going to war."

The trip "through the country white with tents, all alive with patriotism, and already red with blood" sobered even more the nervous Louisa, who wasn't sure whether she would end this adventure "alive or dead." As soon as she arrived in Georgetown, after a brief night's sleep she "began my new life by seeing a poor man die at dawn." It was the start of a taxing but fascinating few weeks that would help propel Louisa May Alcott to the extraordinary literary success she achieved. Her journal gives a fairly matter-of-fact account of those tough days and nights when she was "surrounded by 3 or 4 hundred men in all stages of suffering, disease & death." But she later turned the experience into one of her "tales," and her somewhat fictionalized *Hospital Sketches* enjoyed such success when serialized in the *Boston Commonwealth* that book publishers came knocking on her door, much to Louisa's "surprise and delight." A few years later, Roberts Brothers asked her to write a story for girls. *Little Women* has never been out of print since it first appeared in bookstores in 1868.

That the story would have such a happy ending was not at all likely, as the neophyte nurse worked "giving out rations, cutting up food for helpless 'boys,' washing faces, teaching my attendants how beds are made or floors swept, dressing wounds, taking Dr. Fitz Patrick's orders (privately wishing all the time that he would be more gentle with my big babies)" in the Union Hotel hospital, with air "bad enough to breed a pestilence." The pestilence that grabbed Louisa was typhoid fever, putting a quick end to her nursing career. As the young woman lay sick in bed, Dorothea Dix brought her a basket of get well gifts: "She is a kind soul but very queer & arbitrary," Louisa recorded about the Superintendent of Female Nurses, adding, "no one likes her & I don't wonder," but then she crossed out that somewhat unkind but accurate observation. Dorothea Dix did much better functioning as a one-woman lobbying operation than in an organization where she had to deal with other people.

Seeing how sick her charge was, the head nurse at the Union Hospital summoned Louisa's father to take her home a little more than a month after she had arrived. But Louisa May Alcott's short stint as a nurse allowed her to paint a picture for the country of what life was like in hospitals trying desperately to save the thousands upon thousands of wounded soldiers. "Forty ambulances are at the door," her roommate announced as the casualties from the Battle of Fredericksburg demanded attention. "In they came, some on stretchers, some in men's arms, some feebly staggering along propped on rude crutches, and one lay stark and still with covered face, as a comrade gave his name to be recorded before they carried him away to the dead house." The men did enjoy one ray of Christmas spirit as Elizabeth Smith, the wife of the outgoing secretary of the interior, organized volunteers to decorate the wards and deliver dinners, with donations from Mrs. Lincoln, who never got much credit for her contributions. Adele Douglas, on the other hand, was hailed as an "angel of mercy" for turning her house into a hospital. All the accounts "of the women of Washington attention to the hospitals does them great honor," Lizzie Lee marveled.

INTERIOR SECRETARY CALEB Smith's departure from the Cabinet came without drama as he headed home to Indiana and a judgeship.

But a potential Cabinet shakeup seriously threatened the Lincoln administration that Christmas season. Senate Republicans, upset about the results of the election and the course of the war, wanted someone's head—preferably the president's, but they knew they couldn't depose him. Instead, with some private encouragement from Secretary of the Treasury Salmon Chase, they chose Secretary of State William Seward as their scapegoat. Lincoln managed to face down the Senate, after Seward and Chase each handed in his resignation. The president pocketed both but acted on neither and the crisis passed, but not without Mary Lincoln weighing in. The first lady "regretted the making up of the family quarrel," according to Lizzie Lee, because she thought "there was not a member of the Cabinet who did not stab her husband & the Country daily except my Brother." Lizzie's brother Montgomery Blair, the postmaster general, would cause trouble of his own before the president's term ended. And though the Cabinet was nowhere near as backstabbing as Mary Lincoln suspected, the president's critics continued to hound him.

Lincoln had removed George McClellan from his command of the Army of the Potomac when he failed to pursue Lee into Virginia after Antietam, and placed a somewhat reluctant General Ambrose Burnside in the job. McClellan still had scores of admirers in town and many of them were urging him to run for president in 1864. Lizzie Lee thought that McClellan was likely to go for it, because "everybody over ten years old out of Washington dreams of such things." It was true then, as it remains true today, that presidentitis grabs hold of the powerful in the capital. But here was a president in the middle of a life-or-death war challenged by his Cabinet and his general. Abraham Lincoln, however, still possessed the power of the presidency, and as 1862 came to a close he exercised it in a most forceful way. The New Year dawned with an Emancipation Proclamation.

CHAPTER 6

Left: *Elizabeth Hobbs Keckley, a former slave, became a successful couturière and confidante of Mary Todd Lincoln. She founded an organization to assist and advocate for freed slaves.* Right: *Elizabeth Blair Lee knew every politician from Andrew Jackson on, and wrote clever letters chronicling wartime life in Washington, expressing her own firm political views.*

Lizzie Reports on the Action, Janet Goes to Camp, Louisa Takes Charge

1863

In her quick, sharp way," her son remembered, Mary Lincoln asked the president on New Year's Day what he intended to do about his bold promise to free the southern state slaves. It was a question on many minds that sunny and chilly January 1, 1863, as Washington approached the day with a tense edge of anticipation. Robert Lincoln later recorded his mother's direct inquiry, as well as his father's response: the president looked toward heaven and simply said, "I am under orders." If Lincoln thought God had ordered him to free the slaves, he had only heard that command recently—but for the women and men assembled at Israel Bethel Church it was enough that he heard it at all. Washington's African Americans gathered in churches and at the contraband campsite anxiously waiting to hear the answer to Mary Lincoln's question. Would President Lincoln actually issue his Emancipation Proclamation on that New Year's Day?

It would be a longer wait than Lincoln intended because he had a busy schedule that morning. He had to deal with unhappy generals, who were frustrated by the way the war was going, as he prepared for the annual White House reception, plus the version of the proclamation drafted by his staff needed some stylistic changes. The document went to the State Department for final editing and had not come back to the White House for the official signature by the time the guests started arriving. All those people waiting for word of a presidential signature would have to wait longer.

The reception took hours. First came the officials, including grandly arrayed diplomats. Cabinet members brought their families. Secretary of State Seward's daughter Fanny, excited to be on the guest list now that she had turned eighteen, was impressed by the "very brilliant" scene. Traditionally, members of the cabinet also hosted New Year's open houses after they paid their respects at the White House. At the secretary of the Treasury's house, "Miss Kate Chase . . . stood by the side of her father to do the chiefest graces of the occasion," noted the *National Republican*. Elizabeth Blair Lee remarked that the young woman looked "like a fairy queen—in her light draperies of lace." From Lizzie that was not meant as a compliment; she was no fan of the heralded Kate, whose father often fought the Blair family in trying to influence the president. Dutifully making the rounds of receptions, Lizzie clucked that the "Chases had the roughest set." But the Chase family didn't have to put up with the hordes of visitors from the general public that crushed into the Executive Mansion after the official delegations.

So it was hundreds of handshakes later when Abraham Lincoln was able to pick up his pen with a shaky hand to sign the momentous executive order freeing forever the slaves in the states in rebellion and welcoming them into the Union army. But the president made it clear there was nothing shaky about his resolve. He wanted his signature to show the firmness of his intent. The minister at Israel Bethel, Rev. Henry M. Turner, paced at the offices of the *Washington Star* newspaper until he could grab a copy of the proclamation hot off the press. He fought off the eager mob and went running back to the church— "when the people saw me coming with the paper in my hand they raised a shouting cheer that was almost deafening." Too out of breath from the run to read the document himself, Rev. Turner gave it to a colleague. During the reading of the proclamation "every kind of demonstration and gesticulations was going on. Men squealed, women fainted, dogs barked, white and colored people shook hands, songs were sung, and by this time cannons began to fire at the navy-yard." In a heartbreaking recital of the horrors that would be no more—"no more auction blocks, no more separation of parents and children"— Turner celebrated the scene, "Nothing like it will ever be seen again in this life." From all over town, people gathered at the White House, cheering the president, who appeared at the window to make a bow. The contraband camp rang with the spirituals written in slavery with the hope that this day would someday come. "Go Down Moses" and "I'm a Free Man Now, Jesus Christ Made Me Free" no longer meant these men and women would have to die to break free from the chains of bondage.

Of course, not everyone greeted the epochal emancipation favorably. Whites in Washington and elsewhere harassed and sometimes attacked the people of color in their midst. And in the South, the order of freedom was universally condemned. Jefferson Davis called it "the most execrable measure in the history of guilty man" and pledged that Union officers would be tried as "criminals engaged in inciting servile insurrection." Even before official word of the signing reached Raleigh, North Carolina, the *Daily Progress* editorialized, "we shall now look forward with intense anxiety for the manifesto which is to proclaim freedom to the 'whole world and the rest of mankind.'" Referring to Lincoln as "the Baboon," the newspaper declared, "This proclamation may be issued but it will have no other effect than to make Lincoln and his government the laughing stock of the civilized world. As long as we are able to whip his armies we care not for his proclamations." That was exactly what worried the president. As long as his armies kept losing, not only would the enemy ignore him, but so would the people who were supposed to be his allies.

Republican defeats in the last election spelled trouble for the president politically as Democrats started agitating for peace rather than a continuation of the bloody battles ending in defeat. The ironclad *Monitor* sank at the end of December, making the navy's job tougher, and in the West the army started what turned out to be a long siege of Vicksburg, Mississippi, on the Mississippi River. (Lizzie Lee had her own plan for that battle: surround the city, "besiege the place—& starve them out," which is exactly what happened many months later.) It had been too long since the Union could claim victory. In an attempt to remedy that, General Burnside tried to make another run at Robert E. Lee's Rebel forces in January but the Army of the Potomac was once more thwarted, this time by Virginia loam that trapped the horses and wagons, making a charge impossible. What came to be called the "mud march" ended in ignominious withdrawal to winter quarters. Discouraged troops started deserting at a rate of about two hundred a day. Lincoln once more changed commanders, giving the job this time to Joseph "Fighting Joe" Hooker. Naming yet another general, the president contributed to the more and more widespread view that maybe it was the commander in chief who needed changing.

———————

ONE SKEPTIC ABOUT Lincoln's choice was his confidant's daughter, Elizabeth Blair Lee. "I regret Gen[era]l Hooker's appointment, still it may do—for he has the gift of appreciating clever men & maybe to use them—if so he will get along & well—but I think he lacks everything but courage." Still, like everyone else, including the president, Lizzie was looking for a good general and hoping Hooker might be the one— "a turn in the wheel may as in lotteries turn up a General." She kept a close watch on the war and politics while trying her best to lead a somewhat normal life. Her chief concern other than the welfare of her one child and a promotion for her husband remained the orphanage, where she had moved to first "directress," essentially chairman of the board. "We took a little one in from Fredericksburg—made destitute by the war—two soldiers' orphans—& 3 sailors' orphans—so it is well we are generously dealt by."

The home had just received a number of donations and Lizzie felt a little guilty sitting and counting the money while her brother Frank Blair ducked danger in the campaign against Vicksburg. Still, the needs of the orphan asylum were great. "I took in the Asylum a Secesh baby—whose father was killed in the Army South & the Mother died & left it destitute so I shall call it Secessia—The Army generally take care of their own people but Sailors & refugees give great scope to our charities besides our local calls." She liked the work, "for occupation is happiness," and the first directress was pleased that she had been able to iron out disagreements among board members so that now the place was running contentedly.

Lizzie Lee had a talent for smoothing over divisions, demonstrated by her close ties to Varina Davis even as other friendships frayed. Despite her strong views about the war and the Union, Lizzie kept in constant contact with her relatives on the other side and relished news of her old friends. When a batch of Confederate mail was seized by the Yankees, her brother Montgomery Blair, the postmaster general, read the letters and shared some of them with his wife, Minna. She told Lizzie: "Mrs. Davis & Jeff's photographs were in it—she is looking more coarse & ugly than I thought it possible for her to grow—thick lips gross nose—looked almost *contraband*—Jeff's emaciated and thinner than ever." Much of the information came from servants who seemed to move back and forth to and from Virginia freely. And though she held decidedly racist views—for instance, she hoped to send the contrabands off to Haiti—Lizzie shared warm relations with individual African Americans. Her little boy Blair's nurse, Becky, came back from a holiday with a week's worth of stories about relatives in Leesburg. Most of the slaves had left for freedom, with one of them telling Becky, "colored people was at first as hot Secesh as the 'white folks' . . . but since the Union Army has been there 'we know better.'"

The Union army now included black men. African-American leaders like Frederick Douglass had been agitating for inclusion in the army, firmly believing that once a black man had an "eagle on his button" no power could deny that he had earned the right to citizenship. In late January 1863, Governor John A. Andrew of Massachusetts received permission to raise a regiment of African-American soldiers. And some former slaves had formed their own regiments in areas of the South occupied by the Union—in the city of New Orleans and the coastal islands off South Carolina.

With the Emancipation Proclamation Lincoln had envisaged blacks in support roles rather than in direct combat—if combatants were captured the Confederates would almost certainly kill them. But black men's demand to take up arms combined with white men's readiness to quit fighting led to the formation of all-black regiments. In March, Congress passed the first conscription law (the Confederacy had approved a draft a year earlier) to boost the number of soldiers; later in the year the government established the Department of Colored Soldiers. Southern slaves escaped to join the Union army, causing Lizzie Lee to crack that it was hard on "womankind in the south generally who are unused to waiting on themselves." Even with the additions to the fighting force, a growing number of "Peace Democrats" came to believe the South could not be defeated on the battlefield. *Chicago Tribune* editor Joseph Medill expected an armistice because "the rebs can't be conquered by the present machinery," and a disillusioned veteran of Antietam, Captain Oliver Wendell Holmes Jr., judged that "the South have achieved their independence."

With those attitudes abroad in the land, a little diversion was more than welcome at the White House and in February it came with the visit of Tom Thumb and his new bride. The "pygmy pair," as they were referred to in the *New York Times*, had caused quite a sensation with their Manhattan wedding and now they were making a grand tour. Years earlier P. T. Barnum brought three-foot-tall Charles Sherwood Stratton as a boy from Connecticut to the American Museum in New York, where the showman gave his soon-to-be star performer the stage name General Tom Thumb. His shows—he could sing, dance, and do imitations of famous people—became a spectacular success, earning millions for the little man and his manager. Also part of the Barnum entourage, "the Queen of Beauty," Lavinia Warren, captivated Stratton, who, according to the *New York*

Times, "literally fell desperately in love with her, and vowed his little vows, backed by the sternest of oaths."

The newspaper devoted three columns to their wedding, staged by Barnum in New York's Grace Church, where tickets were in great demand. "There were more than twenty thousand women in this City yesterday morning up and dressed an hour and a half before their usual time, solely and simply because of the approaching nuptials of Mr. Stratton and Miss Warren. They didn't all have cards of admission, oh no, but it wasn't their fault. Fathers were flattered, husbands were hectored, brothers were bullied and cousins were cozened into buying, begging, borrowing, in some way or other *getting* tickets of admission to the grand affair." The police had trouble keeping order on streets jammed with onlookers. General Burnside had a reserved seat in the church, where the groom's best man was another of Barnum's little people, called Commodore Nutt; the bride's maid of honor was her sister, "the dearest little duck of a creature on the face of the globe." A grand reception at the Metropolitan Hotel, where the wedding party was placed on the piano to receive the guests, went on for about ten hours, ending in the bride and groom bowing and blowing kisses from the balcony to the throngs below. And then it was on to Washington to meet the president and first lady, who received them in the East Room of the White House.

———

THERE TO REPORT on the event was Sara Jane Lippincott, a prominent journalist, poet, and lecturer who wrote under the name Grace Greenwood. Or, as President Lincoln called her, "Grace Greenwood the Patriot." In the 1850s, filing stories from Europe as the first woman to write for the *New York Times*, Mrs. Lippincott had achieved fame with her dispatches describing such exciting events as her admission to the House of Lords, where she was privileged to hear Queen Victoria speak (the monarch displayed more "rosy plumptitude than regal altitude"), and her dinners with the likes of Charles Dickens, whose "elegant and simple" lifestyle was demonstrated by his servants' wearing "no livery."

But Mrs. Lippincott didn't confine herself to breezy notes. Her staunch abolitionist stands got her fired from writing for the popular magazine *Godey's Lady's Book*, the bible for women devouring recipes and dress patterns but also the fiction writer's launching pad to success. Supporters of the antislavery cause embraced the young journalist and now, not quite forty years old, her celebrity allowed her to raise funds for the troops with her lectures. The Grace Greenwood name was sought after for endorsements and her monthly children's magazine, the *Little Pilgrim*, was acclaimed by the press. At the beginning of 1863, the Hillsboro, Ohio, *Highland Weekly* recommended the magazine to anyone caring for children: "We believe its beneficial influence upon any family where it is read, is beyond all estimation. In the language of the editor, the gifted 'Grace Greenwood,' we can truly say, 'we believe no child can read it regularly without being greatly benefited in heart, mind and manners. Think of it, fathers and mothers! 50 cents a year for an influence in your homes that may decide for life the characters of your sons and daughters!" But even such a highly touted publication had trouble staying afloat in wartime when Grace Greenwood was out in the camps cheering on the troops or on the stump raising money for their well-being through the Sanitary Commission.

Sara Lippincott was one of several female journalists to descend on Washington during the war. Probably the biggest bomb thrower was Jane Swisshelm, who returned to the capital after writing for and running newspapers in Pittsburgh, Pennsylvania, where she fought for the property rights of married women, and St. Cloud, Minnesota, where she battled against slavery. She turned ardent abolitionist during a sojourn with her husband in Louisville, Kentucky, giving her an up close look at "the peculiar institution." And abolition topped her agenda when she first came to the Federal City in 1850 as a correspondent for the *New York Tribune*, which soon featured "Mrs. Swisshelm's Letters" on page one. The intrepid journalist convinced Vice President Millard Fillmore to let her report from the Senate Press Gallery, the first woman to do so. But she got thrown out in short order. Infuriated by Daniel Webster's support for the Compromise of 1850 and its Fugitive Slave Law, Mrs. Swisshelm repeated rumors that the much-hailed statesman was not only a drunk but also the father of a black woman's children. She broke, as have many women reporters after her, the "boys on the bus" rule dictating that private lives were not public fodder. Though she wrote the story for her hometown Pittsburgh paper, it was reprinted all over the country, embarrassing Webster supporter and *Tribune* publisher Horace Greeley, who promptly fired his female correspondent. The undaunted reporter landed back in Minnesota, where she did battle with established politicians, coming to be called "the mother of the Republican party" in Minnesota. But an Indian raid in that state outraged this great protector of African-American and women's rights and she once again headed for Washington, D.C., to protest what she saw as the lenient treatment of the Native Americans. She had left her domineering husband, James Swisshelm, a failed businessman, and was free to go where she wanted.

Having been told that there was no point in taking her case to the top because "Mr. Lincoln will hang nobody," she went with some trepidation to a reception at the Executive Mansion, where Mrs. Lincoln was entertaining again after her year of mourning for Willie. Mrs. Swisshelm believed that Lincoln "had proved an obstructionist instead of an abolitionist, and I felt no respect for him; while his wife was everywhere spoken of as a Southern woman with Southern sympathies—a conspirator against the Union." After friends convinced the crusading correspondent to come along with them to the White House, she determined to make a quick exit, never stopping to check her coat. Then Jane Swisshelm saw the president's "sad, earnest, honest face" and blurted out, "May the Lord have mercy on you, poor man, for the people have none." Unwittingly, she had tickled Lincoln's sense of humor and when he burst out laughing the ice was broken—not only did she warm to this man who had aroused her suspicions for moving too slowly on abolition, but also to his wife, whose manner "was so simple and motherly . . . she would be incapable of a successful deceit." Maybe the fact that Mary greeted her famous caller by saying, "I have long wished to see you," had something to do with the pair winning over the fierce Jane Swisshelm: "I recognized Mrs. Lincoln as a loyal, liberty loving woman, more staunch even than her husband in opposition to the Rebellion and its cause, and as my very dear friend for life." Mrs. Swisshelm decided to stay in Washington rather than return to newspapering. She landed a job as a clerk in the War Department thanks to the efforts of her old friend Secretary of War Edwin Stanton.

———————

MORE AND MORE jobs in the government were opening up to women as the men left for the battlefield—half of the clerks at the headquarters of Montgomery Blair's U.S. Post Office were female. And new jobs were created with the passage of the Banking Act, which authorized the printing of "greenbacks," paper money to finance the fighting. The treasurer of the United States, General Francis Spinner, saw the wisdom of hiring women as a money saver, since he could pay them less than men and he thought they might actually do a better job. "A woman can use scissors better than a man," he told his boss,

Treasury secretary Salmon Chase. "I want to employ women to cut the Treasury notes." The greenbacks came off the press in large sheets and someone was needed to cut them into individual bills. At first the needy women, left without any support when the men went off to war, were simply handed a pair of scissors and told to go to work for six hundred dollars a year, a substantial salary for a woman. Word spread about the well-paid but finger-blistering jobs and more and more women applied for them. Then Spinner opened additional positions to women, using them to detect counterfeits and count the currency.

Though the treasurer was pleased with his workers, he came in for a good bit of grief for his unorthodox hiring practices, with the women's teakettles in the Treasury windows providing a source of great amusement and ridicule. Congress eventually capped the women's salaries at $900 regardless of the work they were doing even as men doing lesser jobs made $1,200. A Union officer in Washington, William E. Doster, noted in his diary that a "feature on the streets of the Capital is the female Government employees; especially the Treasury girls." He pointed out that many were from "good families—for it takes some influence to get into a department." But "black sheep" also collected government paychecks, forced to supplement their salaries with unsavory occupations because their pay didn't cover their living expenses as Washington rents increased, with board at $30 a month, and a regular room running as high as $20.

Women working in the Printing Offices had the nerve in 1862 to strike for an increase from five dollars a week to a dollar a day but as the war wore on and more women came to town, their attempts to better their situations failed. Members of Congress controlled the purse strings of government agencies and often also controlled who got jobs and who didn't, spraying the "government girls" with a whiff of scandal. "The shameful fact cannot be wiped out that men, high in political power, because they had that power, made womanly virtue its price," bristled journalist Mary Clemmer Ames in describing the Capital City, where "the war had torn the whole social fabric like an earthquake." But by war's end General Spinner saw his experiment as an unqualified success: "The truth is that many of the female clerks now do as much work, if not more, and do it as well, if not better, for $900 per annum, than some of the male clerks are able to do who receive a yearly salary of twice that amount." Later in his life he called his role in "introducing women to employment in the offices of government" more satisfying than "all the other deeds of my life."

———————

As the war effort continued, the war itself, at least in the East, stood at something of a standstill. The cold and wet weather slowed any movement, with thickening mud making the roads impassable. Lizzie Lee was having trouble getting back and forth from Silver Spring to the city, where her work with the orphan asylum took up a good deal of time, as did lobbying for a promotion for her husband. If his wife could make it happen, Flag Officer Samuel Phillips Lee would wear the admiral's insignia. "I have a list of Senators & will give it to Father & get him to speak to a majority of the Senate," she assured Phil as she worked to pass a bill thanking him for his service so he could achieve the higher rank. Several days later another report: "I went with Father to the Capitol & he was so *bitterly opposed* to my seeking conference with the Senators—that I gave it up upon faith & not conviction . . . it is right for women to obey—at the same time I was egotistic enough to think I could get things done he could not."

But her father couldn't keep her from talking to the women: "I have visited people—& that is all I have done—& if able I'll go see Mrs. Lincoln tomorrow after church." The determined wife knew she could have "a pleasant chat" with Mary Lincoln but Lizzie was frustrated by the constraints put on her by both her husband and father: "I must get your appointment if I can and shall go to the City today to see about it—I think I will go straight to the President & Sec[retar]y— although Father & you both will be angry with me for doing so." A few days later her irritation had mounted. She couldn't attempt another lobbying session with the first lady because of the weather and she had been thwarted in her desire to talk to senatorial friends: "Now I want to ask them to go do it—but Father & you have objected to my doing so—I intended to go today to see Mrs. Lincoln—but can't go in a storm." Lizzie suspected that her brother the cabinet member was secretly sabotaging her husband because the two had never liked each other—and she turned out to be right.

The storms of that winter, like the one that kept Lizzie Lee marooned in Silver Spring, also kept the army battened down in camp restively waiting for action. So, in early April the first family decided to celebrate Tad's tenth birthday by taking a trip down the Potomac for a morale-boosting call on the troops headquartered in the Virginia hills between the Rappahannock and Potomac Rivers near Falmouth Station. Though snow forced the presidential party into the safety of a secluded cove the first night, the rest of the visit proved morale building for everyone. Through the swirling storm the family and a few friends took a train to the makeshift city of more than one hundred thousand soldiers built as General Hooker's base.

Bunking down in a well-turned-out tent, the Lincolns enjoyed their time both in formal moments like the cavalry review and in one-on-one conversations with soldiers. Lincoln's friend, the journalist Noah Brooks, traveled with the first family and witnessed the joy of the soldiers as the president "went through the hospital tents . . . leaving a kind word as he moved from cot to cot." The good mood even extended to the famously jealous Mary Lincoln, who forgave her husband despite the attention lavished on him by the notorious "Princess Salm-Salm," the former Agnes Joy. The aptly named red-head had drawn attention to herself as a single woman riding bareback through the streets of Washington and then managed to snare a European prince, albeit a hugely indebted one, named Felix of Salm-Salm. The prince, run out of Europe, had signed up with the Union army and the princess bride went along with him to camp. When she encountered the president she covered him with kisses, but for once Lincoln was able to jolly his wife out of the anger she usually showed if he even politely spoke to another woman. The president summed up the visit to Brooks saying "'It is a great relief to get away from Washington and the politicians,'" so all in all it was a highly successful trip with positive press coverage for the embattled president and even for Mary. Taking credit for this happy moment in a horrible winter was the most unlikely of "advisors"—a spiritualist in Washington frequented by the first lady.

After Willie Lincoln died, on a suggestion from the dressmaker Elizabeth Keckley, his mother sought out the then-popular "mediums" to hold séances, hoping she might "get in touch with" her little boy. Some of the sessions were held in the White House but Mary often traveled to Georgetown, where she participated in séances conducted by a woman named Nettie Coburn, who professed to channel several spirits. Mrs. Lincoln was so taken with Nettie that she secured a job for the medium in the Interior Department guaranteeing that she would stay in Washington. One night one of Nettie's spirits told her the president would be coming that night to her séance and when he actually showed up, one of the party welcomed him by saying, "You were expected." Lincoln asked how that could be since he had just decided on the spur of the moment to accompany his wife to the "circle." The group then sang a few songs—one of the spiritualists was famous for causing pianos to move in time to the music (!)—and then, according to Nettie, Lincoln asked if she had anything to say to him.

A "spirit" took over Nettie's personality and cataloged the disasters befalling Hooker's army. The president agreed that things were as dire as described, and then asked for "the remedy." According to Nettie the spirit replied, "Go in person to the front; taking with you your wife and children; leaving behind your official dignity, and all manner of display. Resist the importunities of officials to accompany you . . . seek the tents of the private soldiers. Inquire into their grievances . . . make them feel that you are interested in their sufferings." The medium claimed that the president responded, "If that will do any good, it is easily done." Before the family left for camp, Nettie visited the White House, where "Mrs. Lincoln informed us that they were being besieged by applications from members of both houses and cabinet officers and their wives, for permission to go with them. And she remarked, in her quick, impulsive way: 'But I told Mr. Lincoln if we are going to take spirits' advice, let us do it fully and then there can be no responsibility resting with us if we fail.'" If the Lincolns really were listening to voices from the otherworld, the president must have been cheered by another piece of news from the spirits: he would be reelected the following year. But as that spring wore on there was less and less reason to believe that.

"PEACE DEMOCRATS," AN ever-growing group ready to end the war, were mounting campaigns in several states, threatening another electoral rout like the one the year before. What Lincoln desperately needed was a military victory. But none came. The whole time he had been in Hooker's camp the president had tried to find out what had happened in Charleston, where he feared a planned attack by the Union navy to retake Fort Sumter had been thwarted. His fear was justified. Nine expensive ironclad ships failed to penetrate the Rebel defenses. One sank. The rest turned back in yet another federal defeat. So a great deal rested on Hooker's enormous and enspirited army when the general finally moved at the end of April.

He maneuvered his massive force across the Rappahannock ready to engage Robert E. Lee at Chancellorsville. The southern general quickly pulled together his Army of Northern Virginia from camps around the state, and once again faced with a superior force—the Union fielded about 130,000 men, the Confederacy about 60,000— Lee and his chief lieutenant, General Stonewall Jackson, devised a plan to surround Hooker's forces while the latter were still making their way through the heavily wooded area called the Wilderness. Taking the risky course of dividing his smaller army, Lee sent Jackson's forces off on a bold sneak attack. That surprise, combined with the hesitancy to move forward on the part of yet another Union general, culminated in a humiliating Yankee defeat, horrible in its toll of more than thirty thousand casualties in the combined armies, including the death of Stonewall Jackson, accidentally shot by his own men, a devastating loss for the South.

For Abraham Lincoln the devastation was even greater. Noah Brooks was in the White House when the president read the telegram informing him that the army he had so proudly inspected just a few weeks earlier had withdrawn across the Rappahannock. "Never, as long as I knew him, did he seem to be so broken, so dispirited, and so ghostlike. Clasping his hands behind his back, he walked up and down the room saying, 'My God! My God! What will the country say! What will the country say!'"

It took a while for the country to learn the details of the defeat. While the battle was still going on, Lizzie Lee "saw hundreds of ambulances moving in the streets—but could not find out where they were going so followed them a while & saw them make for the steamboat wharves. I came home with a heavy heart as there was nothing of a battle in the papers even in the second edition which I got as it was issued on the Avenue—Silence is ever ominous." Even the first lady was in the dark about what was going on. Nettie Coburn dropped by the White House to find that "Mrs. Lincoln, in a loose wrapper, her long beautiful hair down her back and over her shoulders, was distractedly walking up and down the room." Mary was clearly in a state, telling Nettie, "'such dreadful news; they are fighting at the front; such terrible slaughter; and all our Generals are killed and our army is in full retreat.'" Nettie then summoned a spirit who assured the first lady and then the president that all was well. This time the spirit was wrong.

After reading the fateful telegram, President Lincoln headed to Hooker's encampment, departing a city filled with rumors. The war, Lizzie Lee noted, was "the perpetual theme of everybody's talk . . . at home—on the pavements," and on May 6, the last day of the battle, "Nobody *knew* in the city what was going on in Hooker's army—or Stoneman except the President—who they say excludes the War Dept." General George Stoneman of the Union army led the cavalry across the Rappahannock and Lizzie Lee was ready to heap praise on him: "Everyone is full of Stoneman's achievements & even Secesh admit the efficacy & gallantry of his raid." But Hooker was another story.

Word was out, perhaps unfairly, that the general in charge of the battle "was drunk all the time & that after the first day's battle was unfit for duty." Preston Blair had feared Hooker's proclivities from the start and "asked the P. on his return from Falmouth if his Gen[era]l was drunk or sober when he inspected him." A letter from a member of Hooker's staff "discloses the particulars & winds up & 'thus we are disgraced.'" One General Lizzie did admire—Stonewall Jackson. "He was an able Gen[era]l & an earnest man & I hope is taken away to be spared the sorrow which I think the Cause he earnestly espoused is to come to . . . we as a Nation will take pride in his heroism even in spite of the miserable Cause which won his heart." Though she despised the southern cause, Lizzie still had many southern friends, and when she heard that Robert Brown, the son of a former Mississippi senator, had been brought to Washington as a prisoner she rushed "to the City in this rain to see him & his comforts." The Confederate cause was one thing; close companions were another.

During the days when the armies around Chancellorsville, Virginia, fought to their gruesome conclusion, the spiritualist Nettie Coburn visited Washington's Mount Pleasant Hospital, where both her father and brother were recuperating from one of the many diseases that swept through the camps. "Its thousands of clean, white empty tents, full of little cot-beds, suggested the possibilities of war, but presented none of the horrors." By the next week nothing was the same: "Soldiers were everywhere, rushing in all directions. . . . Threading our way through what seemed hardly familiar lines of tents; we were shocked to find that nearly every tent was filled with mutilated occupants; every bed having its tenant, and fresh arrivals constantly being added to the number." Her father, now well enough to assist the other soldiers, asked if Nettie and her friends had "nerve enough to help us." One "started on her round, but the first sight that greeted her eyes was one of horror—a poor soldier boy bleeding to death from a wound in the neck. Turning deadly faint, she retreated to the open air. A few moments and she rallied and bravely returned to her work." It was a story repeated over and over during the long war as women sadly got used to such scenes and then took charge.

———————

WITH GENERAL HOOKER'S retreat back across the Rappahannock, Washington again feared invasion. After the early panic at the beginning of the war, the army built forts and earthworks all around the capital, providing it with ample protection. Now the troops occupying the fortress mini-cities went on alert, preparing to fight if necessary and breaking up what had been a somewhat familial atmosphere in the camps. At Fort Mansfield, on the upper northwest side of town, Janet Seward packed up with her baby and the baby's nurse and headed home to New York to wait out the expected siege. Mrs. Seward's father-in-law served as secretary of state and her brother-in-law, Frederick Seward, as assistant secretary. Another brother-in-law, Augustus, was a colonel in the Union army but until the summer of 1862 her own husband, William Seward Jr., kept to the quiet life of a banker in the small upstate city of Auburn, New York.

Before he enlisted, William and his wife had visited their distinguished family members in Washington, and Janet—called Jenny— had accompanied her sister-in-law to the White House, where she found Mary Lincoln's "wreath of large white roses around her head . . . not very becoming." She also visited officers' wives quartered at Mary and Robert E. Lee's confiscated Arlington House and was somewhat nonplussed when "one of the ladies invited us to her room, and gave us pieces of the china that was presented to Martha Washington by General Lafayette, she having found a box of broken pieces in the attic." But the days at Fort Mansfield, with William in the army, would be a very different Washington experience from the time spent at cabinet dinners and White House receptions as the guests of prominent personages.

Not long after Seward volunteered and the Ninth New York Heavy

Artillery regiment was ordered to Washington, Janet gave birth to their first child, a girl they named Nellie. William established himself at the fort just outside the District of Columbia boundary and then summoned his wife from Auburn to bring the baby and join him in a log cabin there. "There were a great many discussions in the families. Both our mothers said 'Go' but the family physician, when consulted, said, 'Well, if you do go, you will bring a dead baby home with you.'" Despite that scary advice, Janet's mother-in-law, who chose to live most of the time in Auburn rather than with her husband in Washington, scoffed, "Nonsense; think of all the babies that have been born and brought up in log cabins." So off she set in the dead of an upstate New York winter with a three-month-old, a baby nurse, and her sister, plus her husband's aunt.

Crossing the ice-caked Hudson River at Albany by ferry, her sister took the baby and jumped several feet onto the ice because the boat couldn't reach the dock. "We were women alone," but apparently women with a great many "bags and bundles" that were then tossed onto the ice and collected for the train ride to Washington. After a night in the comforts of the secretary of state's mansion, Janet, the baby, and the nurse moved to their new home, a snug log cabin several miles from the center of town. It was far from a typical army wife's life, even though the cabin was small and simple: "We had a great many callers from Washington and Auburn at different times—the president, members of the Cabinet, foreign ministers and others, all curious to see how we lived in camp."

Forced occasionally to move in with her in-laws when her husband was sent away on various missions, Janet loved returning to "our little cabin." And though she was there through the winter and spring of miring mud, one of the soldiers managed to plant a flower garden for her. But then came May and "the long roll, the signal of attack, was sounded." With the nurse and baby Janet made her way into Washington "in a little one-horse wagon" by the light of the full moon. "Upon arriving at the house, we astonished and frightened the family, by the news that we were running from the enemy." No Rebels attacked but it was the end of Mrs. Seward's idyll at Fort Mansfield, "much to my regret, as there were frequent alarms, and raids by the guerillas." And rumors rushed around the Capital City that General Lee was marching north.

———

"YESTERDAY THERE WAS a panic in town made by the ambulance trains, which were so large & enough to affright the people but it was the sick from Fredericksburg hospitals, & not the wounded from any battle," Lizzie Lee reported in mid-June. "It is a race between Hooker & Lee . . . the result I think will not be brilliant but there are men enough & good gen[era]ls enough to take care of us." Despite the roar of gunfire a few days later, she kept to her home certain there were "no Rebels nearer than Harper's Ferry & Centreville." And even in the midst of the panic Lizzie was able to stage a successful benefit for the orphan asylum.

Advertised in the *National Republican* as a "Grand Vocal and Instrumental Concert," featuring ballads like "Her Bright Smiles Haunt Me Still" and a "Scene de Ballet" for violin and piano, the event at the Odd Fellows' Hall raised five hundred dollars and alleviated any worries about money for the summer ahead. Lizzie admitted to her husband, "my heart is so much in this establishment that I can no longer call it a work." But soon fear that the war was about to arrive on the doorstep wiped away all other concerns. Lizzie first heard that the Rebels were in Hagerstown, Maryland, not far at all from Silver Spring, then in Chambersburg, Pennsylvania. "The Army of the Potomac may hug

Washington but that will make it secure for a while only. The President said today he got rid of McC[lellan] because he let Lee get the better of him in the race to Richmond & he seemed to have it in his mind that if Hooker got beat in the present race he would make short work of him, but prudence forbids my saying even this much." That was June 23. Five days later Lincoln replaced Hooker with General George Meade, making him the fifth commander of the Army of the Potomac in three years. But Lizzie Lee didn't yet know about Meade as she moved back and forth between Silver Spring and Washington looking for safe haven. She could "hear every battle" but believed she could "get out of the way if we are defeated." Defeat was all the Army of the Potomac had known for months and defeat seemed likely again.

The next day, June 24, a portion of the Rebel army crossed the Potomac River, passing very near Silver Spring, so Lizzie moved into the house in Washington just as she learned that "Hooker is at last deposed. Meade has a good reputation & is a sober man & a good soldier & may prove a lucky appointment." The Blairs backed Meade, but Montgomery's enemy in the cabinet, Salmon Chase, was distressed at Hooker's dismissal as he told his daughter Kate, "You must have been greatly astonished for the relieving of General Hooker; but your astonishment cannot have exceeded mine." Chase was angling for a presidential run against Lincoln and putting down a marker in case Meade lost the battle.

Monty Blair sent his family out of town for safety and Kate Chase kept to the protection of faraway New York. But Lizzie Lee hunkered down in her house across the street from the White House, though she heard from one of the Union men taken prisoner by Confederate General J. E. B. Stuart that " 'but for his jaded horses he would have marched down the 7th Street Road, took Abe & Cabinet prisoners.' " Lizzie added ruefully, "for the life of me I cannot see that he would have failed had he tried it." Stuart's men were moving closer and closer to Silver Spring and when the Union army captured some of them they "were full of talk about the plan for capturing 'Old Blair,'" bragging that catching the "Old Fox & his cub the Yankee P[ost] M[aster] Gen[era]l we would have all the pluck out of that Washington concern and soon end the war." It was pretty scary stuff for Lizzie there without her husband, but she pluckily promised, "We are very comfortable—laugh and eat & sleep—hope & pray. Still firmly trusting in Him who is our ever present help in time of trouble." Even so, the tension was hard on her parents, who seemed "enfeebled and broke down by this experience." The senior Blairs stayed at Silver Spring, too close to the skirmishing between the armies for Lizzie's comfort, so she was vastly relieved when her seventy-something parents came riding their horses into Washington on July 2, though there was no guarantee of safety there, either: "Rob[er]t Lee's whole object is in my opinion Washington."

When the skirmishes turned into full-fledged warfare it happened eighty miles north of Washington, in a Pennsylvania town called Gettysburg. "We are here on tiptoe with all eyes turned towards the north West where I have felt all day that a mortal combat was going on for our Country's life," Lizzie quivered on July 3, the third day of the battle. "A letter today from Meade to the P says yesterday at 3 o'clock he had all his Army concentrated but 2 corps were so prostrated from an immense march that he would not attack until today." The close relationship between Lincoln and her father allowed Lizzie to keep close tabs on the action and she placed her hopes on Meade not only because he came from a talented and energetic family but especially because "as he was born in Spain he can never be President—thus will not be warred upon by politicians." Timid Union generals had repeatedly held back their armies and Lizzie, like many others, thought they were calculating the political odds of their actions. But now victory in the East seemed possible at last. Plus she had word from her brother Frank that Vicksburg was within Grant's sights.

Still, having weathered so many disappointments, Lizzie didn't dare jump for joy. On July 4, "the news from the Armies is favorable but scarcely decisive enough for my appetite." Though it looked like Lee had retreated, Meade wasn't convinced—the southern general might be searching for a "good stronghold at which to have another fight," and the newly assigned Commander Meade claimed he couldn't pursue the enemy because he had to stop to feed his men. Lizzie learned this from the president himself when she took Blair to the White House to watch the Independence Day fireworks, "in which he was disappointed."

"I think the 4th of July of 1863 will stand by that of 76 in the annals of Country," Lizzie exulted a few days later, breathlessly telling her husband, "I feel too full of joy to wait until the morrow to tell it over to you altho you may know it now & revel in the Good tidings." Not only had the Union won at Gettysburg, but now Vicksburg had finally fallen. "EXTRA," the *National Republican* screamed, "Glorious News!" celebrating the Vicksburg victory, and added from the Battle of Gettysburg, "Lee Retreating." The tide, at last, had turned. When word reached Lizzie, she and fellow board member Mary Merrick were in a meeting about mattresses for the orphanage. Lizzie tamped down her excitement about Vicksburg and her brother Frank Blair's role as a leader in the Union army there because her friend Mary's two brothers had fought off that army from inside the Confederate fortress. "She looked at me with a quiet sadness when my heart overflowed in thankfulness and only remarked, 'Oh the sea of blood this dreadful war has cost.'" More than 50,000 casualties at Gettysburg, almost 20,000 at Vicksburg. But that number doesn't reflect the true costs of the months-long battering of the fortress city that starved soldier and civilian alike until Confederate general John C. Pemberton was forced to surrender to Ulysses S. Grant. It was a crucial victory— "Vicksburg is the key," Lincoln had bluntly declared almost two years earlier, echoed by Jefferson Davis. "Vicksburg is the nail head that holds the South's two halves together"—and it made Grant's career. It took almost two years and several failed attempts but now the North could cut off the supply lines to the Rebel troops. "Now that the Mississippi is open," Lizzie, along with much of the country, prayed, "I take hope that the war will be over before very long."

Back at Silver Spring, Lizzie Lee found herself "too happy to grumble at anybody," but the huge celebrations held around the North at the news of the double victories died down as the public and the president came to understand that Meade had failed to pursue Lee's army as it retreated into Virginia. Lizzie summed up the situation: "Meade's mistake was altogether a want of judgment . . . they supposed Lee would attack them & he out *wised* them for he made all the appearances of an immediate attack & *thus* saved himself. . . . I fear we will never have such an easy prey within our grasp again." The canny southern general had saved himself and what was left of his army but the line of his wounded stretched on for fourteen miles. "Lee made a most desperate & false step by this invasion," Lizzie concluded; "maybe his best excuse is the calculation that Hooker was to be our general." Both Lee and Meade had made mistakes; both offered their resignations and neither was accepted. And the war with its terrible toll raged on for almost another two years.

More fighting meant more soldiers, and on July 11 the first draftees in American history learned their names had been pulled from a giant spinning wheel in New York City. The conscription law contained a provision that allowed a man to get out of the draft by either paying three hundred dollars or finding a substitute. "Rich man's war and poor man's fight" resounded as more than a political slogan as an angry mob of men and boys took to the streets of New York, first destroying the draft office and then taking out their venom on any policeman or black person who had the misfortune to be in their path. They burned an orphanage for African-American children and for five days sacked hundreds of stores, including the well-known provider of Union uniforms—Brooks Brothers. (But the police were able to thwart the "gang attempting to break into the Lord & Taylor store.") More than one thousand people died or were wounded. Lizzie Lee worried that the riots might prolong the war and no one knew what would happen in other cities when the conscripts' names were announced.

Janet Seward's mother-in-law had already been the target of an attack in Auburn, New York. Someone threw a stone through a window where Frances Seward usually sat reading, "and if she had been sitting in the chair she would have been hurt. When she came to tell me about it, she said, 'You had better take baby and go to your mother's; we may have the house burned or something worse.'" Janet took her prize possession—a picture of her husband—to her mother's but she and Baby Nellie stayed put, despite the fact that "the Copperhead element was very active in the North, and we were frequently threatened with violence." The so-called "Peace" Democrats had been behind some of the violence and their faction came to be known by their enemies as "Copperheads" for the poisonous snake that sneaks up and bites without warning. The person they most wanted to strike was Abraham Lincoln.

MARY LINCOLN AND her two surviving sons left Washington for a vacation in New Hampshire and Vermont that particularly hot summer in Washington when malaria felled both humans and horses. The first lady was recuperating from a head injury she received in a frightening fall on the second day of the Battle of Gettysburg. She and the president were returning to the White House from a stay at their Soldiers' Home retreat; he went by horseback, and she followed by carriage. It turned out that the carriage had been sabotaged in what was probably an assassination attempt on Lincoln. Someone had loosened the screws holding the driver's seat to the chassis and when the seat came loose the driver fell out and the horses took off at a gallop. Mary jumped out of the runaway carriage and landed on her back, hitting her head on a sharp stone. The wound was tended to in a nearby military hospital but infection set in so the president called on their friend Rebecca Pomroy to take charge. Mary and Rebecca had stayed close since the nurse had taken care of Tad after Willie died. And a few months earlier, after she had started entertaining again, the First Lady had invited the nurses and soldiers from Rebecca's hospital to one of her receptions.

Mrs. Lincoln tended to confide in the women who worked for her, perhaps because the women of Washington were so unfriendly. She had leaned on Mrs. Pomroy in the forlorn weeks after Willie's death, trying to understand how the nurse had survived the loss of two of her own sons and her husband. The president too "went to her in his troubles as to a family friend," she later revealed. Given the tinkering with the carriage, Mrs. Pomroy feared for Lincoln's life, and when she asked him, "'what will you do about showing yourself in public?' he said, 'I can do nothing different from what I'm doing. I shall leave it all with my Heavenly father.'"

But Mary couldn't stay so sanguine in the face of regular death threats arriving by mail—she constantly worried about her husband. Another of her confidantes, her dressmaker, Elizabeth Keckley, heard many a conversation between the couple on the subject. As Lincoln prepared to go to the War Department one night Mary warned: "'You should not go out alone. You know you are surrounded with danger.'" The reply, "'Don't worry about me, Mother, as if I were a little child, for no one is going to molest me,'" did nothing to comfort her. Neither did the president's response to Mary's refusal to allow their son Robert, then a student at Harvard, to enlist in the military, an ongoing argument heard by Mrs. Keckley. Mary Lincoln: "I cannot bear to have Robert exposed to danger. His services are not required in the field, and the sacrifice would be a needless one." The president's rejoinder: "The services of every man who loves his country are required in this war. You should take a liberal instead of a selfish view of the question, mother." But she did not, despite Robert's pleas so there must have been some tension between mother and son on that long summer sojourn. For his part, Robert believed that his mother "never quite recovered from the effects of her fall . . . it is really astonishing what a brave front she manages to keep when we know she is suffering." By the time the president's son joined the army the war was almost over.

But Mary Lincoln did have some relatives fighting in this war. Unfortunately for her, they were on the wrong side. Lending credence to the charges that the first lady was a southern sympathizer at best, a spy at worst, four of her brothers and three brothers-in-law fought in the Rebel army. While she was still away on vacation—with the president telling her, "I really wish to see you"—the Union lost another big battle, this one at Chickamauga in Georgia. Again at horrible loss of life and limb—more than 16,000 northern casualties, more than 18,000 southern, among them Confederate general Ben

Helm, married to Mary's much younger and much-beloved half sister, Emilie. Both the president and his wife were very fond of the thirty-two-year-old southern general—at the beginning of the war Lincoln had offered him a job as paymaster in the Union army and Mary had hoped that Emilie would join her as a White House hostess. But Ben signed with the South and now he had lost his life.

A visitor to the White House soon after the battle found the president "in the greatest grief." But Mrs. Lincoln, who learned of the death through a telegram from her husband, was forced to do her mourning in private because she knew, said her niece, "that a single tear shed for a dead enemy would bring torrents of scorn and bitter abuse on both her husband and herself." Even with her close companion Elizabeth Keckley, Mary refused to show sadness. First her half brother Samuel Todd was killed at the Battle of Shiloh and then another half brother, Alexander "Alec" Todd, who had been like her own baby, lost his life at the age of twenty-three in the Battle of Baton Rouge. When he died Mary told the seamstress: " 'He decided against my husband, and through him against me. He has been fighting against us; and since he chose to be our deadly enemy, I see no special reason why I should bitterly mourn his death.' "

That provided proof enough for the former slave Lizzie Keckley that Mary "had no sympathy for the South" and that those who thought she did were "widely mistaken." Mary's niece later wrote: "the Northerners had no sympathy for a Southern-born woman whose brothers were in the rebel army. . . . On the other hand, the Southerners shouted that she was hard-hearted, callous . . . so flinty-hearted that she showed no emotion, not even a trace of feeling at the loss of her brothers and friends." Mary couldn't help but show emotion a few weeks after Ben Helm's death when his young widow showed up at the White House bringing her little girl with her.

Emilie Todd Helm, the first lady's half sister, had been in Alabama to be near her soldier-husband and been summoned by the Confederate army to Atlanta for his burial. Now she desperately wanted to go home to her mother in Kentucky. Mrs. Todd, Mary Lincoln's stepmother, appealed to the president to provide Emilie with a pass to travel through enemy lines. The young woman got as far as Fort Monroe in Virginia when a Union officer demanded that she take an oath of allegiance to the United States before proceeding. Emilie refused, declaring it would be "treason to her dead husband, to her beloved Southland," her daughter later recounted. The dutiful soldiers trying to carry out standard orders didn't know what to do with the distraught young woman until one of them came up with the idea of telegraphing the president personally. Lincoln answered directly: "Send her to me. A. Lincoln." And so it was that a Confederate widow took up residence for a week in the Lincoln White House.

Emilie kept a diary of those days, detailing how "Mr. Lincoln and my sister met me with the warmest affection, we were all too grief-stricken at first for speech . . . we could only embrace each other in silence and tears." The sisters tried sticking to neutral subjects, talking about old friends in Kentucky, steering clear of any discussion of the "frightful war" that separated them. "Sister is doing everything she can to distract my mind and her own from our terrible grief, but at times it overwhelms us; we can't get away from it, try as we will to be cheerful and accept fate." Now Mary could reveal how she suffered over the death of her brother Alec: "he was so young, so loving, so impetuous, our dear, red-headed baby brother!" Her hard-hearted statement to Lizzie Keckley was clearly for public consumption.

Though the first lady always put on a smile for her husband, according to Emilie, the "thin and care-worn" president was still worried about his wife. "Her nerves have gone to pieces; she cannot hide from me that the strain she has been under has been too much for her mental as well as her physical health," Lincoln told his sister-in-law as he invited her to spend the next summer with the family at the Soldiers' Home. Emilie agreed that her sister was "very nervous and excitable . . . if anything should happen to you or Robert or Tad it would kill her." Mary in turn asked Emilie whether she thought "Mr. Lincoln was well." When the younger sister tried to deflect the question by simply saying how thin the president looked, Mary responded, "Oh Emilie, will we ever awake from this hideous night-mare?" The toll of the war on the White House was becoming clearer and clearer to the young visitor.

Later that night Mary shocked her sister when she crept into Emilie's room to reveal her nighttime visits with her dead son Willie, how he appeared at the foot of her bed sometimes bringing with him her dead baby Eddie or her little brother Alec. Emilie divulged to her diary: "It *is* unnatural and abnormal, it frightens me. It does not seem like Sister Mary to be so nervous and wrought up." The young widow tried to keep out of sight during her visit, knowing that her presence was a problem for her hosts. But one day when General Dan Sickles and New York senator Ira Harris came calling they asked to see her under the pretense of catching up on some friends in the South. Harris clearly wanted to pick a fight, baiting Emilie about the war until finally he succeeded in getting a Rebel retort.

That gave him an excuse to attack Mary: " 'Why isn't Robert in the Army? . . . He should have gone to the front some time ago.' " Mary's stiffly polite answer, " 'I have insisted that he should stay in college a little longer,' " only seemed to rile Harris up. " 'I have only one son and he is fighting for his country . . . and if I had twenty sons they should all be fighting the rebels.' " Emilie took the bait, " 'And if I had twenty sons . . . they should all be opposing yours.'" She fled from the room, soon followed by her sister, who "was powerless to protect a guest in the White House from cruel rudeness." The men then stormed upstairs demanding to see the president, shouting at him "'You should not have that rebel in your house.'" Refusing to be intimidated by the uninvited intruders, Lincoln instructed them that he and his wife would choose their own guests and that his wife's sister was there because he sent for her.

Emilie knew the situation was untenable: "I feel that my being here is more or less an embarrassment to all of us and I am longing for Kentucky and mother." The time had come to go—among other irritants, the Lincolns' little niece, who grew up to author a book about her aunt Mary, kept insisting to her cousin Tad that Jefferson Davis was the president. When Lincoln handed Emilie Helm her pass to go home, he didn't say a word about an oath of allegiance, instead voicing his trust that "'I know you will not embarrass me in any way on your return to Kentucky.'"

Mary Lincoln did keep embarrassing her husband. The charges that she was a southern sympathizer might not have been fair but there were plenty of other complaints about the first lady that were justified. Her spending was out of control—at one point she ordered three hundred pairs of gloves—and too often so was her temper. She was disdainful of the cabinet and hardly hid her feelings. And with Lizzie Keckley in the room she didn't bother to hide them at all. "'Seward! I wish you had nothing to do with that man,'" she ranted to the president about his secretary of state. "'He cannot be trusted.'" And Treasury secretary Chase "'would betray you tomorrow'" if he thought it would help him, she contended. Mary's view on Chase was correct—he was plotting for the presidency. But her main objection to the man, in Mrs. Keckley's view, was the popularity of his daughter, who "was quite a belle in Washington, and Mrs. Lincoln, who was jealous of the popularity of others, had no desire to build up her social position through political favor to her father."

KATE CHASE'S SOCIAL position needed no bolstering—her coming wedding to Senator William Sprague was already the hottest topic in town other than the war. The *New York Herald* suggested that Mrs. Lincoln offer to hold the wedding in the East Room of the White House "in order that in view of a certain possible event she may have an opportunity of judging how its associations suit her." Everybody knew Chase was eyeing Lincoln's job and Kate was masterminding the campaign. And it looked to political Washington that the marriage was part of the plan. Chase was in debt. Sprague was rich. An unfriendly newspaper account of the wedding sneered, "Personally Mr. Sprague is not attractive, pecuniarlially he is—several millions."

When Kate and her much younger sister Nettie were off for a northern vacation the summer before the nuptials, their father's letters were full of warnings about how much his older daughter was spending: "Not that I am pinched or what I *call* poor—though New Yorkers would so *call* me—but that I cannot afford to be extravagant, since I am determined to be honest." In fact Chase didn't have the money for Nettie's school tuition. So it must have been something of a relief when the soon-to-be son-in-law bought the expensive house the Chases were renting, though the Treasury secretary complained that he hadn't been consulted about the renovations Sprague had commissioned before he moved in with the inseparable father and daughter. Originally the groom-to-be balked at the idea of sharing his father-in-law's home but shortly before the wedding he sent Chase a reassuring letter promising to "never be happier than when contributing to continue the same relation between father & daughter—that has here-tofore existed, excepting if possible to share something of it myself."

The Treasury secretary had good reason to keep Kate close—to shield her from the hard-drinking Sprague, whose character left a good deal to be desired even if his bank account did not. Chase might have been aware that his daughter's betrothed had abandoned a pregnant girlfriend in Providence, Rhode Island, which might have contributed to the couple's on-again, off-again relationship for the last two years. As early as 1861, then-fourteen-year-old Nettie told her big sister she should marry the textile heir, but they didn't get engaged until the spring of 1863. At about that time they were to-gether at the Blair home in Silver Spring when Lizzie Lee noticed Kate's unhappiness when her fiancé agreed with Preston Blair on an issue instead of Salmon Chase. But throughout the summer protes-tations of love filled Kate and William's correspondence and when the couple got together in New York that August, the young wom-an's father feared for her virtue: "Be careful to do nothing which will in the slightest degree diminish his respect for you; for love cannot be perfect where respect is impaired." If she was going to marry Sprague, Chase thought, the wedding should be sooner rather than later, but Kate had planned a November wedding and Kate always got her way.

The day of the grand event, November 12, the Washington *Chron-icle* reported "a large crowd of all sexes, ages and conditions began to assemble around the mansion of Secretary Chase." Fifty people were invited to the wedding in the parlor, five hundred to the reception to follow. The showstopping bride was "dressed in a gorgeous white velvet dress, with an extended trail, and upon her head wore a rich lace veil" topped with a diamond and pearl tiara, a gift from the groom, bought at Tiffany's for $6,500. She made a dramatic entrance down the staircase and the Marine Band played "The Kate Chase Wedding March," specially composed for the occasion. President Lincoln slipped in just in time for the ceremony but his wife refused to come, choosing not to "bow in reverence" to Kate and her father. Chase's enemy in the cabinet, Montgomery Blair, declined as well, but his daughter Betty and father, Preston Blair, joined the party and declared it "a great display of elegance & riches," though "the gaiety was very lame.... Father enjoyed the wedding ... & Betty says he was quite the belle of the occasion." The newspaper account concluded "there was nothing calculated to offend the eye or taste." (The next story in the newspaper: "Jealous Husband Blows His Brains Out.")

AFTER SOME SKIRMISHING in Northern Virginia in mid-October, with the war's heavy fighting concentrated in Tennessee and Georgia, Washington enjoyed a more serene season than it had in a while. Soldiers jammed the racetrack near the National Insane Asylum betting on horses with names like General McClellan. The new theaters, Ford's and Grover's, showed Shakespeare and newer plays including *The Marble Heart*, starring John Wilkes Booth. Real estate boomed with an influx of northerners "coming down to Washington in fashionable force," Lizzie Lee marveled as she started redecorating the house and itemizing the cost of everything. ("Dining room furniture alone will cost four hundred dollars....") Government contracts for military supplies were making people rich and the prewar population of a little more than sixty thousand had grown exponentially, though another census would not confirm that until the end of the decade. The fields around the city yielded bountiful harvests and the shops overflowed with luxury goods coming in from Europe and northern manufacturers.

For Lincoln the election brought great relief as Republicans won in Ohio, with Salmon Chase's well-publicized help, and Pennsylvania. The president traveled to Gettysburg for the consecration of the cemetery there and delivered a short address that has become one of the best known and most memorized speeches in history. And then came more good news in late November—General Grant had successfully driven the Confederate army out of the railroad hub of Chattanooga, Tennessee. The October presidential proclamation of an official Thanksgiving Day, declared at the suggestion of the magazine *Godey's Lady's Book* editor Sarah Josepha Hale, for the last Thursday of November seemed very well timed. And then for the cherry on the sundae, the Statue of Freedom took her place atop the Capitol dome.

"The statue of Freedom was lately placed on the dome of the Capitol," Louisa Meigs cheered to her husband, who had been so instrumental in the engineering of the dome and the expansion of the now almost-finished building. "I went with Mary to watch the ceremony but arrived too late to see anything but the statue hoisted to its position and dimly discernable amid the scaffolding—It made me sad to think of all the changes that had taken place since you first began your career on these great works." Some of the men who had worked with Montgomery Meigs on the Capitol, foremost among them Jefferson Davis, were "now traitors to their Country & fighting to dishonor its flag—some of them dead & almost forgotten in the great struggle for our National existence." But the great vision they had shared was now almost a reality.

President Lincoln ordered that work continue on the Capitol during the war as a symbol of a unified and enduring nation. The great dome slowly rose through the conflict and its crowning glory, a huge bronze statue of a female figure titled Freedom, would add a sense of completion, though there was still work to be done on the dome itself. Montgomery Meigs, then the Capitol's construction superintendent, commissioned Thomas Crawford to sculpt the monumental piece and along with then Secretary of War Jefferson Davis approved the final design. But Crawford died before he was finished, so it took a good deal of effort plus some creative thinking by enslaved worker Philip Reid to assemble the pieces of the fifteen-thousand-pound creation atop its pedestal. On December 2, 1863, the final piece, Freedom's head and shoulders, joined the rest of the statue, saluted by thirty-five guns at the Capitol, echoed by artillery at the forts surrounding the city. Louisa Meigs, with her daughter Mary, attended the event and gave her report to her husband in Chattanooga.

Quartermaster General Meigs had eventually succumbed to his wife's pleas to allow her to return to their home in Washington from her evacuation outpost in Pennsylvania. But now he was gone, having headed to Chattanooga months earlier on a secret mission to organize supplies for the campaign. Louisa didn't know what her husband was doing there and why he was gone for so long. "People here do not exactly know what to think of your absence and have an idea that you have been relieved of your duties," she fussed at him in October when she thought his mission must have been accomplished by then. Their oldest daughter, Mary, had a suitor whose "devoted attention has made a deep impression on her heart." With her father gone, Mary's mother would have to be the one to approve an engagement. "He came upstairs to see me and asked my permission to have Miss Mary who had desired him to come to me before she would consent to engage herself to him."

Taking on the unexpected role, Louisa must have given her consent because a month later, with General Meigs still in the field, Lizzie Lee told her husband, "Mary Meigs is said to be engaged to Hancock Taylor." Even so, Louisa advised Mary against rushing into anything; as she told Montgomery, she would like to protect their daughter from the "trials of marriage" as long as possible: "I do not wish to interfere with their happiness but the truth is that only a wife & mother can know the cares and anxieties that follow a young woman on her entrance into married life—A man has not the trial or the suffering which a woman has & his mind and his feelings are so different that he cannot even understand them." That was the kind of thing women talked about among themselves; it's somewhat surprising to see it in a letter from a wife to her husband. (Twenty-year-old Mary Meigs married Major Joseph Hancock Taylor a little more than four months later.) But Louisa had always been frank in her letters—as an eleven-year-old child she had written to her brother telling him their siblings "continue to go to school to Mr. Washington and do not learn much."

Though she was born in Georgetown, Louisa's father, Commodore John Rodgers, a naval hero in the War of 1812, moved the family to Lafayette Square across from the White House a couple of years before she was married. Montgomery Meigs, an army engineer with a degree from West Point, came to Washington in 1841; met and married the "fascinating" woman he deemed "amiable, intelligent and sprightly"; and promptly embarked on a peripatetic military life as he oversaw the construction of forts and she, often in primitive situations, produced seven children, including a stillborn baby girl. In 1853, after the family moved back to Washington, two other children, nine-year-old Charles and two-year-old Vincent, both died within weeks of each other of what their father called "disease of the brain."

Somehow Louisa always seemed to keep up her spirits, though when she was away from home, she longed to see her mother, and fantasized about "what a convenient thing Aladdin's carpet would be." From far-off army bases she doled out advice to her younger sister, warning "Nannie" in 1845 against throwing herself into the Washington social season: "It leaves I can assure you by my own experience an aching head an aching heart and aching void in the mind of every one who engages to the full in all its follies." From Detroit, where

Monty was building Fort Wayne, she asked her sister wistfully, "Do you ever go to the Capitol not to lounge in the library . . . but to feast your reason & imagination upon the sundry wisdom of eloquence there so abundant?" Louisa was always trying to persuade her family to come visit her, complaining in 1848, "Detroit has been very dull this past winter," so she was thrilled when Monty was briefly reassigned to Washington the next year.

Moving back to her much-missed hometown "seems to me like a dream," she told her off-at-sea brother; "things seem little changed since I was last here—even the very signs and names on the shop doors are the same as used to grace them in days of yore—So that I seem to have slept four years and suddenly waking up, found myself in W[ashington]." Louisa and Montgomery and their children had a pleasant stay "under the maternal roof," but then they were off to northern New York, where she discovered she was pregnant again, admitting to her sister that she had tried to keep it secret because "I know it will annoy Mother."

But her mother must have been pleased when the family settled in Washington in 1853, with Montgomery Meigs assigned to work on the aqueduct and then the extension of the Capitol. He closely collaborated with Jefferson Davis on those projects and Davis helped get the Meigs' oldest son, John Rodgers Meigs, into West Point. Once enrolled, the cadet received regular instructions from his mother— "When you write me word that your nails are of a proper & becoming length I shall feel as if you had accomplished a victory." He shouldn't spoon his food, he should always carry a handkerchief, he should put on lavender water before visiting young ladies, take dancing lessons, stop earning demerits; "you know how I used to have to *watch* you before you left me."

John had left and now Montgomery was gone as well, and her

daughter was about to get married. Louisa would have to manage on her own. She explained to her absent husband: "It is not worthwhile to trouble you with my accounts as I have no advice or assistance from you in management of the household. Rather you will have to leave it to my judgment to decide whether or not my expenses have been useless or extravagant." But her judgment about him and his career had changed, at least in theory. "I used to fancy that I should like to see you at the head of one of our great armies but I think I am cured of that ambition." She was, after all, a commodore's daughter. But she missed her husband, admitting to her father-in-law, "I feel his absence from home more than I can describe and have lost all dreams of military ambition which would take him into the field or place him at the head of a great army." Not only did Louisa want Montgomery to come home; she had also seen what happened to generals who met with defeat: "The instant a man falls from his position he is dragged down and reviled & persecuted by the hounds of the press and by private malice accused of crimes which no one would have dared to whisper while he still held the reins of power." At that moment, with Meigs off in Tennessee, no one was quite sure whether he still held the reins of power: "I am amused & provoked both to see the way in which people enquire for you. They do not seem to know exactly how they ought *to look* when they enquire for you—*regretfully* or *sympathizingly* or *naturally*. . . . I always hasten to assure them of your good health & spirits & that I am expecting you 'very soon.'" She was probably hoping to lure him home with fears for his reputation if he stayed away.

Louisa wrote that letter the day of the victory at Chattanooga, and once she knew of the great success she didn't think it fair that her husband, who was "as much exposed as any of the commanding Generals," didn't share the credit: "If your precious life had been lost to your Country & to us—You would have gained no reputation added to your fame because you had no command there." Apparently she hadn't lost her ambition after all. Louisa was also curious about what would happen next: "I should not wonder if Gen[era]l M[eade] were removed. . . . Will they bring up 'Unconditional Surrender Grant' *and place* him at the head of the Army—How extraordinary success is." This military wife, daughter, and mother wasn't used to being so out of the loop: "We live very quietly in your absence and I see few people who have any knowledge of military affairs—I met Mr. Seward a few days since—he enquired for you." Louisa's speculation was of course on the mark. In a few months, Ulysses S. Grant's success would place him in command of all Union armies

---

PRESIDENT LINCOLN HAD a touch of smallpox when he sent his State of the Union message to Congress in early December. Always ready with a joke, the president quipped, "Now I have something I can give everybody." The disease wasn't the only thing ailing him. With a presidential election year approaching, politicians on all sides were ready to take shots at him, and they all had different views of how he should be prosecuting the war, dealing with slavery, and preparing for eventual peace.

Lincoln used his message to Congress to propose a plan that was essentially his vision for Reconstruction. Any Confederate who took an oath of allegiance to the United States, except high ranking civilian officials and military men, would be pardoned and allowed to keep all property except slaves. If 10 percent of the number of 1860 voters in any state took the oath, including the acceptance of emancipation, the United States would recognize that state's government. No one would be sent back to slavery. No southern lawmaker who supported secession would return to Congress. This "Proclamation of Amnesty and Reconstruction" managed miraculously to bring together all sides. Lizzie Lee was amazed that even the Radical Republicans "now all subscribe to the message." Christmas was coming—"I bought a toy for Blair from you & one from myself"—with peace in the party. It would not last for long.

CHAPTER 7

LEFT: *Surgeons and nurses with the United States Sanitary Commission at Camp Letterman, Gettysburg. Funded mainly by women, the USSC supplied hospitals and provided nurses.* RIGHT: *Sojourner Truth preached the gospels of emancipation and suffrage, electrifying audiences around the country.*

Anna Speaks, Jessie Campaigns (Again), Sojourner Visits

1864

Washington had never seen anything like this before—a *woman* would be speaking at the Capitol. On January 14, 1864, the *National Republican* ran a notice announcing the "Address by Miss Anna E. Dickinson in the Hall of the House of Representatives." Vice President Hannibal Hamlin, Speaker Schuyler Colfax, and more than one hundred other members of the House and Senate signed the request for Miss Dickinson to appear; the paper published the invitation plus the reply: "Accepting it, I would suggest the 16th of January as the time; desiring the proceeds to be devoted to the help of the suffering freedmen."

The twenty-one-year-old Philadelphia woman had become a Republican darling in the last year when at the behest of the party she traveled through New England and the Northeast successfully stumping for congressional candidates. Her fierce fighting style in defense of the war roused the crowds to hall-shaking frenzy and the politicians actually gave her credit for rallying Republican voters to the polls—the invitation from Congress acknowledged her "services in the campaigns in New Hampshire, Connecticut, Pennsylvania and New York." Of course, as a woman she could not be a voter herself, and it was as a supporter of women's rights that Anna Dickinson came to attention not quite four years earlier. No one could have imagined then that she would speak in the Capitol of the United States, with the vice president on one side of her, the Speaker of the House on the other.

At a Quaker meeting of the "Friends of Progress" in Philadelphia, the then-seventeen-year-old startled the crowd when she spontaneously rose to reply to a speaker who had criticized women for moving outside the "domestic sphere." That impromptu rebuttal defending a woman's right to participate in public debate launched Anna Dickinson well beyond domesticity. She became a star on the lecture circuit, sharing the stage with such other reformers as Quaker antislavery activist and feminist Lucretia Mott. Anna hailed from an abolitionist Quaker family herself. Her father died when she was two, leaving his wife and children in poverty, which eventually burdened the young girl with the responsibility of helping support her mother and sister. First she followed the traditional female path as a teacher, then in order to boost her salary she took a job at the U.S. Mint in Philadelphia, where she was paid twenty-eight dollars a month for eleven hours a day, six days a week. It was still more than her teacher's pay.

Soon her freelancing as a forceful pro-war speaker got her fired from her government position. Her crime: she denounced Philadelphia hero General McClellan as a traitor, accusing him of purposely losing the Battle of Ball's Bluff. Abolitionist newspaper publisher William Lloyd Garrison brought her to Boston to earn money on the lecture circuit, but the fees she could command—twenty dollars a speech—weren't enough to sustain her family and her sister pressured her to come home and teach. Then Anna Dickinson got her big break. Famous anti-slavery speaker Wendell Phillips canceled an appearance at the Boston Music Hall due to illness and with five thousand people in the audience the spotlight came up on the fiery young woman. She was such a hit that she went on to appear with renowned African-American leader Frederick Douglass at the Boston Tremont Temple and the secretary of the New Hampshire Republican Committee hired her for that season's political campaign.

From New Hampshire Anna moved on to Connecticut, where the officers of the Republican State Central Committee endorsed her heartily: "Prejudiced against her at the start, we had great misgivings as to the propriety of inviting her to take a part in our campaign. She had not spoken ten minutes before all prejudices were dispelled; thirty minutes, and not a man could be found who would admit that he ever had any prejudices; sixty minutes, and she held fifteen hundred people breathless with admirations and astonishment; two hours, and she had raised the entire audience to a pitch of enthusiasm which was perfectly irresistible. She is really a wonderful woman, and you ought to invite her to speak in New York." Anna Dickinson did speak in New York at the Cooper Union for the Advancement of Science and Art, where thousands paid their twenty-five cents—fifty cents for reserved seats—to hear her denounce McClellan and promote abolition.

The Brooklyn Academy of Music had refused to allow her to speak, with some dispute in the newspapers about whether it was because she was a woman or because she was a partisan. In defending the Academy, the *Brooklyn Eagle* opined, "there is, we are glad to see, something novel in a young woman mixing in the dirty puddle of party politics. It will always we trust be a novelty; for the women of the land will never forget their inherent modesty so far as to make exhibitions of themselves." Eschewing "inherent modesty," Miss Dickinson continued to campaign for Republicans in New York and in Pennsylvania, where not all audiences appreciated her strong pro-war sentiments. At one Pennsylvania gathering a man opposing the draft fired his gun and shot off a lock of her hair, coming close to killing her. Anna just went on talking. The success of those campaigns brought her that January night in 1864 to the Hall of the House of Representatives in the United States Capitol.

Twenty-five hundred people crammed into every possible space in the chamber and the galleries, "made gay with the bright attire of ladies, velvets, flowers, and brilliant hues," reported Noah Brooks to his California readers, and "a splendid burst of applause" greeted Anna Dickinson as the vice president introduced his prize as akin to Joan of Arc—a fighter for the Union cause. A close friend of the president, Brooks knew that Vice President Hamlin and Speaker Colfax were both Radical Republicans, who likely expected Miss Dickinson to rail against the president's moderate reconstruction proposals, as she had in other speeches, assailing Lincoln as too weak in his dealings with the Rebels.

Anna had launched into her criticism when in walked Mr. and Mrs. Lincoln, taking seats of honor right in front of her, causing the young woman hurriedly to change her tune and endorse the president's re-election. Brooks admitted that the speaker "has an apt and telling way of putting things which brings down the house with thunders of applause," but he predicted "she will flash out her brief and splendid career and then subside in the destiny of all women and be heard of no more." (It took more than twenty years for him to be proved right, and in the interim, as Anna Dickinson's speaking fees spiraled upward, Brooks revised his view, saying that Anna's appearance at the Capitol came as she was "just beginning her long and picturesque career.") The opposition party took a decidedly different view—the Democrats saw the lady as a threat.

"Anna E. Dickinson was granted the use of this Hall to deliver a public address . . . which was a political rhapsody and a partisan support to the present administration, and denunciatory of its opponents, and was evidently designed to influence great measures of legislation before the House." Democrats tried to pass a resolution disapproving "of such a use of this Hall, for political purposes, and regard it as disrespectful to the minority of this House." The resolution didn't go anywhere in the Republican-controlled Chamber, but the Democrats clearly feared this young woman. She could sway votes.

———————

IT WAS AN election year and the Lincolns were ready to use the White House for campaign purposes. Mary officially put away her mourning garb, showing up at the New Year's reception—the first where a handful of African Americans joined the eight thousand guests—in "a purple velvet dress. . . . Valenciennes lace was on the sleeves, and an immense train flowed out behind. Mrs. Lincoln never looked better." Noah Brooks knew his readers in far-off Sacramento, California, would want to know what the ladies were wearing, along with other tidbits from Washington's New Year's ritual, and he tried to oblige them as he traipsed from reception to reception: "The War Secretary was the only man who had a spread of edibles for his guests, and Secretary Chase had the only great rush of callers, except the President." For the Treasury secretary it was not just any New Year's reception—it was election year and he was running for Lincoln's job. "Mrs. Sprague, *nee* Chase, did the honors of the reception in a graceful style and a blue brocade gown with a long tail to it."

With the Union armies in winter quarters, the Republican newspaper proclaimed: "We have a right to be somewhat gay and festive here at the national metropolis . . . hundreds and hundreds of the sovereign people come up to this their metropolis every winter and they naturally desire to see what some affectedly call our 'Republican Court.'" And the Republican Court was on full display. Secretary Seward, with his daughter-in-law Anna at his side, still threw the best parties, but Mary Lincoln was determined to compete this campaign season. She was desperate to see her husband reelected; she feared his defeat would expose her debts and make it impossible to pay them. Though her spending sprees had been widely reported and her expensive taste the subject of disapproving comment, she had managed to keep secret, even from her husband, the fact that she was splurging for things like her three hundred pairs of gloves on ever-mounting credit.

But no president had been reelected since 1832 and before he took on the Democrats, Lincoln would have to fight the Radicals in his own party, led by his secretary of the Treasury. Mary, who had always mistrusted Chase, paid particular attention to the first state dinner in late January, traditionally a night for the families of the cabinet and Supreme Court. But when she saw the list, she cut two cabinet family members—Kate Chase Sprague and her husband. The president's secretary, John Nicolay, knowing Mary was making a mistake that was likely to blow up in the newspapers, appealed to his boss. When Lincoln overruled his wife, she caused "such a rampage as hasn't been seen in the House for a year," Nicolay quaked in the face of Mary's rage. As it turned out, the first couple entertained the Treasury secretary and his daughter just as the Chase for President campaign was about to emerge from the back rooms into a full-front public challenge to the sitting president. "The Presidential quest is rife & Abe has the inside of the track," Lincoln supporter Lizzie Lee observed in the middle of January. But by the end of the month, she was less convinced that the president would succeed: "The Radicals will throttle him if he does not soon take them by the throat."

As it turned out, the Radicals ended up throttling themselves. Lincoln had come in for crushing criticism in the torrents of correspondence Chase sent out to politicians and publishers as he allowed his friends to form a committee to promote his presidency, with financing coming from his son-in-law and guidance from his daughter. In late February the work of the committee appeared in print with the publication of a letter over the name of Kansas senator Samuel Pomeroy calling on the Republican Party to dump Lincoln and nominate Chase. The embarrassed Treasury secretary told the president he knew nothing about the effort to elect him—and though there's no reason to think Lincoln believed him, the president chose to keep the treacherous cabinet member in office and then watched as the Chase candidacy collapsed.

Lincoln's supporters, roused by the so-called Pomeroy Circular, organized their state parties to pass unanimous resolutions endorsing the president. After his home state of Ohio backed Lincoln, Chase pulled out of the race, sanctimoniously assuring his daughter Nettie that "a good many of the best and most earnest men of the country desired to make me a candidate," and that though he feared it "would greatly impair my usefulness as Secretary of the Treasury," he had allowed his name to go forward. But, he complained, the "Blairs assailed me" and "my relations with the President were in danger of becoming unfriendly." Then Ohio acted and "I had already said that the wishes of our friends in Ohio would be controlling with me." Lincoln somehow found a way to keep the relations with his cabinet member friendly enough and the Radicals went in search of another candidate.

The Blair brothers—Postmaster General Montgomery and Missouri congressman Frank—had been going at Chase both by name and by inference. Frank had left his place in the army to take his seat in Congress "under orders from the White House," noted his sister Lizzie Lee, and he would return to "the field in the spring." The president needed all the friends he could get in Congress and he knew the Blairs would back him in every way they could. The patriarch, Preston Blair, "gave me *an order* to call on every member & leave his card & his wife if they had any here . . . but think how much easier said than done," Lizzie complained when the Congress convened. By the end of January she had seen about half of the ladies and "where there are no ladies I have left Father's & Frank's card."

The Blairs wanted to be on friendly terms with all the members of Congress as they girded for the campaign ahead. And the first family, in the house across the street, seemed to be paying particular attention to their neighbors, with Lizzie in and out of the White House that winter along with much of the rest of the city. Mrs. Lincoln reinstituted the regular receptions, observed with a wicked eye by her chief aide, William Stoddard: "The Red room does not look unpleasantly red by gas-light, but the prevailing tint has its effect upon any and all other tints exposed to its influence. For instance it heightens the deep crimson shade of the silk that Mrs. Lincoln is wearing this evening . . . you cannot help disliking it." Despite the war, the windows of Washington were ablaze with parties that winter. As Lizzie Lee wearily told her husband: "Nothing tires me more than these parties altho' vastly amused whilst there." And she was impressed with the people she was meeting at these events: "The Congressmen are of a different class of people from those heretofore sent to Congress—far more of refinement in manner and appearance than ever before seen here & many take houses and entertain."

———————

NOT ALL OF the entertaining in the capital was of the savory sort. Washington, where many married men lived without their wives, had long supported its "bawdy houses." Now, with young single soldiers swarming into the city, the "oldest profession" thrived. In January the police staged a raid on all the major establishments and arrested the owners: "Ann Benter, of Tin Cup alley; Ellen Bride, of Pear Tree alley; Mary Heissler, better known as 'Dutch Mary,' of Third Street; and Mary Ann Hall, keeper of the 'old and well established' ranch on Maryland Ave." The women arrived at the courthouse separately, with Mary Hall "in virtuous black." The trial of Mary Ann Hall, the owner of what the *Evening Star* called a house of "national reputation for the last quarter century," mesmerized the city.

Policemen solemnly testified that they had seen "hacks frequently in front of the house," with very few "females" emerging from the taxis, and that they had seen women in the house but no "implements of industry." One thought that "a wedding party was going on—champagne was being handed around—there were six or eight citizens and several officers present"; his sergeant "did not think it was a wedding party." Another policeman told the court that he found the house "very handsomely furnished—first class furniture, very showy." The testimony simply underlined what everyone already knew—Miss Hall, who was something of a personage in the city, ran the best house of prostitution in Washington four blocks from the Capitol, very likely frequented by some of the most important men in town. Hall's house was in a class of its own in the Capital, where an official count the year before turned up almost four thousand prostitutes, both white and black. Most of them had arrived with the outbreak of the war and the influx of the soldiers. In an attempt to control the situation General Hooker had corralled most of the activity into an area near the Treasury Department that wags quickly dubbed "Hooker's Division."

And prostitution was the least of the city's crime problems. In 1863 police made 24,000 arrests, more than "three and a half times the number in Brooklyn, a city with more than twice the population of the District," according to a Washington historian. Thieves ran rampant, with poverty taking hold in overcrowded sections of town, and disease spreading to poor and rich alike. Contrabands—former slaves— crowding into the Federal City threw up shanties for shelter in areas with no water or sewage, overpowering the ability of social welfare societies to aid them and adding to the likelihood of proliferating epidemics requiring the full-time services of the Sisters of Mercy.

But the war brought great wealth as well. Supplies for the soldiers required shipping and storing, so warehouses bulged and wharves burst with goods. Railroads carried tons of freight in and out of the city and real estate prices catapulted to new heights as northern businessmen arrived to take advantage of all the commerce. ("George Riggs has given in cash $25000 for the Digges place," an astonished Lizzie Lee told her husband.) Hotels and restaurants couldn't keep up with the demand. And "every available nook and corner, from cellar to garret," was rented to boarders, according to Lois Adams, who wrote for the *Detroit Advertiser and Tribune*. Services from banks to blacksmiths to bootmakers boomed. And Mary Hall grew rich off her "bawdy house."

When she died in 1886, the *Evening Star* reported her holdings: the house on Maryland Avenue, a farm in Virginia, and "$57,200 in government and railroad bonds." The newspaper also rhapsodically eulogized the "long resident of Washington. With integrity unquestioned, a heart ever open to appeals of distress, a charity that was boundless, she is gone but her memory will be kept green by many who knew her sterling worth." Perhaps appropriately, she is buried at the Congressional Cemetery, with a large statue of a young girl contemplating her grave. Other than that grand marker, her memory disappeared for more than a century. But then in the 1990s, while the foundation was being dug for the National Museum of the American Indian on the National Mall, archeologists came upon Miss Hall's trash heap. "They found gilt-edged porcelain, corset fasteners, seeds from exotic berries and coconuts and bones from expensive meats, including turtle," the *Washington Post* recounted. Also, and not surprisingly, given the police testimony, "They also found 'hundreds' of Piper-Heidsieck champagne corks and wire bales."

Not long after the city (temporarily) cracked down on the "bawdy houses," Congress launched an investigation into goings-on at the Treasury Department. Congressman, later president, James Garfield heard testimony from women working at the place one Capitol insider called "a perfect Sodom." The president had received a letter from a New Yorker horrified that "the Treasury has been converted into the most extensive Whorehouse in the nation." The outraged citizen claimed that members of Congress were stashing "their women" in the department. The committee filed both a majority and minority report as to the accuracy of the accusations, but it's the salacious one filed by the minority charging "a mass of immorality and profligacy" that was repeated in nineteenth-century Washington histories: "these women seem to have been selected . . . for their youth and personal attractions. Neither the laws of God nor of man, the institution of the Sabbath nor common decencies of life seem to have been respected."

Of course the minority might just have been trying to embarrass the Treasury secretary, in the time-honored tradition of congressional investigations. What the members who wrote it succeeded in doing, however, was to besmirch all the young women working for the government. In *The Sights and Secrets of the National Capital*, published a few years after the war, the author, newspaperman John Ellis, asserts, "You will hear it said in Washington that the acceptance of a government clerkship by a woman is her first step in the road to ruin." And though he goes on to defend the "government girls," assuring his readers that the "black sheep are greatly in the minority," Ellis warns, "Strong efforts are made by devils in the form of men, to increase their number, and it is to be feared that these efforts will, in many cases, be successful."

No number of investigations and police raids could keep Washington's attention far from the chief concern of the government—the progress of the war. At the president's request, Congress had resurrected the title of lieutenant general—last held by George Washington—for the man who had claimed victory at Vicksburg and Chattanooga, Ulysses S. Grant. When the general came to town to accept his commission, his appearance at a White House reception caused a sensation. "The mass of people thronged about him wherever he moved . . . the women were caught up and whirled into the torrent which swept through the great East Room; laces were torn, crinoline mashed, and things were generally much mixed." Noah Brooks's readers learned that the crowd stood on sofas and tables to get a look at the general, or to get out of the crush, as everyone wondered what he and the president were plotting.

Grant had never been to Washington before and he wasn't eager to stick around, for fear of getting sucked into its political machinations.

So the city was disappointed when he didn't show up at the theater with the Lincolns that weekend, instead returning to the field to say farewell to his troops in the West before coming back to take command as general in chief of the army. General Henry Halleck moved over to the chief of staff position. Grant also skipped a dinner Mary Lincoln had planned for him, which was probably just as well with her, since she "could not tolerate General Grant," according to her dressmaker, Elizabeth Keckley. "'He is a butcher,' she would often say, 'and is not fit to be at the head of an army.'" But now Grant *was* head of the army and Lincoln was counting on his new commander to end this war successfully and soon. The biggest threat to the president's reelection was not any of the men maneuvering against him but defeat on the battlefield. The country was war weary.

Still, the women didn't flag in their efforts to get food and clothes and medicine to the soldiers. The United States Sanitary Commission grew into a major factor in the war operation, fielding nurses in hospitals around the country and assisting the military with supplies. The women organized massive days-long fairs to raise money that became spectacles in themselves, with huge halls filled with women selling goods, interspersed by theater productions and circuslike sideshows. In Washington the big fair was held at the end of March, and women from every walk of life participated. The *Jewish Messenger* proudly reported: "In the report just published of the Fair lately held here in aid of the Sanitary Commission, I observe that the Hebrew Society's table is credited for $756.95; and when I tell you the entire receipts were only $10,661.47, you will readily perceive how large a proportion of the amount realized is due to the Hebrew congregation. The ladies had the matter in charge and were beaten by only one other table, that of the Treasury Department. All honor to our fair Jewesses!"

Lincoln used the occasion of the Washington fair to make a speech calculated to please an influential, if nonvoting, constituency. Celebrating what he called the remarkable " 'fairs for the relief of suffering soldiers and their families,' " the president proceeded to give credit where credit was due, according to the newspapers: " 'The chief agents in these fairs are the women of America. I am not accustomed to the use of languages of eulogy; I have never studied the art of paying compliments to women, but I must say, that if all that has been said by orators or poets since the creation of the world in praise of women were applied to the women of America, it would not do them justice for their conduct during this war. I will close by saying God bless the women of America!' (Great applause.)" The women of America were also organizing politically, and not necessarily to the president's liking.

In February 1864, Elizabeth Cady Stanton, who had been one of the conveners of the first women's rights meeting at Seneca Falls, New York, in 1848, sent a petition to Massachusetts senator Charles Sumner bearing the names of one hundred thousand women. It was the first installment in what she and the other members of the Women's Loyal National League hoped would be a million signatures calling for a constitutional amendment abolishing slavery. Mrs. Stanton, along with her colleague Susan B. Anthony, led the formation of the league several months earlier, issuing an appeal to the "Women of the Republic" to sign and circulate the petition: "Women, you cannot vote or fight for your country. Your only way to be a power in the Government is through the exercise of this one, sacred, Constitutional 'RIGHT OF PETITION;' and we ask you to use it now to the utmost."

The petition started circulating in January, with the help of Sumner, who allowed the women to use his free mailing privileges. On the first of February Mrs. Stanton delivered the first hundred thousand signatures to the senator with a message: "the mothers, wives, and daughters of the brave men who have fallen in many a bloody battle now pray you to end the war by ending the cause of it, which is slavery. Inasmuch as the 'right of petition' is the only political right woman has under the Constitution, it is the duty of her representatives to give her prayer an earnest and serious consideration." She also asked the Massachusetts Republican to preserve the document "in some enduring form in the national archives, as a part of the history of our second revolution."

Sumner carted the rolls of names to the Senate floor, saying they marked "a stage of public opinion in the history of slavery, and also in the suppression of the rebellion." The women never reached their million-name goal but they did collect more than four hundred thousand signatures and helped propel the Thirteenth Amendment, ending slavery, to passage in the Senate that April. By then Elizabeth Stanton and Susan Anthony had decided on the man they wanted for president, and it wasn't Abraham Lincoln—it was John C. Frémont.

AFTER THE 1856 campaign, when the first nominee of the Republican Party, the dashing explorer John C. Frémont and his alluring wife Jessie garnered such enthusiastic public attention, the couple had stayed active politically. When the general resigned from the Mountain Department of the army in 1862, miffed at his reassignment to report to General Pope, the Frémonts moved to New York, where they lived in limbo with John still in the army, waiting fruitlessly for another military command. Jessie, no longer as alluring (her former friend Lizzie Lee cattily reported the gossip that "she has grown huge"), wrote a not very veiled defense of her husband's handling of his command of the army in Missouri. Publishing *The Story of the Guard* under her own name, Jessie, who had done so much of the writing of her husband's books, now read reviews describing her effort as "a true woman's book" with "no style, or a careless and imperfect one." That was fine with Jessie; the book sold well and she excused her boldness in writing it by saying that the proceeds would go to the families of the fallen Missouri warriors. When she was able to contribute five hundred dollars for the support of the families, Mrs. Frémont told her publisher that in a difficult period, with her husband pining for an army command, the book "has brought to me from so many quarters the most charming evidences of sympathy . . . I am thoroughly gratified by it."

Jessie had reason to fear criticism. This book about the war wasn't anything like the fictional stories written by the "literary ladies" of the time, so it was important that the public understand she was acting out of charity. This woman who loved the limelight assured her readers that it had been a sacrifice for her to reveal anything about her life; she asked them "to bear this in mind, and not think this attempt to relieve suffering more unwomanly or less needed than any of the other new positions in which women are finding themselves during this strange phase of our national life. The restraints of ordinary times do not apply now." Jessie had never paid attention to the "restraints of ordinary times" but she had to suffer them for a while as the family waited uneasily in New York, expecting that any day Frémont would return to the front.

Surrounded by sympathetic abolitionists who questioned Lincoln's commitment to the antislavery cause, and sycophantic hangers-on who promoted Frémont for president, Jessie held tight to her ambition to occupy the White House. She corresponded with congressmen who made pro-Frémont speeches; she protested against "our own political chiefs," especially the Blairs, and blamed the sluggish course of the war on the "unfaithful watchmen at Washington." After Indiana congressman George Julian praised her husband,

Jessie hounded Horace Greeley, the publisher of the *New York Tribune*, until he reprinted the speech.

To like-minded friends Jessie railed against Washington's refusal to give her husband a command: "The Govt. is simply irresponsible. Thank Heaven & the Constitution that limits them to four years, & more than two are over now," and she sneered at Lincoln's "sly slimy nature." John's situation was awkward—he was still in the military and he and six of his senior staff had been drawing a salary while doing nothing for sixteen months, hoping for reassignment to an army command. Frémont couldn't run for president on that record: "On this showing the General is unwilling to stand before the country," Jessie explained to a friend in Congress as she lobbied for a job for her husband, complaining, "I'm tired of the bad behavior of the people down there." And for the record, she added: "Of the General's pay not one farthing goes to private use . . . it goes to a fund we set aside for our part in relieving the suffering caused by the war." But all of her pleading was of no use. Lincoln wasn't about to appoint a general who was not only incompetent in the field but also a potential political enemy.

Jessie herself was still in demand. She declined an invitation from Elizabeth Cady Stanton to "preside at your meeting of the 21st of May," when the Women's Loyal National League was established, but sent the organization fifty dollars. After spending the summer of 1863 at the beach in Massachusetts, where she formed close friendships with the families of writers John Greenleaf Whittier and Henry Wadsworth Longfellow (Longfellow's take: "Mrs. Frémont is next door to us, which is very pleasant"), she threw herself into any activity where she could be seen sustaining the Union.

Following on the success of Sanitary Commission fairs in other cities, New York determined to outdo them all with an extravaganza in April. Jessie took on the assignment of compiling first-person stories of the war to "form a series of small volumes, bound in uniform style," and she hectored her friends to help produce material for the little tomes, saying they would "have value for History & the deepest interest for such of us as have been deprived of a belief in regular Histories by our own experience." The idea was that she would have some books on hand to sell at the fair and take orders for others because "such books would sell well at Christmas & I think it's a good idea to make a growing fund." Working with her on her committee was the wife of another potential rival for the presidency—Ellen McClellan, married to the general the Democrats were eyeing as their nominee. "We get on very civilly—even amicably," Jessie told Elizabeth Peabody, while pestering the reformer and author to gather writings for her project. But Jessie had no kind words for her husband's other opponent, dismissing Lincoln as the "Pontius Pilate of the slaves."

An enormous undertaking, the fair attracted tens of thousands of people. On one day alone the *New York Times* reported, "The number of tickets taken at the door was twenty-three thousand six hundred and fifty," and the restaurant served ten thousand meals a day. For a "hairy eagle" on the main floor President Lincoln donated his own locks for the head, eyes, and backbone. When it was all over this notice appeared in the newspaper:

To the Editor of the New-York Times:
I take the liberty of sending to you for publication in your journal, the following:
At a meeting of the Ladies' Executive Committee
of the Metropolitan Fair, held May 13, 1864, the following resolution was adopted:
Resolved, That JOHN H. GOURLIE, Chairman of the

**Finance Committee of the Metropolitan Fair, be requested
to place one million dollars in the hands of the United
States Sanitary Commission.**
(Signed) CATHARINE C. HUNT.

The women had done their work well and other organizations solicited Mrs. Frémont to contribute her fame to their causes. In Washington a group of wives of cabinet officers and congressmen plus
"well-known authoresses, women of fashion, mothers who had lost
their sons and wives who had lost their husbands" met to form the
Ladies National Covenant to "unite the women of the country in the
earnest resolution to purchase no imported article of apparel, where
American can possibly be substituted, during the course of the war."
Taking as their example the women of the Revolutionary War era
who "signed a pledge to abstain from tea," the women declared: "We,
the women of '64, have the same object to attain and the same duties
to perform which were so nobly accomplished by the women of '76.
. . . It must not be said of us that we have been willing to give up our
husbands, sons, and brothers to fight or die for the Union, and yet
refuse to renounce our laces, silks, velvets and diamonds." After an
amusing description of the five-hour meeting where the covenant was
amended and approved, correspondent Lois Adams summoned her
Detroit readers to action: "Organizing committees are appointed in
every State, and it is to be earnestly hoped that the ladies of town and
country throughout the Union will join heartily in the grand work of
retrenchment and reform."

The local women of Washington, with Adele Douglas in the lead,
appointed representatives from each state to spread the word, mostly
the wives of officeholders. For New York, in addition to the senators'

and governor's wives the committee included Ellen McClellan and Jessie Frémont. Jessie objected that her name had been included without her knowledge and argued that if Lincoln were reelected "the little our gowns & gloves would amount to" would mean nothing in what she was sure would be a national disaster. Still, a meeting in New York to promote the covenant attracted two thousand women, who were infuriated when they found men trying to run their event. "They patted us on the back and said they were sure we would be good little dears and give up our laces, French bonnets, and sugar plums, if we knew how well the gentlemen would think of us," huffed one of the women organizers; "they would think us just as pretty in homespun." The women persuaded the interlopers to leave so they could get on with their business uninterrupted.

Women were clearly beginning to taste power and Jessie Frémont was once again in the thick of the campaign for the most powerful position in the land. The Republican convention was scheduled for the first week of June in Baltimore, so the Radical Republicans decided to preempt Lincoln's nomination by holding their convention first. Elizabeth Cady Stanton told Jessie in early May that they urgently needed to issue a call for a mass meeting in Cleveland so that the "vacillating—always a large class—may be assured that there is to be a liberal movement, and that Gen. John C. Fremont is its chosen representative." Mrs. Stanton believed that if the Radicals went first, the rest of the party might follow. If not, then she could make the case that it would be the regular Republicans dividing the party: "The Liberals must be made to feel that the responsibility of splitting the Republican party cannot justly be imputed to them, inasmuch as they chose their leader first."

Abolitionists like Frederick Douglass and Wendell Phillips supported Frémont, along with a group of German Americans who had fought under his command in Missouri. Anna Dickinson lent her powerful voice to his candidacy as well. After her spontaneous endorsement of Lincoln in January, with the president sitting right in front of her, the young orator had an unpleasant meeting in the White House where she told her host that she had not come to listen to his always-at-the-ready stories and that she had switched her allegiance to Frémont. But only 156 people showed up at the somewhat quixotic convention in Cleveland and they were roundly ridiculed by the pro-Lincoln *New York Times*: "The platform and the ticket are up, and the witless fellows are gaping now to see the popular applause come rushing in. You would judge by their eagerness that the fate of the nation is depending upon it. They don't seem to have the least suspicion what a precious piece of foolery it all is." But Abraham Lincoln was not amused.

———

THOUGH LINCOLN HAD no trouble winning the Republican nomination in Baltimore with Andrew Johnson of Tennessee, a southern Democrat faithful to the Union, as his vice presidential running mate, he knew his ultimate victory depended on success in the war, and the war wasn't going at all well for the Union that spring. The so-called Peace Democrats were agitating for armistice, ready to readmit the rebellious states into the Union in exchange for peace, with no mention of slavery. The Confederates, though running out of men and money, hoped to hang in on the battlefield long enough for the North to elect a new president more sympathetic to the proslavery cause. And the superior fighting by the southern armies made it look like that strategy just might work.

In February, the Confederate submarine CSS *H. L. Hunley* successfully launched a torpedo against a U.S. ship outside Charleston, the first such attack in the war. In March and April, in the Red River

Campaign, the Union army and navy failed to drive the Confederates out of Louisiana. In Tennessee, the Rebels captured Fort Pillow, protected by a Union garrison including African-American troops who were viciously murdered after they surrendered. In May, Grant's army in Virginia was thwarted in Spotsylvania and in the wooded area called the Wilderness in its attempt to capture Richmond, and Sherman was stopped shy of Atlanta in Georgia. Thousands of wounded soldiers overfilled hospitals in the capital. Just as the Republicans were assembling in Baltimore the bloody Battle of Cold Harbor, Virginia, ended with Robert E. Lee's army still entrenched in its defensive position near Richmond. And in Washington a major tragedy shook the city.

"THE EXCITEMENT ATTENDANT upon the terrible explosion and loss of life at the Arsenal yesterday was kept up throughout the entire day," blared the *Evening Star* on June 18, the day after seventeen young women were killed at the Washington Arsenal. Several more of the injured would die in the coming days. "An excited crowd of relatives of the laboratory employees, parents, brothers, sisters, anxious as to the fate of those dear to them, thronged about the outer gate leading to the Arsenal, and the scenes here were heart-rending." Not only heartrending but grisly. The charred and dismembered bodies of the women still lay there, covered over with canvas, as officials tried to identify them: "Johanna Conner . . . was among those burned to death, but her remains were subsequently recognized by a portion of the dress which remained upon her unconsumed. The whole top of her head was, however gone, and the brain was visible; and but for the fragment of dress it would have been impossible to recognize her. . . . Millie Webster . . . was reported killed, but we have subsequently learned that she was not at work yesterday, and is consequently safe."

A jury was quickly assembled for the inquest and when the canvas was pulled away from the bodies "a most terrible sight presented itself to the view of those standing around." Most of the women were missing limbs, some had their clothes burned off, one had her shoes still intact, and "a singular feature of the sad spectacle was that presented by a number of the bodies nearly burned to a cinder being caged, as it were, in the wire of their hooped skirts." Even in the broiling heat, the young women adhered to the proper dress of the day as they did their dangerous work filling or "choking" cartridges for twelve hours a day, six days a week, for about half of what the men made, if that. Most of the women lived near the arsenal in a neighborhood known as "the Island," where many of the working-class residents were Irish immigrants. One of the victims was only twelve years old, others in their teens. That awful day after the explosion, the inquest determined that the fire had been the result of spontaneous combustion when the sun hit star shells—essentially fireworks designed to light up an enemy's position—that had been left out to dry by the arsenal's pyrotechnist. Then families of three women who had been identified, including Johanna Connor, took them home to bury them. The others would have a joint ceremony, with a procession through the city honoring them as fallen heroes.

"The most solemn pageant ever presented to the citizens of the District of Columbia was the funeral procession which on yesterday accompanied to the tomb the remains of the victims of the explosions at the Arsenal," the *National Republican* somberly stated, adding that the streets were "thronged," the steamboats from Alexandria "crowded and also the cars from Georgetown." The Secretary of War had ordered that the families and friends of the deceased should see the "sympathy of the Government," and so a flag-draped stage erected at the arsenal held the coffins, with eight of them bearing a silver plate marked "unknown" at the mobbed funeral. A Catholic priest and a Protestant minister offered prayers and words of solace as President Lincoln and Secretary of War Stanton sat as silent spectators among the mourners. It was the first public funeral the president had attended since his son Willie had died. Stanton too had lost a little child a couple of years earlier, and brought his surviving young son with him that horribly hot and sad day.

After the service the coffins were placed in hearses and ambulances and "the procession moved onward towards the Congressional Cemetery, where the remains were interred with solemn and appropriate ceremonies. A large concourse of citizens thronged the entire way." A few days later it was reported: "The persons employed in the Washington Arsenal have opened a subscription for a monument in memory of the sufferers by the recent explosion." A year after the disaster a grand memorial was erected at Congressional Cemetery, the tallest marker there. A life-sized downcast maiden titled *Grief* stands atop a long column, and an inscription on the pedestal reads

ERECTED
BY PUBLIC CONTRIBUTIONS
BY THE CITIZENS OF
WASHINGTON, D.C.
JUNE 17TH 1865

WHILE GENERAL GRANT was laying siege to Lee's army in Virginia but failing to take Richmond, and General Sherman was smashing at Johnston's army in Georgia but failing to take Atlanta, Confederate general Jubal Early decided it would be a good time to invade Washington. After all those false alarms from the time of the surrender of

Fort Sumter more than three years earlier, this time it was real. Early intended to draw Union troops away from Virginia, giving the city of Petersburg some respite from the relentless barrage, but he came close to an actual attack on the capital. He stole across the Potomac on July 5 and four days later entered Frederick, Maryland, less than fifty miles from the White House, just forty miles from Silver Spring. Lizzie Lee could hear the cannon fire as she rushed with her mother and son off to the safety of the New Jersey seashore. They got out just ahead of Early's army scorching its way into the Blair family enclave. "Mother is very much overcome by the burning of Silver Spring & the terror felt about the safety of my Father who we learn had returned to Washington." The rebel troops set ablaze Montgomery Blair's house and then settled into Preston Blair's, where they "left demijohns of good Old Bourbon empty under the table & cleaned out the larder & poultry," Lizzie learned.

Grant quickly dispatched an army unit to protect the capital, much to her relief: "If the Rebels had massed on it as we left it, they had little to do but walk in," she fumed from the New Jersey shore. In Washington, the journalist Jane Swisshelm agreed: "When Early appeared before Washington, we all knew there was nothing to prevent his coming in and taking possession. The forts were stripped. There were no soldiers either in or around the city . . . so far as I knew, there was a universal expectation that the city would be occupied by rebel troops that night." Some of the women had been worried about exactly this event: "The total blindness & stupidity about this invasion was extraordinary. Any hint on my part of such a possibility was met with a scorn that withered my courage for any action but to get away with my sick mother," Lizzie Lee seethed, furious that no one would listen to her. She tried at the very least to coax her mother into having someone take her silver to the City: "No she would not have the house pulled to pieces." Now her mother was "for the first time in my memory *cut* down . . . moans over an old age in poverty, homeless & etc. til it makes my heart ache."

Louisa Meigs was also forced to flee. But unlike Lizzie she put no stock in a Rebel raid on Washington: "Knowing how completely it is defended by its chain of forts & also how futile our efforts have been to make an entrance into Richmond in all the raids which have been made for the purpose I have concluded that the people of the city were as safe as those elsewhere," she reasoned. If the Yankees couldn't take Richmond, why would the Confederates be able to take Washington? "I know however what an excitement must have been occasioned by rumors & reports of the advent of the enemy." A couple of days after those first bulletins, Lizzie Lee heard much more encouraging news. "Our losses by the Rebels are so small that can never think of the invasion without a sense of escape & thankfulness. All the crops were left just as they found them . . . all the horses are saved but two."

It turned out that John Breckinridge, a former senator, Buchanan's vice president, and cousin of Preston Blair, had "preserved Silver Spring & made more fuss about things there than if they had belonged to Jeff Davis." Breckinridge remembered his pleasant stays with the Blairs as "his place of refuge & of rest," and Lizzie believed "if our own Army had swarmed over us & encamped there for two days, it would have been quite as bad for us." She was especially cheered by reports that General Early told the neighbors "that the women & old men of Maryland were the bravest Union people he had ever yet met—Maryland women as a general thing gave the Secesh Army a cold welcome." Her mother "brightened up," and all in all they felt they had dodged a bullet. Meanwhile, Lincoln was literally dodging bullets: "Father says the President went to the front where the shot & shell fell thick around him."

The Rebels advanced as far as Fort Stevens, one of the defensive bastions built around Washington—a straight shot to the White House, only five miles away. The army that had been defending the capital was off in other battles with only a few militiamen, invalids, and clerks left behind. Once again, the city was cut off from the rest of the country: "We have no mail, no telegraphic communication, no railroad travel," Noah Brooks lamented. "The city is in a ferment; men are marching to and fro; able-bodied citizens are gobbled up and put into the District militia; refugees come flying in from the country, bringing their household goods with them."

The men Grant sent from Virginia arrived during the night of July 12 and took their position at Fort Stevens as the Rebels attacked. Once Early realized professional soldiers were at their posts he retreated, but not before the president almost got shot. He and Mrs. Lincoln decided to take in the action, so they went to the fort to watch. Curious to see better, the president climbed up on the parapet, there in his high-top hat in plain view of the enemy. When a bullet hit the person next to him, upset officers shouted to their commander in chief to take cover. If he had not, the course of war could have gone very differently, with an election still in the offing. Someone with much less determination to see the conflict through to victory might have easily won at the ballot box.

———

"MRS. LINCOLN WAS extremely anxious that her husband should be re-elected President of the United States," Elizabeth Keckley wrote, remembering all too well the conversations during the campaign. Mary was scheming with men of "a certain class" to get her husband elected, telling her dressmaker: " 'These men have influence, and we require influence to re-elect Mr. Lincoln. I will be clever to them until after the election, and then, if we remain at the White House, I will drop every one of them, and let them know very plainly that I only made tools of them.'" When Mrs. Keckley asked if the president knew about his wife's conniving, "'God! No; he would never sanction such a proceeding,' Mary retorted, shocked. 'He is too honest to take the proper care of his own interests, so I feel it to be my duty to electioneer for him.'"

Mary Lincoln's desperation to see her husband reelected stemmed from personal reasons as well as political ones: "'If he should be defeated, I do not know what would become of us all,' she confided; 'to me, to him, there is more at stake in this election than he dreams of.'" She had continued to accumulate debts, defensively telling Lizzie Keckley: "'To keep up appearances, I must have money—more than Mr. Lincoln can spare for me. He is too honest to make a penny outside of his salary.'" The distraught woman was nothing short of terrified but she couldn't stop herself. "Mrs. Lincoln ransacked the treasures of the Broadway dry good stores," the *New York Herald* shrieked on her last shopping spree just as the women of Washington were pledging their covenant against foreign finery. Mrs. Lincoln's niece later defended her aunt's choice of expensive imports, claiming that the first lady had been told it was her "patriotic duty" because the government needed the taxes paid on them. By the end of the summer a panicked Mary Lincoln had "no hope of the re-election of Mr. Lincoln." President Lincoln didn't have much hope of his reelection either.

He had been nominated on the ticket of the "National Union Party," a name the Republicans gave themselves in the hopes of reeling in Democrats committed to the war, as well as Radical Republicans. The president had finally rid himself of the biggest threat to unity inside his own administration—at the end of June he accepted Salmon Chase's fourth offer to resign as Treasury secretary. Chase was stunned. He expected Lincoln to do what he had always done, refuse the overture and smooth everything over. Not this time. The immediate cause of Chase's latest resignation letter was a disagreement over an appointment in the department. The secretary was stuffing Treasury with his supporters, still hoping that disillusion with the president would throw the race open. But the fact was, as President Lincoln put it with great understatement, "you and I have reached a point of mutual embarrassment in our official relation which it seems can not be overcome." Lincoln named the chairman of the Senate Finance Committee, William Pitt Fessenden of Maine, as Chase's successor.

"The news of the change in the Cabinet took us all by surprise," Lizzie Lee rejoiced as a member of the Blair family, Chase's longtime enemies. Fessenden, though "ill tempered," was "honest & as Mrs. Jeff once said the ablest of all the Republican Senators." Lizzie still remembered her friend Varina Davis's political views. (She had heard earlier that year that Varina had "grown grey & forlorn—is very unpopular & never has moved '*in any style*' in Richmond . . . & talks of the pleasures, friends & etc. she sacrificed 'in having to leave Washington.' This looks like a true picture to me." Varina missing Washington had an air of authenticity, even if it's what Lizzie wanted to believe.) Lizzie learned that her surprise was shared by the ousted Treasury secretary and that "there was a desperate effort made by Chase's friends to save him"; not surprisingly, the Blairs were blamed by Chase supporters for his downfall. Before he kept his commitment to return to Sherman's army, Missouri congressman Frank Blair, Lizzie's brother, made a scathing speech against the secretary. "It was a complete triumph—he made his opponents pop up & down in their seats." Tellingly, when members of Congress assembled at Blair House that night for a congratulatory celebration, "they were mostly Democrats," a fact that the family would come to have reason to regret.

With some bravado former cabinet member Chase told his

daughter Nettie, "I am heartily glad to be disconnected from the administration; though a little sorry to miss the opportunity of doing the great work I felt confident I could with God's blessing accomplish." Nettie was visiting with her sister in Rhode Island, where Kate was spending the summer and clearly fretting over her father's fate as well as itching to get to Washington to try to fix the situation. "Had I chosen I might have held on to the office," Chase falsely assured Kate. "I am very glad that you did not put your idea of coming here into execution. It would [have done] no good at all, & exposed you very unnecessarily." And then he advised her: "If you think me wronged or not appreciated, let nobody *think* you *think* so. People never sympathize with such feelings." Kate must have been feeling so left out of the political maneuverings and there was nothing for her in Rhode Island that could replace her lifelong vocation of electing her father. Things were not going well in the Sprague marriage after the "wedding of the century." When the senator was away from home he almost completely ignored his wife, hardly ever writing to her, and he had started drinking again. But the last person Sprague wanted to know about their problems was his father-in-law. He asked Kate not to "refer any of our differences to your father," warning her that confiding in Chase would "bring on a difference which cannot be healed."

As the summer wore on and the city of Washington filled with more and more of Grant's wounded, the president's reelection looked "deader than dead," in the gleeful words of a Democratic newspaper editor. Some Radical Republicans held on to hope that the party would call another convention to nominate a more electable candidate, and the Chase forces continued to believe their man had a chance. Jessie Frémont insisted to John Greenleaf Whittier that Lincoln couldn't win: "Someone else must be put in his place. It must be some one firm against slavery . . . and the General will thankfully retire & give his most active support to such a man." There was a good deal of pressure on her husband to withdraw and not split the Republican vote but he wouldn't pull out with Lincoln looking so weak. "Lincoln's stock is running down rapidly," Frémont supporter Elizabeth Cady Stanton cheered to Susan B. Anthony. Abraham Lincoln did not disagree.

"This morning, as for some days past, it seems exceedingly probable that this Administration will not be re-elected," the president wrote on August 23 in what has come to be called the "blind memo." He continued: "Then it will be my duty to so co-operate with the President elect as to save the Union between the election and the inauguration; as he will have secured his election on such ground that he can not possibly save it afterwards." It was signed, "A. Lincoln." The deeply discouraged president was sure that the Democrats would promise to end the war with a deal that would permanently destroy the Union, and he was determined to do everything he could to prevent that. He folded the paper in a way that its contents were hidden and then brought it to his cabinet members and asked them to sign it—sight unseen, hence "blind." Their signatures constituted a pledge to accept the results of the election even in the midst of civil war.

The sentiment against the president ran so strong that Jessie Frémont even thought the *Democrats* might support her Radical Republican husband to unify the dump-Lincoln movement. "Jessie never was in such feathers," Lizzie Lee fussed when she heard that some Democratic politicians had been to see her erstwhile friend, who told them "'F. will be nominated by the Chicago Convention as a *political necessity*' . . . there is no end to the nonsense she talks on this text." When the Democrats did meet in Chicago a few days after Lincoln penned the blind memo they nominated General George McClellan for president, a supporter of the war, but then added a "Peace Democrat," Congressman George Pendleton of Ohio, as the vice presidential candidate and inserted a peace plank in the party platform. The president's concerns had proved correct. Though McClellan didn't agree with the platform, his party adopted it and he was the nominee of the party. The way the war was going that summer, the prospect of peace at almost any price looked ever more appealing.

And then everything changed. No one paid much attention when Union admiral David Farragut sailed into Mobile Bay damning the torpedoes, but his capture of that southern port in early August suddenly became one more victory to celebrate when, on September 2, William Tecumseh Sherman's army stormed into Atlanta. Now the politicians suing for peace seemed faithless to the fighting forces. Lincoln's prospects brightened considerably as McClellan's dimmed but the president still had to worry about a split in his own party. He needed the Radical Republican to get out of the race. On September 22, General John C. Frémont withdrew his name. And the next day Lincoln asked Postmaster General Montgomery Blair to resign from his cabinet.

Was it a quid pro quo? Probably, whether it was spoken aloud or not. The Frémonts' resentment of the Blairs was no secret and Radical Republicans, disappointed that they no longer had a candidate in the race, could take satisfaction that their effort had run the most conservative member of the administration out of office. The powerful Blair family served as the symbol of everything those Republicans thought was wrong about Lincoln; Frank Blair's speech attacking Chase galled them and Democrats applauding it galled them even more. So Lizzie's brother would have to take the fall in order for Jessie's husband to do the right thing for the president the Blairs supported.

The patriarch, Preston Blair, deemed the decision "all for the best . . . the true interests of the Country require the reelection of Lincoln." His daughter Lizzie was not so sanguine: "I think I am more hurt than anybody else . . . but I can feel, rather *think* it is for the best

& *feel* uncomfortable at the same time." Preston Blair had sounded out McClellan and come to the conclusion that he would settle for peace with a still-separated Confederacy rather than insisting on union; his election would be a disaster for the country. Most of the Radicals, such as Wendell Phillips and Anna Dickinson, fell in line behind Lincoln, to the dismay of Elizabeth Stanton: "all this talk of the Republicans about loyalty and the good of the country requiring the success of their party is the merest twaddle," she griped to Susan Anthony. Years later Jessie Frémont revealed that three prominent Radical Republicans "came to Mr. Fremont and put before him the peril into which his continuing as a candidate put the success of our party. They were empowered to offer any terms in return for his withdrawing his name—among others the Blairs were not to be in any political position etc." But, Jessie insisted, when Frémont understood what he must do, "he not only withdrew his name but utterly refused any appointments, patronage or retaliation." That would be the end of Jessie and John Frémont's quests for the presidency. And by the middle of October the Union army would have control of Virginia's Shenandoah Valley. Lincoln's prospects dramatically improved.

The president also had a prime plum to offer one of the men of his party when long-serving Chief Justice Roger B. Taney, author of the *Dred Scott* decision, died on October 12. The old man had been failing and would-be successors had already lined up for his job. Lincoln loyalists Montgomery Blair, Secretary of War Edwin Stanton, and Attorney General Edward Bates all expressed interest. So did Salmon Chase. "I heard Mr. Chase had a long confab in his visit to the President yesterday after abusing him everywhere at the North," Lizzie Lee burst with the news. "Tis said he was going to Europe but Sumner persuaded him not to." Kate Sprague too told her father that "feeling seems to be very strong among your friends that you will not leave the country at this time. They seem to depend upon your aid for the coming Presidential Campaign." If Chase wanted the chief justice job, he had better stick around and campaign for Lincoln, and the newly empowered president would insist that Chase extend that aid in his behalf before any job offer was forthcoming.

Lincoln was running on a party platform that declared "we are in favor . . . of such an amendment to the Constitution . . . as shall terminate and forever prohibit the existence of Slavery within the limits of the jurisdiction of the United States." The Senate had passed the Thirteenth Amendment in the current Congress but it failed to achieve the necessary two-thirds vote of the House of Representatives. Fearful that the Emancipation Proclamation, which was enacted by executive order, could be undone by a new president, the amendment's backers enshrined it in the platform, making support for it the official position of the Republican candidate. Lincoln, who had been worried about the political consequences of the amendment, now endorsed it, and shortly before the election he met with one of its most prominent proponents. It was the seamstress Elizabeth Keckley who arranged for Abraham Lincoln to receive Sojourner Truth at the White House.

THE IMPOSING SIX-FOOT-TALL, deep-voiced woman in her sixties had made quite a name for herself since her 1851 speech at the Ohio Women's Rights Convention, when she famously asked, "Ain't I a Woman?" in response to a man's protestations that delicate women needed masculine protection. Pointing to her muscular arm and declaring, "I have ploughed and planted, and gathered into barns, and no man could head me! And ain't I a woman?" the former slave electrified the crowd, and she had been doing it ever since. The bestselling abolitionist author Harriet Beecher Stowe's article about Sojourner

Truth in the April 1863 *Atlantic Monthly* sealed the fame of the illiterate woman who made her living selling her life story, *Narrative of Sojourner Truth*, dictated to a friend.

Born into slavery in Ulster County, New York, before it was outlawed in that state, and given the name Isabella, she had escaped to freedom, but not before she had seen two children sold away from her. She worked for several years as a domestic in New York City but became an itinerant preacher, taking the name Sojourner Truth in 1843 as she walked through New York State and New England, singing and speaking at camp meetings and in churches. When she learned about the abolitionist movement she quickly signed up and brought its gospel west, preaching through Ohio, Indiana, Missouri, and Kansas. And then she learned about the women's rights movement and added that cause to her quiver. With the outbreak of the Civil War and the enlistment of African-American regiments, she solicited supplies for those troops and eventually ended up in Washington to work with the National Freedman's Relief Association, an organization similar to the Contraband Society started by Elizabeth Keckley. When Miss Truth arrived in the Capital City she stayed with fellow feminist Jane Swisshelm and made it known that she would like to meet the President of the United States.

At about eight in the morning on October 29, Sojourner Truth and Lucy Colman, another feminist and abolitionist, were ushered in to Lincoln's outer office: "On entering his reception room, we found about a dozen persons waiting to see him; amongst them were 2 coloured women, some white women also. One of the gentlemen present knew me, and I was introduced to several others, and had a pleasant time while waiting, and enjoyed the conversation between the President and his auditors very much. He showed as much respect and kindness to the coloured persons present as to the whites," Miss Truth assured a friend. When she was introduced she told the president that when he was first elected she thought he would be like Daniel in the lion's den, that if the lions didn't tear him to pieces it would be because God spared him; and she vowed that if God spared her, she would meet him before his term ended. When she pronounced him the best president in the history of the country, he responded that he assumed she was talking about emancipation; then he named past presidents, declaring, " 'they were just as good, and would have done just as I have, if the time had come. And if the people over the river . . . had behaved themselves, I could not have done what I have.' " It was southern secession that made abolition politically possible.

Lincoln then showed her a magnificently bound Bible given to him by the "coloured people"; she gave him some "songs and shadows" and asked him to sign her book. "And with the same hand that signed the death warrant for slavery . . . he wrote 'For Aunty Sojourner Truth, October 29, 1864, A. Lincoln.' " She left even more dedicated to the cause of freedom and equality: "I am proud to say that I never was treated with more kindness and cordiality than I was by the great and good man Abraham Lincoln, by the grace of God President of the United States for four years more." Truth's friend Lucy Colman saw the president's form of greeting—Aunty—as an insult and later penned a less flattering portrayal of the visit with Lincoln but Sojourner Truth was true to her word. She stayed in Washington working for a year in the Freedman's Camp set up on the grounds of Robert E. Lee's estate at Arlington, helping teach the former slaves how to get along in a world where no one provided food and clothing for them anymore, where they would have to find jobs and housing, and where they would have to fight for their rights.

And she kept fighting for her own. Like an early-day Rosa Parks, Sojourner Truth insisted on integrating the new Washington streetcar system. Blacks had to ride outside with the drivers of the segregated horse-drawn rail carriages but Miss Truth refused to do that on several occasions, and even managed a few times to get the conductors on the cars fired. When one of them tried to push her off a whites-only car she had him arrested for assault and battery, declaring, "It's hard for the old slave-holding spirit to die. But *die* it *must*."

———————

"WE ARE ALL excitement here over the election," the nurse Rebecca Pomroy exclaimed that fall. Though residents of the Federal City were denied the right to vote for president (and still have no voting representatives in Congress), the citizens of the city waged enthusiastic campaigns. A huge McClellan and Pendleton sign hung over Pennsylvania Avenue where politicians leading torchlight parades marched to oust the current resident on that thoroughfare. And a straw vote of students at Columbian College—now George Washington University—went to McClellan. Anna Ella Carroll supported the Democratic candidate as well. After attending the Republican convention in Baltimore in June and the Democratic one in Chicago in August, the prickly Miss Carroll abandoned Lincoln, convinced that his party's stand against slavery would destroy the Union, though she had emancipated her own slaves years earlier. But things were looking good for Abraham Lincoln as General Philip Sheridan pushed back a Confederate drive in the Shenandoah Valley, effectively ending the battle for control; the slave state of Maryland voted for emancipation and congressional elections in Pennsylvania, Ohio, and Indiana went Lincoln's way.

"A splendid torchlight procession," sponsored by the Lincoln and Johnson Club, followed the announcement of the Republican victories and impressed journalist Noah Brooks with the "detachment of convalescent wounded soldiers from the hospitals whose ambulances bore such mottoes as 'Ballots and Bullets,' 'We can Vote as well as Fight,' etc." The torches set the McClellan sign on fire and a big hubbub followed but the parade made an important point—the soldiers could vote and the president's people would make sure they did. "All my boys go for Lincoln, and I have no doubt he will be re-elected," Rebecca Pomroy exulted. "I would like to give my vote." The War Department organized to send those soldiers home to the polls. "Many of my boys have gone home on furloughs," the nurse observed in her empty ward as troops and government workers jammed into trains heading to Pennsylvania, Ohio, Maryland, and New York. "All who can by any possibility go home, are going," correspondent Lois Adams wrote approvingly, one of the men telling her, " 'it is not merely a majority that we want, but a majority so overwhelming—a mountain of Union votes so high that treachery, both North and South, shall be crushed out of existence.' " That soldiery spirit meant, Mrs. Adams was certain, that "a grand army of them will come up to the help of the Union, as fearlessly at the ballot-box as in the field."

On Election Day, November 8, the president took up his spot in the War Department next to the telegraph where he customarily waited for news from the front. This day it was election news he was anxious for the clattering machine to bring. When the early returns looked promising, Lincoln asked someone to go to the White House and tell his wife, because "she is more anxious than I." That was something Elizabeth Keckley knew all too well. Most satisfying to Abraham Lincoln in what turned out to be a landslide Electoral College victory, where he garnered 221 votes against McClellan's 21, was his overwhelming support among the soldiers. They had given a huge vote of confidence to their commander in chief. Two nights later, when a great crowd gathered on the White House lawn, the freshly affirmed president solemnly celebrated a remarkable feat: the election demonstrated that "a people's government can sustain a national election, in the midst of a great civil war. Until now it has not been known to the world that this was a possibility."

With the election over, President Lincoln needed to decide on a new chief justice and prepare for the lame-duck session of the old Congress. Plus he had to sit for about a half hour a day for seventeen-year-old sculptor Lavinia "Vinnie" Ream. The young woman had a government job in the dead letter office of the post office but once she had seen the Capitol sculptor Clark Mills's studio, she tried her hand at working clay and turned out to have a talent. She had persuaded other politicians to sit for her but the president refused until he learned that she was a poor girl who needed the work. It was an extraordinary assignment for any woman, much less such a young woman, and it led to her receiving the first congressional commission to a female artist. Her full-length statue of Lincoln stands today in the grand Rotunda of the Capitol.

The Capitol had been one of Abraham Lincoln's projects during his presidency. When the war broke out, work on the expansion of the building and the erection of the new dome stopped. But the president insisted that it start again, feeling that the completed "People's Building" would serve as a symbol of unity in the divided nation. And soon after the election, the newspapers were able to report that the work of many years was almost done: "The exterior of the dome is completed, and workmen are employed removing the scaffolding from the interior, which will leave the Rotunda open, and more clearly indicate the beauty of its proportions when finished." The Congress would be coming back to a building where members could see what the years of construction—of grounds strewn with blocks of marble and building equipment, of hallways made impassable by ladders, unlaid tiles, and paintbrushes—had produced. It would provide a much more complete stage for the coming inauguration, where for the first time in twenty-eight years the man standing on the East Portico swearing in the president of the United States would not be Roger B. Taney. It would be Salmon P. Chase.

Lincoln knew he was disappointing men who had been loyal to him, and infuriating his wife, in picking Chase, but he insisted the choice was right for the country. Still the president didn't show his hand to his former Treasury secretary's allies who had been hounding him. One of the Chase supporters, Congressman John Alley of Massachusetts, emerged from a meeting discouraged by what he heard from Lincoln: "He spoke of Mr. Chase's dislike of the President. He talked feelingly of the many hard things Mrs. Sprague, Mr. Chase's daughter, had said of the President." But in the end, Lincoln told Alley, "I ought not to blame Chase for the things his daughter said about me." Of course, Chase had said plenty of awful things himself and Lincoln's secretary John Hay marveled to his fiancée that no other man would have "the degree of magnanimity to thus forgive and exalt a rival who had so deeply and so unjustifiably intrigued against him." As for Lincoln, he simply worried that his choice had "'the White House fever' a little too bad, but I hope this may cure him and he will be satisfied." In fact, as with so many others who have caught that fever, in Chase's case it was incurable.

On December 15, Salmon Chase was sworn in as the sixth chief justice of the United States. His daughters, Nettie Chase and Kate Sprague, looked on "gorgeous in millinery," according to Noah Brooks. It was a little more than a week after the president had sent up his State of the Union address that embodied what Chase had been fighting for much of his political life. The message was a lengthy and tedious disquisition on the state of the world, the state of the government departments, the state of the country's finances, declaring the national resources "unexhausted" and "inexhaustible," and the still uncertain state of the war: "The most remarkable feature in the military operations of the year is General Sherman's attempted march of 300 miles directly through the insurgent region. . . . The result not yet being known, conjecture in regard to it is not here indulged." It was not designed to inspire.

But then President Lincoln underlined his most immediate goal: passage of the amendment outlawing slavery. Recognizing that this Congress was the same that had failed to approve the amendment earlier in the year, the president argued that his landslide election had shown the will of the people and the strong likelihood that the new Congress with its overwhelming Republican majority would approve the amendment, and so he posed the query: "Hence there is only a question of time as to when the proposed amendment will go to the States for their action. And as it is to so go at all events, may we not agree that the sooner the better?"

Of course not all in Congress did agree, but President Lincoln had put down his marker. The new year would bring fresh debate over outlawing and forever ending slavery in the United States of America. And then General Sherman sent his telegram:

SAVANNAH, GA., *December 22, 1864*
(Via Fort Monroe 6.45 p.m. 25th)
His Excellency President LINCOLN:
I beg to present you, as a Christmas gift, the city of Savannah, with 150 heavy guns and plenty of ammunition, and also about 25,000 bales of cotton.

W. T. Sherman,
Major General

The "remarkable feature" the president had spoken of—Sherman's "March to the Sea"—ended triumphantly, and in Nashville, Tennessee, the Confederate army had been totally defeated. "I now look to the end of the War," Lizzie Lee wrote to her long-absent husband, "but it must come soon."

CHAPTER 8

LEFT: *Mary Todd Lincoln, wife of Abraham Lincoln, created controversy throughout her tenure as First Lady and beyond, never mincing her opinions, political or personal.* RIGHT: *Julia Grant, deeply devoted to her husband, General Ulysses S. Grant, greatly enjoyed her time both in army camps and in the White House.*

One Mary Leaves, One Mary Hangs, and Lois Writes About It All

1865

O h you Rascal, I am overjoyed to see you," Varina Davis greeted Francis Preston Blair when he arrived in Richmond in early January. For his part, Blair reported that the First Lady of the Confederacy "never looked as well in her life, stout but fairer well dressed & even a better talker than ever." Elizabeth Blair Lee had received periodic reports of her friend over the years, but here was a firsthand account from her father, back from a secret mission for the Union. For some time the newspaper publisher Horace Greeley had been encouraging the senior Blair to use his connections with both Abraham Lincoln and Jefferson

Davis to try to initiate peace talks. The carnage on the battlefields had reached such horrendous numbers that even dedicated Unionists were looking for some way to end the war. So Blair devised an excuse to go to Richmond. He claimed that important papers had been taken from his house at Silver Spring during the Confederate invasion that summer and that he needed to find out if someone in the Rebel capital knew what had happened to them.

Lincoln, who trusted the old newspaperman and thought there would be no harm in him sounding out Jefferson Davis, issued Blair passes to go through Union lines to Richmond and return, though the family was nervous about the seventy-three-year-old setting out in such cold weather. "He feels that tis *a call* of duty & that no one must now shrink from that in these days of trial & trouble," Lizzie fretted, "& will not return until he sees my Oakland patient for her good & ours I hope." She knew that her husband could decipher her code—he would remember how Lizzie had nursed the terribly sick Varina Davis when they all spent a summer together in Oakland, Maryland, a few long years ago. Despite the efforts at secrecy, word of Blair's trip got out and Lizzie found herself quizzed at parties, but "luckily most people begin with the story about his papers," so that ruse seemed to be working; "the Rebel papers announce his arrival in Richmond." While he was there, Blair presented a far-fetched scheme whereby North and South would pause the war to come together to challenge the French, who had installed a puppet regime in Mexico. The unauthorized proposal provided an opening for further talks and Blair came home with the report that Davis would send commissioners to Washington "with a view to secure peace between the two countries."

Her father arrived "overwhelmed with the excitement & fatigue of the past 10 days," to a relieved Lizzie, who felt "no small sense of joy to know that he is in his own bed & sleeping with Mother by his

side happier than I have known her to be for sometime past." Refusing as always to recognize the concept of "two countries," Lincoln
dispatched Blair back to Davis with the message that the President
of the United States would receive commissioners "with a view of
securing peace to the people of our one common country." With
that missive in hand, "Another visit to my Oakland patients is to be
made," Lizzie confided to Phil. "I hope it will cure all their maladies." Her attempts at communicating in code were comical—it was
the height of the social season and everywhere she went people were
talking about her father's meetings and pumping her for information. To one pointed inquiry: "I replied I knew nothing of the Davis'
since the war & descanted on Mrs. Davis as I knew her tone, her wit
& etc." The newspapers were full of Blair intrigue, though no one
knew what it might be.

———————

SPECULATION ABOUT THE mission was just one of many distrac-
tions that January in postelection Washington. The annual New
Year's "squeeze," held on January 2 because the first of the month was
a Sunday, revealed the toll taken on the White House by the Lincolns'
open-door policy of allowing anyone to wander around the mansion.
The rooms that Mary had so splendidly refurbished at such great cost
now looked shabby and shamefully vandalized. Tourists and invited
guests alike not only stained the settees with dirty shoes and ruined
the rugs with tobacco juice, but they actually carved up the carpets
and curtains, cutting out large swaths of fabric as souvenirs. "The
edges of the carpets have been snipped off wherever they could be
got at by scissors or knife, and so presented the appearance of having
been nibbled at by a regiment of rats in pursuit of winter-bedding,"
Lois Adams informed the readers of the *Detroit Advertiser and Tribune*.

"Last fall from the drapery of one window in the Green Room silk enough had been abstracted to make a good sized apron." A government clerk herself, Mrs. Adams was horrified to discover that one of the perpetrators of the pilferage was "a salaried clerk in one of the Government Departments!" When the man was fired from his job, he "proved himself a genuine son of Adam," laughed the moonlighting reporter. "He said, 'The women who were with me, they tempted me and I did steal.'"

Another group of women arrived at the White House with a more constructive agenda item. A protest meeting of workingwomen in Philadelphia had voted to deputize a committee to call on President Lincoln to petition for the restoration of their former pay scale at the arsenal there. They had been working directly for the government making uniforms for the soldiers but the military brass decided to contract out the work, and the contractors were reducing both the number of assignments and the pay for each item, so the women's incomes had dropped substantially. Refusing to take the cuts without a fight, the women formed a labor-union type association, called a mass meeting, and decided on political action. Newspapers covering the session printed the series of resolutions the women adopted, including: "*Resolved*, That we appeal to Abraham Lincoln, the President of the United States, in whom we recognize an honest man, the noblest work of God, and trust and firmly believe he will have the arsenal work restored." A committee was appointed and the very next day the members came to Washington to put their case before the president. They succeeded in extracting a message from Lincoln to the office of the Quartermaster General with the instruction that "if he could administer his department as to secure employment for the women at the wages ordinarily paid, he would regard it as a personal favor, provided he could do so without interfering with the public interest or disturb private contracts." The direct intervention of the president did improve the women's situation, at least for a while.

The war and its implications for workers no longer topped the city's conversations when the Smithsonian Institution caught fire. "The loss is very serious, including the lecture-room, the philosophical instrument apartment and most of the valuable instruments," the *New York Times* reported on January 25, the day after the destruction of a large part of the cultural center built from the legacy of the Englishman James Smithson. Lois Adams had been looking at paintings in one of the exhibit halls just minutes before "the roof over that part fell crashing in, and the immense room with all its contents, was one seething mass of flames." Crowds gathered in the ice and snow, among them Lizzie Lee, who fumed at the sight. "I saw the Smithsonian Institute burn down today with real sorrow, it was lost by the most miserable imbecility in the Fire Dept." Apparently the alarm box froze, delaying the arrival of the firefighters, and in the interim, according to the *Washington Star*, "Much damage was done to articles removed in consequence of the crazy manner in which they were thrown from the windows by excited individuals." And a few days later there was a murder at the Treasury building.

"Miss Mary Harris, of Chicago, killed Mr. Burroughs, a clerk in the Treasury Department, by shooting him through the heart. The tragedy has created a good deal of sensation in the United States," reported the *Richmond Daily Dispatch*, just one of many papers screaming the story. After she was arrested Miss Harris told a reporter that Burroughs had promised to marry her "and she killed him for not keeping his promise. . . . She had loved him, she said, since she was a child, and though he had at one time urged her to marry him, which was opposed by her parents, he had since married another." Apparently Mary Harris had originally intended simply to sue the spurner, but: "'A few days before starting from Chicago (two weeks ago), I was walking along the street and saw some pistols in a shop window. Having learned that many of the ladies in Chicago carried pistols, especially when traveling, I determined to buy one . . . the day that I left Chicago I examined the printed directions upon the wrapper accompanying the pistol and cartridges, and by following them, succeeded in loading it.'"

That success was unfortunate for Burroughs, though Miss Harris claimed she still had no intention of using the gun, which she carried—loaded—with her to the Treasury Building. She hid herself under a headscarf and veil, asked where to find her target's office, worked up the courage to push open the door, "and saw him at his desk. The moment I looked at him, sitting there so comfortably, the thought of all I had suffered, and of his being the cause, enraged me, and my hand involuntarily pulled back the trigger of the pistol in my pocket." Unseen by Burroughs, she closed the door and waited. "'Then I placed myself where I know he would have to come near me in going to the staircase. When he appeared, I felt suddenly lifted up, my arm was extended as stiff as iron, and I saw him fall. I knew nothing more until I was called back as I was leaving the building.'"

Miss Harris insisted "there had been nothing improper between her and Mr. Burroughs." And further reporting by the newspaper determined that Burroughs was an upstanding citizen: "He attended the Baptist church in this city with his wife every Sunday." The grieving widow believed her husband had always tried to help the distraught young woman and he rejoiced when he thought, erroneously as it turned out, that she had happily married. The murderess, the newspaperman wanted his readers to know, "is of good figure, rather slight; has a well-formed head, dark hazel eyes, fine hair, which seemed, in the light in which we saw it, to be black, cut short and worn in curls; is graceful in her manners; naturally intelligent." Several members of Congress were seen visiting the young lady "of good figure" in her jail cell and for once the city had something to talk about other than war and politics. But that could never last for long.

───────────

WHILE PRESTON BLAIR pursued peace in Richmond, a combined operation of the federal army and navy took Fort Fisher, North Carolina, meaning that the last open port of the Confederacy—Wilmington—would soon be under Union control. Robert E. Lee had told his civilian commanders that without Wilmington he would not be able to supply his army, which was being hammered by Grant and Sheridan's forces in Virginia. And while the armies fought it out, the politicians debated *for the last time* the issue that started the war in the first place—slavery. On January 6, as Lincoln had requested in his State of the Union message, the House of Representatives once again took up the Thirteenth Amendment to the Constitution:

SECTION 1. **Neither slavery nor involuntary servitude, except as a punishment for crime whereof the party shall have been duly convicted, shall exist within the United States, or any place subject to their jurisdiction.** SECTION 2. **Congress shall have power to enforce this article by appropriate legislation.**

That was it. The bondage that had caused so much bloodshed could be wiped away by an aye vote on those two simple sentences.

"The large majority in Congress will clean out slavery in a regular lawful way, which will settle that question for all time I hope," Lizzie Lee, the former slave owner, declared soon after the big Democratic defeat in the fall elections. Believing that party members had been "chastened" by their losses, as they often are when they meet in a lame-duck session, she thought the House would answer the president's call to pass the amendment sooner rather than later: "A large number of Democrats are willing to vote for it now. Our people are working hard for it." Not only were the Blairs working it hard; so was the President of the United States. He called Democratic congressmen to the White House and reminded them that he could offer them or their friends and family all kinds of perks, positions, or pardons because of his "immense power." Lincoln's main message—the South would see that the Border States no longer supported slavery. The game would be up, and the war would soon end. But then whispers of a Peace Commission began to circulate. If the war was going to end anyway, why should these Democrats go out on a limb on an issue that could offend many constituents, not to mention the leaders of their party? Those leaders were warning that passage of the amendment would kill any peace attempts the emissaries might propose. Fortunately for Lincoln, the congressional rumors had it that the commissioners were coming to Washington, so the president was able to assure his supporters truthfully that "there are no peace commissioners in the City, or likely to be in it."

The conversations about peace were taking place elsewhere. Preston Blair had returned to Richmond with Lincoln's message that he would discuss peace for "our one common country." After some discussion, Jefferson Davis decided to name commissioners with vague instructions and send them to Washington. On January 29 the three-man Rebel delegation had made it as far as City Point, Virginia, where the Union army was camped. From there they would need passes to cross through enemy lines. Their arrival was telegraphed to Lincoln, who sent a message insisting that they agree in writing to the "one country" basis for negotiations before proceeding farther. The instructions bought Lincoln time. The vote on the Thirteenth Amendment was scheduled for the afternoon of January 31.

"Big Guns fired over the passage of the act to amend the Constitution prohibiting slavery forever," Lizzie Lee wrote as Washington celebrated with cannons and choirs after the vote. "They passed it by six more than enough, which was four more than they expected." All of the lobbying by her family and the president had paid off, plus "the rumor that the mission was a failure got abroad." If the peace mission had indeed fallen apart, perhaps passage of the amendment would hasten an end to the bloodshed. Southern leaders would be demoralized, the argument went, knowing that the rest of the country had rejected slavery. "The galleries, corridors, and lobbies were early crowded with an expectant assemblage . . . even the sacred precincts of the floor of the House were swarming with anxious magnates and semi-officials," an excited Noah Brooks recounted. Salmon Chase was circulating on the House floor along with his longtime rival Montgomery Blair—the two former cabinet members on the same side of this momentous question. "Ladies in fine dresses occupied the boxes around the main floor, and many held seats usually reserved for the press. NO desk was unattended, no aisle unfilled," *Harper's Weekly* reported in sketching the scene.

As the tense final debate began, the outcome remained uncertain. The men who had voted against the amendment in the first session of Congress stood to explain their changes of heart, opponents had their last say, and then the roll was called. Speaker Colfax asked that his own name be read so that he could be recorded on this historic issue. And then the Speaker announced the results: 119 yea, 56 nay (8 members deliberately did not vote, making it easier to achieve the two-thirds mark of "those present and voting"). "Thereupon rose a general shout of applause. The members on the floor huzzaed in chorus with the galleries. The ladies in the House assemblage waved their handkerchiefs, and again and again the applause was repeated. The audience were wildly excited and the friends of the measure jubilant." The *Cleveland Daily Leader*'s story appeared in a column under the headlines:

Slavery Forever Abolished
Ten Thousand Cheers for Freedom
All Honor to the 38th Congress

President Lincoln signed the amendment the next day, though a presidential signature on a constitutional amendment is not required, and immediately the states began ratifying it. Illinois did that very day. A less noticed but also momentous event occurred the day after the vote when Chief Justice Salmon Chase admitted the first black man to the Supreme Court bar. The high court that had handed down the *Dred Scott* decision not quite eight years earlier now would see an African American arguing before it. Moreover, the lawyer for Scott's owners, Senator Reverdy Johnson, had voted for the amendment forever outlawing the institution of slavery. Only one thing marred the joy of the victorious antislavery forces—on February 2, President Lincoln traveled to Fort Monroe in Norfolk to negotiate with the Confederate delegation. The Radical Republicans, who had never trusted Abraham Lincoln in the first place, now worried that he would sell them out for a quick peace.

Lincoln made his decision to meet the Rebel commissioners himself after he received a communication from General in Chief Ulysses S. Grant. Without expectations of success, given what he viewed as Jefferson Davis's intransigence, the president had chosen Secretary of State Seward to deal with the three-man Confederate team. But Grant had been talking with the men while they waited at his camp and he had come to believe that they sincerely wanted to end the war. When the general telegraphed that message to Washington, Lincoln set out at once to see if he could stop the fighting that had sacrificed hundreds of thousands of lives.

The answer was no, he could not. As Lincoln and Seward discussed terms with the three southerners on board the *River Queen* in what's come to be called the Hampton Roads Peace Conference, the president held fast to his insistence that a cease-fire of any kind could only be ordered if the South agreed to reunification. Otherwise, all those lives would have been lost in vain; the North had gone to war to save the Union. Other topics were discussed—the president raised the possibility of the government compensating southern slaveholders for their loss of property—in what were described as friendly and informal talks where no notes were taken and no one but the principals present. But in the end, the two sides were no closer than they had been. The war would go on. General Sherman had moved his army out of Savannah and was ready to begin his march through the state that had started it all, South Carolina.

———————

THE JOINT SESSION of Congress held to announce the official Electoral College vote count on February 8 was a humdrum affair, as they usually are. None of the anxiety that hovered over the event four years earlier marred the meeting this time around. But a few days later there was some excitement in the Capitol as it filled with "soldiers, officers, civil and military members of Congress, strangers, and citizens, with their wives and daughters," for a first-of-its-kind event. A black man would be "preaching against slavery from the Speaker's desk in the House of Representatives," Lois Adams marveled. "The galleries were thronged on all sides, the majority of the occupants being of the dusky race." Following a hymn sung by the choir of his 15th Street Presbyterian Church, Rev. Henry Highland Garnet, a former slave, called on Congress to "Emancipate, Enfranchise and Educate." A wide-eyed Mrs. Adams posed the question: "After an event like this the world may well ask: 'what next?'" The immediate reply came from Sherman's army marching through South Carolina.

"The birthday of Washington, crowned by the glorious news of the fall of Charleston and the re-occupation of Fort Sumter by loyal troops, fired the populace with a wilder enthusiasm than has been caused by any other event or combination of events since the war began," Lois Adams excitedly informed her Detroit readers. The symbolism of the Union retaking the first field of battle gave the capital an excuse to celebrate, with "gay, rejoicing crowds" streaming into the streets. Flags flew from every "tower and spire and flag staff" and at noon all the forts surrounding the city fired cannons for a solid hour, "till the very earth trembled." At the "superbly draped and festooned with flags and ensigns" War Department hung "a large transparency bearing these words: SUMTER 1861.UNION.SUMTER 1865." It seemed like the war might actually be coming to an end.

Confederate deserters appeared daily in the capital—more than one thousand came in February, almost three thousand in March—to take the oath of allegiance to the Union; they would no longer fight what was clearly a losing battle. Another southern soldier also showed up in town, this one still loyal to the cause. Roger Pryor, the firebrand former congressman from Virginia, had been released from Fort Lafayette, the Union prison on an island in New York harbor, and was now in Washington calling on the president with a request. Here was the man who had pressed for the attack on Fort Sumter as a way to induce his state to secede now coming as a supplicant to the "Black Republican" whose election Pryor had declared sufficient reason to leave the Union.

But Pryor had allies. He had been a newspaper editor, and other newspaper editors—Horace Greeley in New York and Washington McLean in Ohio, along with John W. Forney, a former Pryor colleague at the *Washington Union*—petitioned for their Rebel friend's release. First General Grant said no; then Secretary of War Stanton much more emphatically said no: "He shall be hanged! Damn him!" So the editors took their case to the president. Lincoln, knowing that Pryor had treated Union prisoners well earlier in the war and that his wife, Sara, had fed federal soldiers at Petersburg, Virginia, signed the parole. Here then was the hotheaded former lawmaker back in the city Sara loved so well, asking the president for a stay of execution for a Confederate soldier sentenced to death. Lincoln didn't grant the reprieve, but he did protect Pryor's whereabouts from his infuriated secretary of war and then sent the parolee on to General Grant to effect a prisoner exchange. Here was one Rebel soldier who would be going home to his wife.

"GREAT PREPARATIONS ARE being made for the second inauguration of President Lincoln," Lois Adams observed a couple of weeks before the event. People from all over the country swarmed into town to partake of the festivities, as the Congress feverishly tried to finish up its work. Mary Lincoln invited Lizzie Lee and her niece Elizabeth Blair to go to the Capitol with her to witness the typically chaotic closing hours of the Thirty-Eighth Congress. "Mrs. L was kind & confidential," Lizzie contentedly told her husband. Hordes of Washingtonians were there that night, including the well-known actor John Wilkes Booth, and many visitors as well. "Halls are crowded with strangers, thousands of them witnessing for the first time these august assemblies of the nation's lawgivers," Mrs. Adams looked on the spectacle with dismay. "With shame be it said, they too often witness scenes fitter to be enacted in the bar-room of a country tavern than in these national halls of legislation."

The lawmakers churned out bills far into the night as the president sat in the ornate room off the Senate chamber either signing them into law or not. One that he did affix his signature to: the creation of a Freedmen's Bureau to assist former slaves, the first federal government social welfare agency. A few hours' sleep and a huge thunderstorm capped the night. Early the next morning Lincoln arrived at the Capitol alone to deal with the last of the legislative list, so he missed the muddy procession that had been planned for his journey from the White House, leaving Mary Lincoln to be escorted by the President's Union Light Guard.

With the rain letting up just in time, the parade "embraced two regiments of the invalid corps, detachments of cavalry and artillery, several companies of colored troops (a most unusual spectacle on such an occasion), and numerous civic dignitaries and associations," recounted the *Vermont Transcript*. Dignitaries crowded into the Senate chamber, with ladies filling the galleries, as the current vice president, Hannibal Hamlin, prepared to swear in his successor, Andrew Johnson. But before he took the oath the vice-president-to-be delivered an incoherent, rambling speech, leading everyone to assume that he was more than slightly drunk. One newspaper kindly reported that the speech "was almost inaudible on account of the talking of the women in the galleries," but it did print the now-infamous story of Johnson turning to the cabinet members and addressing them by name until he came to the secretary of the navy, at which point he asked "(to a gentleman near by, sotto voce, 'who is secretary of the navy?' The person addressed replied in a whisper, 'Mr. Welles.')" Nobody could make him stop and everyone, including Lincoln, sat there in embarrassed horror until Johnson finally wound down. It's the kind of performance that's never forgotten in Washington.

But for the moment, it was on to the main event. Abraham Lincoln strode through the Capitol corridors, into the resplendent Rotunda, and out onto the East Portico to a platform before the now-completed grand dome. There, as the sun emerged from the clouds, he pledged with "malice toward none; with charity toward all . . . to finish the work we are in; to bind up the nation's wounds; to care for him who shall have borne the battle, and for his widow, and his orphan—to do all which may achieve a just and lasting peace among ourselves, and with all nations." As Lincoln took the oath and kissed the Bible, the crowd of forty thousand people stretching over the Capitol grounds, on across to the Old Capitol Prison and the buildings beyond, cheered boisterously while cannons boomed their applause. Sitting on a platform for honored guests was John Wilkes Booth, courtesy of one of his girlfriends, the daughter of a former senator from New Hampshire. Booth could have ended it all right then but Lincoln would live to see the South surrender.

"He is going back to the White House, a second time made President by a freedom loving people," Lois Adams celebrated, though the "mud was deep, and prancing horses splashed it upon each other and upon the people, but nobody seemed to care." In the parade of military men, firemen, policemen, "each with banners and bands of music," there marched "part of a colored regiment, a large company of colored Odd Fellows in full regalia." As Lincoln rode in an open carriage with his young son Tad by his side and Mary Lincoln followed in a carriage of her own, amid all the pageantry one float particularly stood out to the reporter. It represented the "Temple of Freedom," and "within this temple, as one of its pillars, stands a black man. He is at the rear end of the edifice, but the tallest man in it, and the only one standing." Assuring her readers of the symbolism of the day, Mrs. Adams finished with what lay ahead for the president: "Tonight he holds a levee at the White House, and everybody will be there to shake his hand in congratulation. So the Inauguration day passes in peace."

Thousands did shake Lincoln's hand over more than three hours straight. "Everybody was there, and we should say everybody's relations," the correspondent for the Wisconsin *Appleton Motor* beheld the "great jam" with amazement. He, like many others, commented on the "care-worn appearance" of the president, who had lost about thirty pounds and been up much of the night before. Lincoln's newly installed bodyguard remembered the reception for the "havoc it wrought. The White House looked as if a regiment of rebel troops had been quartered there—with permission to forage. . . . A great piece of red brocade, a yard square almost, was cut from the window-hangings of the East Room . . . some arrests were made after the reception, of persons concerned in the disgraceful business." It was almost impossible to manage these huge White House receptions.

In order to protect the president, the security forces had recently initiated a system that required visitors to check their wraps before greeting the first couple. "It would be the easiest thing in the world for a would-be assassin to smuggle weapons in under the voluminous cloaks then worn," the bodyguard William Crook explained. But he hadn't reckoned with one insistent guest who "wore a wrap that completely hid her dress. She could have brought in a whole arsenal of weapons under its folds." When he told the "handsome young woman" that she had to check her cloak she became indignant: "'Do you know who I am?' she demanded, haughtily." When the poor security man admitted he did not, she told him, "'I am Mrs. Senator Sprague.'" Crook recalled, "I had heard of Kate Chase Sprague, of course, as had everyone else in Washington," but he explained, she still had to remove her cloak. It was a dicey moment and he still smarted about it years later.

The pregnant Mrs. Senator Sprague didn't draw much attention at the Inaugural Ball, held on March 6 at the Patent Office building. It was her younger sister Nettie, in "rich white moire antique with bertha and skirt of point lace," who garnered the press coverage as she arrived on the arm of the eminently eligible General Joseph Hooker. Also of note to the *Cleveland Daily Leader* correspondent was Miss Harlan, the daughter of Iowa senator James Harlan, who accompanied the president's son, Robert Lincoln. "This couple attracted much attention, by reason of certain rumors of more than ordinary feelings of friendship towards each other, which may lead to a more lasting attachment." (The couple married three years later.) And then there was the famous author E.D.E.N. Southworth wearing a "heavy black velvet dress, trimmed with black lace."

But of course the most coverage went to the first lady, who entered the ballroom escorted by Senator Charles Sumner, giving joy to his Radical Republican colleagues. "Mrs. Lincoln was attired in faultless taste. She wore . . . a splendidly and most elaborately worked white lace dress over the silk skirt. A bertha of point lace and puffs of silk, and a white fan trimmed with ermine and silvered spangles, white kid gloves and lace handkerchief, and a necklace, bracelet and earrings of pearls. Her hair was brushed closely back from the forehead and a head-dress, composed of a wreath of white jasmines and purple violets, with long-trailing vine, completed a most *recherché* costume." As for Mr. Lincoln, he "was dressed in a full suit of black, with white kid gloves." And the correspondent added in amazement, "Among other curious features we noticed several ladies whose locks were powdered with silver and golden dust."

Those white kid gloves always worn by President Lincoln had special meaning for Mrs. Lincoln's friend and seamstress, Elizabeth Keckley. All through the election Mrs. Keckley had been assuring Mary that her husband would win. To prove how certain she was, the dressmaker asked a favor: "I should like for you to make me a present of the right-hand glove that the President wears at the first public reception after his second inaugural." Mary was somewhat taken aback since the glove would "be so filthy when he pulls it off, I shall be tempted to take the tongs and put it in the fire." As Lizzie Keckley wrote those words in her memoir, her most prized possession was President Lincoln's glove.

———

ONE WEEK AFTER the inauguration, Sherman's army, having slashed its way through South Carolina, moved into Fayetteville, North Carolina. With more and more of the country under Union control, supplying the armies of occupation became a major task. Quartermaster General Montgomery Meigs went to assist Sherman. "As he expected to be quite independent having his own party & all his own arrangements he concluded to let Monty accompany him," Louisa Meigs told her sister. Montgomery Meigs Jr. had just turned eighteen and was "highly delighted" at his mother's insistence that his father take him along because this might be the only opportunity he would have "to see anything of the Army life." It's somewhat surprising that Louisa wanted to expose her surviving son to the military; she had been having a very hard time since the death of her beloved firstborn, John Rodgers Meigs, who was shot and killed by Confederate soldiers five months earlier under circumstances that remained murky.

Fellow soldiers thought the twenty-two-year old army engineer had been murdered in cold blood, not shot down in battle, and outrage over the death led them to burn down the town of Dayton, Virginia, in retaliation. The president and cabinet attended John's funeral but the shows of sympathy, "letters from every quarter . . . to assure us how much he was loved, & what a reputation he had already achieved," only contributed to Louisa's grief. Unable to shake her heartbreak, she sadly explained to her sister, "It seems an increase of agony to know what a brilliant future was before him. All that he was, and all that we have is lost." The death of the boy she had nagged to start taking dancing lessons and stop biting his nails left her in deep despondency. "I love much to sit alone for I find even the cheerful conversation of the family often jars upon me," she wrote the month after John died. "It cannot be expected that anyone can mourn as I do, I, *the Mother* who bore him and have lost him." How many hundreds of thousands of other mothers were pounded with that pain as the war entered its fourth year?

While Sherman marched north through the Carolinas, Grant prepared to launch his spring campaign against Lee's army in Virginia. But first, at his wife Julia's instigation, the general invited the president to come to his camp at City Point. "The papers daily announced the exhausted appearance of the President," Julia Grant reasoned, so "I petitioned the General with hospitable intent to invite Mr. and Mrs. Lincoln down to visit the army." Though several of

Lincoln's advisors thought the trip was unsafe, he made up his mind to go anyway, then Mary and Tad decided to come along. Robert Lincoln had finally joined the army, against his mother's wishes, and was serving on Grant's staff—this would be a chance to see him as well as to enjoy some nice spring weather outside the city. The party, along with Lincoln's bodyguard and Mary's maid, boarded the *River Queen*, the same ship on which the Hampton Roads Peace Conference had fallen apart, and under the protection of Captain Penrose of the army and with the expert navigation of Captain Bradford of the navy, they set out on March 23 to sail down the Potomac, headed for Chesapeake Bay and then the James River.

By the time they docked at City Point the night of the twenty-fourth all of Washington was wondering what was going on. "There is much talk about the object of the President's visit to the Army & its peace purpose," Lizzie Lee informed her husband. If fighting continued, it was the fault of the stubborn southern politicians, she protested: "the Leaders alone are for keeping up the war & there was a regiment of deserters passing here yesterday." Lizzie had a patient in her charge—after his disgraceful performance at the inauguration, Vice President Andrew Johnson had been bundled off to "recuperate" at Silver Spring, where the Blairs, a political family of the same ideological stripe, could keep an eye on him.

At City Point, the Grants welcomed their guests, and as Julia noted: "Our gracious President met us at the gangplank, greeted the General most heartily, and, giving me his arm, conducted us to where Mrs. Lincoln was awaiting us." The men went off to talk privately, leaving the women by themselves. An awkward moment followed when Julia sat on the same settee as Mary. When the first lady seemed offended, the general's wife offered apologies. It was just the beginning of what would be a disastrous visit for Mary Lincoln.

When the party went to review the troops, the men traveled on horseback to the parade area. Mrs. Lincoln and Mrs. Grant rode in a bumpy Army ambulance and arrived after the exercises had begun. The wife of General Edward Ord, jauntily dressed in a "Robin Hood" hat with a large feather, galloped up on her horse to greet them and encountered an incensed Mary Lincoln. She was furious that Mrs. Ord had been riding in the place of honor next to the president, the place where she should be. The first lady proceeded to dress down the general's wife in such withering language that Mrs. Ord left in tears. Neither the president nor anyone else could reason with his wife, who ranted into the night, heaping abuse on her husband and demanding that he fire General Ord. After that Mary took to her stateroom for the next few days, probably too embarrassed to emerge.

"It is believed here that there is a huge fight going on between Gen[era]l Grant and Gen[era]l Lee's armies," Lizzie Lee advised her husband on March 27. "This idea may have been induced by the fact that the President was expected here early today but his non arrival has started dame rumor in fresh business." Lincoln was still at City Point when William Tecumseh Sherman showed up at the army camp. Consulting with Grant, the two generals came to the conclusion that there would be one more bloody battle ahead. The military men then reported to their posts for what they fervently hoped would be the last push of the long war. President Lincoln waited vigil at City Point. Everyone assumed he was working on a peace deal, especially after Secretary of State Seward joined him. "The peace talk is on every lip as the wish is in all our hearts," Lizzie wrote. "I fear there is a huge battle going for these two days --there is an anxious look about some people's faces . . . this seems now to be a *crisis* & everybody watches the signs as events are now so portentous." What was it? Peace? A major battle? Both? No one knew. But on April 1, Seward returned, bringing the secluded Mary Lincoln with him and leaving her husband and son behind on the James River.

The president could see the flash of cannon fire from his ship that night as Grant's army, including Robert Lincoln, besieged the Rebel defenses of Petersburg. He kept Mary apprised of the action through a stream of telegrams and then the next day rode out to see it for himself. That night Lincoln received the word he had been waiting for from Grant—the long-fought-over prize would soon be his. The end of the war was truly in sight. On April 3, the Union army took possession of Petersburg; Grant sent for the president to meet him in the forsaken town. The starved survivors told Lincoln's bodyguard that they were grateful that the army had come. Also, "a little girl came up with a bunch of wild flowers for the President. He thanked the child for them kindly, and we rode away." Back at City Point, they learned that the Confederate government had fled. Richmond had been evacuated.

The newspapers trumpeted the news: "Glory!!! Hail Columbia!!! Halleluia!!! Richmond Ours!!!" From the War Department, Secretary Stanton delivered a prayer of thanksgiving to the expectant crowd outside: "Praise God from whom all blessings flow." The people took up the hymn, "then added the 'Star Spangled Banner,' and finished up with Yankee Doodle and deafening cheers," Lois Adams marveled. "People seem almost to have gone mad with joy." The government agencies shut down, as did most shops; public schools allowed the children to join in the glee. "Flags were up everywhere, and bands of music; and impromptu processions were got up, marching here and there . . . cannon from the far-encircling forts rolled their white wreaths around the horizon and shout victory and freedom across the broad valley where the city lies." In Elizabeth Keckley's shop her workers "were particularly elated, as it was reported that the rebel capital had surrendered to colored troops."

Louisa Meigs was not ready to join in the celebration, but with Montgomery Meigs still in North Carolina, one of his men brought her a flag to display. "I told him I thought it unnecessary as Gen[era]l M was absent & for myself I had too sad a heart to wish to make any show of rejoicing." The soldier advised her to "show some sympathy with the National feeling," so she followed her friends and neighbors and raised her flag. Her husband's reaction: "You were very right dear Lou to put up the Flags." The next night all the public buildings and many private ones appeared as cathedrals of candlelight, and thousands of fireworks blazed into the sky over the Capital City, creating one shining scene of unrestrained (and not-so-sober) exultation. When she came in from Silver Spring, Lizzie Lee "found this city in a tumult of great joy over the fall of Richmond," but for herself, "I confess to great disappointment when I found the Rebels had escaped."

From the battlefield, Robert E. Lee had sent word to Jefferson Davis that the army could no longer defend Richmond. The Confederate president quickly fled—his wife and children were waiting in Charlotte, North Carolina, for word from him of what they should do next. The breakaway states no longer had a capital and had very little left of an army. Despite the danger, Abraham Lincoln decided to visit the city the Union had tried for so many years to topple. He and Tad and the bodyguard, Captain Crook, traveled up the booby-trapped river, maneuvering around sunken boats and dead horses and torpedoes edging so close "that we could have put out our hands and touched them." As they approached the city they saw crowds of gleeful African Americans lining the riverbanks. "They had heard that

President Lincoln was on his way . . . by the time we were on shore hundreds of black hands were outstretched to the President."

Soldiers formed a protective phalanx around Lincoln as he "walked up the streets of Richmond not thirty-six hours after the Confederates had evacuated." Nervously they stepped through the empty streets, aware that someone might come out from behind a building, or raise a window and shoot at any minute. Captain Crook was much relieved when they reached the place the army had set up headquarters—at the house where Jefferson Davis's family had lived. A black servant left in charge told the bodyguard "that Mrs. Davis had ordered him to have the house in good condition for the Yankees," and then she had bid farewell, saying, "I am going out into the world a wanderer without a home." Young Constance Cary witnessed the president's return to his ship. "Today, Mr. Lincoln, seated in an ambulance with his son Tad upon his knee, drove down Grace Street, past this house, a mounted escort clattering after." That ride had been a very long time coming.

Lincoln returned to Grant's camp at City Point expecting Lee's surrender any day. Mary Lincoln soon joined him there. She brought a party of dignitaries with her and invited along her friend the seam-stress Elizabeth Keckley, who was especially excited to be back in the state of her birth. In Richmond they roamed through the desecrated Confederate Capitol, where Mrs. Keckley happened to pick up "the resolution prohibiting all free colored people from entering the State of Virginia." They moved on to the Davis mansion, where "the ladies who were in charge of it scowled darkly upon our party as we passed through and inspected the different rooms." How surprised those ladies would have been to learn that Varina Davis had asked Elizabeth Keckley to move south with her as Mississippi prepared to secede. That evening back on the *River Queen* a young officer managed to raise Mary Lincoln's wrath once again, by telling her that Lincoln "is quite a hero when surrounded by pretty young ladies." Mary turned on the young man. "Quite a scene followed, and I do not think that the Captain who incurred Mrs. Lincoln's displeasure will ever forget that memorable evening in the cabin of the *River Queen* at City Point," Mary's defender Lizzie Keckley dejectedly recalled.

Moored just about a hundred yards away was Julia Grant's ship, and though Lincoln had been very courteous to her while Mary was away, once the first lady returned, Julia wasn't invited to join the group on the *River Queen*. "I felt this deeply," Julia later recalled, and "could not understand it. . . . Richmond had fallen; so had Petersburg. All of these places were visited by the President and party and I, not a hundred yards from them, was not invited to join them." Even worse, Mrs. Grant learned that she was not on the guest list for the Lincolns' farewell reception aboard the ship before their return to Washington. So she decided to take her ship out for a pleasant ride up and down the James River and asked that a band come along to entertain her. As she sailed past the *River Queen* the musicians played "Now You'll Remember Me." Clearly there would be no love lost between Julia Grant and Mary Lincoln.

PRESIDENT LINCOLN RETURNED to Washington earlier than he wanted to because his secretary of state, trusted counselor, and good friend William Seward had been in a carriage accident and broken several bones, including his jaw. He was in terrible shape, "so disfigured by bruises, his face so swollen that he had scarcely a trace of resemblance to him," his daughter Fanny divulged in her diary. Lincoln went directly to Seward's house when he got back to the capital on that Palm Sunday night, April 9. Then he went home to the White House for the first time in more than two weeks. It was almost 10 p.m. when his secretary of war rushed in—telegram in hand: Robert E. Lee had surrendered to Ulysses S. Grant at Appomattox Court House, in Virginia. The president went immediately to tell his wife.

"With the dawn of the day began the roar of cannon, the ringing of bells . . . the flash and glow of starry banners floating, streaming, wreathing everywhere." Lois Adams thought the very trees were glorying in the victory as they suddenly burst into bloom in the pouring rain. "The streets were full; bands and batteries playing and firing salutes as they went; steam fire engines decked with flags and screaming desperately; soldiers, sailors and citizens singing 'Rally round the Flag' and Yankee Doodle." A huge crowd assembled at the White House, screaming loud cheers when Tad popped up in a window waving a captured Rebel flag. But it was the triumphant president the people wanted to see and to hear. Hats flew into the air as Lincoln appeared and promised he would speak later, when he had thought through exactly what he wanted to say, but for now he only had a word for the band: "I think it would be a good plan for you to play *Dixie*." The musicians took up the tune and the president went inside to prepare his speech, little knowing it would be his last. For that day it was enough, as the *New York Times* summarized: "The great rebellion is crushed. The Republic is saved. PEACE comes again. To Heaven be the praise." Though General Sherman's army still fought Joe Johnston's in North Carolina, and smaller skirmishes farther west and south meant more blood would be shed, the capital celebrated through the night.

The next day, April 11, Washington amused itself while waiting for the president's speech. Bands pranced around the city playing patriotic ditties, workmen prepared the public buildings for another night of "illuminations," and masses mingled in the streets anticipating another stirring soliloquy, like the one at Gettysburg, or at the Lincoln inaugurals. Finally the throngs that had managed to push their way onto the White House grounds, spilling over onto Pennsylvania Avenue and into the park across the street, were about to get what they had been waiting for. Abraham Lincoln came to the window to huge huzzahs but then he let his listeners down. Instead of his usual poetry or prayer, the president offered a somewhat cerebral presentation outlining an important plan for Reconstruction. It took the next speaker, Senator Harlan, to give the crowd the red meat they wanted. When he asked what should be done with the Rebel leaders, the cry came back "Hang 'em" on that Holy Week Tuesday. Harlan suggested, to great approval, that the country should trust in the president. Then, before anyone else could speak, the band placed a perfect coda on the evening with "The Battle Cry":

> *We will welcome to our numbers the loyal, true and brave,*
> *Shouting the battle cry of freedom!*
> *And although he may be poor, he shall never be a slave,*
> *Shouting the battle cry of freedom!*
> *The Union forever! Hurrah, boys, hurrah!*

> *Down with the traitor, up with the star;*
> *While we rally round the flag, boys, rally once again,*
> *Shouting the battle cry of freedom!*

And with that the people wandered away. In their number was actor John Wilkes Booth, outraged by the president's consideration of suffrage for African Americans; Booth vowed as he departed that Lincoln had just made "the last speech he will ever make." The next day Elizabeth Keckley told Mary Lincoln that she had worried the night before that it would have been easy for someone in the crowd to shoot the president. "The President has been warned so often, that

I tremble for him on every public occasion," the first lady replied. "I have a presentiment that he will meet with a sudden and violent end." That was April 12.

On April 13, when the capital would again celebrate with grand lightings of all the buildings, Ulysses S. Grant and his wife sailed into the city. Julia thrilled at the reception: "Every gun in and near Washington burst forth—and such a salvo!—all the bells rang out merry greetings, and the city was literally swathed in flags and bunting." That night they toured the brightly lighted buildings and then received guests at the home of the secretary of war, with a brief interruption while Grant, at the president's request, escorted Mary Lincoln to see the "illuminations." Julia had insisted that her husband take her first and then collect Mrs. Lincoln, "as it was the honor of being with him when he first viewed the illumination in honor of peace restored to the nation, in which he had so great a share—it was this I coveted." Mrs. Grant knew that the newspapers and the public would be curious about the general's reaction to the laurels for his triumph, and she would be the one at his side, not the woman who had been so rude to her only a few days earlier.

Mary Lincoln enjoyed the spirited days after their return from Richmond. She told her friend Charles Sumner that she thought the celebration after Appomattox was "a happier day than last Monday," after the fall of Richmond. The general joy and goodwill in the city did not give way to the solemnity of Good Friday. It fell on April 14, and in another stark symbol that the war had come to an end, General Robert Anderson returned to where it began, four years to the day earlier. He personally raised the Union flag over Fort Sumter in a ceremony in which the famous author Harriet Beecher Stowe participated. And though Lincoln recalled a disturbing dream where he saw himself in a coffin in the East Room and heard people murmuring, "The president is dead," he was by and large in an expansive mood. That afternoon he and Mary took a carriage ride around the celebratory city, bedecked with bunting and banners—just the two of them—and he told her, "We must *both* be more cheerful in the future—between the war & the loss of our darling Willie—we have both been very miserable." They talked of the future, of going home to Springfield, Illinois, of the traveling abroad they might do. Mary later remembered how cheerful her husband had been that day as he prepared to go to the theater, one of his favorite pastimes.

Lincoln was probably the country's most theatergoing president, apparently enjoying the distraction that stage performances provided in those tough times. But that night he was tired and didn't want to go. Still, the newspapers had announced he would be there with General Grant as his guest and Lincoln preferred not to disappoint the audience, the actors, or the owner of Ford's Theatre. Mrs. Grant had no such compunctions. She absolutely insisted that she and her husband leave Washington *that day* to see their children, who were in school in New Jersey: "As soon as I received the invitation to go with Mrs. Lincoln, I dispatched a note to General Grant entreating him to go home that evening; that I did not want to go to the theater; that he must take me home." Later, Julia realized that a series of strange occurrences took place in the course of that day. A man showed up at her hotel purporting to be a messenger from Mrs. Lincoln and demanding Julia's presence at the theater, which she rejected. Then at lunch at Willard's Hotel she was convinced that same man along with three others sat opposite her and listened to every word she said. On the way to the train station that evening one of those men "rode past us at a sweeping gallop on a dark horse—black, I think. He rode twenty yards ahead of us, wheeled and returned, and as he passed us both going and returning, he thrust his face quite near the General's and glared in a disagreeable manner."

After the Grants declined the invitation, the Lincolns were turned down by several other people they asked to accompany them to the theater, perhaps as a result of Mary's recent displays of bad temper. Finally young Clara Harris, the daughter of the senator who had been so rude to Mary's sister Emilie, said yes and brought along her fiancé, Major Henry Rathbone. The foursome took their box seats a little late and *Our American Cousin* was already under way but the action stopped for the band to play "Hail to the Chief," while the audience rose and applauded. As the comedy resumed the bodyguard who had replaced Captain Crook for the night sat in the audience to watch it, abandoning his assigned post outside the presidential box. So no one was on guard when John Wilkes Booth entered the box and fired his fatal shot. In the ensuing chaos, with Mary Lincoln screaming, "They have shot the President!" Booth jumped to the stage and escaped. A member of the audience, Charles Leale, just out of medical school, rushed into the box, where "Mrs. Lincoln . . . exclaimed several times, 'O Doctor, do what you can for him, do what you can.'" The doctor tried to reassure the first lady, who was "weeping bitterly," but he found the president in "a profoundly comatose condition." More doctors crowded in to the small space and they with young Dr. Leale enlisted some men to move Lincoln across the street to Petersen's boardinghouse to be met by Robert Lincoln and members of the cabinet and White House staff. Dr. Leale stayed through the night, recording that "Mrs. Lincoln . . . came into the room three or four times during the night." In fact, Secretary of War Stanton had tried to keep the hysterical Mary away from her dying husband and she was not in the room at the end: "At 7:20 A.M. he breathed his last and 'the spirit fled to God who gave it.'"

One cabinet member not present in that sad, silent room that night was Abraham Lincoln's dear friend William Seward. The bedridden secretary of state, still suffering miserably from his carriage accident wounds, was also a target of Booth's co-conspirators. Late at night a man who purported to be delivering a message from the doctor appeared at the Seward home on Lafayette Square. The servant who opened the door allowed him in but when the intruder reached the top of the stairs, Seward's son Fred refused to let him disturb the sleeping secretary. When the assassin pulled out a gun Fred lurched at him and received a pistol whipping so severe that his skull was fractured, but so was the gun. The assassin would have to use a knife to kill his prey.

Seward's daughter Fanny was keeping watch by her sick father when the murderer pushed into the room and ran toward Seward's bed. "In his hand nearest me was a pistol, in the right hand a knife. I ran beside him to the bed imploring him to stop. I must have said 'Don't kill him,' for father wakened, he says, hearing me speak the word kill, & seeing first me, speaking to someone whom he did not see—then raised himself & had one glimpse of the assassin's face bending over, next felt the blows." The would-be murderer slashed repeatedly at the figure in the bed and threw Seward to the floor as the male army nurse George Robinson, an invalid himself, attacked the assassin. Fanny, screaming, ran into the hallway to get help. Her screams awakened her brother Gus, who joined in the melee. Then "the assassin rushed headlong down the stairs" and escaped on horseback.

Fanny dashed back to her father's room and cried out, "'Where's Father?' seeing the empty bed. At the side I found what I thought was a pile of bed clothes—then I knew that it was Father. As I stood my feet slipped in a great pool of blood. Father looked so ghastly I was sure he was dead, he was white & very thin with the blood that had drained from the gashes about his face & throat." The men of the household, who were themselves injured from wrestling with the knife-wielding killer, managed to get Seward back in bed. He was able to issue instructions to Fanny, "he spoke to me, telling me to have the doors closed, & send for surgeons, & to ask to have a guard placed around the house." Policemen and the press along with a crowd of people gathered at the door while the surgeon sewed up a huge gash on Seward's face and Fanny found assassin Lewis Powell's hat and gun.

Servants cleaned up the pools of blood as members of the cabinet arrived and informed Mrs. Seward that the president had been shot. The trauma completely overwhelmed the women of the family. Young Fanny, who two years before had been so happy to turn eighteen and be accepted into Washington society, sobbed: "Blood, blood, my thoughts seemed drenched in it—I seemed to breathe its sickening odor. My dress was stained with it—Mother's was drabbled with it—it was on everything." The next day Dorothea Dix offered the services of her nurses and Secretary of War Stanton came to check on Seward and tell his wife that the president was dead. The Seward women never got over the attack. William Seward's wife, Frances, was dead in six weeks and young Fanny would die a year and a half later.

General Grant received the bulletin via telegraph while he and his wife were in a restaurant in Philadelphia waiting to catch the train to Burlington, New Jersey. The couple went on to their destination, where "crowds of people came thronging into our cottage to learn if the terrible news was true." Grant left for Washington by special train and the next morning Julia opened a letter: "'General Grant, thank God, as I do, that you still live. It was your life that fell to my lot, and I followed you on the cars. Your car door was locked, and thus you escaped me, thank God!'" Julia was convinced that this was the man she had seen from the carriage the night before; the lock on the railroad car door saved Ulysses Grant's life. The Vice President of the United States also escaped. The man assigned to murder him, George Atzerodt, lost his nerve at the last minute and instead sat in a tavern drinking as his co-conspirators carried out their dread deeds.

As word of the attacks spread, the city shook with fear. At about 11 p.m., not quite an hour after the president was shot, a soldier rang the bell at the Lee house and "announced the assassination of our President & the attempt upon Mr. Seward." Lizzie Lee, the only family member awake in the household, was trying to digest that "horror" when another ring at the door brought the bulletin that "the provost marshal had ordered a guard of 6 men to protect this house." No one knew if the assassins would strike again.

Elizabeth Keckley also heard a knock on her door at about eleven o'clock when a neighbor broke in "with the startling intelligence that the entire Cabinet had been assassinated, and Mr. Lincoln shot, but not mortally wounded." She "sallied out into the street to drift with the excited throng" and went to the White House, passing the heavily guarded Seward house on the way. Guards surrounded the Executive Mansion as well and she could only garner the news that the president had not been brought back there. As she learned on the street that Lincoln was dying, Mrs. Keckley knew that Mary Lincoln needed her, "as I pictured her wild with grief; but then I did not know where to find her, and I must wait till morning. Never did the hours drag so slowly."

When morning came a carriage from the White House arrived to take Mrs. Keckley to her friend. Elizabeth found the first lady "nearly exhausted with grief." After calming her down, the former slave crept into the guest room to see the body of Abraham Lincoln: "No common mortal had died. The Moses of my people had fallen in the

hour of his triumph." Cabinet members and army officers made way
for the dressmaker, interrupting their own mourning for this woman
who had consoled the president through his own grief: "I could not
help recalling the day on which I had seen little Willie lying in his
coffin where the body of his father now lay. I remembered how the
President had wept over the pale beautiful face of his gifted boy, and
now the President himself was dead."

That realization was just beginning to sink in as the secretary of
war ordered troops to the city to protect other government officials
and find the murderers. Nobody knew if this was a Confederate plot
to disrupt the government so some sneak attack could be launched.
Anxiety mixed with anguish as somber black crepe replaced the gaudy
red, white, and blue hanging from the houses and government buildings. "The revulsion is so sudden from the delirium of joy which had
made the past two weeks one gala-day of delight, that men scarcely
know how to act or what to do," a benumbed Lois Adams recounted.
Church bells tolled, businesses shut down. "Noisy newsboys in the
streets are shouting the particulars of the murder, and in spite of what
we know of the awful truth, we hold our breath in listening for some
word of hope, some contradiction which we long for and yet know too
well can never come."

Elizabeth Blair Lee took down her flag by seven in the morning,
"This whole city is draped in black," she mourned to her long-absent
husband; "the grief of the people here is sincere & intense. Those
of Southern sympathies know now they have lost a friend willing &
more powerful to protect & serve them than they can now ever hope
to find again." Lizzie couldn't know how true those words would be
and, unlike many in the capital, she had faith in Lincoln's successor,
Andrew Johnson.

AT TEN O'CLOCK on the morning of April 15, Chief Justice Salmon
P. Chase, accompanied by members of the cabinet and other notables like Francis Preston Blair, joined Vice President Andrew Johnson
at the Kirkwood Hotel, where Chase administered the oath of office
of the President of the United States. "Mr. Chase came to Father at
the quiet inauguration of today & took his hand & with tearful eyes
said, 'Mr. Blair I hope that from this day there will cease all anger
& bitterness between us.' My Father responded promptly & kindly."
Thus did Lizzie describe the conciliation of the two old enemies, one
who had been such a stalwart of the murdered president, one who had
tried to defeat him. It was a pledge to come together in support of the
government they both believed in. And the head of that government,
Andrew Johnson, would need all the support he could get.

After his humiliating drunken performance at the inauguration,
Johnson had moved in with the Blairs and stayed there until the beginning of April. Lizzie Lee insisted that though "the City and papers are
full of gossip" after Johnson's rambling speech, "he is a sick man." The
vice president was suffering from a lingering case of typhoid fever and
the doctor summoned by the Blairs prescribed "absolute quiet . . . & a
low diet." As Johnson improved he was no longer quiet, "he talks well
& a great deal . . . enjoys his food hugely." While nursing her guest,
Lizzie was also worrying about a lump in her breast. "I have been
trying to get up the courage to consult the Doctor, but so far have not
done so," she fretted, but then went on happily to report: "Mr. Johnson is still with us & improves daily in health & cheerfulness."

Her mother insisted that a doctor look at the lump. He declared
it "a small tumor" and hoped to cure it without surgery, adding "the

knife is a perfectly safe remedy and that too without pain." Though that seemed doubtful, Lizzie claimed not to be "troubled about it," but clearly she was. She tried to convince herself that the discomfort she felt was the result of a crooked whale bone in her corset that poked at her all one day: "The strap which holds my skirts up pressed it on me." The fashions of the time could be treacherous but of course what really concerned Lizzie was breast cancer. After a few days the doctor determined that surgery would be necessary. So it was with great relief that before he operated she was able to report "the tumor has now entirely disappeared from sight." The doctor admitted the next day, the day after the assassination, that he had indeed thought the tumor was cancerous and was happy to see it gone. She had been keeping up such a brave face as she related political news and chatty gossip but had been so frightened by "the knife" that her reprieve allowed Lizzie to make the rare admission to her husband: "You can never know how bitterly I have felt these last months of our long separation." But she quickly put personal concerns aside as she was called on to minister to the deeply distressed Mary Lincoln.

"I shall never forget the scene," Elizabeth Keckley shuddered about that first day at the White House after the president was killed; "the wails of a broken heart, the unearthly shrieks, the terrible convulsions, the wild, tempestuous outburst of grief from the soul." This would go on for about a month, with poor little heartbroken Tad, who had never been far from his father's side, begging his mother not to cry. Some of the women of Washington went to offer their condolences to the inconsolable first lady but were refused admittance. Julia Grant claimed she "went many times to call on dear heart-broken Mrs. Lincoln, but she would not see me." The two women summoned by the doctor to comfort the hysterical widow were Mary Jane Welles, wife of Secretary of the Navy Gideon Welles, and Elizabeth Blair Lee. Lizzie Lee found it tough duty. Though Mrs. Lincoln had "always been marked in her kindness of manner to me," Mary's "pitiable" condition could be hard to witness. Lizzie tried to show sympathy, remarking, "it is a terrible thing to fall from such a height to one of loneliness & poverty," as she considered the former first lady's plight. "No woman ever had a more indulgent kind husband. Some have thought she had not his affections but tis evident to me she had no doubt about it and that is a point about which women are not often deceived after a long married life like theirs."

Instructions awaited Lizzie when she arrived to relieve Mrs. Welles, "She begs me not to smile. Mrs. L. said 'Oh I dread to see *Mrs. Lee's smile.*'" But she had little to smile about that day. While the women kept to their quarters upstairs, downstairs in the East Room six hundred people attended Abraham Lincoln's funeral. Only seven were women, including Nettie Chase and Kate Sprague. The *Cleveland Morning Leader*'s story about the solemnities singled out "The pleasant face of Mrs. Kate Sprague," but added, "such scenes gain little additional power by beauty's presence." Even at the end Kate Chase Sprague outshone Mary Todd Lincoln in her own White House.

The day before the funeral, some twenty thousand people filed tearfully through the East Room to pay their respects to the dead president. Among them was Rebecca Pomroy, now quite ill with typhoid fever herself. "With the strength born of a determined will," the nurse "resolved on seeing the face of her dear friend once more." Helpers at her hospital made her ready so she could "add her tribute of tears to that of hundreds of others who looked upon their beloved friend with unspeakable sorrow and affection." So many people had been turned away at nightfall that another viewing was scheduled for two days later, April 20, this time in the Rotunda of the Capitol. Thousands lined the streets as the melancholy march to the drumbeat of the dirge brought the casket up Pennsylvania Avenue, followed by the fallen president's riderless horse, and hundreds of officers on foot. When a mix-up kept the Twenty-Second Colored Infantry from joining the line along the route, the soldiers smartly took a place instead at the front, leading the other mourners of their emancipator, Abraham Lincoln.

Lizzie Lee stayed with Mary Lincoln all that day until the Lincoln sons came home from the Capitol. "I was so weary from 24 hours of unflagging watching that I undressed & went to bed," she sighed. As exhausted as she was, she felt obliged to give her hectoring husband an account of the family finances. Phillips Lee had grown wealthy in the navy because his job involved intercepting ships trying to break the northern blockade, and he was allowed to keep some of the bounty he confiscated. Lee wanted to know how his wife was spending the money. ("Insurance and water tax $550 . . . Gas & coal 200 . . . Blair's French & dancing 52 . . . meat bills and confectionary $300." And in the postslavery era at the Blair household the total monthly salary for four servants was $49.) It was a brief interruption from her White House duties. "I am surprised to find so far that she has not uttered a word of resignation, or religious submission," Lizzie mused about Mary on April 22, the day after the funeral train left Washington carrying President Lincoln's long coffin and the small one of his little boy Willie home to Illinois. "She constantly refers to his religious faith—but never to her own. I shall return there again this evening & shall continue to go as long as I find I can stand it." The "religion" Mary turned to was spiritualism.

Nettie Coburn was no longer in town. She had left in February to go home to Connecticut to nurse her father but paid a farewell call on the president before she departed. She told him then that the spirits "re-affirm that the shadow they have spoken of still hangs over you." Lincoln admitted he had received letters to that effect from mediums all over the county but that he knew "I shall live till my work is done, and no earthly power can prevent it. And then it doesn't matter as I am ready." But Mary Lincoln was still not ready to leave the White House.

President Johnson, working out of a small room at the Treasury Department, graciously allowed her to stay for more than a month after her husband's death, though the former first lady held it against him that he never paid a condolence call or wrote a sympathy note. But he might have still been smarting from her behavior on the night of the assassination. Mrs. Lincoln, holding a grudge about Johnson's embarrassing performance at the inauguration, refused to allow him in to the house where her husband was dying. In the days since then Mary had become convinced that Johnson was in on the plot to kill the president.

Several of the actual plotters were arrested on April 17 and on April 26 a group of detective Lieutenant L. C. Baker's cavalrymen found John Wilkes Booth and his co-conspirator David Herold, the man who held Lewis Powell's horse outside Seward's house, hiding in a barn on a farm in Virginia. When the men refused to surrender the soldiers set fire to the barn. According to newspaper reports, Herold opened the door to hand himself over, Booth fired at the soldiers, and they fired back and killed him. A few days later, President Johnson named the men he believed to be the masterminds of the conspiracy: Jefferson Davis, Clement C. Clay, and other Confederate officials. He offered a hundred-thousand-dollar reward for the capture of Davis and twenty-five thousand for each of the others.

Johnson's spurious charges were widely believed; journalist Lois Adams dramatically used them to attack Jefferson Davis: "the archfiend of the rebellion stands before the world in his true light at last, branded all over with infamy." By that time Confederate general Joe Johnston had surrendered to Sherman in North Carolina and Davis and some of the others were on the run. On the day that the trial of the true Lincoln assassination conspirators began, May 10, Jefferson Davis was captured in Georgia. Clement Clay turned himself in. Mary Lincoln was still in the White House.

"The White House, so lately the resort of the gay and brilliant throngs of levees and reception days, has now hanging about it the gloom and loneliness of the sepulcher," Lois Adams lamented. "She who bears his now immortal name is a stricken and desolate mourner within. A silence like that of death seems to have settled on all around." Mary wasn't getting any easier to take and it was well past time for her to go. Lizzie Lee dragged herself to the former first lady's side: "she begged me so hard yesterday not to leave her that I feel as if it was a duty to go—yet I do dread it more & more." While Mrs. Lincoln stayed upstairs, out of sight, "the White House was left without a responsible protector. The rabble ranged through it at will," the journalist Mary Clemmer Ames recounted, with outrage at how the place was stripped of china and silver: "It was plundered, not only of ornaments, but of heavy articles of furniture." Though entirely innocent, Mary Lincoln was suspected in the robbery, especially since she brought twenty trunks and fifty to sixty boxes with her when she finally moved out of the Executive Mansion. There was hardly any notice taken of the departure of the controversial first lady who left Washington friendless, just as she had arrived four years earlier. "The silence was almost painful," Elizabeth Keckley recalled. Mrs. Abraham Lincoln chose to go back to Illinois on one of the most remarkable days in the history of the Capital City—May 23, the beginning day of the Grand Review of the Union Army.

EVEN MORE PEOPLE descended on Washington than had gathered for Lincoln's inaugurations or funeral. This was not only going to be a grand spectacle; it would also serve as a great symbol that peace had come at last, the Union was restored. The large reviewing stands in front of the White House must have looked tempting to Tad Lincoln as he readied himself to leave with his mother and brother, plus Elizabeth Keckley and two bodyguards. Starting with the Army of the Potomac, so closely associated with the Capital City, wave after wave of soldiers paraded by, soldiers on horseback, soldiers singing songs that had been fraught with longing—"When Johnny Comes Marching Home Again," and "When This Cruel War Is Over"—now a reality. Flags and flowers festooned the entire city for the two-day celebration, when Washington did nothing but "watch our national heroes marching home," Lois Adams cheered; "as brigade after brigade swept up the noble avenue with their war-worn flags and inspiring music, they were welcomed with cheers and songs, the waving of flags and handkerchiefs, and now and then a showering of bouquets and wreaths of evergreens and beautiful flowers." The signs of mourning still showed, the White House remained draped in black, the flags flew at half-staff, with black crepe attached. But the sadness could not overcome the excitement of saluting 150,000 victorious soldiers as they proudly paraded by.

There's no record that any one of the several hundred women who disguised themselves as men and fought in the Civil War marched with the Grand Army of the Republic that day, but among the lines of men in blue was a woman in calico, riding sidesaddle in her sunbonnet. This was the famous Mother Bickerdyke, scourge of bureaucrats and balky brass, saint to sick and starving soldiers. She had been with Grant's army at Vicksburg and with Sherman's in Georgia. She had bullied anyone who resisted her efforts to clean up the camps, set up hospitals, nurse the soldiers, and provide them with decent meals. Her legend includes the story that she had a surgeon fired because a drunken spree the night before made him late to the hospital the next morning. He had not yet written the special diet list for the patients, who were hungry by the time he showed up as well as being ill. Mary Ann Ball Bickerdyke, called "Mother" by the grateful soldiers, flew into a rage and demanded that he be removed. When the doctor complained to headquarters and General Sherman pressed him about who had caused the discharge, the surgeon reluctantly admitted it was the formidable nurse. "Oh," Sherman is supposed to have said, "well, if it was her, I can do nothing for you. She ranks me." William Tecumseh Sherman became Mother Bickerdyke's great admirer, so he invited her to march with his army on that bright day marking the end of the long and life-draining war. Two days later the Army of the Trans-Mississippi, the last Rebel army, surrendered.

––––––––––––

THE REBEL PRESIDENT had not surrendered; he had been captured by Union soldiers and was now in solitary confinement at Fort Monroe. After the fall of Richmond, Jefferson Davis and some of his cabinet tried to keep operating the Confederacy from Danville, Virginia. But as the Rebel battlefield defeats mounted, the civilians moved farther south with the plan of escaping to set up a government in exile in the West. Varina Davis had sold almost everything she owned to convert it to cash and fled with the children to North Carolina before the fall of Richmond. She too kept moving south with the hopes of getting to Florida and then out of the country. When her now-fugitive husband learned that they were not far apart in Georgia, he met up with her for a night in a campsite by a creek. The next morning Yankee soldiers swooped in and arrested him. In telling the story of his capture, Varina Davis maintained that her husband had thrown her raincoat over his shoulders and that she then tossed her shawl over his head as he went to the creek to wash. But the newspapers printed a different story altogether—a much more ignominious one.

Under the headlines, "The Old Lady Jeff. Davis! How she was Captured—no. 13 Boots and Whiskers!" the Janesville, Ohio, *Weekly Gazette* reprinted a *New York Herald* account. "There appeared at the tent door an ostensible old lady, with a bucket on her arm, escorted by Mrs. Davis and her son; 'Please let my old mother go to the spring for some water to wash in,' said Mrs. Davis in a pleading tone. 'It strikes me your mother wears very big boots,' said the guard as he hoisted the old lady's dress with his sabre, and discovered a pair of number thirteen calfskins, 'and whiskers too,' said the Sergeant, as he pulled the hand from her face, and lo! Jeff Davis in all his littleness stood before them." The party was then carted off to Macon, Georgia. "While on the road they received a copy of President Johnson's proclamation, offering $100,000 for Davis. Davis read it and trembled, his hands dropped to his side, and with a groan, he dropped the paper. His wife picked it up and read it aloud, and the whole party burst into tears." At the same time, Clement Clay, who had already read about President Johnson's charges against the Confederate leaders and the offer of a reward for their capture, turned himself in thinking it the wisest thing to do. "Mrs. Clay remarked, jocularly, that as she had brought in her husband, she would claim the reward offered for him, to which Mrs. Davis responded, 'Yes $100,000 would be considerable of an amount of pocket money to us poor unfortunates. I sold my horses, carriage, silver ware and jewelry, for what little money I had, but it has been stolen from me.'"

It was a livid Varina Davis who related the story to her old friend Montgomery Blair. "Trunks were broken open, letters and clothing scattered on the ground, all the gold taken, even our prayer books and bibles taken . . . my baby's little wardrobe was stolen almost entirely, the other children shared the same fate," she sputtered. She later learned that if Davis had resisted arrest the soldiers were ordered "to fire into the tents (there being only two and those two containing women and children) and 'make a general massacre.' Another said 'bloody work' should have been made of the whole party." After a tearful trip with the Clays to Fort Monroe, the men were taken to prison and Varina sent to Savannah, Georgia, where she was placed under a loose house arrest. The town turned out for the former "First Lady of the Confederacy," as Virginia Clay later recalled: "an impromptu levee was begun which lasted until late in the night. It was followed the next day, by gifts of flowers and fruit, and what was immediately needful, of clothing of every description." The Davis children, except for the baby, were sent to Canada in the care of Varina's mother. Virginia Clay, with a good deal of difficulty, made her way to her in-laws in Huntsville, Alabama. And both women started lobbying campaigns with their former friends in Washington for the release of their husbands.

THE ITEMIZED BILL for President Lincoln's funeral, presented to the Congress by the commissioner of public buildings, includes $360 to Elizabeth Keckley "as first Class Nurse & attendant on Mrs. Lincoln from April 14th to May 26th, 1865." Lizzie Keckley had not wanted to go with Mary Lincoln to Chicago. "You forget my business, Mrs. Lincoln," she protested. "I have the spring trousseau to make for Mrs. Douglas." Adele Cutts Douglas had announced her engagement to Union army officer Robert Williams but Mary Lincoln was insistent: "Mrs. Douglas can get someone else to make her trousseau. . . . I have determined that you shall go to Chicago with me, and you *must* go." Addie Douglas typically gave her blessing: "Do all you can for Mrs. Lincoln. My heart's sympathy is with her." But once Mrs. Keckley settled the Lincolns at a hotel in Chicago, Mary admitted she had no money to keep Lizzie on, so the dressmaker was able to return to her thriving business in Washington and take up the work she most wanted to do—assisting former slaves in adapting to a new life. She had been there and knew how hard it was.

Born a slave in Dinwiddie, Virginia, Elizabeth Keckley grieved through the breakup of her family when the man she believed was her father was taken out of state by his owner, breaking her mother's heart. (Her mother, on her deathbed, confessed to Lizzie that her true father was the master of the household, Colonel Burwell, so the children she cared for were her half siblings.) As a teenager she was sent to work for one of the Burwell sons, whose wife tried "to subdue my stubborn pride" by enlisting Burwell and another man to beat her viciously while she did her best to fight them off. She couldn't fight off a white neighbor who repeatedly raped her, resulting in the birth of her baby boy. The mother and baby were sent to live with a Burwell daughter when she married and moved to St. Louis.

There Lizzie met her husband, James Keckley, and established herself as an accomplished seamstress. She bolstered the income of the family that owned her by making clothes for several women in town, who in turn advanced her $1,200 to pay for freedom for her son George and herself. Lizzie later paid back the loan in full. She left Keckley because of his "dissipation" and headed north, arriving in Baltimore in 1860. Her original plan to open a school for black women to teach them how to sew proved unsuccessful so she moved on to Washington, D.C., and started making dresses for the wives of senators and congressmen. One of her patrons, Elizabeth Blair Lee, made such a splash in a Keckley creation at the ball for the Prince of

Wales that the demand for the dressmaker shot up and Varina Davis hired her on a regular basis.

At the home of Mississippi Senator Jefferson Davis, Lizzie Keckley heard a great deal of political news as the country drew closer to war. "Mrs. Davis was warmly attached to Washington, and I often heard her say that she disliked the idea of breaking up old associations, and going South to suffer from trouble and deprivation." Little did Varina know then, in the winter of 1860, how much trouble and deprivation she would have to endure. Varina tried to convince the seamstress to come south with her, warning that war would turn northerners against African Americans: "The Northern people will look upon them as the cause of the war, and I fear, in their exasperation, will be inclined to treat you harshly." Lizzie wisely stayed in Washington and became the intimate of the first lady, who knew she was a "remarkable woman." But it was true that many blacks were experiencing harsh treatment in the Federal City as more and more arrived from the South. And in the camps set up to accommodate the so-called contrabands, disease ran rampant due to overcrowding and bad sanitary conditions.

A few years earlier Elizabeth Keckley had started the Contraband Relief Association and was elected its president. Her son, George, who had been the focus of her life, was killed in Missouri in one of the early battles of the war; now she threw herself into relief work. She raised funds for the organization when she traveled with Mary Lincoln to New York and Boston, and "Mrs. Lincoln made frequent contributions, as also did the President." After the Emancipation Proclamation, and the freeing of the slaves in the District of Columbia, the name of the society changed to reflect the new realities: the Ladies' Freedmen and Soldiers' Relief Association. Mrs. Keckley was also instrumental in establishing the National Association for the Relief of Destitute Colored Women and Children, which provided a home for elderly black women and the orphans of freedmen and turned out to be enlightened self-interest on her part.

By 1865, after four years of continuous migration to the capital, some estimates put the total number of African-American arrivals at 40,000, quite an adjustment for a city of just over 60,000 before the war. A huge Freedmen's Village was set up on the grounds of Mary and Robert E. Lee's confiscated Arlington House, along with the Union military cemetery there. Volunteers, like Sojourner Truth, arrived to lend a hand but the needs of the former slaves were too great for benevolent citizens and black churches to handle. The difficulties of integrating freed slaves into the wider society, helping them find employment and housing—the problems Elizabeth Keckley had recognized three years earlier—caused Congress to pass legislation in March 1865 establishing the Freedmen's Bureau, a government agency designed to take on the task.

The woman named that summer as the District of Columbia's assistant to the assistant to the commissioner for the bureau had been lobbying for its creation for quite some time. An antislavery activist in Ohio, Josephine Griffing had opened her home to fugitive slaves as part of the Underground Railroad and gone on the road in the 1850s as a paid speaker (and singer) for the Western Anti-Slavery Society. She also served as president of the Ohio Women's Rights Association, so when the war came and feminists Elizabeth Cady Stanton and Susan B. Anthony formed the Women's Loyal National League to petition for a constitutional amendment outlawing slavery, she signed up immediately and traveled the Midwest gathering the signatures of hundreds of women.

As she traveled pushing for freedom, Mrs. Griffing was one of the few abolitionists to consider the future for the slaves if they were in fact freed. She came to Washington in 1864 to lobby for an agency to deal with the questions of employment and education and housing and hunger and saw for herself the desperate situation of many of the new black residents of the nation's capital. This was not a problem for the future, people were in need of services right then, so she moved to the city to try to provide them. Almost immediately she was named "general agent" of the National Freedmen's Relief Association for the District of Columbia and held that job, along with others, until she died.

Leaving her husband behind in Ohio but bringing two daughters with her, Josephine Griffing threw herself into the work of helping African Americans in need. She solicited funds and food and clothing from women's organizations in the North and Midwest. She supervised the establishment of "industrial schools" to teach women how to make a living by sewing. "Much gratitude is manifested by these women for the opportunity of learning to make their own and their children's clothing, and for the employment it affords them, even at a low rate of pay," she reported to the Freedmen's Bureau. The rate of pay was low indeed—the most any woman averaged was seven dollars a month—but it kept starvation at bay. One of the industrial schools operated out of Josephine Griffing's house on Capitol Hill, where she also ran a day-care facility for children and an office to counsel the freedmen on how to handle their money, something they had never done before, along with any family or legal issues. People lined up on her doorstep for the free food and clothing, some lived there for a while if they had no place else to go, and others came by to check the lists of jobs available as employers let Mrs. Griffing know what kinds of workers they needed.

She was so used to running her own show, and doing it well, that she started fighting with the Freedmen's Bureau soon after she went to work there, and she lost the job a few months later. But Josephine Griffing had been sure to make friends in Congress and they continued to encourage her efforts, especially her program of arranging employment for the freedmen in the North. She would often travel with the job seekers, as one newspaper reported: "We would sometimes go to the railroad depot at night to see her start for New York with a chartered car full of these freed people, she going to see that they were put in right hands." Though she battled red tape at the bureau she had been so instrumental in creating, the powers there did cooperate with Mrs. Griffing in her search for freedmen jobs outside of Washington, and the War Department turned over abandoned barracks in Rhode Island for her to use as an employment clearinghouse. More employment offices followed in other cities, and she managed to get some three to five thousand destitute freed people jobs in the North.

For those many thousands more who remained in Washington, Josephine Griffing toiled tirelessly to make sure they were fed, clothed, and housed. She was always badgering the bureaucrats who she thought stuck too close to the rules in the face of desperate need. Part of the resistance to her demands emanated from the Freedmen's Bureau's concern about creating a culture of dependency on government—but Mrs. Griffing contended she was only giving handouts to people who couldn't help themselves, "those broken-down aged slaves whom we have liberated in their declining years, when all their strength is gone, and for whom no home, family, friendship or subsistence is furnished." The bureau also struggled with a constant lack of funds. Congress was never going to appropriate enough to do the job. That made the cause of women's suffrage all the more important to reformers like Josephine Griffing, who believed that if women had the vote the lawmakers would have to be more responsive to their demands for funds for social services. So she redoubled her suffrage efforts as well. A founder and vice president of the American Equal Rights Association, she would join forces with other feminists pushing to include women in the growing movement to enfranchise blacks.

THE SEA OF blue uniforms that washed over Washington for the review of the Grand Army of the Republic slowly subsided that summer as soldiers mustered out and headed home. But the city could not yet turn away from the dramatic events of April as the conspirators in the assassination plot against Abraham Lincoln were tried and sentenced. Secretary of War Stanton took charge of the investigation, arresting anyone who had been in on the plan or had aided and abetted John Wilkes Booth and Lewis Powell (also known as Lewis Payne) in their attacks on the president and the secretary of state. The manhunt quickly took Stanton's troops to the boardinghouse door of Mary Surratt, who had moved from her home in Surrattsville, Maryland, the previous October in order to make a living after her debt-ridden husband died. With one son in the Confederate army and another, John Surratt, a civilian message-runner for the Rebels, Mary Surratt's boardinghouse attracted southern sympathizers like John Wilkes Booth.

Earlier that year Booth hatched a plan with John Surratt to kidnap President Lincoln and hold him hostage in Richmond in return for the release of southern prisoners of war who could help the dwindling Rebel army fight on. The plot was foiled when Lincoln failed to show up at a theater performance where Booth expected him, and with the end of the war, the kidnapping no longer made sense. But the avenging actor then determined to throw the government into chaos by assassinating the president, vice president, secretary of state, and general in chief of the army. John Surratt was not in Washington the night Lincoln was shot and he managed to flee the country, but his mother, along with seven men, was arrested and jailed in an old penitentiary at the Washington Arsenal. In the outrage over the assassination, there was no public outcry when the secretary of war announced that the trial would be conducted by military tribunal with no jury, rather than in a civil courtroom, but such a protest erupted when he tried to exclude the press and the public that Stanton was forced to open the proceedings.

Despite the distance to the arsenal, Lois Adams spotted "hundreds" trekking daily to the trial, hoping to get in. "If provided with proper passes they may go in, and take their chances of ever coming out alive from the small, thronged and crowded room, where Judges, counsel, prisoners, witnesses, and spectators, men, women, and children, are jammed and sweltering together." A small room at the arsenal had been fitted up as a makeshift courtroom filled mainly with the nine-member military commission assigned to hear the evidence and pronounce a verdict, though the outcome was never in doubt. Much of the crowd's curiosity focused on the one woman, Mary Surratt, who, the government argued, assisted the assassins in planning their attacks and provided them with food and shelter. As President Johnson himself judged, she "kept the nest that hatched the egg." Every day she sat there in the courtroom, her face veiled, while the public hurled taunts and threats: " 'Isn't she a devil?' 'She looks like a devil!' 'Hasn't she a horrid face?' 'I hope they'll hang her—tee, hee, hee!' All these remarks and more such, some of them again and again." Jane Swisshelm reported disapprovingly to the *Pittsburgh Daily Commercial*, as she praised the defendant's demeanor, "She made no scenes, as a weak or vain woman would have done." Mrs. Surratt appeared calm and serene though she was suffering from the side effects of menopause; the men, on the other hand, looked disheveled and disoriented when their jailers pulled off the confining hoods Stanton ordered they wear over their heads for the duration of their imprisonment. Not physically in the dock with the prisoners but named in the indictment were the former President of the Confederacy, Jefferson Davis, and other leaders, including Clement Clay, who had spent much of the last year of the war in Canada, where he was alleged to have conspired with Booth.

When the weeks of testimony ended, the verdict of guilty came as expected; what wasn't expected was Mary Surratt's sentence, printed in full by the *New York Times*: "the Commission does, therefore, sentence her, the said MARY E. SURRATT, to be hung by the neck until she be dead, at such time and place as the President of the United States shall direct." No woman had ever before been executed by the United States government. It was a split vote of the military commission, but only two-thirds were necessary to mete out the penalty of death. President Johnson named the time and place by executive order: the hangings would take place on July 7 between the hours of 10 a.m. and 2 p.m., at the direction of the secretary of war. Three of the accused conspirators had been given prison sentences. Four were condemned to die. Johnson did not yield to the request from the minority of the commission to commute the sentence of Mary Surratt. "It was well known that the counsel, family and friends of the culprit were determined to make every exertion, to strain every nerve in a strong pull and tug at the tender heart of the President in her behalf. She was a woman, and a sick woman at that," the *New York Times* reported, congratulating Johnson for resisting the imprecations: "these and like arguments, it was said, would be brought to bear upon the President, backed with certain political strength which could not fail to succeed." One who tried to use her strength to save the life of Mary Surratt was Adele Cutts Douglas.

She arrived at the White House on the day of the executions and found the condemned woman's daughter in tears on the outside steps. The president had refused to see the distraught twenty-two-year-old Anna Surratt. Now she was at her wit's end; all other avenues to save her mother had been blocked. Very early that morning, Mary Surratt's lawyers had awakened Judge Andrew Wylie of the Supreme Court of the District of Columbia and asked him to sign a writ of habeas corpus turning their client over to civil authorities, on the basis that the war was over and the military had no business conducting the trial in the first place. With some trepidation the judge in that federal district court agreed and ordered General Hancock from the Arsenal Penitentiary to bring Mary Surratt to his courtroom at ten that morning. When the general failed to show up, the judge didn't know what to do, finally deciding to "submit to the supreme physical power" of the military, which held Mrs. Surratt in custody. A few hours later, while Judge Wylie was hearing another case, the attorney general of the United States, with General Hancock in tow, appeared in the courtroom and explained that President Johnson had negated the judge's writ and ordered that the executions proceed.

And that's what he did again after he met with Adele Douglas, who pushed past the bayonet-wielding guards to bring Johnson the information that Lewis Powell had that morning proclaimed that Mary Surratt was innocent. It's not known whether Douglas came to the White House for the express purpose of petitioning for Mary Surratt. Both women were Catholic and there was some upset in the community about suspicions of anti-Catholicism in the charges against the boardinghouse owner. The conversation between President Johnson and Mrs. Douglas has never been revealed. But her intervention was to no avail. Even the persuasive Adele Cutts Douglas couldn't shake Andrew Johnson, who had privately told his secretary "there had not been 'women enough hanged in this war.'"

As she was marched out to her death, Mary Surratt's famous composure abandoned her. Her daughter's sobs in the hours before the execution caused her to moan with anguish; "she had apparently lost sight of her own interest in deep solicitude for her daughter, of whom she constantly talked, and repeatedly, frantically and with wringing of hands asked: 'What will become of her—what will be ANNA's fate?'" the *New York Times* informed readers, showing a rare bit of sympathy. She was the first of the condemned prisoners to be led to the gallows. The other three—Lewis Powell, who attacked Secretary Seward; David Herold, who helped both Powell and Booth escape; and George Atzerodt, who plotted to kill the vice president—were all directly involved. The four were placed in their seats, prayers were said, and the nooses were pulled over their heads. "Mrs. Surratt seemed, by a desperate mental effort, to nerve herself up specially for this occasion, looking forward and around her, for the only time, with an air of mingled determination and resignation. Her bonnet and veil were removed previous to putting the noose upon her neck," the New Berne, North Carolina, *Times* reported, noting almost as a throwaway that Powell had made a statement about Surratt "exonerating her from complicity, and that another person subscribed to an affidavit impeaching the testimony of an important witness against her." It didn't matter; the deed was done. The United States government had executed a woman for the first time in history.

Was she innocent? That's still a debated question but most of the evidence points in that direction. Certainly the prevailing public opinion of the time was that she was not. "It is an awful thing to hang a woman," Lois Adams conceded, but she argued that no execution, "though multiplied by thousands, can atone for the wrongs these Southern women are guilty of in connection with the rebellion. All through they have been the bitterest, the most defiant, unreasoning and dangerous enemies the government has had to contend with."

———————

AFTER THE INTERRUPTION by the attorney general on the habeas corpus request for Mary Surratt, Judge Wylie returned to the case he was trying. In this crime there was no question who did the deed. It was the trial of the winsome Miss Harris, charged with murdering Mr. Burroughs at the Treasury Department. And the public was all on the side of the wronged defendant; from her Chicago hotel Mary Lincoln sent flowers. That Mary Harris was the culprit was certain, but would she be found guilty? "The prisoner was tastefully attired in a black silk dress, and a tight-fitting coat or basque of the same material, trimmed with braid and beads; a black bonnet trimmed with straw," swooned the *New York Times*; "her hair was worn in ringlets."

Mary Harris had become quite the favorite of the press since that cold day in January when she shot and killed the man she said had promised to marry her. And despite the fact that she bought a gun in Chicago, loaded it, carried it halfway across the country, concealed it in her bag as she entered the Treasury Department, and then hid in wait for her victim, her lawyers contended there was no premeditation involved. She was "temporarily insane." It was the creative defense dreamed up six years earlier by Edwin Stanton, now the secretary of war, to obtain a not guilty verdict for Dan Sickles, now a decorated Union general, after he had murdered Philip Barton Key.

The judge admitted into evidence letters from the dead man

attesting to his devotion to the woman he then scorned, and a former employer testified that Mary's reaction to the news of Burroughs's marriage indicated a "mental aberration." The superintendent for the federal Government Hospital for the Insane, the highest-ranking person the lawyers could possibly summon to testify about mental illness, the man who ran the hospital that Dorothea Dix founded, gave Miss Harris's condition a name: paroxysmal insanity. He talked about "menstruation hysteria" and all manner of other maladies this fair damsel suffered as a result of her callous lover. She got off.

The jury deliberated for a full ten minutes and returned to the courtroom, which "was densely packed, the attendance of ladies being very large." When the verdict was announced "there was great excitement. The men threw up their hats and burst into loud applause, women waved their handkerchiefs and wept with joy," the Raleigh, North Carolina, *Daily Progress* cheered, though "the acquitted lady fainted." Lois Adams was disgusted. "Her counsel were far nearer crazed than she was, and acted it out in their insane conduct and maudlin huggings and kissings on the closing day of the trial," the journalist scolded; "she goes home stripped of everything that makes pure and dear and blessed the life of woman. She has made her name most unfortunately notorious, and has won an empty acquittal based upon a false pretense: that is all." In fact Mary Harris did turn out to be mentally ill, and not temporarily. She ended up spending close to twenty years in the Government Hospital for the Insane and then when she came out she married her lawyer, Joseph Bradley, by then an octogenarian. Miss Harris was not yet forty.

———

WASHINGTON WAS BEGINNING to realize that the war was actually over. Military camps closed down or filled with freedmen, hospitals emptied as the crippled and careworn returned to their homes, but many people would not go home—they were there to stay. The clerks, male and female, still clocked in every day at the federal departments. The central government had mushroomed into a vast new entity growing from 5,000 employees to more than 15,000 while the nation fought a war over states' rights and the capital had emerged from the conflict as a bustling, burgeoning metropolis. As Lois Adams noted, "Everywhere about the city improvements are going on. Private enterprise seems wide awake, and is reaping rich rewards for all its outlays of energy and expense." The war had forever changed the place Mrs. Adams covered: "The new elements, first drawn here by force, are gathering strength, obliterating the old landmarks . . . scaffoldings everywhere beset the sidewalks . . . handsome blocks and dwellings are filling up hitherto vacant lots . . . the public buildings are also in process of completion and renovation." And the government still had much to do in the wake of the war.

With Congress out of session, President Johnson was issuing Reconstruction decrees sure to incense northern Republicans, allowing states back into the Union with no requirement other than that they ratify the amendment outlawing slavery. As far as he was concerned, the men who had seceded could return to their seats in the Senate and the House and the question of voting rights for African Americans, something Radical Republicans thought would change the social structure of the South, was up to the states. It was sure to be a battle when the Congress reconvened. Until then there was another fallout from the war needing attention—the identification of missing and dead soldiers. The person who almost single-handedly took on that task was Clara Barton.

After the exhilarating and exhausting year on the battlefields of Virginia and Maryland, Clara Barton settled on the Sea Islands off the coast of South Carolina, a Union-controlled area where wounded soldiers from the siege of Charleston were hospitalized. She found the work too easy for her taste, but her brother, who had been assigned to the Quartermaster's Corps, was there too and she didn't want to abandon him. Plus she was having a love affair. She knew it would be brief. Colonel John Elwell was a married man but she enjoyed it while it lasted and ignored the sly looks cast her way when she left his rooms early in the morning. And the abolitionist Frances Gage engaged her interest in the plight of the freedmen on the islands.

But Clara Barton itched for action and so traveled to Washington. After a winter there and plagued with the depression that always overtook her when she didn't have enough to do, she set out for the battlefields of Virginia and was once more caught up in the excitement of war. In the winter hiatus at the beginning of 1865 she came again to Washington, borrowed a green silk skirt to wear to the Inaugural Ball, and kept pushing to see President Lincoln to discuss a project she had in mind. A little more than a month before he died, she received Lincoln's blessing for her plan to help families find missing soldiers and to identify the dead.

It was a short note: "To the Friends of Missing Persons: Miss Clara Barton has kindly offered to search for the missing prisoners of war. Please address her at Annapolis, giving her name, regiment and company of any missing prisoner. Signed A. Lincoln." That was all she needed. She placed the treasured endorsement from the now-dead president in the newspapers and moved to Annapolis, Maryland, where the Union army had established "parole camps" for released prisoners to allow them to recuperate before rejoining their regiments.

As the numbers of parolees grew the camps kept expanding, to the extent that one, called "Camp Parole," housed as many as twenty-five thousand soldiers. That's where Clara Barton set up shop with some assistance from the War Department. She found the records in shambles; no one had adequately processed the released prisoners, so their families didn't know whether they were dead or alive, and thousands of letters asking for information hadn't even been opened, much less answered. With the notice she had placed in the newspapers, thousands more letters poured in. Clara sorted the names by state and published them in local newspapers; then she would hear back from soldiers who had been in the same units about the whereabouts of the missing men. Sometimes she heard from the men themselves. She hit the grim jackpot when a young man named Dorence Atwater, who had been imprisoned at infamous Andersonville, revealed that he had been given the prison assignment of recording the name, rank, and cause of death of every soldier who died there. He secretly copied his lists for himself in order to preserve the record for the Union and now he brought them to Clara Barton. Atwater also mapped out at Andersonville where each man was buried in that bleak Georgia cemetery. With more than half of the Union dead lying in unmarked graves, Atwater's information proved enormously important. And Secretary of War Edwin Stanton decided to act on it.

In July, Clara Barton, Dorence Atwater, and a party of forty workers boarded ship with the prickly Captain James Moore, bound for Andersonville with the mission of marking the graves. Because of Atwater's records, by mid-August they were able to place names on the burial plots of 13,000 soldiers, leaving only 400 with the anonymous "Unknown." It had been a trying time in that horrible place but Clara found that she was something of a celebrity as the "Yankee lady." Local African Americans came to ask questions about whether they were in fact free; white people in the area had told them that Lincoln's death meant that the Emancipation Proclamation was no longer valid. Some of the stories they told her foreshadowed things to come in southern states that would cause major battles between the president and Congress. But for now, Clara Barton could rejoice that she had accomplished what she set out to do—show respect to thousands of dead Union soldiers, recognizing them by name. In the ceremony marking the achievement, it was Clara Barton who was asked to raise the flag. "My own hands have helped to run up the old flag on our great *and* holy ground," she wrote in her diary. "I ought to be satisfied—*I* believe I am."

There was still much work to do, with many thousands of letters to answer. Clara was drawing no salary and running out of money. With a great deal of difficulty she prevailed on Congress to appropriate fifteen thousand dollars to the enterprise. She went herself to testify before the Joint Committee on Reconstruction, perhaps making her the first woman to appear at a congressional panel. By the time her Washington "Office of Correspondence with the Friends of the Missing Men of the United States Army" closed in 1867 she and a small staff had responded to more than 63,000 letters and determined the fate of more than 22,000 men. But Clara Barton's work had just begun.

———————

"TWICE EVERY WEEK during warm weather, Washington gives itself a three hours' play-spell, puts on its holiday clothes, goes into its pleasant parks, walks on the grass, sits under the trees and admires and criticizes itself." As a government worker, Lois Adams enjoyed the 3 p.m. closing time of the agencies on Saturdays, when she and much of the rest of the city gathered on the White House lawn to enjoy the melodies of the Marine Band. The School for Music Boys at the Washington Barracks was turning out talented musicians and the free concerts at the president's house on Saturday and on the Capitol grounds on Wednesday evenings helped settle the

Capital City into a sense of normalcy after the earthquake of events in the spring and early summer. But not everything could return to the way it was. Ford's Theatre tried to stage a new play and the reaction was so strong that the War Department closed it down. (The building was converted to government offices and not restored and reopened as a theater until 1968.) And, of course, there was a new family in the White House.

President Johnson's wife, Eliza, and their two grown daughters, two sons, one son-in-law, and five young grandchildren moved to Washington in September. The other son-in-law, daughter Mary's husband, and the Johnsons' son Robert had died in the war. A house full of family presided over by a first lady with no political ambitions couldn't have marked a sharper contrast to the Lincoln White House. But the president's wife did act as a strong influence on his career. Eliza Johnson had married her husband when she was sixteen years old and "She was the stepping stone to all the honors and fame my father attained," their daughter Martha Patterson attested.

The couple had met when the seventeen-year-old Andrew left Raleigh, North Carolina, to settle in Greeneville, Tennessee, to work as a tailor. Both had grown up poor, but unlike Andrew, Eliza was educated and the story spread that it was she who taught her adolescent suitor the alphabet. During Johnson's years in Congress, his wife spent most of her time in Tennessee, not Washington, so this was not a homecoming for the now fifty-five-year-old first lady and she was not well, probably suffering from tuberculosis. "Mrs. Johnson was a retiring, kind, gentle, old lady, too much of an invalid to do the honors of the house, which care and pleasure she gladly transferred to her two daughters, Mrs. Patterson and Mrs. Stover," Julia Grant recalled; "she always came into the drawing room after the long state dinners to take coffee and receive the greetings of her husband's guests. She was always dressed elegantly and appropriately." Very different from Mrs. Grant's view of Mary Lincoln. As for Mrs. Lincoln, she moaned dramatically to Elizabeth Blair Lee, "the utter impossibility of living another day, so wretched, appears to me, as an impossibility."

Things were not going well for the former first lady, friendless in Chicago. However, her one true friend in Washington, Elizabeth Keckley, stayed faithful to her, keeping up a correspondence. Lizzie was doing some work as well for the current White House hostesses, Martha Patterson and Mary Stover, the Johnson daughters. "Mrs. Patterson and Mrs. Stover were kindhearted, plain, unassuming women, making no pretensions to elegance," Mrs. Keckley recounted with some amazement that one day she found "Mrs. Patterson busily at work with a sewing machine. The sight was a novel one to me for the White House, for as long as I remained with Mrs. Lincoln, I do not recollect ever having seen her with a needle in her hand." Because the White House women could sew for themselves, the relationship with Mrs. Lincoln's dressmaker did not last. They wanted Lizzie Keckley to measure and cut fabric for them to piece together. The proud couturier refused.

With unpretentious women in the White House, it fell to Julia Grant to fill in as Washington's hostess. "Our receptions were brilliant," she immodestly remembered. "The house would not hold our guests. The New York papers used to make wonderful cartoons of General Grant's house and surroundings on reception days and of General Grant's hand after the reception." With "distinguished soldiers and statesmen" paying homage on these "gala days" it was clear that a campaign was under way to make Ulysses S. Grant the next president of the United States. But for now, the man who held that office was Andrew Johnson.

Because he had stayed true to the Union after Tennessee seceded and because he had given speeches all over his state castigating the southern leaders and the plantation aristocracy, the Republicans who nominated Johnson for vice president thought they had picked a like-minded man. By the time the new Congress came into session in December, the singular path Johnson had decided to follow would lead to bitter battles ahead. But on December 18 the now-recovered Secretary of State William Seward formally announced the Thirteenth Amendment as the law of the land. Twenty-seven states, or three-quarters of the thirty-six making up the one United States of America, had ratified the constitutional provision abolishing slavery. It was cause for celebration. And Virginia Clay was back in town.

CHAPTER 9

LEFT: *Sara Agnes Pryor, a successful author and social welfare activist, suffered deprivation and danger in the South during the Civil War.* RIGHT: *Virginia Clay Clopton, the "most brilliant of them all" among the women in Washington's prewar social circles, wrote a compelling memoir and became a stump-speaking suffragist.*

Virginia and Varina Return, Sara Survives, Mary Is Humiliated, Kate Loses

1866–1868

Virginia Clay had no idea what to expect as she sat on the train carrying her back to the city she had so captivated as a leading belle in what seemed like an eternity ago. Back then the respected Alabama senator Clement C. Clay's bright and witty young wife, the undisputed star at Mrs. Gwin's still-talked-about ball, gathered crowds around her in every drawing room. Now she was coming to the Capital City as a supplicant from a defeated land, begging parole for her imprisoned husband. From the moment she received word that President Johnson would consider her "application for permission to visit

Washington," friends and family tried to talk her out of making the trip. It would do no good, they argued, and it might actually do harm to the cause of securing her husband's release from Fort Monroe. "The efforts of the wives of other prisoners," Virginia knew, "not only had been of no avail, but in some instances had made them the direct objects of attack." She particularly had in mind Johnson's reaction to Varina Davis's entreaties, which "became the talk of the whole country." The president had lashed out at the former Confederate first lady, complaining to a visiting delegation from South Carolina that she was an angry woman who lacked the "proper spirit," in remarks that were picked up by the press. Virginia's elderly and ill in-laws especially begged her not to go, convinced she "would be attacked on every side so soon as I entered the Federal Capital." Mainly they wanted her to stay in Huntsville, Alabama, to take care of them, something this spirited woman definitely did not want to do, so she set off for Washington. In her stops along the way, friends from years before offered encouragement, and from the "hour of my arrival in the capital on November 17 my misgivings gave place to courage."

It must have been shocking to see the city, much altered over the years of the war. It would take until the end of the decade and a new census to state officially what was obvious to anyone on the street—there were so many more people than there had been when Mrs. Clay left only five years earlier. The population increased by 75 percent in the 1860s, more than any other decade in the city's history, and the physical appearance of the place had changed markedly, with shops and restaurants Virginia had never seen before lining the streets, government buildings that she had last seen as construction sites—the Grecian temples of the Treasury and Patent Buildings—now elegant in completion, and proudly towering over it all the magnificent Capitol dome with Freedom reigning tall on top. Only the pathetic protrusion of the unfinished and abandoned Washington Monument stood the same.

Virginia took a room at the wonderfully familiar Willard's Hotel and "for the next few days I knew no moment alone." Her old friends gathered round, delighted to have her back, and eager to hear how she had fared through the war. And President Johnson sent word that he would see her in a few days. Clement Clay and Jefferson Davis had been locked up for six months since the government issued the order for their arrest, alleging their involvement in the assassination of President Lincoln. In that time no charges had been filed, no trial date set, and no real evidence brought against them. While she waited to see the president, Virginia consulted with lawyers, building the case for her husband's release.

The newspapers tracked her movements. "Mrs. Clement Clay has an interview with the president today in relation to the release of her husband," one item revealed. She was putting herself at the mercy of a man she wouldn't have paid much attention to in her glory days; when Johnson served in the Senate he "had seldom been seen in social gatherings in the capital." But when she walked into the White House who would be there but one of the stars of those gatherings: "one of the first familiar faces I saw as I entered was that of Mrs. Stephen A. Douglas." Adele had been busy trying to secure pardons for her southern friends and was having some success, including for her husband's running mate in the 1860 presidential campaign, Herschel Johnson. "The amnesty was granted at the intercession of Mrs. Douglas," according to the newspaper reports. Now Virginia's friend from the time of "flounces and furbelows" offered to intercede for her, "with the affectionate warmth so well-known to me in other and happier days."

The women were ushered in to see the president who appeared deaf to their pleas; Addie Douglas burst into tears and threw "herself down on her knees before him." But Virginia refused to follow suit: "I had no reason to respect the Tennessean before me . . . my heart was full of indignant protest that such an appeal as Mrs. Douglas's should have been necessary; but that, having been made, Mr. Johnson could refuse it, angered me still more." The president dismissed the women saying he would consult with his cabinet and suggesting Virginia try her luck with the secretary of war, Edwin Stanton.

Knowing that Radical Republican Stanton was the puppet master behind Johnson's accusations against her husband, Mrs. Clay prepared for disappointment as she "briefly, but bravely, proceeded with my story." In an unpleasant interview Stanton claimed to be neither Clay's judge nor accuser. She took this bit of information as a good sign, though her legal team seemed less encouraged, and moved on to her next target—General Grant. At his house she found a far more sympathetic soul. The stern and vindictive Stanton was replaced by a gracious Grant, ready to hear her out. If it were up to him, he told the amazed woman, all the prisons would be opened and every prisoner released "unless Mr. Davis might be detained for a while to satisfy public clamour." He assured her, "Your husband's manly surrender entitles him to all you ask." Thrilled, Virginia asked Grant to put his words in writing, whereupon he called his wife to act as stenographer. Julia Grant "shook my hand with the cordiality of a friend" and chatted about acquaintances they had in common. It was all so strange and disconcerting. Here was Virginia Clay in a house in Georgetown that had once belonged to a fellow Alabaman, enjoying a pleasant conversation with the man being hailed as the "Hero of the Hour," and "Our next President," when only a few months before he had been leading an army that had kept her on the run for most of the war.

IN THE FIRST months after secession, the new capital in Richmond seemed much the same as the old one in Washington for the members of the Confederate government. Many of the families knew each other well and they fell into a comfortable pattern of dinners and entertainments—Virginia's acting talents once again came to the fore, this time as Mrs. Malaprop—similar to the ones they had left behind. As in the federal capital, once the fighting started the hospitals filled quickly with the women rushing to provide aid. But as the war wore on and the Union blockade closed down southern ports, making imports impossible and cutting off the revenue from exporting cotton, prices shot up and scarcity took hold. "The price of board for my husband alone now amounted to more than his income," Virginia later decried the situation in the Confederate capital; "our treasury was terribly depleted, and our food supply for the army was diminishing at a lamentable rate."

The Clay hometown of Huntsville had come under Union control, so Virginia couldn't go there, but the high prices and empty shelves in Richmond meant she couldn't stay there for long, either, so she moved from one relative's house to another. She and the other women "sat and planned and compared our news of the battle-fields, or discussed the movements of the army," while they "did a prodigious amount of sewing for our absent husbands." Luckily for her life as a refugee, Virginia had no children to worry about, and after her mother died when she was three years old, she had spent much of her childhood in the homes of aunts and uncles. The little girl learned early that charming her relatives—all of them politicians—worked for her and she operated on the assumption that charm and pluck could get her through almost anything, including war. "Women of the Confederacy cultivated such an outward indifference to Paris fashions as would have astonished our former competitors in the Federal Capital," Virginia joked, turning necessity into virtue.

"A general gloom prevails here because of the scarcity and high price of food," Clement Clay wrote to her in 1863 from Richmond, where the soldiers were subsisting on half rations with no vegetables or fruit or coffee or sugar. "Don't mention this, as it will do us harm to let it get abroad." The southern press tried to suppress the bad news but on April 2athe sight of thousands of weapons-wielding women descending on the shops and warehouses of Richmond demanding "bread or blood" couldn't be kept secret. So the Clays were not all that sorry when Clement lost his bid for reelection to the Confederate Senate in 1863. As the couple contemplated the next move, Jefferson Davis assigned his friend to a new mission: Clay was to go to Canada as part of a recently created Secret Service with the twofold goal of creating disruptions on the northern border and sounding out the prospects for peace.

When Clement Clay left for Canada in 1864, his wife decided to go south to Georgia. Unfortunately for her, William Tecumseh Sherman was headed in that direction as well, so she moved farther and farther into Confederate territory, first to Columbus, Georgia, then to Macon, and finally to Beech Island, South Carolina, a town near Augusta. The deprivation of Richmond now spread wide across the Confederacy. "Potato coffee" and "peanut chocolate" substituted for the real thing and "needles were becoming precious as heirlooms; pins were the rarest of luxuries . . . writing paper was scarcely to be had." With no reliable lines of communication the couple occasionally resorted to placing "personals" in the newspapers to inform each other as to their whereabouts but now Virginia felt completely cut off. She was hoping for word from her husband—or someone—to tell her what to do, beyond helping hide the silver, as Sherman made his march from Atlanta to the sea. "Great excitement all over the country caused by *Sherman's advances*. God in mercy help us now!" Virginia beseeched in her diary, a more raw account of the story than the witty memoir she authored years later.

"No letters, no telegrams! What am I to do?" She anguished both for herself and for Clement; "no letter or intelligence from my husband! Will he *ever* come?" And then in the house where she was staying the baby died. "I miss her all day! Her dear presence, merry laugh, her cherub form!" And the news of the outside world, to the extent that she could ascertain it, was bleak: "great loss of officers & men in Tennessee." And then on December 22, "*Savannah has fallen!* Oh! My country—" Rumors swirled—Davis was dead, went one; Richmond evacuated, another; Clay headed to Mexico, yet another. Over that lonely Christmas, "homeless, husbandless, childless," Virginia kept following the routes of approaching ships, praying each one might bring her husband, wondering each night if he "ran the fearful blockade last night, or will he tonight, while I lie safe in my bed?"

But she couldn't be sure she really *was* safe at Beech Island so after she found "a suitable escort" she moved on to Macon, where in early February her husband finally arrived. He had barely made it—unable to break the blockade, he had to wade into shore under gunfire—but he was there. And that's where they were when they learned that President Andrew Johnson had put a price on Clement Clay's head. "We receive the President's Proclamation offering $100,000 for my dear husband's arrest as the murderer of Lincoln!" a terrified Virginia Clay recorded in her diary on May 11. Macon was now under the control of the Union army and the couple had just the day before heard of the capture of Jefferson Davis. Clement Clay decided to turn himself in. His wife was sure he would hang.

They boarded the same train with Varina and Jefferson Davis and their four children, plus Varina's sister Maggie Howell and some nurses for the children. Then it was on to a "brig-rigged steamer," the *Clyde* guarded by the Fourth Michigan Regiment on board and the gunship *Tuscarosa* alongside. On the trip up the Atlantic to an uncertain fate there was a moment's respite from fear on "the water deeply, darkly, beautifully blue & the porpoises in shoals . . . chasing each other." But then as they dropped anchor in the waters outside Fort Monroe, Mrs. Clay shuddered, "I sadly fear that they will land my darling at this fort. God forbid!" Before the men were taken away, Virginia and Clement said their farewells privately in their stateroom. The Yankee press told a different version of the story: "The parting of Mr. and Mrs. Clement C. Clay was more demonstrative and affecting than the separation of traitor Jeff. and his Serena [*sic*]. . . . Mrs. Davis bore the parting remarkably well and it did not seem to cost her much effort to do so." In fact the Davis family was in distress, with the "weeping of children and the wailing of women" informing the secluded Virginia that the men had been taken ashore.

Then the women found out what was in store for them as they were summarily strip-searched and informed they could neither leave the country nor go north to New York or Baltimore. So it was back south, past Fort Sumter—"Desolate, historic Sumter! Flag floating & sentry walking"—and on to Savannah and the famous Pulaski House hotel, where the town turned out to greet them. The federal soldiers patrolling the city drilling outside included, to Virginia's horror, "a regiment of Negroes in full dress!" It would be a new world for these southern slave owners. Leaving the Davis brood behind in Savannah, Virginia worked her way to Huntsville, where she found the Clay family house occupied by the Union army, and her seventy-five-year-old in-laws in terrible shape, with their son's imprisonment landing a final blow after a wartime of want. And the news from prison was bad.

Some reports had the men in chains, kept in solitary cells, with no books allowed and no visitors, guarded by soldiers tramping up and down twenty-four hours a day. That meant no lawyers for the trial expected at any time. Virginia heard rumors that Clay and Davis would be tried by a military tribunal, like Mary Surratt, and she was terrified that they would come to the same end. She *had* to do something; it would be "impossible for a wife, knowing her husband to be innocent, and resenting the ignobleness of a government which would thus refuse to a self-surrendered prisoner the courtesies the law allows to the lowest of criminals, to rest passively under conditions so alarming." She had been writing to everyone she knew, but to no avail. It was time for her to go to Washington herself. "If you come North," a letter from her husband warned, "you must come prepared to hear much to wound you, and to meet with coldness and incivility where you once received kindness and courtesy. Some will offend you with malice, some unwittingly and from mere habit, and some even through a sense of duty." So it was with more than a little surprise and gratitude that Virginia Clay found she was treated kindly not only by her old friends but also by the enemy general in chief himself.

The letter Ulysses S. Grant dictated to his wife, Julia, could not have been more direct: "As it has been my habit heretofore to intercede for the release of all prisoners who I thought could safely be left at large, either on parole or by amnesty, I now respectfully recommend the release of Mr. C. C. Clay." It was addressed to the President of the United States. An ecstatic Virginia Clay thought she had won. She rushed to the White House, letter in hand, asking permission to visit her husband at Fort Monroe and to be "furnished with copies of the charges against him." No answer. Despite repeated sallies into the president's office, Virginia wasn't making any progress. Finally, Johnson tried to send her back to Stanton, provoking an outburst: "I will *not* go to Mr. Stanton, Mr. President! *You* issued the proclamation charging my husband with crime!" Johnson meekly replied that he had been forced to do so "to satisfy public clamour," since Clay was in Canada at the same time as the Lincoln assassination conspirators. An enraged Virginia Clay demanded to know if Johnson thought the charges were true: "Do you, who nursed the breast of a Southern mother, think Mr. Clay could be guilty of that crime?" The president did not. But he also would not release the prisoner or allow her to visit him.

Andrew Johnson was already in political hot water with Congress, which was about to come back into session. He had spent the summer and early fall instituting his own form of Reconstruction, which included liberal pardons parceled out by the thousands. He didn't raise an objection as states enacted repressive "Black Codes," treating the freedmen as little different from slaves, and he looked the other way at violence against the formerly enslaved men and women of the South. But releasing one of the Confederacy's top men would be a step too far, Johnson believed, and the Republicans in Congress would have his head. Still, Virginia, who now haunted the White House daily, was able to extract a promise that the prisoners would not be tried by a military commission, and at last Johnson provided her with a permit to visit her husband. First she would go to New York City to consult with some of the men who had been agitating for Clay's release, among them the newspaper publisher Horace Greeley. Their conversation took place in a busy hotel hallway, "now thronging with Southern guests." Virginia couldn't help laughing when she saw some "prominent Southern generals" staring at them "with a look of surprise that said very plainly, '*Well!* If there isn't Mrs. Clem. Clay hobnobbing with that old Abolitionist!'" Little did she know then that she would hobnob with Horace Greeley on many a platform as she became a prominent public voice for women's suffrage in later years.

When Virginia Clay arrived at Fort Monroe, despite her pass from the president the authorities would not let her in nor permit her to contact Johnson asking him to give the word. Only after much negotiation was she allowed to spend a few depressing hours with her husband. Clement Clay, convinced that the secretary of war was ready to see him hang, dispatched her back to Washington with even greater urgency: "You must not get discouraged!" he pleaded. "*My life depends upon it, I fear!*" Though she had not been partaking of the social season in her quasi-widow position, Mrs. Clay decided it would be wise to show up at a White House reception, "as a stroke of policy." She had been warmly received by the president's daughters, who served as his hostesses, and now that they were showing off the freshly repaired and redecorated Executive Mansion, Virginia thought that attending the event would "further win the President's good offices." Just as she was preparing to leave the house where she was staying, she learned that her husband's mother had died, poignantly asking as she expired, "What of my son?"

The news had the effect of infuriating Virginia, who tore into the president's office the next day demanding, "Who *is* President of the United States." To the reply, "I am supposed to be," she flew at him: "But you are *not!*" She berated him with the information about her treatment at Fort Monroe and he promised that she could go back whenever she wished and for a longer time. But when she pressed him on paroling Clay, he reverted to his excuse that it was up to the War Department. This time she was having none of it. Trying to appease her, the president told her to write up her case and pledged to read it at the next cabinet meeting. "'You will Not!' I answered hotly. 'Why?' he asked, cynically. 'Because,' I replied, 'you are afraid of Mr. Stanton!

He would not allow it! But let *me* come to the Cabinet meeting, and *I* will read it. . . . I do not fear Mr. Stanton or anyone else.'" And with that she flounced off to see her husband at Fort Monroe.

SO VIRGINIA CLAY was not in the city when Adele Cutts Douglas married for the second time, on January 23, 1866. (Adele's old rival, Harriet Lane, had married for the first time just twelve days earlier.) Virginia might not have been invited under any circumstances since "the marriage was quite private," according to the *Norfolk Post*, "the company on the part of the groom being limited to less than half a dozen of his immediate military circle." Major Robert Williams was a West Point graduate from Virginia, but unlike many of his fellow alumni, he had chosen to stay in the U.S. Army when the Civil War began. The Capital approved of the pairing if the Washington *Evening Star* is to be believed. Still referred to as "one of the handsomest and most brilliant women in America," Adele this time around was marrying "one of the finest looking and most fascinating men in the country, so the match is on all sides looked upon as singularly felicitous and fit to be made." A far cry from the reaction to Adele's first marriage, when Varina Davis fumed that the Cutts family was marrying her friend off to the malodorous Stephen Douglas for his money.

But Adele and Douglas had formed a tight partnership; she traveled with him as he debated Abraham Lincoln while running for the Senate, stayed by his side as he campaigned or president in 1860, and nursed him through his illness and death at the age of forty-eight in 1861. She turned the mansion Douglas built not far from Capitol Hill into an important Washington social center, having learned how to bring people with differing viewpoints together from the master of that craft, her great-aunt Dolley Madison. When war came Adele handed the house over to the military for a hospital and moved into the "Cutts Cottage" with her family, and it was there that she and Major Williams said their vows.

The wedding ended years of speculation about who the winsome young widow might marry. For a while it was "reported and believed in the City" that Salmon Chase was the lucky man, said Elizabeth Blair Lee, until Adele denied the rumor. A few months later Lizzie's father dropped by to see the devout Catholic woman and discovered "Mrs. Douglas—who he found reading Cicero's orations in Latin to one of the Holy Fathers looking exquisitely beautiful—& charming. She says she cannot marry without *descending* to do it & is too proud for that. Mother's comment was witty but looks hard written so I'll spare it." (Eliza Blair had probably made a crack about Stephen Douglas, who was definitely not the favorite of the women of Washington.) There was even talk that Mrs. Douglas might enter the convent, become a Sacred Heart nun.

Adele didn't need a husband in order to hold power, as her free rein in the White House made clear. Frequently an item would appear in the newspapers attesting to her access: "Mrs. Stephen Douglas and Mrs. Surgeon General Barnes who were in attendance this morning were both granted special interviews with President Johnson." For Virginia Clay to have Addie Douglas fighting for her was helpful indeed and now the Alabama woman was also getting help from even more useful quarters.

"When will wonders cease?" she asked her diary in mid-February. "Who but Hon. Mr. Wilson of Mass. has called! Voluntarily to say he will do anything in his power for me or Mr. Clay! Knows he is innocent. Believes Mr. Davis to be also innocent. Was kind & I melted." This was a big breakthrough! A political opponent from the deeply abolitionist

state of Massachusetts, Republican Senator Henry Wilson, was coming
to her aid. When she told the president about Wilson's endorsement
in one of her almost daily forays to the White House, Johnson scoffed
that the congressman would never put it in writing for fear of the Radical press. But the persistent Mrs. Clay soon produced a letter from the
senator saying he had "no hesitation in recommending" the favorable
consideration of her request. The leader of the Radicals in the House,
Thaddeus Stevens of Pennsylvania, also backed the parole. Public opinion had begun to turn. Clay and Davis had been held now for almost ten
months with no charges brought against them and no trial date set. But
still fearful of the "public clamour" Johnson wouldn't budge.

As the president became engaged with the Civil Rights Act and his
highly controversial veto, Mrs. Clay took some time off from her relentless lobbying, with a visit to Vinnie Ream's studio at the Capitol, where
the young woman was busy working on her statue of Lincoln. In early
April Virginia traveled to Baltimore for the fair of the Ladies' Southern
Relief Association, which raised more than $160,000 to help the desti-
tute South just a year after the bitter war had ended. By the middle of
the month, the newspapers reported that "Mrs. Clement C. Clay . . . has
laid before the President recommendations for her husband's release on
parole from such officials as General Grant, Senator Wilson and Thad.
Stevens." In a smart public relations move, the tenacious woman had
gotten the word to the press. The president no longer had any reason
to fear the "public clamour" and on April 17 Andrew Johnson handed
Virginia Clay the papers for her husband's parole. It was all her doing—
and everyone knew it, including Jefferson Davis.

———

"THE HAPPIEST EVENT for me which has occurred here was
the release of my friend and fellow sufferer Mr. Clay," the former

Confederate president told his wife, Varina; "he was not allowed to take leave of me, and his wife was unable to obtain the permission she sought to visit me." Jefferson Davis had not been allowed much in his eleven months at Fort Monroe. At first he had been placed in chains and shackled to his cell but the public uproar that followed news reports about his treatment served to free him from his manacles; still, little else changed. He could not receive mail or books, he could only sleep about two hours at a stretch, and his always fragile health was rapidly deteriorating. Varina Davis, in Savannah with her four children, the oldest of whom had just turned ten, was frantic about her husband's condition and her own.

Guards watched her at her hotel, and all of her communications with family and friends had to go through official channels, limiting her words as well as her movements. And though the local Savannah families were kind, Varina agonized when some of the Yankee tourists told the children their father would be hanged; one woman told eight-year-old Jeff that his father was a "a rogue, a liar, an assassin, and that means a murderer, boy; and I hope he may be tied to a stake and burned a little bit at a time." Union soldiers taught three-year-old Billy Davis to sing, "We'll hang Jeff Davis on a sour apple-tree." She had to get her children out of there. Her request for permission to move to Augusta was denied but then the children were allowed to leave for Canada, along with her mother and a former slave, Robert Brown, who remained loyal to the family.

Her husband in jail, under conditions so dire that she was afraid he was dying, and her small children sent off thousands of miles away, Varina was left with only the baby, one-year-old Winnie, her little "Pie Cake," as she puzzled over her prospects. For the present, her main objective was humane treatment for her husband. "Shocked by the most terrible newspaper extras issued every afternoon, which represent my husband to be in a dying condition, I have taken the liberty, without any previous acquaintance with you, of writing to you," she bravely addressed the doctor in charge at Fort Monroe, the first of many letters she sent without ever hearing back from him. Dr. John Craven too was under orders not to communicate.

Varina's letters to the doctor were just some of the many she was mailing out from what was little better than house arrest—she was allowed to go out in Savannah but not to leave the city. When she learned that her husband had been shackled in chains she penned a blistering missive to her old friend Francis Preston Blair: "Shame-shame upon your people! . . . May God except you from the curse which He will surely visit upon such sin." Preston Blair tried to assist Varina, telling President Johnson that it would make him look good if he showed a "tenderness" to Davis's wife, even if he didn't want to show any to the Confederate president himself. To the former tailor Johnson, Jefferson Davis epitomized the southern aristocracy, which the president hated; he rejected Blair's appeal. Varina didn't have any better luck with another old friend, Montgomery Meigs.

Meigs and Jefferson Davis had worked closely together building the Capitol and the Aqueduct, their wives were friendly, and Davis had helped the Meigs' son John get into West Point. But John's death had erased any hint of friendship in Meigs's mind. He refused to answer Varina himself, instead sending word to her through the Union army in Savannah that her husband's health had improved. Meigs harbored no sympathy for the women of the South. "Let the rebels take care of their own widows," he remarked; they had "filled" the North with widows aplenty. Not only were her current letters producing no results, but Varina saw some of her past correspondence spread all over the newspapers. When the government searched through her husband's papers and discovered her letters, they were leaked to the press.

An insulted Varina protested to the secretary of state about releasing her mail to "newsmongers." She vacillated between her temper and her terror as she tried in vain to help her husband.

Varina begged President Johnson to let her join her children in Canada but he didn't reply, and she was incensed when she read what he said to the South Carolina delegation about her being an angry woman; she protested that she had never written to him in anything but a courteous vein. Even though, she told a friend, "his unmanly persecution of me has been very often a great temptation," she knew better than to attack the president, because it would only hurt her husband. "Mr. Johnson's theories about my character are of small importance, because I have never been in the same room with him in my life, unless unconsciously. . . . I pray God I may bear all the insults, and agonies of the life to come with the same quiet fortitude which I have evinced in the past." She had had to show fortitude in the past because Varina had a hard time as first lady in Richmond, not at all unlike her counterpart a little over a hundred miles away, in Washington.

Just as Mary Lincoln had been suspect in the Union capital because of her southern family, Varina Davis's northern roots raised eyebrows in the Confederate seat of power. Her grandfather, Joseph Howell, had been governor of New Jersey and she herself had gone to school in Philadelphia. The women of Richmond, particularly those hailing from the snobbish First Families of Virginia, didn't hide their disdain for the newcomers who came with Confederate officeholders. Varina in particular bore the brunt of their snubs and snide remarks. With her olive complexion—"tawny," according to a hostile Richmond editor—she didn't even look like a true southern belle. (Years later, when southerners objected to the First Lady of the Confederacy moving to New York, she declared to her daughter that she could do what she wanted because she was "free, brown, & 64.") She was tagged,

just as Mrs. Lincoln was, as a "coarse Western woman." And she possessed a famously cutting wit, which she often didn't hold in check.

The women of Richmond did show some sympathy to Varina
Davis when her five-year-old son fell off a balcony and died of a fractured skull. Unlike Mary Lincoln after the death of Willie, Varina
carried on her duties in her grief, joining the thousands of mourners
at the little boy's funeral, though she was eight months pregnant. The
welcome birth of the new baby girl in June 1864 marked a moment
of happiness but the war soon took its inexorable turn, leading to her
husband's imprisonment and her inability to do anything about it. Not
that she wasn't trying. She wrote to everyone she could think of, including General Grant and Horace Greeley, people she would have
never have had anything to do with only a few months earlier.

Though Dr. Craven at Fort Monroe wasn't responding to her letters, he did use her information to make Jefferson Davis's situation
more comfortable and then, at last, the prisoner received permission
to exchange letters with his wife. She informed him of her efforts: "I
have appealed again and again to go to you, but never an answer. President Johnson stated to one of a committee who called upon him that
my application were not in a proper spirit"; this was the now-famous
statement to the South Carolina men. "Perhaps he may change his
mind. I do not know." She was upset that some of her mail had not
reached her husband; she didn't think it was because of anything she
said in her censored letters. "God knows I repress all which might be
offensive to anyone." Davis probably had trouble believing that about
his tart-tongued wife, and he tried to call her off: "Let me beg you to
address all your energies to the heavy task imposed on you in having
sole charge of the children. You cannot effect anything for me and
would probably meet wounding repulse in any attempt to do so."

It's not that Jefferson Davis didn't think women were capable of swaying men in power. He had sent the famous spy Rose Greenhow to England as an unofficial emissary for the Confederacy. While there she published her prison story and stirred up sympathy for the southern cause. (When she returned in 1864 the ship carrying her ran afoul of the Union blockade and the lifeboat she transferred to was swamped. The two thousand dollars in gold pieces sewn into her dress weighed her down and drowned her.) So he knew how to use women for propaganda purposes. He might have thought that his wife would do more harm than good; she told him herself that the president didn't think her requests were proper. But then Clement Clay was set free, and it was clearly Virginia's doing.

By then President Johnson had given Varina permission to travel. First she went home to Mississippi to inspect their devastated property, then to New Orleans to the welcome arms of old friends, and from there to Canada, where she could join her children and mother and sister. While she was there she heard that her husband was gravely ill. This time when she shot off a telegram to the president, asking, "Is it possible that you will keep me from my dying husband? Can I come to see him?" The answer was yes. The press tracked her progress from Canada. "Mrs. Jeff Davis has left here to visit her husband. She is described as of superior personal appearance and manners with highly cultivated mind and admirable power of conversation," came the report from a Montreal correspondent. A Charleston, South Carolina, newspaper described her arrival at Fort Monroe:

> Mrs. Jefferson Davis accompanied by two servants and her youngest child, an interesting little girl about two years old, arrived here at an early hour this morning. . . . Immediately

on receiving the gratifying intelligence of the permission allowed her by President Johnson to visit her husband confined
here, Mrs. Davis . . . left Montreal. She made no stoppage
on the way, but came through direct, and made very quick
traveling time.

It had been almost a year since Varina had seen her now achingly
emaciated husband. She was shocked at what she saw when she entered
his barren cell with its rude necessities—a horse bucket for water, a
mattress infested with lice. He looked awful, though the doctor assured her that his condition was not fatal. General Nelson A. Miles,
the commander at Fort Monroe, had fired Dr. Craven for being too
friendly to the former Confederate president, which left the doctor
free to publish a book sympathetic to Davis, including all of Varina's
unanswered letters, softening public attitudes toward the prisoner
Horrified by her husband's condition, Varina again begged President
Johnson for his intervention, beseeching him to let Davis have "a quiet
dark room at night" and "the power to walk about at will during the
day," but even those modest requests got nowhere. So Varina Davis
decided the only thing for her to do was go to Washington herself.

It was quite a moment when the former cabinet wife, Senate wife,
and first lady of the Confederacy showed up in the Federal City. The
New York Tribune reported with wonder "the great sensation" of Delaware senator Willard Saulsbury actually appearing in public with
Varina. He took her to church "clothed and in his right mind," the reporter joked, adding, "Mrs. Davis has received very marked attention,
and many distinguished personages have made unseemly haste to pay
their respects to her." Varina was back in the city she loved, with the
people she had missed longingly during the years when she had to
carry the burden of a cause she knew was doomed from the beginning.

She was especially glad to see "my dear friends" Montgomery Blair and his sister Lizzie Lee. But Senator Wilson also "called with kind words of sympathy" and General Grant promised he "would be glad if he could serve me in any way," Varina remembered appreciatively in her memoir. It was just the president who was a problem. "He sent me a verbal message of discourteous character" telling her to go see senators instead. But senators had no control over General Miles at Fort Monroe. Several of her political friends interceded and Johnson agreed at last to see her: "This was my first and last experience as a supplicant."

Andrew Johnson repeated to Mrs. Davis the same thing he told Mrs. Clay: his hands were tied by public opinion. Varina reminded him that he was the person who had stirred up the public with his proclamation charging Davis with conspiring to assassinate Lincoln. Johnson admitted he didn't believe those charges, explaining he "was in the hands of wildly excited people," but when she pressed him for a retraction he replied, "*I would if I could but I cannot.*" His standing with the Congress was too precarious, he whined, and if members could find any excuse to impeach him they would. Just then a senator she didn't know burst into the room and berated the president so shockingly that Varina left feeling "sorry for a man whose code of morals I could not understand." Though she walked away from her unpleasant interview empty-handed, she soon did manage to find a way to improve her husband's treatment at Fort Monroe through the intervention of the new doctor. Then Davis's tormentor, General Miles, was reassigned. Montgomery Blair's wife, Minna, guessed Varina had manipulated the move: "I see by the *Herald* Gen. Miles is removed. If so I congratulate you upon it." Mrs. Davis had made no secret of her views.

Now that she had succeeded in making his life better in prison, with friends visiting regularly and bringing good food and drink, Varina could marshal her forces for the ultimate goal: her husband's release. She decided to follow Virginia Clay's example and pay a visit to Horace Greeley. He wrote a helpful editorial as she lined up more support, traveling to Baltimore, where she was introduced to John W. Garrett, president of the Baltimore & Ohio Railroad and a close friend of Secretary of War Stanton. That did the trick. Garrett, after some considerable argument, prevailed on Stanton to instruct the attorney general to release Davis for trial.

Two years and a day after his capture, thanks to the efforts of his wife, Jefferson Davis walked out of Fort Monroe. With an entourage of lawyers and aides, he and Varina traveled to Richmond, where they stayed in the same hotel room they had moved to six years earlier as the new President and First Lady of the Confederacy. The next day, Horace Greeley and radical abolitionist Gerrit Smith were among those supplying the $100,000 bail Davis posted in a courtroom set up in his old office. He walked out a free man. He and his wife could go to Canada to reunite with their children and figure out their futures.

WHILE VARINA DAVIS and Virginia Clay lobbied for freedom for their husbands, Elizabeth Blair Lee pushed for a promotion for hers. Throughout the entire war Lizzie had browbeat members of Congress and the executive for an admiralty for Samuel Phillips Lee, with her father as her staunch ally. But Lizzie's brother Montgomery Blair blocked all of their moves, still smarting over a falling-out he had had with Lee years before. Now that the war had ended, another matter thwarted Lee's push for a higher rank—money: he had too much, having commanded the largest squadron in the navy for two years, enforcing the Union blockade. The sale of the ships and their cargoes confiscated by the blockade reaped huge rewards for the Union sailors on all ships within range of the one captured—they all received a percentage of the total sale. It was an even better deal for the commander, who took home a twentieth of every single prize from every ship under him. And Lee's take of the booty from confiscated ships came to more than $100,000. It was a sum sure to arouse envy among fellow officers and the public. Lizzie's case in trying to help her husband was almost as unpopular as the ones of the southern women.

Lee had stayed on duty until the bitter end of the war, though he had asked to come home when Lizzie found the lump in her breast, which did eventually require surgery. Secretary of the Navy Gideon Welles wanted Lee to hold his position as commander of the Mississippi River Squadron in case Confederate leaders tried to escape to the West. So it was not until August 1865 that the long-absent Lee returned to his wife and son. Lizzie was thrilled to have her husband home as she went about her much-loved duties running the orphan asylum. But then a bolt hit them from the Department of the Navy. Secretary Welles assigned Phillips Lee—still not an admiral—to California. The Blair family, except Montgomery, went into action. Lee himself ignored the chain of command and went directly to the president, the man his wife had nursed for a month. Preston Blair stormed into Johnson's office as well but the navy secretary held firm.

Finally, after his father had begged him to "bury this feud before you bury your parents," Montgomery Blair went to Welles arguing that it would be a horrible blow to his elderly parents for Lizzie and her son to move to California. They needed her and adored her little boy, who at age eight had lived with them his whole life. An even more potent lobbying force greeted Welles when he went to the White House and found that Lizzie had enlisted the support of her most heartrending troops: sixty to eighty orphans from the asylum. The matron with them implored him "for the children's sake, to revoke the orders, that Mrs. Lee could remain." Welles thought it was a cheap trick; why couldn't Lizzie and little Blair stay in Washington while Lee moved to California? But at last he relented and substituted an assignment in Hartford, Connecticut, as president of a newly created Board of Examiners to hear applications of volunteer officers who wanted a permanent commission.

As the military created new entities to deal with the end of the war, they closed old ones. Dorothea Dix shuttered her office as superintendent of nurses in September 1866. Her high standards and strict rules combined with her imperious manner had so irritated senior officers that they curtailed her power midway through the war by giving the surgeon general a shared say in the appointment of nurses, along with Miss Dix. But she stayed on duty securing pensions for the wounded, visiting those still in the hospitals and responding to requests. When she was ready to depart, Secretary Stanton asked what she wanted for her extraordinary service. "The flag of my country," she replied. Stanton did better than that. Three years later, accompanying a special stand of three flags presented to her was a congressional resolution acknowledging "the inestimable services rendered by Miss Dorothea L. Dix for the care, succor, and relief of the sick and wounded soldiers of the United States on the battlefield, in camps, and hospitals during the recent war, and for her benevolent and diligent labors and devoted efforts to whatever might contribute to their comfort and welfare, it is ordered that a stand of arms of the United States colors be presented to Miss Dix." General Sherman did the honors of making the presentation.

Clara Barton finished up her work at the Missing Persons Office and went on the lecture circuit for a couple of years, until a breakdown in her health sent her on a rest cure to Europe, where a whole new mission would await her. As she left she was beginning to realize that the war that allowed her to be of such use had changed life for women in America, later reflecting "woman was at least fifty years in advance of the normal position which continued peace . . . would have assigned her."

———————

IT DIDN'T TAKE long for peacetime politics to heat to a boiling point, with northern Republicans increasingly disillusioned with the new president. Lizzie Lee briefly moved with her husband to Hartford, where the local sentiments worried her: "The tone of talk is exactly like that of the secessionists before the war—and our side are disheartened," she fretted. "But we women kind can only hold our tongues and pray." The divisions over Johnson's Reconstruction plans grew wider, and the arguments over civil rights for African Americans louder. Though Andrew Johnson in his conversations with Varina Davis and Virginia Clay seemed to quake in his boots about the Congressional reaction to releasing their husbands, he showed no qualms about handing out thousands of pardons for other Confederates, much less taking on the lawmakers over policy. Johnson's Reconstruction allowed southern states to reenter the Union without having enacted any social or economic reforms or any provisions for freedmen suffrage. When Congress came back to Washington for the session following the assassination, members found a completely different road map for the future from what they were ready to accept. And they set about redrawing it.

First they refused to seat members of Congress from the Confederacy. Then they proceeded to pass landmark legislation—the nation's first civil rights bill, stating that "all persons born in the United States," with the exception of American Indians, were "hereby declared to be citizens of the United States." Congress then approved a bill expanding the Freedmen's Bureau to include land distribution to African-Americans, plus schools and legal protections. President Johnson vetoed both bills. Congress overrode both vetoes, at the time an unprecedented move on such major legislation. And two-thirds of each House also sent to the states a Fourteenth Amendment to the Constitution directing that no state could "deprive any person of life, liberty, or property, without due process of law; nor deny to any person within its jurisdiction the equal protection of the laws." In a section on apportionment of House seats, the amendment inserted the word *male* in the nation's governing document for the first time to the distress of women's rights advocates.

Andrew Johnson strongly believed that all of these measures infringed on states' rights and he decided to take his case to the people. In what came to be known as his "swing around the circle" tour, the president went on the road stumping for his candidates for Congress and against the Radical Republicans. Calling Johnson "faithless & unscrupulous," Mary Lincoln escaped to Springfield, Illinois, when the campaign circus swung into Chicago, complaining to her friend Charles Sumner, "he is endeavoring to ignore all the good, that has been accomplished and returning the slave, into his bondage."

It was considered beneath the dignity of the president to campaign personally, and Johnson added to the lack of dignity by his haranguing, vituperative speeches, where onlookers suspected he was drunk much of the time. It was a disaster. The Republicans gained veto-proof majorities in both the House and Senate. They used them in 1867 to override Johnson in approving the Tenure of Office Act, requiring the president to obtain Senate consent before firing a cabinet member and to extend suffrage in the District of Columbia to all males over the age of twenty-one. It was the first success in the move to provide voting rights for African-Americans. But supporters of women's suffrage were bitterly disappointed to have been excluded. The Congress also instituted a Reconstruction plan for the South administered by the federal military, passing several pieces of legislation to effect that highly controversial end. These were still essentially battles over race—how African Americans would be treated in the postwar period when the terrorist organization the Ku Klux Klan had already raised its sheeted head.

———

BUT WITH THE end of the war other matters also came before a Congress now able to look to a future with a soon to be united and still expanding country; one surprising new addition came with the purchase of Alaska in 1867, the same year Nebraska was admitted as the thirty-seventh state. American businesses, especially the railroad companies laying tracks across the nation as fast as they could, sent lobbyists to Washington looking for congressional subsidies to pad their pockets. Reporting on the Fortieth Congress, newspaperman John Ellis looked on these agents with amusement; "Women make excellent lobbyists, as they are more plausible than men, and cannot be shaken off as rudely." Some of the favor seekers offered outright bribes, while others employed more subtle approaches. "The female lobbyist is called in to exert her arts, which are more potent than those of the sterner sex," Ellis observed. "Congressmen and officials are famous as being the most susceptible men in the world, and the fair charmer is generally successful. Men in public life are very obliging when they choose to be, and these women know how to win favors from them." Wives of members also were often enlisted by lobbyists, who would give "magnificent presents" requiring the recipient to show "some especial civility." The wife and the lobbyist would form a friendship; the wife would become convinced of the rightness of the cause and in turn convince her husband. As first lady, "Mrs. Lincoln was much sought after by the lobbyists, who, knowing that they would not dare to hint at a bribe to the President, loaded her with flattery and presents. She was not deceived by them, however and made good use of them to secure the re-election of her husband."

———————

THOSE PRESENTS WERE about to come back to humiliate Mrs. Lincoln, who was now doing a good deal of lobbying of her own, not in the halls of the Capitol but by mail from Chicago. She had left the White House strapped with debt and tried desperately to persuade the Congress to contribute her husband's full four-year salary to her support. The unpopular former first lady instead received Lincoln's paycheck for one year—$25,000. That plus $1,700 a year from the interest on her husband's estate and $300 from the rental of the Springfield, Illinois, house would not be enough for her to live according to her "station," and certainly not enough to pay off her debts. She tried to shame Congress into seeing the sum as an insult to the martyred president: "in return for the sacrifices my great and noble husband made, both in his life and in his death the paltry first year's salary is offered us; under the circumstances, such injustice has been done us as calls the blush to any true, loyal heart," Mary seethed to a friend.

At her wits' end, Mary Lincoln decided to raise some cash by selling off her finery from the White House years, now that she had adopted mourning black as her only attire. She prevailed on Elizabeth Keckley to help her with the sale and the two met in New York, where Mrs. Lincoln tried to hide her financial embarrassment by calling herself "Mrs. Clarke." Well acquainted with the New York shopping scene, Mary thought she could discreetly unload her goods to secondhand shops. But she was soon recognized by a pair of unscrupulous businessmen, brokers named Brady and Keyes, who promised they would be able to raise $100,000 fast by selling her things to Republican politicians who would want to keep the public from knowing about Abraham Lincoln's widow's financial plight.

At his direction, Mary wrote a couple of letters to Brady that he would be able to show to the people he was trying to extort for funds. In the backdated letters she explained her situation and asked him to sell her "personal property," listing some of the articles, with their estimated worth: "1 black center camel's hair shawl $1500 . . . 1 Russian sable boa $1200 . . . also many other articles, including diamonds, rings, etc." She put the total value at $24,000 (but said she would settle for $16,000) and described the items as "gifts of dear friends." She called her position "painfully embarrassing" and reminded her readers that "I am passing through a very painful ordeal, which the country, in remembrance of my noble and devoted husband, should have spared me." When Brady and Keyes showed the pathetic missives to Republican politicians, they were unmoved. Mary then took the scheme a step further: she released the letters to the New York *World* and prepared to put her wardrobe on public display. The day the newspaper published the letters, a heavily veiled Mary Lincoln, aka Mrs. Clarke, boarded the train home to Illinois. So she had no idea what a sensation she had caused, though she told Elizabeth Keckley that she overheard people in her car talking about her clothes sale.

It was all anyone was talking about. The next day when her son Robert accosted her, "almost threatening his life," Mary Lincoln began to understand what she was in for: "I shall have to endure a round of newspaper abuse from the Republicans because I dared venture to relieve a few of my wants." She didn't yet know how much of an understatement that would be. Mrs. Lincoln had named names when accusing Republican politicians of blocking a public subscription for her benefit—with William Seward, Henry Raymond, and Thurlow Weed topping her villains' list. Political boss and New York newspaperman Weed fought back, and he could fight a good deal harder than the former first lady: "If the American Congress or the American people, have failed to meet the peculiar expectations of Mr. Lincoln's widow, it is because that personage failed, during his life and since his death, to inspire either with respect or confidence," he lashed out in the *World*. "Had Mrs. Lincoln, while in power, borne herself becomingly, the suggestion of a Lincoln fund, by voluntary contributions would have been promptly responded to." He noted the public had handsomely provided for General Grant, and in case anyone had not noticed it, he pointed out that presents worth $24,000 were "suggestive, at least, of offices and contracts, unless the more charitable construction is reached through the assumption that they were expressions of regard and friendship. But it is not known that the wife of any other President, however estimable, was so loaded with shawls, laces, furs, diamonds, rings &etc."

Mrs. Keckley tried vainly to defend her friend and former employer, reminding the newspaper editors that women in European royalty had not been attacked when they sold their clothes, but the criticism just kept coming. "The Republican papers are tearing me to pieces," Mary wailed to Lizzie. "If I had committed murder in every city in this *blessed* Union, I could not be more traduced." The *Cleveland Herald* demanded to know "what was in the 40 boxes" Mary took when she left the White House. The *Cincinnati Commercial* slammed her as an "intensely vulgar woman . . . her conduct throughout the administration of her husband was mortifying to all who respected him . . . she was always trying to meddle in public affairs and now she will have it known to the whole world that she accepted costly presents from corrupt contractors"; plus, in case anyone had forgotten, her relatives were secessionists. Added the *Brooklyn Eagle*, "In the meantime Mrs. Lincoln's peculiar wardrobe continues on exhibition at Brady's where 'all sorts and condition' of men, women, and artists continually visit it, but unfortunately not to buy."

That was not the worst of it. Not only did Mary Lincoln get dragged through the mud, she also made no money. So many curiosity seekers stopped in at the showroom that Lizzie Keckley, who stayed in New York to manage the sale, suggested that Brady place a subscription book at the door so everyone could pledge a dollar for the grieving widow. That too was unsuccessful. The loyal Mrs. Keckley then asked famous African-American abolitionists Frederick Douglass and Henry Highland Garnet to stage a series of lectures for Mary's benefit. They readily agreed but Mrs. Lincoln refused the offer as she sent letter after letter hectoring Lizzie, who was forced to take in sewing to support herself for the two months she tried to assist Mary Lincoln. Sorrowfully, Mary confessed, "I am feeling so *friendless* in the world. I remain always your affectionate friend."

By the next year that friendship would be shattered. While she was in New York trying to sell Mrs. Lincoln's clothes, Elizabeth Keckley worked with an editor, James Redpath, to write a memoir, *Behind the Scenes: Thirty Years a Slave and Four Years in the White House*. She claimed she had done it in order to defend Mrs. Lincoln after the abuse piled on her by the newspapers. But she included her former employer's letters, along with conversations between Mary and Abraham Lincoln. The publisher, Carleton & Company, touted it as "the great sensational disclosure by Mrs. Keckley." Mary Lincoln of course felt betrayed and the two women never spoke again. Reviewers asked in horror, "Where will it end? What family that has a servant may not, in fact, have its peace and happiness destroyed?" Mrs. Keckley's business was ruined. Just a few years earlier, the popular journalist Mary Clemmer Ames had declared: "Lizzie is an artist, and has such a genius for making women look pretty, that not one thinks of disputing her decrees." Now the fashionable modiste who had dressed the leading women of Washington had trouble finding a client.

——————

THERE'S NO RECORD that Sara Pryor was among the people pawing over Mary Lincoln's clothes that fall. She certainly would not have gone as a shopper, since she wouldn't have been able to afford any of the items. But she was in New York, where the hotheaded secessionist Roger Pryor had come to find work after the war and his family had now joined him. It had been a very long time since the family had been together, after Sara so sadly left Washington in 1861 as the southern states were seceding. Roger had gone back to the capital briefly for his meeting with President Lincoln, who arranged for his parole as a prisoner. It had been a long and hard war for the Confederate soldier; it was no shorter nor easier for his wife.

When Roger Pryor was elected to Congress at the age of thirty-one, and Sara and their five little children moved to a big house on New York Avenue, she was delighted: "We had come to stay!" she rejoiced in a memoir. It was a safe congressional district "and his constituents were devoted to him. They would never supplant him with another . . . we were going to be happy young people." She had been an active member of the Washington social set, particularly friendly with Adele Douglas but also close with Varina Davis and Virginia Clay. Her husband's propensity to get into duels somewhat marred her enjoyment, but the couple "knew everybody—and what is more I, for one liked everybody. It takes so little to make a woman happy!" The last thing on earth Sara Pryor wanted to do in early 1861 was leave the Capital City to go to Richmond and prepare for war.

But this dutiful wife was soon caught up in the cause. Roger, who had no military training, was placed in charge of a regiment, somewhat to the dismay of the men under him, and Sara joined with the other women in sewing anything they could think of for the sake of the soldiers. "We embroidered cases for razors, for soap and sponge, and cute morocco affairs for needles, thread . . . with a little pocket lined with a banknote." She laughed "'How perfectly ridiculous!' do you say? Nothing is ridiculous that helps anxious women to bear their lot—cheats them with the hope that they are doing good."

But even as she stitched away Sara didn't really grasp what was about to happen: "War? Oh surely, surely not! Something would prevent it. Surely, blood would not be shed because of those insulting words in the Senate and the House." She had followed those arguments closely, and she had been the person who informed President Buchanan that South Carolina had seceded, but the reality of war did not hit her until wounded soldiers filled the hospitals and homes of Richmond. "Every house was opened for the wounded. They lay on verandas, in halls, in drawing rooms of stately mansions. Young girls and matrons stood in their doorways with food and fruit for the marching soldiers and then turned to minister to the wounded men within their doors." The Union politicians who kept pushing the generals to take Richmond didn't see that the city was already under siege and soon there would be no food or fruit.

Unable to sit still in her sewing circle, Sara volunteered for duty in one of the hospitals and sent word to her family in Petersburg to tear up all of her household linens, including slipcovers, as bandages.

"My spring like green and white chintz bandages appeared on many a manly arm and leg." Everything was make-do; "the war had come upon us suddenly. Many of our ports were already closed and we had no stores laid up for such an emergency." The South was not prepared for the necessities of nationhood and the Pryor family had made no plans for the emergency upon them. The two girls had gone to their aunt Mary's near Charlottesville and the three little boys stayed with their mother, who made the decision in the winter of 1862 to join Roger at camp in the Blackwater, at the edge of the Great Dismal Swamp, because, she explained, "I now had no home." Her clergyman father-in-law in Petersburg had abandoned the parsonage to join the army as a chaplain and turned his congregation over to another minister.

She arrived by train at nightfall, with three children and a couple of trunks. No one knew she was coming and she had nowhere to go. At the station she saw the postmaster locking up for the night and asked him where she might stay; he took her home. The next day she got a message to Roger, who negotiated with the kindly Quaker postmaster to make his house the camp headquarters. Though fairly cut off from the outside world, they did hear the news of the Emancipation Proclamation in January 1863. Since the Pryors had never owned slaves—they hired other people's slaves as servants and paid them—the proclamation didn't mean anything to them personally and it "did not create a ripple of excitement among the colored members of our households in Virginia."

Occasionally Sara received mail from her friend Agnes in Richmond, who enclosed in one letter "a copy of Victor Hugo's last novel, 'Les Miserables,' reprinted by a Charleston firm on the best paper they could get, poor fellows, pretty bad, I must acknowledge." Things were "pretty bad" all over the South, especially in Richmond, where Agnes joked, "Do you realize we shall soon be without a stitch of clothes?" But the city was putting on a brave face. "A sort of court is still kept up

here. . . . Mrs. Davis is very chary of the time she allots us." At Varina
Davis's most recent reception, Agnes wore the gown she had last worn
to Adele Douglas's in Washington. "Doesn't it all seem so long ago—
so far away?" With the arrival of spring, Agnes, writing with red "ink"
drawn from an oak tree on pages torn out of a scrapbook, had more
severe shortages to report as she witnessed the crowd of "more than
a thousand women and children" expand "until it reached the dignity
of a mob—a bread riot." The men in town assured her that everything would improve "if we can win a battle or two (but, oh, at what a
price!)." The price would climb much higher in the course of the year.
When Washington celebrated victories at Gettysburg and Vicksburg,
on the other side of the lines Sara Pryor wept: "Surely and swiftly the
coil was tightening around us. Surely and swiftly should we too, be
starved into submission."

Sara and her little boys were left as refugees when Roger struck
camp at the Blackwater and went back into battle. She tried to reach
her aunt where her daughters were staying, and one of her sons had
also gone, but the guerrilla fighting all over Virginia made the journey
too dangerous, plus she was pregnant. She managed to get to Petersburg where her brother-in-law allowed her to use a primitive house
abandoned by one of his workers, and it was there that she gave birth
to a baby girl. Then General Grant opened his guns on Petersburg
"without giving opportunity for the removal of non-combatants, the
sick, the wounded, or the women and children."

At one point Roger showed up with some captured Union prisoners and Sara fed them out of their meager provisions—though
the hired man John objected to baking for Yankee soldiers. Food
was too scarce to share with the enemy. "We are slowly starving to
death," Sara's friend Agnes sighed to her from Richmond, where the
sight of emaciated women infuriated her. "Ah! these are the people

who suffer the consequence of all that talk about slavery in the territories you and I used to hear in the House and Senate Chamber. Somebody, somewhere, is mightily to blame for all this business, but it isn't you nor I. . . . It is all so awful."

Blitzlike, the shelling of Petersburg continued for months as Sara and the children repeatedly repaired to a neighbor's cellar to wait out the bombardment, so it was a happy day when her brother-in-law told her he had had enough. He would go to North Carolina and she could move out of the firing range to his farm. "Cottage Farm" came with two servants, in addition to the two traveling with Sara, and little furniture, but when Roger's father, the chaplain, moved in as well, he suggested that she get her trunk from Washington out of storage in Petersburg so they could set up housekeeping. This brief moment of pleasantness after the nonstop battle suddenly ceased when tents popped up in the garden and Robert E. Lee's army made camp all around her—then word came that her husband had been captured. And for a while it looked like the servant John would be taken away as well. His owner, wanting to protect his property, planned to send all the enslaved workers south to Louisiana for safety. A distraught John believed the move would kill him but the only way to stop it was to buy him. Sara took the last of her money, $106 in gold pieces sewn into a money belt, and turned it all over in order to save John and make him a free man. But she had no money to pay him and no money to buy food beyond the few rations allotted them by the army.

Racking her brain for a way to bring in income, Sara remembered the contents of her trunk. Out came the dresses that had glittered in Washington salons, including the one from the night when "Mrs. Douglas and I had dressed alike in gowns of tulle," and off came their lace decorations, their flowers and feathers. "These were my materials. I must make them serve for the support of my family." She worked long hours making lace collars, cuffs, and sleeves and sent them off to a store in Richmond, where they were snatched up by the ladies still gracing "the Confederate court." She sold off her silk dresses, opera cloak, and "point lace" handkerchiefs and then started in on artificial flowers. With the decorations stripped from her muslin dresses she proceeded to embroider them with a fine blue yarn she had discovered in the bottom of her trunk. "I traced with blue a dainty vine of forget-me-knots on bodice and sleeves, with a result that was simply ravishing!" Then it was the turn of her husband's dress coat, transformed by the enterprising Mrs. Pryor into gloves that "yielded me hundreds of dollars." She took her proceeds and bought a barrel of flour, costing $1,300. Sara would not see her family starve. And an old pocketbook plus some leather bags found in the field were turned into shoes for the children by the hands of a shoemaker soldier. For herself, "my own prime necessity was for the steel we women wear in front of our stays." She "suffered so much for want of this accustomed support" that she was pleased to find an army gunsmith to make a pair.

General Lee stopped by to ask if she could house a member of the Irish parliament who was coming to camp and when assured that the guest would "mess with the General" so she wouldn't have to feed him Sara readily agreed. After his stay, the Honorable Conolly declared Sara "one of the nicest ladies I ever saw," promising her he would go home "'and tell the English women what I have seen here: two boys reading Caesar while the shells are thundering, and their mother looking on without fear.'" Her reply: "'I am too busy keeping the wolf from my door . . . to concern myself with thunderbolts.'" And she was trying to get Roger out of prison.

When she heard that southern peace commissioners were going to meet with President Lincoln and that they would pass through Petersburg on the way to Fort Monroe, she asked for a ride out to the front to talk to them as they crossed the line into enemy territory. Soldiers on both sides cheered the men as Sara approached one of them, Senator Robert M. T. Hunter, and implored him "to remember your friend General Pryor. . . . Beg his release from Mr. Lincoln." He promised he would but the conference fell apart and Roger Pryor languished in his cell at Fort Lafayette until his newspaper friends interceded. The news of his release came to her personally from none other than Robert E. Lee. Twenty days later the general would surrender at Appomattox.

In those twenty days, despite the joy of Roger's return, the ominous handwriting was on the Richmond wall. "I don't like the looks of things here," Agnes worried, she had recognized "some of Mrs. Davis's things" in the stores, "and now comes the surprising news, that she has left the city with her family. What does this all mean?" The first lady of the Confederacy could sell her clothes with barely a mention. But her departure told the story. One last Union push toward Richmond drove the Pryors off the exposed farm and back into town, where they found an empty house and listened to the battering that finally broke the Confederate line. Sara knew the end had come when "the firing had all ceased." The next day the Rebel government evacuated Richmond. "At ten o'clock the enemy arrived—ten thousand negro troops, going on and on, cheered by the negroes on the streets," Agnes recounted in despair as she described President Lincoln's brief tour through the town, and concluded, "there is really no hope now of our ultimate success."

The next news from Agnes, in early May, revealed that she and "the Colonel" were heading to New York, where he had taken a job in a publishing house, and she was ready to take on the challenge of a move to what had been enemy territory only a few weeks earlier. "All the setting, the *entourage* of a lady is taken from me but the lady herself has herself pretty well in hand." Eventually Roger Pryor's friends convinced him to try his luck in New York as well, so Sara hocked everything she could find in order to buy him clothes and passage for the trip. She and their six children, now all together, would stay behind until he made enough money for them to join him. It would be two long years of deprivation, living under Union occupation for a while, forced to share her house with strange soldiers and line up for food for her family. As a sad little note in the Washington *Evening Star* informed her friends in the capital, "Mrs. Gen. Roger A. Pryor comes up regularly to our commissary at Petersburg to draw rations designated for the poor of the city." But true to form, Sara found a way to make do for herself and the children. (The servants who had stood by her with no salaries finally left when she insisted they go find paying jobs.) She persuaded friends and neighbors to send her their children for music lessons. And the "Rebel Pryor," as the newspapers called Roger, started finding clients.

Though the lawyer experienced some hostility as a former enemy leader, New York had become something of a gathering place for southerners. But Roger missed his wife and children terribly and prevailed on them to join him in the summer of 1867, when they were still eking out an existence. Besides caring for the children, and a new baby girl who arrived in 1868, Sara Pryor put her endless energies into relief work for various causes in New York, including the Home for Friendless Women and Children, whose suffering she could understand. She also helped establish Memorial Day to honor the soldiers who had fallen all around her. "They died because their country could devise, in its wisdom, no better means of settling a family quarrel than by slaying her sons with the sword."

As EARLY AS 1866 the word *impeachment* was whispered in Washington. When she was trying to scare him into doing what she wanted,

Virginia Clay had warned Andrew Johnson that she had heard "hints of 'impeachment' uttered in connection with the dissatisfaction resulting from your administration." By the following January, capital conversation about removing the president was out in the open, and the House Judiciary Committee had the matter under consideration. The House had passed a resolution instructing the committee to "inquire into the official conduct of Andrew Johnson"; at a wedding reception, Elizabeth Blair Lee heard an English newspaper correspondent ask a couple of congressmen if impeachment was merely meant as a threat: "One Republican replied, 'Yes we only intend it to keep Johnson in *torment*.' Old Stevens spoke up quick by & said, 'You are very much mistaken. To carry out the views of our party, we must have the Executive power & we intend to have it & pretty quickly too.'"

"Old Stevens" was Pennsylvania Republican Thaddeus Stevens, a leader of the Radical Republican faction in Congress and a fierce fighter against what he saw as Andrew Johnson's lenient treatment of the South in his Reconstruction protocols. After hearing witnesses for several months, the Judiciary Committee, by a vote of 5 to 4, refused that June to send articles of impeachment to the full House of Representatives. But Stevens persisted in his staunch opposition to the president as he proceeded to try to pass a Reconstruction plan of his own. The Confederate states seeking readmission should be treated like any territory applying for statehood, in his view, with the extra dimension of land reform. He would confiscate the large plantation properties from their owners and divide them, in forty-acre parcels, to the freedmen. This would give the formerly enslaved people land to work in order to make a living and change the political dynamics of the South.

These ideas had been talked about for a few years though it was not the path Abraham Lincoln chose when he presented his

Reconstruction proposal allowing the Rebels, other than the highest-ranking military and civilian leaders, to keep their property except for slaves. But Stevens's plan gained support as black codes were enacted across the South and violence against freedmen became common-place. And when the southern states elected the politicians who had seceded in the first place, the Congress refused to seat them and then abolished the state governments and required ratification of the Four-teenth Amendment for any state wanting readmission. The South was divided into military districts, with the Union Army protecting African-Americans. And the Union army operated under the orders of Secretary of War Edwin Stanton.

Andrew Johnson hated Stanton. In fact no one seemed to like him very much. In a letter to his daughter Nettie, Chief Justice Salmon Chase called his former fellow cabinet member "obstinate & self-willed yet changeful & capricious! a sincere lover of his country, but prone to sacrifice just interests to private hates or gusts of caprice." Stanton and his wife had not been regulars in the parlors of Wash-ington, according to Lizzie Lee, who confided that nobody ever "went near Mrs. Stanton . . . until they were in the Cabinet—when they had been here several years before—un-noticed & unknown & she is very bitter on this point." Mrs. Stanton had reason to become more bitter in the summer of 1867 when Johnson asked for his sec-retary of war's resignation. Stanton refused. Then Johnson fired his cabinet member in violation of the Tenure of Office Act. It was one of the many laws the Congress passed over Johnson's veto and it took direct aim at presidential power by requiring Senate approval of a presidential decision to remove someone from office. Johnson ac-tually did submit the dismissal for approval; the Senate, unsurpris-ingly, turned him down. Johnson then fired Stanton anyway, declar-ing that he believed the law to be unconstitutional and planning to take the case to the Supreme Court. But on February 24, 1868, the House of Representatives voted 126 to 47 to impeach the president.

On March 30, the Senate began the trial, with Chief Justice Salmon P. Chase presiding. His daughter Kate Sprague walked with him to the Capitol almost every day of the proceedings. Kate had recently raised eyebrows at one of her receptions when she "unreservedly" supported the president in his "controversy with Congress," because the time had come "to save the Constitution." After her baby was born, Kate had taken a grand tour of Europe with her sister Nettie and the little boy, with her husband showing up from time to time. Things were not going well in the marriage and being back in her familiar role as Washington hostess seemed to please her, plus it was an election year and Kate had an even worse case than her father of the White House fever Lincoln thought infected Salmon Chase. The impeachment trial would be a good opportunity for her to make an impression on the public stage.

The proceedings of course attracted huge crowds but only those with tickets could get in. "And it is a most significant fact that women hold nearly all the tickets," observed Emily Briggs, writing for the *Philadelphia Press*. "They sail into the gentlemen's gallery like a real 'man of war,' shake out the silken, feathery crinoline, rub their little gloved hands in an ecstasy of delight" while everyone scans the crowd looking for a familiar face. "Why, that is the queen of fashion—the wife of a Senator, the daughter of Chief Justice Chase." Mrs. Briggs wrote under the pen name "Olivia" and her letters from Washington were a popular feature, so Kate must have been delighted midway through the trial to read Olivia's latest: "Paris has its Eugenie; Washington has Mrs. Senator Sprague, the acknowledged queen of fashion and good taste," the correspondent gushed. "Her costume is just as perfect as the lily or the rose . . . a single flower, of lilac tinge, large enough for the 'new style' rests upon her head, and is fastened to its place by lilac tulle so filmy that it must have been stolen from the purple mists of the morning." though Mrs. Briggs conceded that Kate was not perfect: "she shrinks from the hard and lowly task of visiting the wretched hut, the sick, and the afflicted." So too did the queens of Europe avoid those tasks, argued "Olivia," defending her own queen. But not all of the coverage was so kind.

Mary Lincoln's friend, and Andrew Johnson opponent, Jane Swisshelm had another take on Kate Sprague, one that described her lobbying, not her lilacs. "A paragraph is going the rounds of the papers to the effect that Mrs. Sprague is bringing her influence to bear on her husband and father in favor of President Johnson and Against impeachment," the Radical Republican wrote for the *Pittsburgh Gazette*. "Mrs. Sprague's desire to be 'First Lady' amounts almost to a mania; and, no doubt, has much to do with her father's Presidential aspirations." As Mrs. Swisshelm saw it, Kate wanted to keep Johnson in the White House because his wife and daughters didn't threaten her position as queen of society, but if he were removed, the president pro tempore of the Senate, Benjamin Wade of Ohio, would become president. And Mrs. Wade could be a formidable opponent: "If she goes into the White House there will be no room for dispute as to who is 'First Lady,' in this Democratic land."

The current women in the White House bore the whole spectacle with grace. "Whatever Andrew Johnson was or was not, no partisan foe was bitter or false enough to throw a shadow of reproach against the noble characters of his wife and daughters," judged the journalist Mary Clemmer Ames approvingly. "There was no insinuation, no charge against them . . . nor could anyone say that they had received costly presents," she concluded in a not-so-veiled attack on Mary Lincoln. Apparently the trial was harder on the Johnson family than the public knew. "But for the humiliation and Mr. Johnson's feelings," Eliza Johnson reportedly told a friend, "I wish they would send us back to Tennessee . . . give us our poverty and our peace again."

Interest in the trial did not flag as the weeks of arguments dragged on. And the coverage of Kate Chase Sprague continued, most of it of the lilac-and-tulle variety. But even the favorable coverage managed to sneak in digs at Kate. A report on the "Ladies Gallery" that made the rounds of the newspapers described the women witnessing the trial of the president of the United States—among them the suffragist Anna Dickinson, the Confederate spy Belle Boyd, the sculptor Vinnie Ream, and the newspaperwoman Mary Clemmer Ames. The correspondent deemed the women in the gallery "fairer than any Grecian form chiseled from Parian marble and in the front of this brilliant galaxy is Mrs. Kate Sprague, who is the acknowledged peerless leader of Washington society . . . she would adorn the White House so elegantly if her father should ever become President, for with her natural beauty and many accomplishments, the enormous wealth of her husband, she would make it appear more like a royal than a republican court." Still the reporter jabbed, "she lives happily with her husband, newspaper reports to the contrary notwithstanding."

The press had sniffed out the troubles in the Sprague marriage. Kate's husband was abusive, a drunk, and a philanderer. But the rumors were that she was angry because she couldn't convince him to vote for Johnson's acquittal. She left for Rhode Island shortly before the vote, and a letter from her father makes it clear that the husband and wife had had a terrible fight. Bemoaning the fact that Sprague had

been "almost unmanned—moved to tears" by "the difference that occurred between you just before you went away," he advised her not to
forget "that the happiness of a wife is most certainly secured by loving
submission & loving tact." Moving on to the news of the trial, Chase
revealed his views: "My own judgment & feeling favors acquittal; but
I have no vote & do not know how the Senators will vote." On May 16
the Senate voted 35 to 19 to remove Andrew Johnson from office. It was
one vote shy of the two-thirds necessary to convict. William Sprague
voted with the majority. Salmon Chase's handling of the trial was considered fair and nonpartisan. It ruined him with the Republican Party.

"I FELT SORRY for the Johnsons and was glad it ended as it did," Julia
Grant recalled. "I could not free myself from the thought that the trial
savored of persecutions and that it was a dangerous precedent." Julia
thought that if her husband were president and any cabinet officer
should try him "as Stanton had tried Johnson there would be another
impeachment." And it was looking more and more certain that Grant
would be the next president. As the Republican convention was about
to open in Chicago, Julia asked him: "'Ulys, do you wish to be President?' He replied: 'No, but I do not see that I have anything to say
about it. The convention is about to assemble and, from all I hear, they
will nominate me; and I suppose if I am nominated, I will be elected.'"

It was impossible to imagine that the general who had won the
war would be defeated at the ballot box. But at least two people did
imagine it—Salmon Chase and Kate Sprague. If the Republican Party
wouldn't have her father, Kate would make him the Democratic nominee. If Grant had fought the war, Chase had financed it. His longtime
opposition to slavery meant he would still stand in good stead with antislavery Republicans who hadn't joined forces with the Radicals, and

his nonpartisan handling of the impeachment trial should make him attractive to Democrats—that was the reasoning. The fact that Chase had run against the party she wanted to embrace him didn't deter the determined daughter. In fact he had once been a Democrat, briefly; the chief justice had worn just about every political stripe over the last thirty plus years, leading his opponents to conclude that he belonged only to the Chase party. But as with so many other politicians who once thought the White House could be theirs, encouragement from a few friends led the Chief Justice to believe he could win the nomination.

A confident Kate would handle the campaign at the convention in New York's Tammany Hall when the delegates met that July. It would require adroit maneuvering to line up the votes in just such a way so that they would fall to her father. There was a crowded group of candidates and some would have to drop out before the convention would move to Chase as a compromise. The sitting president, Andrew Johnson, was out after the first ballot. As the voting went on and on, Kate worked the delegates while keeping her father apprised of the situation: "There is growing confidence everywhere that you will ultimately be the choice—there are snares & pitfalls everywhere." She signed her letter, "Affectionately & ambitiously for Country—the Democracy, & its Noblest Patriot & Statesman, Your daughter, K. C. Sprague." She was clearly enjoying herself and made no pretense about her role, which was widely reported: "Mrs. Kate Sprague, daughter of Chief Justice Chase, has had an interview with Samuel J. Tilden, August Belmont and other leading politicians in order to induce them to cast the vote of New York for her father. For years while at Washington and Columbus, Mrs. Sprague, then Kate Chase, notoriously managed the political affairs of her father, and for years has been permeated with the indomitable resolution that she would live to see her father President of the United States."

The New York vote was key and it looked like she had snared that delegation, that it would move to Chase after the candidate they had been backing, Indiana senator Thomas Hendricks, had lost. But then, unexpectedly, on the twenty-second ballot the Ohio delegation cast its votes for the convention chairman, former New York governor Horatio Seymour, who had already declined the nomination. Seymour protested but was drafted and elected by acclamation. Once again, his home state of Ohio had done in Salmon Chase. And to make it worse, Seymour picked Frank Blair, Lizzie Lee's brother, as his running mate. After all these years of the Blair-Chase rivalry the Blairs had won. When he got the word, Chase asked, "Does Mrs. Sprague know? And how does she take it?" She was indignant, insisting that they had been sold out by one of their lieutenants. And she was ridiculed in the press. "Mrs. Kate Sprague was in New York and engaged up to the latest moment of hope in lobbying and log-rolling for her father," one account read, adding that she "burst into tears" when Seymour got the nomination.

———

THAT WAS IT. Kate Chase Sprague would not preside at the White House. That honor would go to Julia Grant. In the first postwar election the general who had brought the peace won in a landslide. Salmon P. Chase would be administering rather than taking the oath of office that misty day in March when Ulysses S. Grant was inaugurated. It was a day Julia Grant remembered fondly: "I went with a large party to the Capitol, where I heard the oath of office and listened with pride and emotion to the first inaugural address of my husband, the President."

As he gave that address looking out from the East Portico of the Capitol, President Grant saw a city that buzzed with people and purpose, with women permanently working in government agencies, for newspapers and magazines, in the new schools now opening and in the hospitals where nursing had in the course of the war become a woman's job. And the women, black and white, who worked in the social service agencies dedicated to helping those in need were bringing their advocacy skills, many of them honed in the war, to bear on the men in power, while pushing to share in that power. The place to make that push would be in this city, under this dome. In fact it had already begun.

The National Woman Suffrage Convention had assembled in Washington several weeks earlier. There Elizabeth Cady Stanton declared after a war that left more than six hundred thousand Americans dead, "the history of American statesmanship does not inspire me with confidence in man's capacity to govern the nation alone, with justice and mercy." It would be another half century before women were included in the nation's central charter, the Constitution, but the services and sacrifices, the abilities and accomplishments of women in the Civil War had changed the face of Washington, just as Washington had changed the place of women.

Washington Monument, with no money to go any higher than 153 feet, stood abandoned during the Civil War. Photographed by Mathew Brady.

Epilogue

CLARA BARTON

Traveled to Europe to recuperate after her years of wartime service and discovered something called the Red Cross. The first Geneva Convention in 1864 had established the principles that ambulance and sanitary personnel traveling under the symbol of a red cross on a white background, the obverse of the Swiss flag, could move onto battlefields as unmolested neutrals in order to treat the wounded on both sides of a conflict. The Red Cross was right up Clara's alley but she was distressed to learn that the United States Department of State had refused to consider the Geneva treaty, for fear of "entangling alliances." She would eventually come home to lobby for ratification but first there was another war where victims needed her services—the Franco-Prussian War, where she worked with the

International Red Cross. When Miss Barton returned to America
in 1873 she began a full-scale lobbying campaign involving Congress, the press, and the public for U.S. approval of the Geneva
treaty. She stressed the need for organized relief in natural disasters as well as war and in 1881 established the American Red Cross,
with Clara Barton as president. At last, after nine years of labor,
the Senate ratified and President Chester A. Arthur signed the
Geneva treaty in 1882, affiliating the American Red Cross with its
international counterpart. As the U.S. representative to the Geneva
Convention of 1884, Clara Barton was able to attach the "American
amendment" to include natural disasters in the organization's mission of mercy. And then she was off to deliver the goods—to victims
of the Russian famine in 1892, the Sea Islands tidal wave in 1893,
the Johnstown Flood in 1894, the yellow fever epidemic in Florida,
and the Armenian massacre in 1896. During the Spanish-American
War, President William McKinley requested that Miss Barton, now
seventy-seven, go to Cuba in 1898 and work with American soldiers,
Cuban refugees, and prisoners of war. Her last personal foray into
the field was in Galveston, Texas, where six thousand people died in
the flood of 1900. She raised the money for the Red Cross's endeav-
ors privately, fearful of government control. But her lax ways with
the books eventually got the better of her. She was deposed as president in 1904 and never had anything more to do with the organization. In the course of her tenure the American Red Cross provided
relief in twenty-one disasters and Clara Barton collected medals
and meritorious citations from around the world. In her last years
she organized the National First Aid Association of America and
spent her time writing and working with women's rights advocates.
When she died of pneumonia at age ninety in 1912, her obituaries
ran under headlines like "CLARA BARTON—HEROINE," and

"CLARA BARTON—a Mother to Humanity." Flatly stating that her death "created sorrow throughout the nation" and that "rulers in every country have delighted to do her honor," the stories also quoted from an interview Miss Barton gave at age eighty-seven: "I am strong and well . . . and thanking God hourly that I have never known what it is to be without work."

Anna Ella Carroll

Stayed active in politics and propaganda but was frustrated for decades trying to wrestle compensation for her wartime work from Congress, particularly for the "Tennessee Plan," which she continued to contend she had strategized. In various sessions one house or the other would vote in her favor but never both houses in the same Congress. The women's suffrage movement adopted her and championed her cause as an example of the government's injustice to women. Books and pamphlets ballyhooed her case but they didn't put food on the table and after suffering a stroke she died in poverty in 1894 at the age of seventy-eight. In her death she received the accolades denied her in life. Newspaper headlines heralded the "Heroine of the War" and "Military Genius," and the stories castigated Congress for failing to heed her claims. Several biographies and fictionalized accounts have kept her claim alive.

Virginia Clay

Moved back to Alabama with her husband, who tried to make a living farming and selling insurance. She traveled as much as she could to escape the dull life of Huntsville and for a while received flowery love letters from the still-married Jefferson Davis. Her husband died and at the age of sixty-two she married Alabama Supreme Court justice David Clopton, who had been in Congress with Clay before the war. When he died in 1892 she took up suffrage as a cause. The

Alabama Equal Rights Association gained prestige and credibility with Mrs. Clay-Clopton, as she styled herself, as its president. At the fiftieth anniversary of the Seneca Falls meeting, the National Woman Suffrage Association convened in Washington in 1898. There Virginia proved herself "a powerful speaker for the cause which holds her enthusiastic allegiance," according to the newspapers. And she started using her acting abilities to raise money for charity. In her diary she intermingled the notations of the accounts she was keeping to run her farm with entries like "spoke on women suffrage at City Hall with Miss Anthony" and "played Mrs. Partington for United Charities." Her appearances with notables like Horace Greeley and the wife of leading abolitionist William Lloyd Garrison garnered a good deal of press attention, as did her memoir *A Belle of the Fifties*, published when she was seventy-five. When she died at age ninety in 1915, her obituary appeared in newspapers all over the country with its two final sentences describing the trajectory of her life: "She was a belle at Washington during the Pierce administration. She was first president of the Alabama Suffrage association."

VARINA DAVIS

Stayed with her husband and children in Canada for a while and then endured years in unhappy circumstances while Jefferson tried to make a living and she tried to make a life. The couple spent some time together in Europe, but they also spent a good deal of time separated from each other, with Varina often depressed and dispirited. Jefferson Davis pursued an infatuation with Virginia Clay though there's no evidence he acted on it. He did, however, move into the Mississippi Gulf Coast home of widow Sarah Dorsey, where he wrote his memoirs, and eventually Varina begrudgingly moved there as well. After Davis

died Varina authored a massive work stoutly defending the husband
she had so often found churlish and difficult. The two-volume tome
failed both critically and financially but throughout the pages are
sprinkled her own highly perceptive political insights. Realizing that
she needed to make a living, Varina Davis, with her daughter Winnie,
the baby "Pie Cake," decided to move to New York, much to the shock
and horror of true believers in the "lost cause" of the Confederacy.
She thoroughly enjoyed life there, running something of a salon out
of her rooms in the Majestic Hotel, supporting herself writing for the
New York *World* plus several magazines, sometimes expressing views
about women's equality and political issues that would have gotten her
in trouble had her husband been alive, and befriending Julia Grant.
Since she was still a very public persona, her initial meeting with Mrs.
Grant made page one news in the *New York Times*. Varina recognized
the symbolism that their relationship provided toward regional reconciliation and made a point of attending the dedication of the Grant
Memorial in New York. Her sons met with early deaths and then she
suffered the almost unbearable loss of her thirty-four-year-old daughter Winnie, who had become a published novelist and a darling of
the South as the "Daughter of the Confederacy." Despite repeated
attempts by the people of Richmond, Virginia, to convince Varina to
move there, even offering her a house, she held firm to New York and
from time to time visited her old friends in Washington. When she
died of pneumonia at age eighty in 1906, her illness had been tracked
in the newspapers for days; fifty thousand people lined the streets of
Richmond for her burial procession, with military escort provided by
the son of Ulysses S. Grant. Republican president Theodore Roosevelt sent a wreath. In Washington memorials staged by Confederate veterans and the United Daughters of the Confederacy filled

Willard's Hotel and overflowed the Confederate Memorial Hall, recently opened in the Union capital. Some of the front page coverage of her in death rebuked the "unjust censure" heaped on her for moving north; all of it reflected her importance in her husband's work and her own intelligence and erudition. "The years she lived in Washington," went one typical account, "were, she often said, her happiest."

DOROTHEA DIX

Returned to the work of inspecting mental hospitals, especially concentrating on those in the South that had been badly damaged during the war. Her efforts over the years resulted in the establishment of more than one hundred institutions in the United States before her death and two in Japan. She was directly involved in the creation of thirty-two state hospitals, including the one in New Jersey where she lived out the last years of her life when she became too old and infirm to travel. The notices of her death from heart disease in 1887 at the age of eighty-five described her advocacy for "criminals, paupers and the insane. . . . She lectured in all the states of the Union in their behalf and was instrumental in founding many institutions." Barely mentioned was her service as superintendent of nurses in the Civil War. Miss Dix herself looked back on those years as a low point in her life of activism but her time in the Capital City did give her a new cause: fund-raising for the completion of the Washington Monument.

ADELE CUTTS DOUGLAS

Went with her husband Robert Williams to the "far northwestern territory, almost beyond the limits of civilization . . . where for several years they lived in the barracks of a border garrison," according to a newspaper account. Six children came along as the couple moved from army post to army post, returning to Washington when Williams became adjutant general at the War Department. After years living mainly out of the public eye, newspapers ran huge stories referring to her as a "popular idol" when she died of heart failure in 1899 at age sixty-three. "She had a social and political career extending from Washington to the Mississippi Valley . . . as she grew older her reputation as the reigning belle of the Capital City was spread over the country." Her contributions to Stephen Douglas's career were cited, judging that "by her tact and keen intuition she made herself a strong factor in his chances of success." And finally, "to the last she retained the exquisite charm in conversation and manner."

JESSIE BENTON FRÉMONT

Supported her family with great energy and éclat through her writing after the never-reliable John went bankrupt. She contributed regularly to many magazines, compiled her writings into several popular books, and, just as she did as a new bride, acted as ghostwriter for Frémont's memoirs. He was appointed territorial governor of Arizona in 1878 and she joined him there briefly as they both engaged in get-rich-quick schemes that failed to make them money but succeeded in sullying their names. Back in New York one bright spot was a visit from Elizabeth Blair Lee. In 1883, after all those years of bitterness and battles, the two old friends reconciled, much to Jessie's delight. She and John moved to Los Angeles thinking they might be able to restore their fortunes there, but on one of his many trips east and away from her John died suddenly, leaving Jessie devastated and broke. A government widow's pension of two thousand dollars a year came to her aid along with the women of Los Angeles, who raised money for a house where she and her daughter Lily lived for the rest of Jessie's life. In Los Angeles Jessie Benton Frémont contributed her fame and forcefulness to the women's movement and as an advocate for education; her house, according to the newspapers, was "the Mecca toward which the footsteps of distinguished visitors have turned." President McKinley visited Jessie Frémont on a West Coast tour and delivered his one public speech at her house, where he presented "'the respects not only of himself and Mrs. McKinley, but the affection and esteem of the American people.'" A bad fall resulting in a broken hip made her an invalid and at seventy-seven she died in her sleep of pneumonia. It was just after Christmas in 1902 and obituaries from around the country recounted her belleship in Washington, elopement with the Pathfinder, her brave treks to California (repeating the off-told tale that "Mrs. Frémont's influence was instrumental in bringing California into the Union as a free state"), the political campaign of 1856 and the trip after that defeat to Europe, where "the beauty and wit of Mrs. Frémont made a great impression," then her move to Los Angeles, where she maintained "keen interest in national and international affairs." Some of the obituaries also managed to list her impressive body of published works. In 2014 the House of Representatives passed a bill to change the name of Mammoth Peak in Yosemite National Park to Mount Jessie Benton Frémont in recognition of the work she did to preserve the Yosemite Grant for the nation when she was living at nearby Las Mariposas. The Senate failed to act.

JULIA DENT GRANT

Thoroughly enjoyed her husband's two terms in the White House, declaring herself very fond of society. She didn't mind the big receptions, enjoyed hosting comfortable friends like the Blairs and Lizzie Lee, threw a huge White House wedding for her daughter Nellie, and was not at all happy when her husband rejected the idea of running for a third term. After they left office, the Grants embarked on a two-year world tour, with the princes and potentates and pashas of Europe, Africa, and Asia fawning over them wherever they went. When they returned to America they were so well received on a trip around the country that Grant made a bid for the Republican nomination in 1880. Despite Julia's pleas, he refused to go to the convention in Chicago and lost out to James Garfield, so she would not be enjoying a homecoming in the White House she loved. Instead they settled in New York, where Julia came to know both Varina Davis and Sara Pryor. The Grants' money was tied up in a firm where their son was a partner—the other partner got involved in a scam that resulted in them losing everything. Desperate to provide for his family, Grant wrote his memoirs as he was dying of throat cancer. It was an excruciating ordeal for the pain-stricken general but it worked; his book, published posthumously with the help of Mark Twain, proved so successful that his family was left with a great deal of money and Julia moved back to Washington to be among friends. When Julia died of bronchitis at age seventy-six in 1902 she was hailed as "her husband's faithful helpmeet, both when he was a great General and afterwards when he was chief executive of the nation." Some of the obituaries noted that "for a number of years she devoted herself to the preparation of her book of reminiscences of her husband." But the first first lady to author a book couldn't find a publisher. It wasn't until 1975 that *The Personal Memoirs of Julia Dent Grant* saw the light of day.

Elizabeth Keckley

Didn't fare well after her memoirs were published. Many white patrons abandoned her and some blacks shunned her for being disloyal to their hero Abraham Lincoln. A vicious racist parody of her book was published and must have produced more pain. Trying to carry on, she did some work training young African-American seamstresses and in 1892 took a job in Ohio as head of Wilberforce University's Department of Sewing and Domestic Arts. But a stroke ended her teaching career and she returned to Washington. Elizabeth moved into the Home for Destitute Colored Women and Children, the home she had helped establish, and died there in 1907 at the age of eighty-nine. Unsurprisingly, given the era, there are no published notices of the death of this woman who knew President Lincoln intimately and had met and worked with some of the leading political families of the country.

Harriet Lane

Had a difficult time through the years of the Civil War when her uncle was vilified and humiliated. She quietly married a banker, Henry Johnston, and moved with him to Baltimore from Buchanan's home in Pennsylvania. They had two sons but both boys died in their teens, in successive years. And then their father died. She moved back to Washington, the city where she had gone to school and where she had in some of the most difficult years in the history of the country presided with grace at the White House. In those years she had advocated for a national art gallery and she continued on that quest after she returned to the Capital City. She also worked to erect a monument to President Buchanan, which, with the help of Congress, she succeeded in doing. It stands shrouded in obscurity in Meridian Hill Park. When Theodore Roosevelt took his turn in the White House, Mrs. Johnston was called on from time to time to assist Mrs. Roosevelt in entertaining there. But she didn't abandon Baltimore entirely. Her work for poor and sick children in that city grew into what is now one of the premier pediatric medical centers in the country—the Harriet Lane Clinic at the Johns Hopkins Children's Center. One obituary declared, "There has never been a more gracious woman in the White House than Harriet Lane." She did not achieve her goal of starting an art gallery in her life but she did in her death from cancer in 1903 at seventy-three, having bequeathed her art collection for a "national gallery of art." The legislation establishing the Smithsonian Institution had included provisions for art collections, and the Smithsonian claimed Harriet's bequest, which spurred it to fulfill her vision and establish a National Gallery of Art.

ELIZABETH BLAIR LEE
Continued her work with the Washington Orphan Asylum, which still exists today as Hillcrest Children & Family Center, providing services to kids with mental health needs and their families. Her husband finally got his promotion and retired as an admiral to the Blair country house in Silver Spring, Maryland, where he tried to farm after all his years at sea. Their one child, born late in their marriage and doted on by all the Blair family, followed in the family tradition, becoming a United States senator—the first to be directly elected by the voters after the Seventeenth Amendment to the Constitution took that privilege away from the state legislatures. The house that Lizzie Lee lived in in Washington, across the street from the White House, and the one her brother Montgomery Blair occupied next door to it have been combined into Blair House, the home to visiting heads of state and other dignitaries. Lizzie also helped found the Daughters of the American Revolution, an organization after the Civil War that could leap back in history to a time when the country was united and find common ground between North and South. Sara Pryor joined

her in that enterprise. Despite a lifetime of bad health, she lived until she was eighty-nine, dying at home in Silver Spring in 1906. Her obituaries, while repeating her father's joke that because she was raised on Andrew Jackson's knee she was "brought up in caucus," and reminding readers that as a child she was known as "the little Democrat," also gave credit to her work in the community, praising her "life-long devotion . . . to the Washington City Orphan Asylum, manager for 57 years and first directress for 44 years." The newspapers noted that she had "learned to weigh political opinions and keep political secrets" and, remarkably, presented her own views as a moderate between southern secessionists and northern radicals. In sum, "very few women have had so broad a political experience, and it is doubtful if any other American woman has been conversant with political leaders and movements for so long a period."

MARY TODD LINCOLN

Left for Europe with Tad soon after Elizabeth Keckley's book came out. She put the boy in schools in Germany and England while she lived nearby and pestered Congress for a pension. She finally was awarded $3,000 annually and after almost three years abroad she brought her son back to Chicago. There he developed either tuberculosis or pneumonia and died at the age of eighteen. It was the last straw for the boy's mother. Robert Lincoln took his little brother's body to Springfield, Illinois, to be buried next to his father and brothers. Mary's distress became a matter of public comment, according to the newspapers "She spent her time in overhauling her many trunks, complaining that she was very sick and ate full meals of substantial food three times a day." Robert Lincoln called for a sanity hearing and the court declared Mrs. Abraham Lincoln insane. Mary's confinement in a private mental hospital got the attention of Myra Bradwell, one of the first women lawyers in the country, who took the case back to court, and this time Mary won. Embarrassed by the insanity verdict, she fled to Europe, made her base at Pau, France, suffered a fall, and in 1880, after four years abroad returned miserable to America, where she renewed her battle with Congress for more money. She moved in with her sister and brother-in-law in Springfield, though she had had a falling-out with them years earlier. Congress did increase her pension to $5,000 in 1882 and not long after that she died at the age of sixty-three. The former first lady's press was no better in death than it was in life: "though fond of society and brilliant company her reign at the White House was not socially successful," the reports agreed; "ever since the death of her husband she has simply been a physical and mental wreck."

Louisa Rodgers Meigs

At the end of the war, without Montgomery Meigs's knowledge, she wrote to Secretary of War Edwin Stanton telling him her husband was ill and needed a vacation. She knew the quartermaster general would not approve of her meddling so she told him after the fact. And she relayed Stanton's reply that he "thought it would be best to put the sea between you & your work." And so he did. Louisa and Montgomery and two of their children went on a European grand tour. They returned to Washington, where Montgomery remained quartermaster general and later took his wife on another European sojourn to inspect European armies for President Grant. Louisa's funeral was held at home in Washington when she died at the age of sixty-three in 1879 and "the parlors were crowded by prominent residents of Washington and strangers."

SARA AGNES PRYOR

Struggled through the early years in New York as her husband tried
to establish a law practice and she agonized over the probable suicide
of her brilliant young son Theodorick, a student at Princeton at the
time. Another son also died before she did. Roger went into partnership with Benjamin Butler, one of the Union generals most hated in
the South, and eventually went on the New York bench, rising to the
position of justice on the New York Supreme Court. Sara mused in
her writings over whether that would have ever happened if he had
fired that first shot at Fort Sumter instead of giving that "honor" to
another. The newspapers pick up the story from there: "when he retired and his income was reduced Mrs. Pryor at the age of 63 began
writing articles for newspapers and magazines and like her distinguished husband her efforts were crowned with success." Sara wrote
several well-received books, including two memoirs describing her
belleship in Washington, her harrowing experiences in the Civil War,
her postwar friendship with Julia Grant and her role in establishing
the Daughters of the American Revolution, the Colonial Dames, and
the Jamestown Association. But she told one of her daughters that she
took the most pride in her relief work. She organized the women of
New York into the Ladies' Florida Relief Society to aid that state in
battling a yellow fever epidemic, and issued a similar appeal for the orphans of the Galveston flood, where the funds she raised through fairs
and theater performances added up to enough to build an orphanage.
When she died in 1912 just shy of her eighty-second birthday she was
remembered as having the "reputation of being one of the most clever
and beautiful women in Washington" and a "noted writer and prominent figure in New York and the South." Sara Pryor herself had this
to say about her early-twentieth-century work: "It is often said that it
is still too early to write the story of our Civil War. It will soon be too

late. Some of us still live who saw those days. We should not shrink from recording what we know to be true. Thus only will a full history of American courage and fidelity be preserved,—for we all were Americans."

Kate Chase Sprague

Tried one more time to get her father elected president, in 1872 after Salmon Chase had had a stroke. She hosted a reception for him in Washington, where she tried to hide his shaking hands and he tried to control his slurred speech. Horace Greeley was chosen instead to run against Grant for a second term, which the incumbent president won easily, and Chase died in 1873. It was downhill from there for Kate, who had a miserable marriage but still managed to produce four children. She took up quite publicly with powerful and philandering Senator Roscoe Conkling, a married New York political boss, and entertained him at the over-the-top sixty-room estate, Canonchet, she had built at Narragansett Pier, Rhode Island. When William Sprague found Conkling in his home the irate husband came after his wife's reputed lover. The details varied with each story after the incident hit the press; some had Sprague wielding a shotgun, some had Conkling jumping out of a window to escape. Sprague and Kate divorced, Sprague lost his fortune, Kate and Conkling ended the relationship, and Kate moved to Europe with her three girls while her ex-husband kept their only son. When she returned to the Chase estate in Washington it was with limited resources, so she repeatedly mortgaged the Edgewood property. Her son committed suicide and her older girls grew up and moved out, leaving her with the youngest, who was mentally disabled. Slowly Kate sank into poverty. When the house was foreclosed on, some of her father's old friends came to her aid and paid for the house, but she had nothing to live on. The former queen of Washington went door-to-door selling eggs and milk from the Edgewood estate. She disappeared from the parlors of the powerful and the pages of the press until she died in 1899 shortly before her fifty-ninth birthday. Her death brought her back to the front of the nation's newspapers: "Nothing in her whole career was commonplace . . . her failures, it has been remarked, were the inevitable reverses of a brainy and beautiful woman compelled by her sex to devious paths of social and political strategy." In telling the story of her life the obituaries agreed that "from the time she was 16 years old she was a shrewd politician," and that "Kate Chase ruled as no other American woman ever reigned at the capital, unless Dolly Madison is excepted." Dolley Madison ended her life as a poor woman as well but was loved, respected, and highly honored until the end.

THE WASHINGTON MONUMENT

In 1866, on George Washington's birthday, President Andrew Johnson presided over a meeting of the Washington Monument Society. "Let us *restore the Union*," proclaimed the president who was locked in a battle with Congress on that very subject, "and let us proceed with the Monument *as its symbol*." Despite the stirring words, Johnson didn't have any cash to offer from the depleted coffers of the federal government at the end of the war, so the building fund limped along just as it had from the beginning. Various proposals put before Congress went nowhere, although some state governments appropriated money, as did fraternal organizations, in a push to finish the memorial in time for the centennial of the Declaration of Independence, July 4, 1876. But that effort failed as well. Instead on July 5, 1876, Congress finally took over the job. The construction assignment went to the Army Corps of Engineers and the task was at last completed on December 6, 1884, with the placing of the 3,300-pound capstone atop the obelisk, which at the time was the tallest building in the world. The formal dedication ceremony came in time to celebrate George Washington's birthday the next year. Inscribed on the east face of the capstone are the words "Laus Deo," or, "Praise be to God." It was finally done.

Author's Note and Acknowledgments

When I go to my mother's grave in New Roads, Louisiana, I see nearby the marker on her grandfather's tombstone. He was her beloved Biz who I heard about all of my life until my mother died. I'm sure I would have loved him too. The stone reads:

LOUIS B. CLAIBORNE, LOUISIANA,

PVT POINTE COUPEE ARTY CSA,

AUG 24 1842 NOV 29 1934

That is "Private, Pointe Coupee Parish Louisiana Artillery, Confederate States Army."

My father's great uncle, General William Robertson Boggs, CSA, after whom my grandfather and my baby brother were named, surrendered the army of the Trans-Mississippi six weeks after Appomattox. I grew up with the tales of awful Yankee atrocities. In every plantation house someone pointed out where the family hid the silver during the war. (I don't know why the Yankees didn't catch on that a lot of it seems to have been hidden in the fan windows above the front doors.) I say all this by way of saying that I love the South. But that might not be clear to the readers of this book. That's partly because the book is set in Washington, D.C., where the fate of the Union was the question at hand, but it is also because I think the Southern politicians' decision to secede was one of the most profound tragedies ever brought on by human beings.

Four years and six hundred thousand lives after the firing on Fort Sumter, the South was left with cities burned—the worst, by the way, being Richmond, torched by the Confederates as they evacuated—its fields ravaged, its coffers empty, and a stronger central government in Washington. The great good to come out of the war, the abolition of slavery, was what the South was fighting against. And as I have read the letters of the women who were married to those politicians I have learned that they saw the catastrophe as it was unfolding. As one of them wrote from Richmond as the body count mounted from the tens of thousands to the hundreds of thousands: "These are the people who suffer the consequences of all that talk about slavery in the territories you and I used to hear in the House and Senate Chamber. Somebody, somebody is mightily to blame for all this business but it isn't you nor I." When we took our grandkids on a tour of Fort Sumter a few years ago, the youngest boy typically asked as he was trying to pick out a souvenir in the gift shop, "Whose side are we on?" My daughter answered, "Well, everyone in our family fought for the South, but it was good for the country that the North won." There it is.

The fact that I even feel a need to explain all of that tells me how much that awful war still sears the soil and the soul of the South. Abraham Lincoln told Sojourner Truth that he would not have been able to emancipate the slaves if the South had not seceded. I would like to believe the politicians might have eventually found a way, but it's hard to see it when reading how hostile they were. So yes, a great good came out of the carnage—the end of the great moral stain of slavery. But I have also learned in researching and writing this book that the war brought about another positive development, the advancement of women in American society, South and North. And it created a cohesive country, no longer "these" United States but "the" United States with its Capital City on a firm foundation in Washington, D.C.

As always in writing women's history, there's a lot of detective work involved and I've had a great deal of help along the way. The research was a family affair starting with Steve's cousin Miranda Sachs spending a summer noodling around in the Library of Congress and at Princeton University. She turned up some good leads and turned in some good letters having started the painful process of deciphering the handwriting of these women. Then my daughter-in-law, Liza Roberts, took up the quest at the University of North Carolina and Duke and then my daughter Rebecca Roberts added to the effort new batches of material from the archives at the Historic Congressional Cemetery, along with more letters from the Library of Congress. Rebecca then introduced me to two absolutely essential team members. Jeanine Nault first helped with some newspaper research and then did the painstaking work of footnoting the entire manuscript. Laura Nelson has taxed her eyes reading hundreds of handwritten letters and a few diaries and transcribing them all. Steve's student Julie Alderman compiled the bibliography. Some transcription help came as well from William Kurtz and Adrian Brettle at the University of Virginia, introduced to me by Holly Shulman, the creator of the Dolley Madison Digital Edition, and a great resource on any history project. My friend Ann Charnley, who has moved away so is no longer able to help with research, found the absolutely fascinating unpublished diary of Ann Green from 1861. Many thanks to her descendant Cathy

O'Donnell for sharing the diary and allowing me to use it. And thanks to all of the wonderful people at the libraries and historical societies around the country: Kate Collins and Elizabeth Dunn at the David M. Rubenstein Rare Book & Manuscript Library, Duke University; Rena Schergen at the Special Collections Research Center, University of Chicago; the Princeton University Library Department of Rare Books and Special Collections, where my great-niece Caroline Davidsen was of assistance; my many friends at the Massachusetts Historical Society and The Historical Society of the Washington, D.C., plus the incredibly knowledgeable people in the Manuscript Division at the Library of Congress. Rod Ross at the National Archives was particularly helpful and he introduced me to David Gerleman of the Papers of Abraham Lincoln Project and provided me with the excellent paper on Josephine Giddings by Keith Melder. Kathryn Jacob, Curator of Manuscripts at the Schlesinger Library, Radcliffe Institute at Harvard, was wonderfully giving of her time and knowledge. Special thanks also to Sister Mada-anne Gell, VHM, the Archivist at the Georgetown Visitation Monastery. She not only provided me with valuable material, she let me join the nuns for lunch in the refectory. A special thanks as well to Dayle Dooley at the Historic Congressional Cemetery.

In addition to the people who helped me directly, I also had the advantage of many resources that were not available when I first started doing historical research. The digitization of newspapers and documents has lightened the load immeasurably. Two sites for newspapers: one free, chroniclingamerica.loc.gov, funded by the National Endowment for the Humanities, and one subscription, newspapers.com, make the ability to get the news as the people of the time were receiving it invaluable. The only problem is that they are so interesting you can spend all day reading them. The *New York Times* website also has an archive going back to the beginning. My friend Mary Regula has created a first rate research center at the National First Ladies' Library, firstladies.org, and the Lincoln Institute, a project of the Lehrman Institute, has a very useful website, mrlincolnswhitehouse.org. A few more: the Civil War Preservation Trust, civilwar.org, is great on battles, the National Park Service is great on places, nps.gov, and the well-worth supporting National Women's History Museum, nwhm.org is great on women.

There are two terrific books about Washington in the Civil War, the 1941 classic by Margaret Leech, *Reveille in Washington: 1860–1865*, is beautifully written but totally unsourced, which makes it tough for those of us coming after her. In his 2007 *Freedom Rising: Washington and the Civil War*, reporter Ernest B. Furgurson thankfully reveals his sources. Pat Furgurson was also very kind about getting back to me when I asked him for suggestions about women. Two other books that served as bibles: James McPherson's *Battle Cry of Freedom* and Doris Kearns Goodwin's *Team of Rivals*.

And now I must thank all of the people who have put this book and my life together. First, my friend and fabulous editor who keeps me laughing while she does great work, Claire Wachtel, and her assistant, Hannah Wood, who has had to take me on as a fulltime job and has done it graciously. Also at HarperCollins, Cindy Achar, John Jusino, and Lydia Weaver who did magic tricks to make the production of this book go as fast as it had to; Fritz Metsch did the interior design and Milan Bozic who designed the beautiful cover. And a big thanks to the big bosses, Jonathan Burnham and Michael Morrison, who are incredibly supportive and encouraging. DeeDee DeBartlo is the best publicist anyone can have and I am grateful to Harper for bringing her on to work with me again under the guidance of the great Rachel Elinsky. No project of mine would happen without Bob Barnett, dear friend and wise counselor. My good friends at work, Robin Sproul at ABC and Ellen McDonnell at NPR, help me patch up the holes I leave when I'm on deadline. Kim Roellig is my longtime friend and total support system. Without her my whole life would fall apart during a project like this. And then there's my unbelievable husband of almost forty-nine years, Steven. He is always my biggest cheerleader but with this book he's also had to be chief shopper and errand-runner, has had to put up with my hermit-like existence, looking none too lovely chained to my computer, and he's done it with humor and understanding because he loves me. For that I thank him most of all. And I hope none of the humans are insulted that I am also grateful to our chocolate Lab Ella. She stays by my side, occasionally asking for a pet or giving me a lick, making me happy.

Cast of Characters

POLITICAL WOMEN

Abigail Brooks Adams

Anna Ella Carroll

Virginia Tunstall Clay

Varina Howell Davis

Adele Cutts Douglas

Jessie Benton Frémont

Julia Dent Grant

Rose O'Neal Greenhow

Harriet Lane

Elizabeth (Lizzie) Blair Lee

Mary Todd Lincoln

Dolley Madison

Louisa Rodgers Meigs

Katherine Chase Sprague

LITERARY WOMEN

Lois Adams

Mary Clemmer Ames

Emily Briggs

Elizabeth Lomax

Sara Rice Pryor

Jane Swisshelm

Mary Jane Windle

ACTIVIST WOMEN

Clara Barton

Anna E. Dickinson

Dorothea Dix

Josephine Griffing

Elizabeth Keckley

Sojourner Truth

POLITICAL MEN

Charles Francis Adams—Husband of Abigail Brooks Adams

Thomas Hart Benton—Father of Jessie Benton Frémont

Montgomery Blair—Brother of Elizabeth (Lizzie) Blair Lee

James Buchanan—Uncle of Harriet Lane

Salmon P. Chase—Father of Kate Chase Sprague

Jefferson Davis—Husband of Varina Howell Davis

Stephen Douglas—Husband of Adele Cutts Douglas

John Charles Frémont—Husband of Jessie Benton Frémont

Samuel Philips Lee—Husband of Elizabeth (Lizzie) Blair Lee

Abraham Lincoln—Husband of Mary Todd Lincoln

William Seward—Father-in-law of Janet Seward

William Sprague—Husband of Kate Chase Sprague

MILITARY MEN

General Ulysses S. Grant—Husband of Julia Grant

"Fighting Joe" Hooker

Robert E. Lee—Husband of Mary Custis Lee

General George B. McClellan—Husband of Ellen Marcy McClellan

Montgomery Meigs—Husband of Louisa Rodgers Meigs

William Tecumseh Sherman—Husband of Ellen Ewing Sherman

Notes

INTRODUCTION

1 took advantage of the GI Bill: U.S. Department of Labor, Women's Bureau, *Women Workers in Ten War Production Areas and Their Postwar Employment Plans*, Bulletin 209 (Washington, DC: U.S. Government Printing Office, 1946); "History Matters: The U.S. Survey Course on the Web," George Mason University, last modified June 11, 2014, http://historymatters.gmu.edu/d/7027/; "Partners in Winning the War: American Women in World War II," National Women's History Museum, last modified 2007, http://www.nwhm.org/online-exhibits/partners/exhibitentrance.html.

2 mothers in the workforce: "Employment Characteristics of Families—2013," Bureau of Labor Statistics, last modified April 25, 2014, www.bls.gov/news.release/famee.nr0.htm.

3 "but talent outranks it": Margaret Howell to Joseph Howell, October 29, 1854, in *Jefferson Davis: Private Letters, 1823–1889*, ed. Hudson Strode (Boston: Da Capo Press, 1995), 79.

4 new federal agencies: "The Civil War—150 Years: National Park Service Sesquicentennial Commemoration," National Park Service, last modified February 2, 2011, www.nps.gov/features/waso/cw150th/reflections/legacy/page3.html.

5 "a sphere of life and action": Linus Pierpont Brockett and Mary C. Vaughn, *Woman's Work in the Civil War* (Philadelphia: Zeigler, McCurdy, 1867), e-book, loc. 1501.

CHAPTER 1: MEET THE WOMEN OF WASHINGTON

7 "opposite and distant parts of the Union": Catherine Allgor, "The Politics of Love," *Humanities* 31, no. 1 (January/February 2010).

7 bright sunlight greeted them: *Daily National Intelligencer*, July 6, 1848, http://www.genealogybank.com/gbnk/.

8 "the residence of Congress": Frederick L. Harvey, *The History of the Washington National Monument and of the Washington National Monument Society* (Washington, DC: N. T. Elliott, 1902), e-book, loc. 38.

8 "aid in collecting funds": Ibid., 554.

8 "collected about $87,000": Constance McLaughlin Green, *Washington Village and Capital, 1800–1878* (Princeton, NJ: Princeton University Press, 1962), 171.

8 "weighing twenty-four thousand five hundred pounds": Harvey, *National Monument*, 621.

8 "touchingly and eloquently": *Daily National Intelligencer.*.

9 "picture of Gen. Washington is secured": Madison to Lucy Payne Todd, August 24, 1814, in *Selected Letters of Dolley Payne Madison*, ed. David B. Mattern and Holly C. Shulman (Charlottesville: University of Virginia Press, 2003), 193.

10 "liberal sentiment to a practice": Paul M. Zall, *Dolley Madison: Presidential Wives Series* (Huntington, NY: Nova History Publishers, 2001), 61.

10 specially cast silver medal: Allgor, "The Politics of Love."

10 most famous woman in the land: *Daily National Intelligencer*, July 17, 1849, http://www.genealogybank.com/gbnk/.

10 "our grandchildren were grown": Louisa Catherine Adams, February 27, 1823, microfilm edition of the Adams family papers, Massachusetts Historical Society.

10 "delighted with the whole aspect": Frances Milton Trollope, *Domestic Manners of the Americans* (New York: Whittaker, Treacher, 1832), e-book, loc. 107.

11 "beauty and majesty": Ibid., loc. 107.

11 "fashionable watering places": Ibid., loc. 108.

11 "cultivation of the mind": *National Intelligencer*, November 27, 1848, quoted in Green, *Washington Village*, 170.

11 "tobacco-tinctured saliva": Charles Dickens, *American Notes for General Circulation*, vol. 1 (London: Chapman & Hall, 1843), 272.

11 metropolis of 52,000: U.S. Department of Commerce, Bureau of the Census, *Historical Statistics of the United States: Colonial Times to 1970, Bicentennial Edition, Part 1* (Washington, DC: U.S. Government Printing Office, 1975), 42.

11 long lines called "slave-coffles": Damani Davis, "Slavery and Emancipation in the Nation's Capital: Using Federal Records to Explore the Lives of African-American Ancestors," *Prologue* 42, no. 1 (Spring 2010), www.archives.gov/publications/prologue/2010/spring/dcslavery.html.

12 Washington's slave population: J. D. B. DeBow, *The Seventh Census of the United States, 1850* (Washington, DC: Robert Armstrong, 1853). There is some discrepancy in the census records themselves. The 1970 publication puts the total population at 8,000, with 6,000 whites and 2,000 "Negroes," not delineated by slave or free. The 1853 one counts more than 14,000 residents in 1800, and gives the breakdown by free and slave status. The two documents agree on the total number for 1850.

14 further splitting the Whigs: James McPherson, *Battle Cry of Freedom: The Civil War Era* (Oxford: Oxford University Press, 1988), 88.

14 "banished all animation": Jessie Benton Frémont, *Souvenirs of My Time: Primary Source Edition* (Boston: D. Lothrop, 1887), 103.

14 "never become a social center": Mrs. Roger A. Pryor, *Reminiscences of Peace and War* (New York: Grosset & Dunlap, 1904), 19.

14 "evolving novel social relaxations": Virginia Clay Clopton, *A Belle of the Fifties: Memoirs of Mrs. Clay of Alabama, covering social and political life in Washington and the South, 1853–66, put into narrative form by Ada Sterling* (New York: Doubleday, Page, 1905), 29.

14 "so many beautiful women": Virginia Tatnall Peacock, *Famous American Belles of the Nineteenth Century* (Philadelphia and London: J. P. Lippincott, 1900), 175.

15 "the most brilliant woman of her time": Pryor, *Reminiscences*, 81.

15 "genuine loveliness of character": Peacock, *American Belles*, 176.

15 "queenly apparition": Henry Villard, *Memoirs of Henry Villard, Journalist and Financier, 1835–1900*, vol. 1, 92, quoted in George Fort Milton, *The Eve of Conflict: Stephen A. Douglas and the Needless War* (1934; reprint, New York: Octagon Books, 1963), 256.

16 "beautiful as a pearl": Pryor, *Reminiscences*, 68.

16 "and sweetness of nature": Frémont, *Souvenirs of My Time*, 115–16.

16 "the effect she had on strangers": Clopton, *Belle of the Fifties*, 35–36.

16 "never trick myself out in diamonds": Pryor, *Reminiscences*, 69.

16 "sailed fearlessly about": Ibid., 71.

16–17 "buried my only child": Clopton, *Belle of the Fifties*, 25.

17 "to mourn in secret": Varina Davis, *Jefferson Davis, Ex-President of the Confederate States of America V1: A Memoir by His Wife* (1890; reprint, Baltimore: Nautical and Aviation Publishing Company of America, 1990), 534–35.

17 "every Tuesday morning a reception": Varina Davis to Margaret Howell,

January 1854, in *Jefferson Davis: Private Letters 1823–1889*, ed. Hudson Strode (1966; reprint, Boston: Da Capo Press, 1995), 74.

17 "formal calls were paid": Clopton, *Belle of the Fifties*, 27.

18 once went to the opera: David W. Miller, *Second Only to Grant: Quartermaster General Montgomery C. Meigs* (Shippensburg, PA: White Mane Books, 2000), 67.

18 "poor and the helpless": Penny Coleman, *Breaking the Chains: The Crusade of Dorothea Lynde Dix* (Lincoln, NE: ASJA Press, 1992, 2007), e-book, loc. 910.

18 "the property of the people": Ibid., loc. 939.

19 the indomitable advocate: Ibid., loc. 948.

19 supported her demand: Ibid., loc. 955.

19 the care of the poor: Ibid., loc. 971, and Green, *Washington Village*, 202.

20 "our political system": Anna E Carroll to Millard Fillmore, May 28, 1852, quoted in Janet L. Coryell, *Neither Heroine nor Fool: Anna Ella Carroll of Maryland* (Kent, OH: Kent State University Press, 1990), 7.

20 "even one cent": Harvey, *National Monument*, 685.

20 similar appeals: Ibid., 702.

20 "signalize his name and glory": *Daily National Intelligencer*, March 4, 1854, quoted in ibid., 719.

21 pitched it into the Potomac River: Ibid., 735.

21 new gas lamps: Green, *Washington Village*, 209.

21 "I fear the poor will suffer": Louisa Rodgers Meigs to Nannie, September 6, 1854, Rodgers Family Papers, Naval Historical Foundation Collection, Manuscript Division, Library of Congress, Washington, D.C.

21 an economic downturn: "US Business Cycle Expansions and Contractions," National Bureau of Economic Research, last modified April 23, 2012, www.nber.org/cycles/cyclesmain.html. December 1854 is cited as the first economic "trough."

CHAPTER 2: JESSIE RUNS FOR PRESIDENT BUT HARRIET TAKES THE WHITE HOUSE AND MARY JANE REPORTS

23 "your nomination by that party": Anna Ella Carroll to Millard Fillmore, May 15, 1855, in Janet L. Coryell, *Neither Heroine nor Fool: Anna Ella Carroll of Maryland* (Kent, OH: Kent State University Press, 1990), 11.

24 "between Christianity and Political Romanism": *Daily Dispatch* (Richmond, Virginia), April 30, 1856, Chronicling America: Historic Newspapers, Library of Congress, http://chroniclingamerica.loc.gov/lccn/sn84024738/1856-04-30/ed-1/seq-2/.

24 "a woman has ventured openly": Anna Ella Carroll to Millard Fillmore, June 26, 1856, in Coryell, *Neither Heroine*, 25.

26 "most flagging goose-quill to flowing": Mary Jane Windle, *Life in Washington, and Life Here and There* (Philadelphia: J. B. Lippincott, 1859), hardpress.net e-book, 83.

26 "he is a *public man!*": Ibid., 242.

26 "'throw away the scabbard'": Elbert B. Smith, *Francis Preston Blair* (New York: Free Press, 1980), 224–25.

27 nursed by the Blair women: Ibid., 227.

27 "historic assault on Mr. Sumner": Virginia Clay Clopton, *A Belle of the Fifties: Memoirs of Mrs. Clay of Alabama, covering social and political life in Washington and the South, 1853–66, put into narrative form by Ada Sterling* (New York: Doubleday, Page, 1905), 95.

27 "a meeting ground for conspirators," and "Have we a Presidentess among us": Frémont to Elizabeth Blair Lee, March 8, 1856, and Frémont to Elizabeth Blair Lee, April 18, 1856, in *The Letters of Jessie Frémont*, ed. Pamela Herr and Mary Lee Spence (Urbana and Chicago: University of Illinois Press, 1993), 94 and 97–99.

27 "triumph with us": Frémont to Elizabeth Blair Lee, June 9, 1856, in ibid., 106.

27 "let us see Jessie": *Albany Evening Journal*, quoted in Michael D. Pierson, *Free Hearts and Free Homes: Gender and American Anti-Slavery Politics* (Chapel Hill: University of North Carolina Press, 2003), e-book, loc. 2539.

28 "astonished even me": Frémont to John Charles Frémont, June 18, 1846, in Herr and Spence, eds., *Letters*, 25.

28 "cut loose from everything": Jessie Benton Frémont, *A Year of American Travel* (1878; reprint, Big Byte Books, 2014), e-book, loc. 138.

29 "undefined for the future": Ibid., loc. 160–72.

29 "I had no idea": Ibid., loc. 389.

30 "burned to death": Ibid., loc. 400.

30 "canvas and blanket tents": Ibid., loc. 831.

30 "San Francisco society": Ibid., loc. 856.

30 "quite a town": Ibid., loc. 893.

30 "the example of happiness": Ibid., loc. 1213.

31 "a new sense of power": Ibid., loc. 1300.

31 "too costly an amusement": Frémont to Francis Preston Blair, August 14, 1851, in Herr and Spence, eds., *Letters*, 46.

31 "She is very outspoken": Pamela Herr, *Jessie Benton Frémont: American Woman of the 19th Century* (New York: Franklin Watts, 1987), 234.

32 "advice and friendly counsel": Frémont to Francis Preston Blair, August 27, 1855, in Herr and Spence, eds., *Letters*, 71.

32 "I refused to buy a slave": Frémont to Lydia Maria Child, July, August, 1856, in Herr and Spence, eds., *Letters*, 121.

32 "a wayfaring man": Pierson, *Free Hearts*, loc. 2548.

32 "than five stump orators": *Western Reserve Chronicle* (Warren, Ohio), July 2, 1856, Chronicling America: Historic American Newspapers, Library of Congress, http://chroniclingamerica.loc.gov/lccn/sn84028385/1856-07-02/ed-1/seq-2/.

33 FOR PRESIDENT: *M'arthur Democrat* (McArthur, Vinton County, Ohio), July 17, 1856, Chronicling America: Historic American Newspapers, Library of Congress, http://chroniclingamerica.loc.gov/lccn/sn87075163/1856-07-17/ed-1/seq-1/.

33 *she is a crown to his head*: Catherine Coffin Phillips, *Jessie Benton Frémont: A Woman Who Made History* (1935; reprint, Lincoln: University of Nebraska Press, 1995), 210.

34 "the safest chance": *New York Times*, June 6, 1856, http://timesmachine.nytimes.com/timesmachine/1856/06/06/issue.html.

34 "more than a Jessie Fremont": Anna Ella Carroll to Millard Fillmore, October 31, 1856, quoted in Coryell, *Neither Heroine*, 29.

35 "the engrossing excitement": Frémont to Elizabeth Blair Lee, November 18, 1856, in Herr, *American Woman*, 143–45.

35 "fashionable and political circles": George Fort Milton, *The Eve of Conflict: Stephen A. Douglas and the Needless War* (1934; reprint, New York: Octagon Books, 1963), 257.

35 "put me out of patience": Varina Howell Davis to her parents, September 15, 1856, in *Jefferson Davis: Private Letters 1823–1889*, ed. Hudson Strode (1966; reprint, Boston: Da Capo Press, 1995), 80–81.

36 "brought from the street pump": Louisa Rodgers Meigs to Nannie, September 1854, Rodgers Family Papers, Naval Historical Foundation Collection, Manuscript Division, Library of Congress, Washington, D.C.

36 "and a reception to give": Varina Howell Davis to her father, January 13, 1857, in Strode, ed., *Private Letters*, 83.

36 "Free-Soilers, Black Republicans and Bloomers": Clopton, *Belle of the Fifties*, 43.

36 "as plenty as blackberries": Ibid., 98.

36 "the Civil War of Kansas!": Ibid., 58.

37 "accomplished, and clever wife": Thomas Keneally, *American Scoundrel: The Life of the Notorious Civil War General Dan Sickles* (New York: Anchor Books, 2003), 72.

37 "the soul of every company": Mrs. Roger A. Pryor, *Reminiscences of Peace and War* (New York: Grosset & Dunlap, 1904), 80–81.

37 "What's all this noise": Clopton, *Belle of the Fifties*, 104.

37 "the women composing our circle": Ibid., 45.

38 "publish the ages": Ibid., 77.

38 named after Clay: Ibid., 65–66.

38 "the prestige of your patronage": Anna Cora Ritchie to Adele Cutts Douglas, July 29, 1857, Box 46, Folder 4, Stephen A. Douglas Papers 1764–1908, Special Collection Research Center, University of Chicago Library.

38 "offered prayers this day": Margaret Hertford to Adele Cutts Douglas, December 7, 1857, Stephen A. Douglas Papers 1764–1908, Special Collection Research Center, University of Chicago Library.

38 "the uncrowned queen of Capitol society": Milton, *The Eve of Conflict*, 258.

39 "a remarkable sway for years": Clopton, *Belle of the Fifties*, 35.

39 "the engrossing subject of discourse": Windle, *Life in Washington*, 88.

39 1,200 quarts of ice cream: Milton Stern, *Harriet Lane: America's First Lady* (Lulu.com, 2005), e-book, locs. 191, 21.

39 "an extra force of Shuckers": *Evening Star* (Washington, D.C.), March 3, 1857, Chronicling America: Historic American Newspapers, Library of Congress, http://chroniclingamerica.loc.gov/lccn/sn83045462/1857-03-03/ed-1/seq-2/.

39 "the grandest affair of the kind": *Nashville Union and American*, March 13, 1857, Chronicling America: Historic American Newspapers, Library of Congress, http://chroniclingamerica.loc.gov/lccn/sn85038518/1857-03-13/ed-1/seq-2/.

40 "the favorite of the evening": *Semi-Weekly Standard* (Raleigh, N.C.), March 11, 1857, Chronicling America: Historic American Newspapers, Library of Congress, http://chroniclingamerica.loc.gov/lccn/sn83045450/1857-03-11/ed-1/seq-3/.

40 "the duties of the White House": *Nashville Union and American*, March 13, 1857, Chronicling America: Historic American Newspapers, Library of Congress, http://chroniclingamerica.loc.gov/lccn/sn85038518/1857-03-13/ed-1/seq-2/.

41 "Honorary Ambassadress": Stern, *Harriet Lane*, 810.

41 "your position in this country": Sophia Plitt to Harriet Lane, James Buchanan and Harriet Lane Johnston Papers, Manuscript Division, Library of Congress, Washington, D.C.

41   "any foreign airs & graces": James Buchanan to Harriet Lane, October 12, 1855, James Buchanan and Harriet Lane Johnston Papers, Manuscript Division, Library of Congress, Washington, D.C.

43   "poet's ideal of an English dairymaid": Clopton, *Belle of the Fifties*, 114–15.

43   "so interesting a relative": Windle, *Life in Washington*, 144.

43   "she made no enemies": Pryor, *Reminiscences*, 53.

44   "'Take it away!'": Ibid., 52.

44   "your Virginia ham will be perfect": Sarah Agnes Pryor to Adele Cutts Douglas, n.d., probably 1860, Box 46, Folder 6, Stephen A. Douglas Papers 1764–1908, Special Collection Research Center, University of Chicago Library.

44   "an 'Art Association' recently formed": Windle, *Life in Washington*, 147.

44   "a black bertha of lace": Varina Howell Davis to Margaret Howell, December 16, 1857, in Strode, ed., *Private Letters*, 97.

45   "rounded length of a pretty arm": Clopton, *Belle of the Fifties*, 89.

45   "the days of the Goths and Vandals": Windle, *Life in Washington*, 264–65.

46   "withering sarcasm and crushing invective": Ibid., 266.

46   a member's wig was pulled off: "35th Congress (1857–1859)," History, Art & Archives, U.S. House of Representatives, accessed December 12, 2014, http://history.house.gov/Congressional-Overview/Profiles/35th/.

46   "Mrs. Gwin's 'fancy ball'": Windle, *Life in Washington*, 329.

47   "radicals and fire-eaters": *New York Times*, April 13, 1858, http://timesmachine.nytimes.com/timesmachine/1858/04/13/issue.html.

47   "the onus of such egotism": Clopton, *Belle of the Fifties*, 128.

47   "angry and menacing look": Windle, *Life in Washington*, 333–35.

48   "the sentiment and romance of life": Ibid., 353–54.

48   "The gay season is over": Ibid., 354.

49   "ugly and dirty this city is": Adele Cutts Douglas to her mother, June 24, 1857, in *Letters of Stephen A. Douglas*, ed. Robert W. Johannsen (Urbana: University of Illinois Press, 1961), 384.

49   "upon his enemies": R. F. Merrick to Adele Cutts Douglas, May 7, 1858, Box 46, Folder 4, Stephen A. Douglas Papers 1764–1908, Special Collection Research Center, University of Chicago Library.

49   "furnish you with your 'confectionery'": Eckardt & Co., July 14, 1858, Box 46, Folder 4, Stephen A. Douglas Papers 1764–1908, Special Collection Research Center, University of Chicago Library.

49   combatants remained cordial: Milton, *Eve of Conflict*, 332.

50   a bleak reminder: Frederick L. Harvey, *The History of the Washington National Monument and of the Washington National Monument Society* (Washington, D.C.: N. T. Elliott, 1902), e-book, loc. 982.

CHAPTER 3: VARINA LEADS AND LEAVES AS ABBY DROPS BY

52 "the well bred of both sections": Varina Davis, *Jefferson Davis, Ex-President of the Confederate States of America, V1: A Memoir by His Wife* (1890; reprint, 1990, Baltimore: Nautical & Aviation Publishing Company of America, 1990), 574.

52 "confine ourselves to trivialities": Mrs. Roger A. Pryor, *Reminiscences of Peace and War* (New York: Grosset & Dunlap, 1904), 82–83.

52 "a rather unwelcome guest": *New York Times*, February 19, 1859, http://timesmachine.nytimes.com/timesmachine/1859/02/19/78885361.html.

53 "haystacks of spun sugar": Pryor, *Reminiscences*, 58.

53 "stirred Washington to its centre": Virginia Clay Clopton, *A Belle of the Fifties: Memoirs of Mrs. Clay of Alabama, covering social and political life in Washington and the South, 1853-66, put into narrative form by Ada Sterling* (New York: Doubleday, Page, 1905), 97.

54 newly minted congressional wife: Thomas Keneally, *American Scoundrel: The Life of the Notorious Civil War General Dan Sickles* (New York: Anchor Books, 2003), Kindle ed., 64.

54 "an accumulation of heartless cruelties": Frémont to Elizabeth Blair Lee, April 2, 1859, quoted in Pamela Herr, *Jessie Benton Frémont: American Woman of the 19th Century* (New York: Franklin Watts, 1987), 213.

55 "no punishment upon its author": Clopton, *Belle of the Fifties*, 97.

55 Key got what was coming to him: Sam Roberts, "Sex, Politics and Murder on the Potomac," *New York Times*, March 1, 1992.

55 "filth, filth": Davis to Margaret Howell, July 2, 1859, quoted in Joan E. Cashin, *First Lady of the Confederacy: Varina Davis's Civil War* (Cambridge, MA: Belknap Press of Harvard University Press, 2006), 85.

55 "stirring around like mad": Varina Howell Davis to Margaret Howell, March 1, 1859, in *Jefferson Davis: Private Letters 1823–1889*, ed. Hudson Strode (1966; reprint, Boston: Da Capo Press, 1995), 102.

56 "yet he is a Democrat!": Varina Howell Davis quoted in Cashin, *First Lady*, 35.

56 "she has a fine mind": Jefferson Davis quoted in Ishbel Ross, *First Lady of the South: The Life of Mrs. Jefferson Davis* (New York: Harper & Brothers, 1958), 8.

56 "a 'comfortable' dress": Carol Berkin, *Civil War Wives: The Lives and Times of Angelina Grimké Weld, Varina Howell Davis, and Julia Dent Grant* (New York: Knopf, 2009), 119.

56 "a pretty good seam": Davis, *Volume I: A Memoir*, 254.

56 "I think it is a trick": Ibid., 226.

57 "a proud young creature": Ibid., 245.

57 "not an impressive man": Ibid., 267.

57 "impossible for us ever to live together": Berkin, *Civil War Wives*, 133–34.

58 "thoughtless, dependent wife": Varina Howell Davis to Jefferson Davis, January 25, 1849, in Strode, ed., *Private Letters*, 58.

59 "dissatisfied with the Administration": Davis, *Volume I: A Memoir*, 548.

59 "biting him on the nose": Ibid., 559.

59 "his own fine horses": Ibid., 571.

60 "all 'the passing show'": Ibid., 579.

60 "the most unexpected kindnesses": Ibid., 583.

60 "relief and confidence about her": Ibid., 38.

61 "These reminiscences of Boston": Ibid., 39.

61 "lose the objects of those cares": Varina Howell Davis to her mother, November 21, 1858, in Strode, ed., *Private Letters*, 11.

61 "lovely sometimes to cut duty": Varina Howell Davis to her father, November 14, 1858, quoted in Berkin, *Civil War Wives*, 150.

62 "offered for keeping peace": Jefferson Davis to Margaret Howell, March 28, 1859, in Strode, ed., *Private Letters*, 103.

62 "Don't feel uneasy about me": Varina Howell Davis to Jefferson Davis, April 3, 1859, ibid., 105.

62 "every day to rear him": Varina Howell Davis to Jefferson Davis, April 17, 1859, ibid., 107.

62 saving Varina's life: William Ernest Smith, *The Frances Preston Blair Family in Politics*, vol. 2 (New York: Macmillan, 1933), 323.

63 "here and out of danger": Elizabeth Blair Lee to Francis Preston Blair, May 21, 1859, Blair and Lee Family Papers; 1764–1946 (mostly 1840–1920), Manuscripts Division, Department of Rare Books and Special Collections, Princeton University Library.

63 "part of a powerful party": Varina Howell Davis to Jefferson Davis, July 2, 1859, in Strode, ed., *Private Letters*, 111.

63 "Mrs. Davis is parting for Washington": Elizabeth Blair Lee to Francis Preston Blair, 16 September 1859, Blair and Lee Family Papers; 1764–1946 (mostly 1840–1920), Manuscripts Division, Department of Rare Books and Special Collections, Princeton University Library.

63 "not subject to taxation": quoted in Constance McLaughlin Green, *Washington Village and Capital, 1800–1878* (Princeton, NJ: Princeton University Press, 1962), 206–7.

64 "Here, the lock is off": Washington *Star*, October 3, 1859, quoted in Green, *Washington Village*, 227.

64 "Poverty, squalor, prejudice, and violence": Ibid., 228.

64 the overcrowded public schools: Ibid., 213.

65 "nothing but starvation or beggary": E.D.E.N. Southworth, *The Hidden Hand*, first serialized in *New York Ledger*, 1859 (reprint, New York: Hurst, 1907), Kindle e-book, loc. 628.

65 an abridged version of the tract: James McPherson, *Battle Cry of Freedom: The Civil War Era* (Oxford: Oxford University Press, 1988), 199.

66 "mutual hatred between North and South": Davis, *Volume I: A Memoir*, 648.

66 "pestilent, forceful man": Ibid., 644.

67 "churches were draped in mourning": James Buchanan, *Mr. Buchanan's Administration on the Eve of the Rebellion* (New York: D. Appleton, 1866), Google e-book, 63, also quoted in Davis, *Volume I: A Memoir*, 644–45.

67 "wild with passion": Pryor, *Reminiscences*, 92–94.

67 "punch a head or two": Abigail Brooks Adams to Henry Brooks Adams, December 26, 1859, microfilm edition of the Adams family papers, Massachusetts Historical Society.

69 "my most hearty approval": Rose Greenhow, *My Imprisonment and the First Year of Abolition Rule at Washington* (London: Richard Bentley, 1863), Internet Archive e-book, 65–66.

69 "a little more upper crust": Abigail Brooks Adams to Henry Brooks Adams, December 26, 1859, microfilm edition of the Adams family papers, Massachusetts Historical Society.

69 "the unfortunate affair of Brown": Pryor, *Reminiscences*, 95.

70 "tell him the whole truth": Anna Ella Carroll to Thurlow Weed, January 27, 1860, quoted in Janet L. Coryell, *Neither Heroine nor Fool: Anna Ella Carroll of Maryland* (Kent, OH: Kent State University Press, 1990), 43.

70 "made a dozen mistakes": Abigail Brooks Adams to Henry Brooks Adams, February 1, 1860, microfilm edition of the Adams family papers, Massachusetts Historical Society.

71 "never appeared at Miss Lane's receptions": Pryor, *Reminiscences*, 98.

71 "were stately & elegant": Abigail Brooks Adams to Henry Brooks Adams, February 8, 1860, microfilm edition of the Adams family papers, Massachusetts Historical Society.

72 "never invite any of us to dinners": Abigail Brooks Adams to Henry Brooks Adams, February 26, 1860, microfilm edition of the Adams family papers, Massachusetts Historical Society.

72 filling its tail with cannon balls: Green, *Washington Village*, 204.

73 "thousands of patriotic hearts": *Weekly Standard* (Raleigh, N.C.), February 29, 1860, Chronicling America: Historic American Newspapers, Library of

Congress, http://chroniclingamerica.loc.gov/lccn/sn83045706/1860-02-29/ed-1/seq-3/.

74 "I am treated like a queen": Abigail Brooks Adams to Henry Brooks Adams, March 4, 1860, microfilm edition of the Adams family papers, Massachusetts Historical Society.

75 "headstrong, willful, fighting": Abigail Brooks Adams to Henry Brooks Adams, March 30, 1860, ibid.

75 "met several nice people": Abigail Brooks Adams to Henry Brooks Adams, March 24, 1860, ibid.

75 "the bitterest opponent Grandpapa ever had": Abigail Brooks Adams to Henry Brooks Adams, April 4, 1860, ibid.

75 "even Mrs. Jeff Davis": Abigail Brooks Adams to Henry Brooks Adams, March 11, 1860, ibid.

75 "Don't let any of them in but Mrs. Lee": Smith, *Blair Family in Politics*, vol. 2, 258.

76 "I stick to the Seward colors": Abigail Brooks Adams to Henry Brooks Adams, March 11, 1860, microfilm edition of the Adams family papers, Massachusetts Historical Society.

76 one of the leading ladies of Washington: Abigail Brooks Adams to Henry Brooks Adams, April 29, 1860, ibid.

77 "turned a cold shoulder to its guests from the North": Pryor, *Reminiscences*, 95–96.

77 "I shall become a *pauper*": F. O. Prince to Adele Cutts Douglas, April 26, 1860, Box 46, Folder 5, Stephen A. Douglas Papers 1764–1908, Special Collection Research Center, University of Chicago Library.

78 "Visits are falling off": Abigail Brooks Adams to Henry Brooks Adams, May 5, 1860, microfilm edition of the Adams family papers, Massachusetts Historical Society.

78 "I gave him a piece of my mind": Abigail Brooks Adams to Henry Brooks Adams, April 9, 1860, ibid.

79 "He is a trial to his party": Abigail Brooks Adams to Henry Brooks Adams, May 5, 1860, ibid.

79 "fell from the lips of the men": Pryor, *Reminiscences*, 101.

79 "chat & gossip, & laugh & spend money": Abigail Brooks Adams to Henry Brooks Adams, May 13, 1860, microfilm edition of the Adams family papers, Massachusetts Historical Society.

79 "twenty thousand dollars to put it in repairs": Abigail Brooks Adams to Henry Brooks Adams, April 9, 1860, ibid.

80 "every show that comes along": Pryor, *Reminiscences*, 63.

80 "crowding curiously to gaze at them": Clopton, *Belle of the Fifties*, 111.

80 "some sat for their photographs": Abigail Brooks Adams to Henry Brooks Adams, May 13, 1860, microfilm edition of the Adams family papers, Massachusetts Historical Society.

80 "imagined oneself at a funeral": Pryor, *Reminiscences*, 63–64.

81 "all inelegant": Abigail Brooks Adams to Henry Brooks Adams, May 13, 1860, microfilm edition of the Adams family papers, Massachusetts Historical Society.

81 "stoop to such tricks": Abigail Brooks Adams to Henry Brooks Adams, May 17, 1860, ibid.

82 "the embodiment of the enmity": Davis, *Volume I: A Memoir*, 685.

82 "Jeff Davis & Douglas make speeches & quarrel": Abigail Brooks Adams to Henry Brooks Adams, May 28, 1860, and June 3, 1860, microfilm edition of the Adams family papers, Massachusetts Historical Society.

83 "first lady in the land": "Harriet Lane Biography," National First Ladies' Library, accessed December 13, 2014, http://www.firstladies.org/biographies/firstladies.aspx?biography=16.

84 "a great slave sale": "The Prince in Washington," *New York Times*, October 6, 1860, http://timesmachine.nytimes.com/timesmachine/1860/10/06/77869690.html.

84 barely anyone had voted for the new president: "1860 Presidential General Election Results," Dave Leip's Atlas of Presidential Elections, accessed November 15, 2014, http://uselectionatlas.org/RESULTS/national.php?year=1860.

85 "the dissolution of the Union": Elizabeth Lindsay Lomax, *Leaves from an Old Washington Diary, 1854–1863*, ed. Lindsay Lomax Wood (Mount Vernon, NY: E. P. Dutton, 1943), 133.

85 "the reputation of Sodom": George William Bagby, quoted in Ernest B. Furgurson, *Freedom Rising: Washington in the Civil War* (New York: Vintage, 2005), 15.

85 "crime goes unpunished": Louisa Rodgers Meigs to Montgomery C. Meigs, January 6, 1861, Montgomery C. Meigs Papers, Manuscript Division, Library of Congress, Washington, D.C.

85 "talked of forts and fusillades": Clopton, *Belle of the Fifties*, 138.

85 "the lurid picture of disunion and war": Pryor, *Reminiscences*, 98.

85 "'*spunk* however justified'": Louisa Rodgers Meigs to Montgomery C. Meigs, November 29, 1860, Montgomery C. Meigs Papers, Manuscript Division, Library of Congress, Washington, D.C.

86 "'The papers are teeming with secession . . . . God defend us from civil war'": Lomax, *Leaves*, 134–35.

86 "event which was to change all our lives": Pryor, *Reminiscences*, 111–12.

87 "unfurling of our national flag": Louisa Rodgers Meigs to Montgomery C. Meigs, December 6, 1860, Montgomery C. Meigs Papers, Manuscript Division, Library of Congress, Washington, D.C.

87 "peaceable secession is a fallacy": Lee to Samuel Phillips Lee, December 25, 1860, in *Wartime Washington: The Civil War Letters of Elizabeth Blair Lee*, ed. Virginia Jeans Laas (Urbana and Chicago: University of Illinois Press, 1999), 19.

87 "a defiance of public feeling": Louisa Rodgers Meigs to Montgomery C. Meigs, January 17, 1861, Montgomery C. Meigs Papers, Manuscript Division, Library of Congress, Washington, D.C.

87 "but this day is oh, so different": Lomax, *Leaves*, 138.

87 "North and South mingled fraternally": *Frank Leslie's Illustrated Newspaper*, January 19, 1861, quoted in Ann Blackman, *Wild Rose: Rose O'Neale Greenhow, Civil War Spy, A True Story* (New York: Random House, 2005), 20.

87 "resolved itself literally this year": Pryor, *Reminiscences*, 117.

87 "At the elbows of Senators": Clopton, *Belle of the Fifties*, 142.

87 "pregnant with storm and cloud": Louisa Rodgers Meigs to Montgomery C. Meigs, January 3, 1861, Montgomery C. Meigs Papers, Manuscript Division, Library of Congress, Washington, D.C.

88 "Political events breathe defiance": Lomax, *Leaves*, 140.

88 blow her brains out": Louisa Rodgers Meigs to Montgomery C. Meigs, February 8, 1861, Montgomery C. Meigs Papers, Manuscript Division, Library of Congress, Washington, D.C.

88 "women grew hysterical . . . before the evil": Clopton, *Belle of the Fifties*, 147–48.

89 "his desire for reconciliation . . . 'May God have us in His holy keeping'": Davis, *Volume I: A Memoir*, 696–99.

89 "many, we knew, would be final": Clopton, *Belle of the Fifties*, 151.

89 "break any *bonds* between us": Lee to Samuel Phillips Lee, December 17, 1860, in Laas, ed., *Wartime Washington*, 18.

89 "We left Washington 'exceeding sorrowful'": Varina Davis, *Jefferson Davis, Ex-President of the Confederate States of America, Part Two V2: A Memoir By His Wife* (1890; reprint, Baltimore: Nautical and Aviation Publishing Company of America, 1990), 5–6.

90 "giving up whatever of social dominion": *New York Herald*, February 7, 1904, quoted in Pryor, *Reminiscences*, 82.

90 "no friend either North or South": Louisa Rodgers Meigs to Montgomery C. Meigs, January 17, 1861, Montgomery C. Meigs Papers, Manuscript Division, Library of Congress, Washington, D.C.

90 "we do not feel in a party mood": Lomax, *Leaves*, 142.

91 "Mrs. Davis is a warm personal friend": Lee to Samuel Phillips Lee, February 8–9, 1861, in Laas, ed., *Wartime Washington*, 33.

91 "signal of every Northern lady's leaving": Anna Ella Carroll to Thomas Hicks, January 30, 1861, quoted in Coryell, *Neither Heroine*, 50.

91 "children out to the far west": Lee to Samuel Phillips Lee, February 5, 1861, in Laas, ed., *Wartime Washington*, 32.

92 "bid adieu to the bright days": Pryor, *Reminiscences*, 118–19.

CHAPTER 4: ROSE GOES TO JAIL, JESSIE GOES TO THE WHITE HOUSE, DOROTHEA GOES TO WORK

93 "counting the president's votes": Elizabeth Lindsay Lomax, *Leaves from an Old Washington Diary, 1854–1863*, ed. Lindsay Lomax Wood (Mount Vernon, NY: E. P. Dutton, 1943), 143.

94 "a very military appearance:" Louisa Rodgers Meigs to John Rodgers Meigs, February 16, 1861, in *A Civil War Soldier of Christ and Country: The Selected Correspondence of John Rodgers Meigs, 1859–1864*, ed. Mary A. Giunta (Urbana and Chicago: University of Illinois Press, 2006), 99–100.

94 "the grandest parade": Ann Green, February 22, 1861, in "The 1861 Diary of Ann (Forrest) Green of Rosedale," unpublished diary, courtesy of her great-great granddaughter, Catherine O'Donnell, 13.

94 "a united and happy people": Lomax, *Leaves*, 143.

94 "Mrs. Lincoln and son came in the afternoon": Ibid., 143–44.

95 "extensive and organized conspiracy": David Gollaher, *Voice for the Mad: The Life of Dorothea Dix* (New York: Free Press, 1995), 393.

95 "the knowledge of the people": Green, February 23, 1861, "1861 Diary," 13.

95 "awfully western, loud and unrefined": Harriet Lane to Sophia Plitt, 24 February 1861, James Buchanan and Harriet Lane Johnston Papers, Manuscript Division, Library of Congress, Washington, D.C.

95 "in triumph all the way": Lee to Samuel Phillips Lee, February 15, 1861, in *Wartime Washington: The Civil War Letters of Elizabeth Blair Lee*, ed. Virginia Jeans Laas (Urbana and Chicago: University of Illinois Press, 1999), 37.

96 "a worthy successor": *New York Times*, February 21, 1861, http://timesmachine.nytimes.com/timesmachine/1861/02/21/issue.html.

96 "'not bad looking by any means'": *Lewistown Gazette* (Lewistown, Pa.), February 28, 1861, Chronicling America: Historic American Newspapers, Library of Congress, http://chroniclingamerica.loc.gov/lccn/sn83032276/1861-02-28/ed-1/seq-2/.

97 "The city thronged with strangers": Lomax, *Leaves*, 144.

97 "hated by half the people": Mary Montgomery Meigs to John Rodgers Meigs, January 6, 1861, in Giunta, ed., *Selected Correspondence*, 88.

97 "everything went off peacefully": Green, March 4, 1861, "1861 Diary," 15.

97 "no doubt of its sanity": Lomax, *Leaves*, 144–45.

98 "found no quarters": *New York Times*, March 5, 1861, http://timesmachine. nytimes.com/timesmachine/1861/03/05/issue.html.

98 " 'But he will never come back alive' ": Julia Taft Bayne, *Tad Lincoln's Father* (1931; reprint, Lincoln: University of Nebraska Press, 2001), e-book, 7.

98 "fair ladies by the score": *New York Times*, March 5, 1861, http://timesma-chine.nytimes.com/timesmachine/1861/03/05/issue.html.

99 "the least dislike to his living": Clara Barton to Annie Childs, March 5, 1861, in Elizabeth Brown Pryor, *Clara Barton: Professional Angel* (Philadel-phia: University of Pennsylvania Press, 1987), 75.

99 "the belle of the evening": *New York Times*, March 5, 1861, http://timesma-chine.nytimes.com/timesmachine/1861/03/05/issue.html.

100 "the nasal twang of the strong-willed Puritan": *Cincinnati Daily Press*, March 8, 1861, Chronicling America: Historic American Newspapers, Library of Congress, http://chroniclingamerica.loc.gov/lccn/sn84028745/1861-03-08/ ed-1/seq-1/.

100 "holy hands of horror": Bayne, *Tad Lincoln's Father*, 6.

100 "the fatigue of the two and a half hour siege": Gilson Willets, *Inside History of the White House: The Complete History of the Domestic and Official Life in Washington of the Nation's Presidents and Their Families* (New York: Christian Heralds, 1908), 312.

101 "I will not dress": Elizabeth Keckley, *Behind the Scenes, or Thirty Years a Slave and Four Years in the White House* (New York: G. W. Carleton, 1868), 71.

102 "susceptible of a double construction": *New York Times*, March 5, 1861, http://timesmachine.nytimes.com/timesmachine/1861/03/05/issue.html.

103 "as she did secession": Lee to Samuel Phillips Lee, February 12, 1861, in Laas, ed., *Wartime Washington*, 36.

103 "the south wing of the Treasury Building": Lomax, *Leaves*, 148.

104 "God only knows": Ibid., 149–50.

104 "men bold and brave enough": *Richmond Enquirer*, December 25, 1860, quoted in John Lockwood and Charles Lockwood, *The Siege of Washington: The Untold Story of the Twelve Days That Shook the Union* (New York: Oxford University Press, 2011), e-book, 22.

105 a cocky Varina Davis: Ibid., 99.

106 hoarded food and supplies: Ibid., 215.

106 "Heaven only knows": Louisa Rodgers Meigs to Minerva Rodgers, April

28, 1861, Montgomery C. Meigs Papers, Manuscript Division, Library of Congress, Washington, D.C.

107 "fearful apprehensions rule the hour": Green, April 19, 1861, "1861 Diary," 23.

107 "martial law will be proclaimed": Ibid., April 20, 1861, 23–24.

107 "condition of siege": Lockwood and Lockwood, *The Siege of Washington*, frontispiece.

107 "All the statuary in the rotunda had been boxed": Bayne, *Tad Lincoln's Father*, 28.

108 "to defend their capital and your own": Anna Ella Carroll to Thomas H. Hicks, April 21, 1861, in Janet L. Coryell, *Neither Heroine nor Fool: Anna Ella Carroll of Maryland* (Kent, OH: Kent State University Press, 1990), 52.

108 "The rumor of invasion and battle was startling": Green, April 25, 1861, "1861 Diary," 24.

109 "God alone knows": Ibid., April 25, 1861, 25.

109 "will astound and appall the South": Louisa Rodgers Meigs to John Rodgers Meigs, May 2, 1861, Montgomery C. Meigs Papers, Manuscript Division, Library of Congress, Washington, D.C.

109 Mrs. Lincoln's Zouaves: Adam Goodheart, *1861: The Civil War Awakening* (New York: Knopf, 2011), 275.

110 "disgraced with Lincoln's low soldiery": Virginia Clay Clopton, *A Belle of the Fifties: Memoirs of Mrs. Clay of Alabama, covering social and political life in Washington and the South, 1853–66, put into narrative form by Ada Sterling* (New York: Doubleday, Page, 1905), 151.

110 "like one grand water closet": Thomas Walter to Amanda Walter, quoted in Guy Gugliotta, "1861, The U.S. Capitol at War," *Capitol Dome* 49, no. 1 (Winter 2012): 19.

110 "which often precedes the storm": Louisa Rodgers Meigs to Minerva Rodgers, April 28, 1861, Montgomery C. Meigs Papers, Manuscript Division, Library of Congress, Washington, D.C.

110 "the common sense of silence": Green, April 29, 1861, "1861 Diary," 26.

111 "impelled them to this sacrifice": Louisa Rodgers Meigs to John Rodgers Meigs, May 2, 1861, Montgomery C. Meigs Papers, Manuscript Division, Library of Congress, Washington, D.C.

111 four hundred left to take positions: Ernest B. Furgurson, *Freedom Rising: Washington in the Civil War* (New York: Vintage, 2005), 114.

111 "Troops are still pouring in": Green, May 7, 1861, "1861 Diary," 29.

111 "receiving fourteen hundred and fifteen soldiers": Ibid, May 6, 1861, 28.

111 "Virginia troops had attacked Washington": S. A. Douglas Jr. to Adele Cutts

Douglas, May 8, 1861, Box 46, Folder 8, Stephen A. Douglas Papers 1764–1908, Special Collection Research Center, University of Chicago Library.

112 "the fanatical Mrs. Lee": Clopton, *Belle of the Fifties*, 152.

112 "a very nice set of teeth": Green, May 22, 1861, "1861 Diary," 33.

112 "an attack on Alexandria is expected": Lomax, May 1, 1861, *Leaves*, 152.

112 "we would be in no danger": Ibid., April 23 1861, 151.

113 "kill my own people": Ibid., May 7, 1861, 152–53.

113 "the outcome of this frightful war": Ibid., May 11, 1861, 153.

113 "with a sad heart": Ibid., May 12, 1861, 154.

113 "the clang of their weapons": Louisa Rodgers Meigs to Minerva Rodgers, May 26, 1861, Rodgers Family Papers, Naval Historical Foundation Collection, Manuscript Division, Library of Congress, Washington, D.C.

114 "his horse covered with a black pall": Green, May 26, 1861, "1861 Diary," 34.

114 "The Zouaves followed the hearse": Louisa Rodgers Meigs to Minerva Rodgers, May 26, 1861, Montgomery C. Meigs Papers, Manuscript Division, Library of Congress, Washington, D.C.

115 "All a false alarm": Green, May 26, 1861, "1861 Diary," 34.

115 "but what a changed scene": Ibid., June 2, 1861, 35.

115 "be illy spared by the nation": "Death of Stephen A. Douglas," *New York Times*, June 4, 1861, http://timesmachine.nytimes.com/timesmachine/1861/06/04/issue.html.

115 "extremely jealous of her superior attractions": Keckley, *Behind the Scenes*, 74.

116 "the cold shoulder in the City": Lee to Samuel Phillips Lee, July 14, 1861, in Laas, ed., *Wartime Washington*, 61.

116 "the good taste of Mrs. Lincoln": *Washington Star*, quoted in "Downstairs at The White House: State Dining Room," Mr. Lincoln's White House, accessed December 14, 2014, http://www.mrlincolnswhitehouse.org/inside.asp?ID=75&subjectID=3.

116 "will take any part in this war": Lee to Samuel Phillips Lee, June 1, 1861, in Laas, ed., *Wartime Washington*, 40.

117 "our horses are fast": Lee to Samuel Phillips Lee, June 4, 1861, ibid., 43.

117 "I wish her no ill": Lee to Samuel Phillips Lee, June 11, 1861, ibid., 47.

117 "serious consequences might have ensued": *National Republican*, June 26, 1861, p. 2, http://www.newspapers.com.

118 "one universal grumble": Lee to Samuel Phillips Lee, June 25, 1861, in Laas, ed., *Wartime Washington*, 51.

118 "pouring in to the city": Lee to Samuel Phillips Lee, July 3, 1861, Ibid., 57.

118 "some good result": Green, June 20, 1861, "1861 Diary," 39.

118 "far exceeding in splendor": *National Republican*, July 3, 1861, 3, http://www.newspapers.com.

119 "but I held my tongue": Lee to Samuel Phillips Lee, July 17, 1861, in Laas, ed., *Wartime Washington*, 63.

119 "its perusal by the people": Sarah Ellen Blackwell, *A Military Genius: Life of Anna Ella Carroll of Maryland* (Washington, DC: Judd & Detweiler, 1891), e-book, 54.

119 "Overwhelming forces": Green, July 16, 1861, "1861 Diary," 43.

120 "All sorts of barbarous acts": Ibid., July 17, 1861, 44.

120 "the *roar* in my ears": Lee to Samuel Phillips Lee, July 21, 1861, in Laas, ed., *Wartime Washington*, 65.

120 "I still cling to the idea": Green, July 12, 1861, "1861 Diary," 45.

120 "rocking our boy to sleep": Lee to Samuel Phillips Lee, July 21, 1861, in Laas, ed., *Wartime Washington*, 65.

121 "the army is completely routed": Louisa Rodgers Meigs to Minerva Rodgers, July 28, 1861, quoted in Furgurson, *Freedom Rising*, 121.

121 "tales of carnage and bloodshed": Green, July 22, 1861, "1861 Diary," 45.

121 "the southern victory": Ibid., July 23, 1861, 46.

121 "our boasted free country": Ibid., June 27, 1861, 41.

121 "A tradition only": Rose O'Neal Greenhow, *My Imprisonment and the First Year of Abolition Rule at Washington* (1863; reprint, Whitefish, MT: Kessinger, 2010), 15.

122 "via Fairfax Court House and Centerville": Rose Greenhow quoted in Ishbel Ross, *First Lady of the South: The Life of Mrs. Jefferson Davis* (New York: Harper & Brothers, 1958), 100.

123 "we are ready for them": Greenhow, *My Imprisonment*, 5.

123 "well-informed person": "Condition of Affairs at Manassas; Reports of a Returned Prisoner," *New York Times*, August 3, 1861, http://timesmachine.nytimes.com/timesmachine/1861/08/03/issue.html.

123 "The Confederacy owes you a debt": Greenhow, *My Imprisonment*, 6.

123 "pell-mell into the Potomac": Ibid., 6.

123 "a general massacre": Ibid., 8.

124 "conscious of the great service": Ibid.

124 "clear of all secessionists": Florence Greenhow Moore to Rose O'Neale Greenhow, July 23, 1861, in Ann Blackman, *Wild Rose: Rose O'Neale Greenhow, Civil War Spy, A True Story* (New York: Random House, 2005), 35.

124 "The alarm-guns of the Yankees": Greenhow, *My Imprisonment*, 12.

125 "shoot her at sunrise": Bayne, *Tad Lincoln's Father*, 60.

125 "until evidence was shown": "The Great Rebellion: Important News from the National Capital," *New York Times*, August 26, 1861, http://timesmachine.nytimes.com/timesmachine/1861/08/26/issue.html.

125 "'Mother has been arrested'": Bayne, *Tad Lincoln's Father*, 62.

126 "The Sixteenth-street gaol": "Political Prison for Ladies in Washington," *Freeman's Journal*, Dublin, Ireland, February 19, 1862, http://www.newspapers.com.

126 "a detective stood sentinel": "What Mrs. Greenhow Says of Her Imprisonment," *McArthur Democrat*, Vinton County, Ohio, January 9, 1862, http://www.newspapers.com.

126 "a note informing the lady": "The Immense Armament Secured by the Government," *New York Times*, December 31, 1861, http://timesmachine.nytimes.com/timesmachine/1861/12/31/issue.html.

126 "a quart of wine a day": "Items from Washington," *Cleveland Morning Reader*, January 8, 1862, http://www.newspapers.com.

127 "the old Capitol prison": Greenhow, *My Imprisonment*, 8.

127 "steamed all night": Green, July 23, 1861, "1861 Diary," 46.

127 "completely demoralized": Ibid., July 25, 1861, 47.

128 "McDowell and Tyler were drunk": Ibid., July 26, 1861, 47.

128 "great exertions to reorganize the Army": Ibid., July 31, 1861, 48.

128 "the opinion of everybody": Francis Preston Blair to Elizabeth Blair Lee, August 4, 1861, Blair and Lee Family Papers; 1764–1946 (mostly 1840–1920), Manuscripts Division, Department of Rare Books and Special Collections, Princeton University Library.

128 "even 'around Silver Spring vicinity'": Lee to Samuel Phillips Lee, August 14, 1861, in Laas, ed., *Wartime Washington*, 71.

128 ducking bullets: Green, August 3, 1861, "1861 Diary," 49.

128 "fifteen thousand troops about Tennallytown": Ibid., August 14, 1861, 52.

129 "Southerners were confidently expected": Ibid., August 15, 1861, 52.

129 "I looked at the shot hole": Ibid., August 16, 1861, 53.

129 "every particle of poultry gone": Ibid.

129 "All our peaches": Ibid., August 4, 1861, 49.

129 "finished on the fruit": Ibid., September 1, 1861, 57.

129 "dear little boy": Ibid., August 6, 1861, 50.

129 "enjoy my other grandchildren": Ibid., September 22, 1861, 63.

130 "separation with all its restrictions": Ibid., September 13, 1861, 61.

130 "About the war we know nothing": Ibid., September 17, 1861, 62.

130 "they will never do it": Francis Preston Blair to Elizabeth Blair Lee, August

21, 1861, Blair and Lee Family Papers; 1764–1946 (mostly 1840–1920), Manuscripts Division, Department of Rare Books and Special Collections, Princeton University Library.

130 "slept on their arms": Elizabeth Blair Lee to Francis Preston Blair, August 30, 1861, ibid.

130 "this wicked conspiracy": Elizabeth Blair Lee to Francis Preston Blair, September 7, 1861, Ibid.

131 "no matter what danger": Varina Howell Davis to Margaret Howell, June 1861, in *Jefferson Davis: Private Letters 1823–1889*, ed. Hudson Strode (1966; reprint, Boston: Da Capo Press, 1995), 124.

131 "devotedly in love with him": Elizabeth Blair Lee to Francis Preston Blair, September 7, 1861, Blair and Lee Family Papers; 1764–1946 (mostly 1840–1920), Manuscripts Division, Department of Rare Books and Special Collections, Princeton University Library.

131 "old Jeff is still alive": Lee to Samuel Phillips Lee, September 12, 1861, in Laas, ed., *Wartime Washington*, 77.

131 "*lukewarm hands heads & hearts*": Lee to Samuel Phillips Lee, August 19, 1861, ibid., 72n.

133 "I have begged Mr. Fremont": Frémont to Elizabeth Blair Lee, July 27, 1861, in *The Letters of Jessie Frémont*, ed. Pamela Herr and Mary Lee Spence (Urbana and Chicago: University of Illinois Press, 1993), 255.

133 "miracles on the Mississippi": Frémont to Montgomery Blair, July 28, 1861, ibid., 257–58.

133 "begging and bullying": Frémont to Montgomery Blair, August 5, 1861, ibid., 260.

133 "the absolute want of arms": Frémont to Abraham Lincoln, August 5, 1861, ibid., 262.

133 "I am mistaken in the men": Lee to Samuel Phillips Lee, August 20, 1861, in Laas, ed., *Wartime Washington*, 74.

134 "only *infer* from *signs*": Lee to Samuel Phillips Lee, September 12, 1861, ibid., 77.

135 "suits the President's convenience": Frémont to Abraham Lincoln, September 10, 1861, in Herr and Spence, eds., *Letters*, 264.

135 "'A. Lincoln. Now'": Jessie Benton Frémont and F. P. Frémont, *Great Events During the Life of Major General John C. Fremont . . . and of Jessie Benton Fremont*, unpublished manuscript, 1891, Bancroft Library, University of California, Berkeley, quoted in Herr and Spence, eds., *Letters*, 265.

135 "an audience with me at midnight": John George Nicolay and John Hay,

Abraham Lincoln, A History, vol. 4 (New York: Century, 1909), Google e-book, 414–15.

136 "tomorrow or the day after": Frémont and Frémont, *Great Events*, quoted in Herr and Spence, eds., *Letters*, 265–66.

136 "a lady who has lost her temper": Catherine Coffin Phillips, *Jessie Benton Frémont: A Woman Who Made History* (San Francisco: John Henry Nash, 1935), quoted in Pamela Herr, *Jessie Benton Frémont: American Woman of the 19th Century* (New York: Franklin Watts, 1987), 339.

136 "not fit for a woman": Frémont and Frémont, *Great Events*, quoted in Herr and Spence, eds., *Letters*, 267.

137 "a very *high* look": Lee to Samuel Phillips Lee, September 17, 1861, in Laas, ed., *Wartime Washington*, 79.

137 "made that investigation necessary": Frémont to Abraham Lincoln, September 12, 1861, in Herr and Spence, eds., *Letters*, 270.

137 "any hostility towards him": Abraham Lincoln to Frémont, September 12, 1861, in ibid., 271n.

137 "Mrs. Fremont left there": "Rumor That Gen. Fremont Is to Be Superseded," *New York Times*, September 14, 1861, http://timesmachine.nytimes.com/timesmachine/1861/09/14/issue.html.

138 "pride precedes a fall": Elizabeth Blair Lee to Francis Preston Blair, September 18, 1861, Blair and Lee Family Papers; 1764–1946 (mostly 1840–1920), Manuscripts Division, Department of Rare Books and Special Collections, Princeton University Library.

138 "the General and his Body Guard": "The Preparation in Missouri," *New York Times*, October 3, 1861, http://timesmachine.nytimes.com/timesmachine/1861/10/03/issue.html.

138 "his attention to that lady": Louisa Rodgers Meigs to Montgomery C. Meigs, October 4, 1861, Montgomery C. Meigs Papers, Manuscript Division, Library of Congress, Washington, D.C.

138 "travels with a grand cuisine": Lee to Samuel Phillips Lee, October 16, 1861, in Laas, ed., *Wartime Washington*, 86.

139 "Father was most incautious": Lee to Samuel Phillips Lee, October 7, 1861, ibid., 83.

139 "She is perfectly unscrupulous": Montgomery Blair to W. O. Bartlett, September 26, 1861, Blair and Lee Family Papers; 1764–1946 (mostly 1840–1920), Manuscripts Division, Department of Rare Books and Special Collections, Princeton University Library, quoted in Herr, *American Woman*, 342.

139 "his groveling nature": Lee to Samuel Phillips Lee, October 14, 1861, in Laas, ed., *Wartime Washington*, 85.

139 "He is too prejudiced against me": Frémont to Ward Lamon, October 26, 1861, in Herr and Spence, eds., *Letters*, 283.

139 "good brain & bad heart": Frémont to Dorothea Dix, late October 1861, ibid., 285–86.

140 "this tenderness toward slavery": Frémont to Thomas Starr King, December 29, 1861, ibid., 304.

140 "actually owning slaves": Bayne, *Tad Lincoln's Father*, 6.

142 "the General has decided": "General Butler and the Contraband of War," *New York Times*, June 2, 1861, http://timesmachine.nytimes.com/timesmachine/1861/06/02/issue.html.

142 "beginning of a battle": Montgomery C. Meigs to Louisa Rodgers Meigs, October 5, 1861, Montgomery C. Meigs Papers, Manuscript Division, Library of Congress, Washington, D.C.

142 "keeps me very anxious": Green, October 6, 1861, "1861 Diary," 67.

143 "disburse special supplies": Penny Colman, *Breaking the Chains: The Crusade of Dorothea Lynde Dix* (Lincoln, NE: ASJA Press, 1992, 2007), e-book, 1312.

144 "she wore men's clothes": Bayne, *Tad Lincoln's Father*, 72.

144 "male surgeons may take the credit": Coleman, *Breaking the Chains*, 1377.

145 "the whole benevolence of women": Katherine Wormeley, *The United States Sanitary Commission: A Sketch of Its Purposes and Work* (Boston: Little, Brown, 1863), 3.

146 "mere formalists, idlers, and evildoers": Gollaher, *Voice for the Mad*, 415.

146 "fallen in the fight": Julia Ward Howe, *Reminiscences, 1819–1899* (Boston and New York: Houghton, Mifflin, 1899), Kindle e-book, loc. 2607.

146 "'most things that I have written'": Ibid., locs. 2635–51.

147 "he meant well": Ibid., loc. 2621.

147 "The character of the war": Green, November 16, 1861, "1861 Diary," 74.

148 "secured a tutor for the boys": Bayne, *Tad Lincoln's Father*, 65.

148 "in and out of the White House": Ibid., 66.

148 "what she wanted she wanted when she wanted it": Ibid., 20.

148 "No lady of the White House": "Press Hounding Mrs. Lincoln," *Chicago Tribune*, August 31, 1861, quoted in Catherine Clinton, *Mrs. Lincoln: A Life* (New York: Harper Perennial, 2010), 151.

149 "'Lady President'": Doris Kearns Goodwin, *Team of Rivals: The Political Genius of Abraham Lincoln* (New York: Simon & Schuster, 2006), 385.

150 "gave that paper an advantage": Harold Holzer, *Lincoln and the Power of the Press: The War for Public Opinion* (New York: Simon & Schuster, 2014), 369–72, and Clinton, *Mrs. Lincoln*, 154.

150 "climate congenial to them": Furgurson, *Freedom Rising*, 149.

151 "Now Fortune turn thy wheel": Frémont to Thomas Starr King, Herr and Spence, eds., *Letters*, 305.

151 "I cannot help feeling sorry": Louisa Rodgers Meigs to Montgomery C. Meigs, November 21, 1861, Montgomery C. Meigs Papers, Manuscript Division, Library of Congress, Washington, D.C.

151 *"back down flat"*: Lee to Samuel Phillips Lee, December 23, 1861, in Laas, ed., *Wartime Washington*, 93.

152 "an explosive condition": Lee to Samuel Phillips Lee, December 30, 1861, ibid., 94.

CHAPTER 5: ROSE IS RELEASED, CLARA GOES TO WAR,
LOUISA MAY BRIEFLY NURSES

153 "state of crude incompleteness": Mary Clemmer Ames, *Ten Years in Washington: Life and Scenes in the National Capital, as a Woman Sees Them* (1874; reprint, Ann Arbor: University of Michigan Library, Michigan Historical Reprint Series, 2005), 67–68.

153 "the nation's neglect and shame": Ibid., 70.

154 "money will again be subscribed": Anthony Trollope, *North America*, vol. 2 (New York: Harper & Brothers, 1862), Project Gutenberg e-book, locs. 230–245.

154 "more given to enjoy hospitality": Ibid., locs. 385–99.

154 "service against the rebels": David Herbert Donald and Harold Holzer, eds., *Lincoln in the Times: The Life of Abraham Lincoln as Originally Reported in the New York Times* (New York: St. Martin's Press, 2005), 135.

155 "I told him you had enemies": Ellen Ewing Sherman to William T. Sherman, January 19, 1862, William T. Sherman Family papers, University of Notre Dame Archives.

156 "Public receptions are more democratic": Elizabeth Keckley, *Behind the Scenes, or Thirty Years a Slave and Four Years in the White House* (New York: G. W. Carleton, 1868), 80.

156 "abrogate state dinners": Catherine Clinton, *Mrs. Lincoln: A Life* (New York: Harper Perennial, 2010), 164.

157–58 "costly and inappropriate festivity": *Cincinnati Daily Press*, February 10, 1862, Chronicling America: Historic American Newspapers, Library of Congress, http://chroniclingamerica.loc.gov/lccn/sn84028745/1862-02-10/ed-1/seq-1/.

158 "a ghastly failure": Pamela Herr and Mary Lee Spence, eds., *The Letters of Jessie Frémont* (Urbana and Chicago: University of Illinois Press, 1993), 313n.

158 "a complete success": Frémont to Frederick Billings, February 7, 1862, ibid., 311.

158 "our soldiers are sick, suffering and dying": *Emporia News* (Emporia, Kan.), February 15, 1862, Chronicling America: Historic American Newspapers, Library of Congress, http://chroniclingamerica.loc.gov/lccn/sn82016419/1862-02-15/ed-1/seq-1/.

159 "a season of mutual congratulations": *National Republican* (Washington, D.C.), February 19, 1862, Chronicling America: Historic American Newspapers, Library of Congress, http://chroniclingamerica.loc.gov/lccn/sn82014760/1862-02-19/ed-1/seq-2/.

159 "the children have a good time": Julia Taft Bayne, *Tad Lincoln's Father* (1931; reprint, Lincoln: University of Nebraska Press, 2001), e-book, 47.

159 " 'he will call for me' ": Ibid., 82.

159 "his rugged nature": Keckley, *Behind the Scenes*, 85–87.

159–60 "sent for Bud to see Willie": Bayne, *Tad Lincoln's Father*, 82.

160 " 'Try and control your grief' ": Keckley, *Behind the Scenes*, 87.

160 "ten times better looking than Mrs. Lincoln": Lee to Samuel Phillips Lee, March 1, 1862, in *Wartime Washington: The Civil War Letters of Elizabeth Blair Lee*, ed. Virginia Jeans Laas (Urbana and Chicago: University of Illinois Press, 1999), 104.

160 "was tearful but very kind": Lee to Samuel Phillips Lee, March 27, 1862, ibid., 104n.

160 "I am so completely unnerved": Mary Todd Lincoln to Julia Ann Sprigg, quoted in Mark Hartsell, "A Mother's Grief," *Library of Congress Magazine*, November/December 2012, 27, http://www.loc.gov/lcm/pdf/LCM_2012_1112.pdf.

161 "I shall be glad for *you* to call on *me*": Ernest B. Furguson, *Freedom Rising: Washington in the Civil War* (New York: Vintage, 2005), 134.

162 "In fact she married him": Bayne, *Tad Lincoln's Father*, 35–36.

162 "extensive purchases at Lord & Taylor's": *New York Daily Tribune*, May 14, 1861, quoted in Clinton, *Mrs. Lincoln*, footnote to 134, 358.

162 "Mrs. Lincoln 'shopped' ": Ames, *Ten Years in Washington*, 237–38.

163 "making too much of the Negro": Clinton, *Mrs. Lincoln*, 171, and Ishbel Ross, *Proud Kate: Portrait of an Ambitious Woman* (New York: Harper & Brothers, 1953), 90.

163 "A humbug": Keckley, *Behind the Scenes*, 115.

164 "the champagne and oyster suppers": Edwin Stanton to Charles A. Dana, January 24, 1862, quoted in Frank Abial Flower, *Edwin McMasters Stanton: The Autocrat of Rebellion, Emancipation and Reconstruction* (Akron, OH: Saalfield, 1905), Google e-book, 125.

165 "life and motion into the inert army": Salmon P. Chase to Katherine Chase, January 11[?], 1862, in *"Spur Up Your Pegasus": Family Letters of Salmon, Kate and Nettie Chase, 1844–1873*, ed. James P. McClure, Peg A. Lamphier, and Erika M. Kreger (Kent, OH: Kent State University Press, 2009), 193.

165 "evacuated without a fight": Lee to Samuel Phillips Lee, April 5, 1862, in Laas, ed., *Wartime Washington*, 123.

166 "diminish their means of war": Lee to Samuel Phillips Lee, March 18, 1862, ibid., 112.

166 "a huge Newfoundland dog": Lee to Samuel Phillips Lee, March 20, 1862, ibid., 115.

166 "McClellan invested Yorktown": Lee to Samuel Phillips Lee, April 10, 1862, ibid., 125.

166 "He wants more troops": Ibid., 127.

166 "Yorktown siege will be slow & long": Ibid., 127.

166 "on the lips of all": Ibid., 129.

166 "now turned to New Orleans": Ibid., 137.

166 "the Yorktown line under eclipse": Ibid., 139.

167 "the biggest feeling in my heart": Lee to Samuel Phillips Lee, May 8, 1862, ibid., 141n.

167 "Frenchmen & quadroons": Lee to Samuel Phillips Lee, April 10, 1862, ibid., 126.

167 "'dear unto life's end'": Lee to Samuel Phillips Lee, March 13, 1862, ibid., 110.

168 "the slaves who are released from bondage": *Raftsman's Journal* (Clearfield, Pa.), April 23, 1862, Chronicling America: Historic American Newspapers, Library of Congress, http://chroniclingamerica.loc.gov/lccn/sn85054616/1862-04-23/ed-1/seq-2/.

168 "beyond the limits of the United States": Furgurson, *Freedom Rising*, 173.

168 "Miss Kate's father": Lee to Samuel Phillips Lee, April 14, 1862 in Laas, ed., *Wartime Washington*, 130n.

169 "Prince George's and St. Mary's counties": "Hurrying them Off," *National Republican*, April 18, 1862, http://www.newspapers.com.

169 "renewed the rebellious spirit": Lee to Samuel Phillips Lee, April 19, 1862 in Laas, ed., *Wartime Washington*, 130.

169 provided ready cash: Mary Mitchell, *Divided Town: A Study of Georgetown, DC During the Civil War* (Barre, MA: Barre, 1968), 64.

169 "delighted that her children are free": Lee to Samuel Phillips Lee, April 18, 1862, in Laas, ed., *Wartime Washington*, 130–31.

169 "as the Yankees had the Pequots": Lee to Samuel Phillips Lee, May 20, 1862, ibid., 151n.

170 "poor women! poor slaves!": C. Vann Woodward and Elisabeth Muhlen-feld, eds., *The Private Mary Chesnut: The Unpublished Civil War Diaries* (New York: Oxford University Press, 1984), 21.

171 "I intend to dance and sing 'Jeff Davis is coming'": Rose O'Neal Greenhow, *My Imprisonment and the First Year of Abolition Rule at Washington* (1863; reprint, Whitefish, MT: Kessinger, 2010), 74.

171 "charged with insanity": "Important from Washington," *Evening Bulletin* (Charlotte, N.C.), April 15, 1862, http://www.newspapers.com.

171 "a stern joy in your martyrdom": Greenhow, *My Imprisonment*, 96.

172 "cherish my own political faith": Ibid., 96.

172 "my being immediately sent South": Ibid., 105.

172 "thought differently": Ibid., 106.

172 "past all endurance": "Traitors in Crinoline and in Congress," *Goodhue Volunteer* (Goodhue, Minn.), April 16, 1862, http://www.newspapers.com.

172 "with swords and carbines": Greenhow, *My Imprisonment*, 108.

173 "their brethren of the South": Ibid., 109.

173 "in sight of the promised land": Ibid., 110.

174 "proudest moment of my life": Ibid., 111.

174 "shaken by mental torture": Ann Blackman, *Wild Rose: Rose O'Neale Greenhow, Civil War Spy, a True Story* (New York: Random House, 2005), 241.

175 "Secesh surrenders the sea": Lee to Samuel Phillips Lee, May 11, 1862, in Laas, ed., *Wartime Washington*, 142n.

175 "spiked & filled with sunken vessels": Lee to Samuel Phillips Lee, May 18, 1862, ibid., 147.

175 "kept them inviolate": Lee to Samuel Phillips Lee, May 20, 1862, ibid., 149n.

175 "I'll not wound any who like him": Lee to Samuel Phillips Lee, May 19, 1862, ibid., 148.

176 "he looks thin but well": Lee to Samuel Phillips Lee, June 15, 1862, ibid., 157.

176 "a street joke": Lee to Samuel Phillips Lee, May 26, 1862, ibid., 150.

176 "feel alien to the Rebels": Lee to Samuel Phillips Lee, July 7, 1862, ibid., 162.

176 "Heaven save our poor country!": Salmon P. Chase to Kate Chase, July 11, 1862, in McClure, Lamphier, and Kreger, eds., *Family Letters*, 209.

177 "Miss Carroll's usual vigor": "Miss Carroll on the Relation of the National Government to the Revolted Citizens," *National Republican* (Washington, D.C.), June 3, 1862, http://www.newspapers.com.

177 "as long as the Declaration of Independence": Janet L. Coryell, *Neither Heroine nor Fool: Anna Ella Carroll of Maryland* (Kent, OH: Kent State University Press, 1990), 79.

177 "'any government on earth'": Ibid., 80.

177 "Mr. President, there is another subject": Ibid., 70.

178 "substantial and liberal recognition": Anna Ella Carroll to Abraham Lincoln, June 21, 1862, ibid., 79.

179 "hot, hotter, hottest": Salmon P. Chase to Kate Chase, July 7, 1862, in McClure, Lamphier, and Kreger, eds., *Family Letters*, 208.

179 "retrieve its disasters": Salmon P. Chase to Kate Chase, July 6, 1862, ibid., 207.

180 "a repetition of McClellanism": Salmon P. Chase to Kate Chase, July 11, 1862, ibid., 209.

180 "deemed captives of war": James McPherson, *Battle Cry of Freedom: The Civil War Era* (Oxford: Oxford University Press, 1988), 500.

180 "persons of African descent": Ibid., 499.

181 "I hope he will": Margaret Leech, *Reveille in Washington 1860–1865* (New York: Harper, 1941), 224.

181 "oppress those around me": Lee to Samuel Phillips Lee, September 12, 1862, in Laas, ed., *Wartime Washington*, 180.

181 "Our cause is righteous": Lee to Samuel Phillips Lee, September 13, 1862, ibid., 180n.

181 "lose the fruits of this hard won fight": Lee to Samuel Phillips Lee, September 16, 1862, ibid., 182.

182 "not a bandage, rag, lint, or string": Stephen B. Oates, *A Woman of Valor: Clara Barton and the Civil War* (New York: Free Press, 1994), 85.

182 "a ball had passed between my body": "Aftermath of Antietam—September 1862: Clara Barton—The Angel of the Battlefield, 'God has indeed remembered us,'" The American Civil War: Battle of Antietam/Sharpsburg, accessed January 4, 2015, www.brotherswar.com/Antietam-8.htm.

183 *"the angel of the battlefield"*: Elizabeth Brown Pryor, *Clara Barton: Professional Angel* (Philadelphia: University of Pennsylvania Press, 1987), 99.

183 "born believing in the full right of woman": Ibid., 6.

183 "less than a man's pay": Ibid., 23.

184 "impropriety of mixing two sexes": Ibid., 59.

184 "gnaws at my peace": Ibid., 71.

185 "does not hurt me to pioneer": Ibid., 76.

185 "stand and feed and nurse them": Ibid., 80.

188 "must change our tactics, or lose the game": Emancipation Proclamation Summary Facts, accessed January 4, 2015, http://www.historynet.com/emancipation-proclamation.

188 "all that could be done to hurt our cause": Lee to Samuel Phillips Lee, September 23, 1862, in Laas, ed., *Wartime Washington*, 186.

188 the Republicans emerged with a majority: McPherson, *Battle Cry of Freedom*, 561.

188 "the country's well being": Lee to Samuel Phillips Lee, November 8, 1862, in Laas, ed., *Wartime Washington*, 209–10n.

189 "we *assure* freedom to the *free*": "Annual Message to Congress—Concluding Remarks," Abraham Lincoln Online: Speeches and Writings, accessed January 5, 2014, http://www.abrahamlincolnonline.org/lincoln/speeches/congress.htm.

189 "high crime against the Constitution": McPherson, *Battle Cry of Freedom*, 562.

189 "an idle, dependent race": Keckley, *Behind the Scenes*, 95.

189 "any bits of carpeting to cover themselves": Mary Todd Lincoln to Abraham Lincoln, November 3, 1862, in *Women in the Civil War: Warriors, Patriots, Nurses, and Spies*, ed. Phyllis Raybin Emert, Perspectives on History Series (Boston: History Compass, 2007), 68.

190 "the comfort of the sick and dying": Scott Korb, "Harriet Jacobs's First Assignment," *New York Times*, September 6, 2012, http://opinionator.blogs.nytimes.com.

190 "I heard was in flames": Lee to Samuel Phillips Lee, December 12, 1862, in Laas, ed., *Wartime Washington*, 213.

190 "your place is here": Pryor, *Professional Angel*, 106.

190 Nearly 200,000 soldiers skirmished over four days: "The Battle of Fredericksburg," Civil War Trust, accessed January 4, 2015, http://www.civilwar.org/battlefields/fredericksburg.html.

191 "broken by this woeful war": Lee to Samuel Phillips Lee, December 16, 1862, in Laas, ed., *Wartime Washington*, 216.

191 "Our city is being filled with hospitals": Lee to Samuel Phillips Lee, June 15, 1862, ibid., 157.

191 "Our church has not been converted": Dr. John Blake to Harriet Lane, May 16, 1862, James Buchanan and Harriet Lane Johnston Papers, Manuscript Division, Library of Congress, Washington, D.C.

191 "neglecting the soldiers": Lee to Samuel Phillips Lee, June 25, 1862, in Laas, ed., *Wartime Washington*, 158.

191 "a great want of good nurses": Lee to Samuel Phillips Lee, July 2, 1862, ibid., 159n.

192 "I am quite a skillful nurse": Louisa Rodgers Meigs to Montgomery C. Meigs, September 2, 1862, Montgomery C. Meigs Papers, Manuscript Division, Library of Congress, Washington, D.C.

192 "my family are far from the center": Montgomery C. Meigs to Louisa

Rodgers Meigs, September 12, 1862, Montgomery C. Meigs Papers, Manuscript Division, Library of Congress, Washington, D.C.

192 "bring his wife to that beleaguered city": Louisa Rodgers Meigs to Montgomery C. Meigs, November 18, 1862, Montgomery C. Meigs Papers, Manuscript Division, Library of Congress, Washington, D.C.

192 "all so badly ventilated": Lee to Samuel Phillips Lee, July 5, 1862, in Laas, ed., *Wartime Washington*, 161.

193 "decided to go to Washington as a nurse": Joel Myerson and Daniel Shealy, eds., Madeleine B. Stern, assoc. ed., *The Journals of Louisa May Alcott* (Athens: University of Georgia Press, 1997), November 1862, 110.

193 "the son of the house going to war": Ibid., December 1862.

193 "all stages of suffering, disease & death": Ibid., January 1863, 113.

193 "surprise and delight": Ibid., June 1863, 119.

193–94 "breed a pestilence": Ibid., January 1863, 113–14.

194 "very queer & arbitrary": Ibid., 116.

194 "no one likes her": Ibid., 123n.

194 "a comrade gave his name to be recorded": Louisa May Alcott, *Hospital Sketches* (Boston: J. Redpath, 1863), e-book, 39.

194 decorate the wards and deliver dinners: Leech, *Reveille in Washington*, 279.

194 "angel of mercy": Doris Kearns Goodwin, *Team of Rivals: The Political Genius of Abraham Lincoln* (New York: Simon & Schuster, 2006), 459.

194 "does them great honor": Lee to Samuel Phillips Lee, August 9, 1862, in Laas, ed., *Wartime Washington*, 175.

195 "who did not stab her husband & the Country": Lee to Samuel Phillips Lee, January 14, 1863, ibid., 231.

195 "dreams of such things": Lee to Samuel Phillips Lee, November 10, 1862, Ibid., 203.

CHAPTER 6: LIZZIE REPORTS ON THE ACTION, JANET GOES TO CAMP, LOUISA TAKES CHARGE

197 "I am under orders": Allan C. Guelzo, *Abraham Lincoln: Redeemer President* (Grand Rapids, MI: Eerdmans, 1999), 345, quoted in "Final Proclamation: January 1, 1863," Mr. Lincoln and Freedom, the Lincoln Institute and the Lehrman Institute, accessed January 24, 2015, http://www.mrlincolnand-freedom.org/inside.asp?ID=47&subjectID=3.

198 "very brilliant" scene: Fanny Seward diary entry, January 1, 1863, the Papers of William Henry Seward, microfilm set in Department of Rare Books and Special Collections Reels, University of Rochester Library, quoted in Doris

Kearns Goodwin, *Team of Rivals: The Political Genius of Abraham Lincoln* (New York: Simon & Schuster, 2006), 498.

198 "Chases had the roughest set": Lee to Samuel Phillips Lee, January 1, 1863, in *Wartime Washington: The Civil War Letters of Elizabeth Blair Lee*, ed. Virginia Jeans Laas (Urbana and Chicago: University of Illinois Press, 1999), 224.

199 "Men squealed, women fainted, dogs barked": James MacPherson, *Marching Toward Freedom: Blacks in the Civil War 1861–1865*, Library of American History (New York: Facts on File, 1994), 21, quoted in "Final Proclamation: January 1, 1863," Mr. Lincoln and Freedom, the Lincoln Institute and the Lehrman Institute, accessed January 24, 2015, http://www.mrlincolnandfreedom.org/inside.asp?ID=47&subjectID=3.

199 "Nothing like it will ever be seen again": Ernest B. Furgurson, *Freedom Rising: Washington in the Civil War* (New York: Vintage, 2005), 220.

200 "inciting servile insurrection": James McPherson, *Battle Cry of Freedom: The Civil War Era* (Oxford: Oxford University Press, 1988), 622.

200 "we care not for his proclamations": *Daily Progress*, Raleigh, NC, January 2, 1863, http://www.newspapers.com.

200 "starve them out": Lee to Samuel Phillips Lee, January 8, 1863, in Laas, ed., *Wartime Washington*, 229n.

201 "he lacks everything but courage": Lee to Samuel Phillips Lee, January 27, 1863, in ibid., 237n.

201 "turn up a General": Lee to Samuel Phillips Lee, January 28, 1863, in ibid., 236.

201 "two soldiers' orphans—& 3 sailors' orphans": Lee to Samuel Phillips Lee, January 6, 1863, in ibid., 228.

201 "The Army generally take care of their own people": Lee to Samuel Phillips Lee, November 17, 1862, in ibid., 229n.

202 "emaciated and thinner than ever": Lee to Samuel Phillips Lee, January 14, 1863, in ibid., 232.

202 "'we know better'": Lee to Samuel Phillips Lee, December 30, 1862, in ibid., 222.

203 "womankind in the south": Lee to Samuel Phillips Lee, August 23, 1863, 301n.

203 "the rebs can't be conquered": Joseph Medill to Elihu Washburne, January 16, 1863, quoted in McPherson, *Battle Cry of Freedom*, 648.

203 "the South have achieved their independence": *Touched with Fire: Civil War Letters and Diary of Oliver Wendell Holmes, Jr., 1861–1864*, ed. Mark deWolfe Howe (Cambridge, MA: Harvard University Press, 1946), 73, quoted in McPherson, *Battle Cry of Freedom*, 648.

204 "the dearest little duck": *New York Times*, February 11, 1863, http://timesma-chine.nytimes.com/timesmachine/1863/02/11/issue.html.

204 "Grace Greenwood the Patriot": Furgurson, *Freedom Rising*, 225.

205 "no livery": *New York Times*, September 7, 1852, http://timesmachine.ny-times.com/timesmachine/1852/09/07/issue.html.

205 "'the characters of your sons and daughters!'": *Highland Weekly News*, Hills-boro, Ohio, January 1, 1863, http://www.newspapers.com.

206 "the mother of the Republican party": Donald Ritchie, *American Journal-ists: Getting the Story* (New York: Oxford University Press, 1997), Google e-book, 73–74.

207 "a loyal, liberty loving woman": Jane Swisshelm, *Half a Century* (Chicago: Jansen, McClurg, 1880), Gutenberg project e-book, 155.

208 "I want to employ women to cut the Treasury notes": Mary Clemmer Ames, *Ten Years in Washington: Life and Scenes in the National Capital, as a Woman Sees Them* (1874; reprint, Ann Arbor: University of Michigan Library, Mich-igan Historical Reprint Series, 2005), 372.

208 as Washington rents increased: "Abraham Lincoln's White House: Other Government Buildings—Treasury Department," Mr. Lincoln's White House, the Lincoln Institute and the Lehrman Institute, ac-cessed January 24, 2015, http://www.mrlincolnswhitehouse.org/inside. asp?ID=166&subjectID=4.

208 more women came to town: Margaret Leech, *Reveille in Washington 1860–1865* (New York: Harper, 1941), 339.

209 "made womanly virtue its price": Ames, *Ten Years in Washington*, 373.

209 "all the other deeds of my life": "Uncle Sam as Woman's Boss," *New York Times*, April 18, 1926, http://www.nytimes.com.

209 "I have a list of Senators": Lee to Samuel Phillips Lee, February 17, 1863, in Laas, ed., *Wartime Washington*, 241.

209 "I was egotistic enough": Lee to Samuel Phillips Lee, February 26, 1863, in ibid., 243.

209 "tomorrow after church": Lee to Samuel Phillips Lee, March 10, 1863, in ibid., 244n.

210 "a pleasant chat": Lee to Samuel Phillips Lee, January 14, 1863, in ibid., 231.

210 "Father & you both will be angry": Lee to Samuel Phillips Lee, March 5, 1863, in ibid., 249.

210 "can't go in a storm": Lee to Samuel Phillips Lee, March 10, 1863, in ibid., 250n.

210 "from cot to cot": Noah Brooks, *Washington in Lincoln's Time* (New York: Century, 1895), Google e-book, 48.

211 jolly his wife out of the anger: Catherine Clinton, *Mrs. Lincoln: A Life* (New York: Harper Perennial, 2010), 200.

211 "'a great relief to get away'": Ibid., 50.

212 "it is easily done": Nettie Coburn Maynard, *Séances in Washington: Abraham Lincoln and Spiritualism During the Civil War*, ed. with commentary Irene McGarvie (1891, as "Was Abraham Lincoln a Spiritualist?" reprint, Toronto: Ancient Wisdom, 2011), Kindle e-book, loc. 862.

212 "if we are going to take spirits' advice": Ibid., 992.

213 "What will the country say!'": Brooks, *Lincoln's Time*, 57–58.

214 "Silence is ever ominous": Lee to Samuel Phillips Lee, April 30, 1863, in Laas, ed., *Wartime Washington*, 265n.

214 "'our army is in full retreat'": Maynard, *Séances*, 1006.

214 "excludes the War Dept": Lee to Samuel Phillips Lee, May 6, 1863, in Laas, ed., *Wartime Washington*, 265–66.

214 "gallantry of his raid": Lee to Samuel Phillips Lee, May 8, 1863, in ibid., 267.

214 "drunk all the time": Lee to Samuel Phillips Lee, May 8, 1863, in ibid., 266.

214–15 "'thus we are disgraced'": Lee to Samuel Phillips Lee, May 8, 1863, in ibid., 268.

215 "take pride in his heroism": Lee to Samuel Phillips Lee, May 13, 1863, in ibid., 267n.

215 "see him & his comforts": Lee to Samuel Phillips Lee, May 6, 1863, in ibid., 266.

215 "none of the horrors": Maynard, *Séances*, 1035.

215 "she rallied and bravely returned": Maynard, *Séances*, 1056, 1069.

216 "wreath of large white roses": Mrs. Janet W. Seward, *Personal Experiences of the Civil War*, January 20, 1898, for the "Fortnightly," Woman's Literary Club, Auburn, New York, reprinted in *History of "The Ninth New York Heavy Artillery"* (Worcester, MA: F. S. Blanchard, 1899), 5.

216 "a box of broken pieces": Ibid., 5–6.

217 "brought up in log cabins": Ibid., 7.

218 "a little one-horse wagon": Ibid., 11.

218 "running from the enemy": Ibid., 11–12.

218 "raids by the guerillas": Ibid., 12.

218 "a race between Hooker & Lee": Lee to Samuel Phillips Lee, June 15, 1863, in Laas, ed., *Wartime Washington*, 275n.

218 "nearer than Harper's Ferry & Centreville": Lee to Samuel Phillips Lee, June 18, 1863, in ibid., 274.

218 "'Her Bright Smiles Haunt me Still' and a 'Scene de Ballet'": "Grand Vocal and Instrument Concert for the Benefit of the Washington City Orphan Asylum," *National Republican*, May 27, 1863, http://www.newspapers.com.

218 "my heart is so much in this establishment": Lee to Samuel Phillips Lee, June 2–3, 1863, in Laas, ed., *Wartime Washington*, 271 and 271n.

219 "if we are defeated": Lee to Samuel Phillips Lee, June 26, 1863, in ibid., 277n.

219 "your astonishment cannot have exceeded mine": Goodwin, *Team of Rivals*, 531.

220 "all the pluck out of that Washington concern": Lee to Samuel Phillips Lee, July 1, 1863, in Laas, ed., *Wartime Washington*, 279.

220 "laugh and eat & sleep—hope & pray": Lee to Samuel Phillips Lee, June 29, 1863, in ibid., 279.

220 "Lee's whole object": Lee to Samuel Phillips Lee, July 1, 1863, in ibid., 280.

221 "he was disappointed": Lee to Samuel Phillips Lee, July 4, 1863, in ibid., 282–83.

221 "Lee Retreating": "Extra," *National Republican*, July 6, 1863, http://www.newspapers.com.

221–22 "sea of blood this dreadful war has cost'": Lee to Samuel Phillips Lee, July 7, 1863, in Laas, ed., *Wartime Washington*, 285.

222 "that holds the South's two halves together": Bob Zeller, "The Long, Gruesome Fight to Capture Vicksburg," *Hallowed Ground*, Summer 2013, at Civil War Trust: Saving America's Civil War Battlefields, accessed January 24, 2015, http://www.civilwar.org/hallowed-ground-magazine/summer-2013/fight-to-capture-vicksburg.html.

222 "the war will be over before very long": Lee to Samuel Phillips Lee, July 16, 1863, in Laas, ed., *Wartime Washington*, 289.

222 "too happy to grumble": Lee to Samuel Phillips Lee, July 10, 1863, in ibid., 287n.

222 "an easy prey within our grasp": Ibid., 284n.

223 "break into the Lord & Taylor store": David Barnes, *The Draft Riots in New York, July 1863, The Metropolitan Police: Their Service During Riot Week, Their Honorable Record* (New York: Baker & Godwin, 1863), Google e-book, 40.

223 More than one thousand people died or were wounded: Goodwin, *Team of Rivals*, 536.

223 "'we may have the house burned'": Seward, *Personal Experiences*, 12.

223 "the Copperhead element was very active": Ibid.

224 "leave it all with my Heavenly father": Rebecca R. Pomroy, *Echoes from Hospital and White House: A Record of Mrs. Rebecca R. Pomroy's Experience in Wartimes*, ed. Anna L. Boyden (Boston: D. Lothrop, 1884), 57–58 quoted at Mr. Lincoln's White House, Rebecca R. Pomroy (1817–1884), the Lincoln Institute and the Lehrman Institute, accessed January 24, 2015, http://www.mrlincolnswhitehouse.org/inside.asp?ID=65&subjectID=2.

225 "a liberal instead of a selfish view": Elizabeth Keckley, *Behind the Scenes, or*

Thirty Years a Slave and Four Years in the White House, (New York: G. W. Carleton, 1868), 55.

225 "what a brave front she manages to keep": Katherine Helm, *The True Story of Mary, Wife of Lincoln: Containing the Recollections of Mary Lincoln's Sister Emilie (Mrs. Ben Hardin Helm), Extracts of Her War-Time Diary, Numerous Letters and Other Documents* (New York: Harper & Brothers, 1928), 250.

226 "a single tear shed for a dead enemy": Ibid., 217.

226 "no sympathy for a Southern-born woman": Ibid., 217–18.

227 "her beloved Southland": Ibid., 221.

227 "Send her to me": Ibid.

227 "in silence and tears": Ibid., 221–22.

227 "to be cheerful and accept fate": Ibid., 223.

227 "our dear, red-headed baby brother!": Ibid., 224.

228 "Her nerves have gone to pieces": Ibid., 225.

228 "it would kill her": Ibid., 225–26.

228 "It *is* unnatural and abnormal": Ibid., 227.

229 "'they should all be opposing yours'": Ibid., 229–30.

229 "powerless to protect a guest": Ibid., 230.

229 "I am longing for Kentucky and mother": Ibid., 231.

229 "'on your return to Kentucky'": Ibid., 232.

230 "quite a belle in Washington": Keckley, *Behind the Scenes*, 58.

230 "judging how its associations suit her": Leech, *Reveille in Washington*, 348.

230 "Mr. Sprague is not attractive": "Marriage in Official Circles," *Brooklyn Daily Eagle*, November 14, 1863, http://www.newspapers.com.

230 "I cannot afford to be extravagant": Salmon P. Chase to Kate Chase, August 17, 1863, *"Spur Up Your Pegasus": Family Letters of Salmon, Kate and Nettie Chase, 1844–1873*, ed. James P. McClure, Peg A. Lamphier, and Erika M. Kreger (Kent, OH: Kent State University Press, 2009), 218.

231 "the same relation between father & daughter": William Sprague to Salmon P. Chase, November 4, 1863, in ibid., 235.

231 "love cannot be perfect": Salmon P. Chase to Kate Chase, August 12, 1863, in ibid., 216.

232 "The Kate Chase Wedding March": Ibid., 239.

232 "bow in reverence": Goodwin, *Team of Rivals*, 581.

232 "the gaiety was very lame": Lee to Samuel Phillips Lee, November 12, 1863, in Laas, ed., *Wartime Washington*, 319.

232 "offend the eye or taste": "Marriage in Official Circles," Washington *Chronicle*, reprinted in *Brooklyn Daily Eagle*, November 14, 1863, http://www.newspapers.com.

232 horses with names like General McClellan: Leech, *Reveille in Washington*, 320.

232 "in fashionable force": Lee to Samuel Phillips Lee, September 30, 1863, in Laas, ed., *Wartime Washington*, 309.

232 "Dining room furniture alone": Lee to Samuel Phillips Lee, October 11, 1863, in ibid., 312.

233 "the great struggle for our National existence": Louisa Rodgers Meigs to Montgomery C. Meigs, December 16, 1863, Montgomery C. Meigs Papers, Manuscript Division, Library of Congress, Washington, D.C.

234 echoed by artillery at the Forts: "The Statue of Freedom," Architect of the Capitol, United States Capitol, accessed January 24, 2015, http://www.aoc. gov/capitol-hill/other-statues/statue-freedom.

234 "engage herself to him": Louisa Rodgers Meigs to Montgomery C. Meigs, October 11, 1863, Montgomery C. Meigs Papers, Manuscript Division, Library of Congress, Washington, D.C.

234 "Mary Meigs is said to be engaged": Lee to Samuel Phillips Lee, November 12, 1863, in Laas, ed., *Wartime Washington*, 319.

235 "his mind and his feelings are so different": Louisa Rodgers Meigs to Montgomery C. Meigs, November 8, 1863, Montgomery C. Meigs Papers, Manuscript Division, Library of Congress, Washington, D.C.

235 "do not learn much": Louisa Rodgers to Brother, December 16, 1827, Rodgers Family Papers, Naval Historical Foundation Collection, Manuscript Division, Library of Congress, Washington, D.C.

235 "amiable, intelligent and sprightly": David W. Miller, *Second Only to Grant: Quartermaster General Montgomery C. Meigs* (Shippensburg, PA: White Mane Books, 2000), 14.

235 "disease of the brain": Ibid., 23.

235 "what a convenient thing": Louisa Rodgers Meigs to Minerva Dineson Rodgers, July 1842, Rodgers Family Papers, Manuscript Division, Library of Congress, Washington, D.C.

235 "the full in all its follies": Louisa Rodgers Meigs to Nannie Rodgers, January 1845, Rodgers Family Papers, Manuscript Division, Library of Congress, Washington, D.C.

236 "feast your reason & imagination": Louisa Rodgers Meigs to Nannie Rodgers, February 1845, Rodgers Family Papers, Manuscript Division, Library of Congress, Washington, D.C.

236 "Detroit has been very dull": Louisa Rodgers Meigs to Nannie Rodgers, April 1848, Rodgers Family Papers, Manuscript Division, Library of Congress, Washington, D.C.

236 "seem to have slept four years": Louisa Rodgers Meigs to Henry Rodgers, November 1850, Rodgers Family Papers, Manuscript Division, Library of Congress, Washington, D.C.

236 "I know it will annoy Mother": Louisa Rodgers Meigs to Nannie, March 1851, Rodgers Family Papers, Manuscript Division, Library of Congress, Washington, D.C.

236 "as if you had accomplished a victory": Louisa Rodgers Meigs to John Rodgers Meigs, September 4, 1861, in *A Civil War Soldier of Christ and Country: The Selected Correspondence of John Rodgers Meigs, 1859–1864*, ed. Mary A. Giunta (Urbana and Chicago: University of Illinois Press, 2006), 110–11.

236 "*watch* you before you left me": Louisa Rodgers Meigs to John Rodgers Meigs, September 1, 1860, in ibid., 72.

237 "useless or extravagant": Louisa Rodgers Meigs to Montgomery C. Meigs, October 28, 1863, Montgomery C. Meigs Papers, Manuscript Division, Library of Congress, Washington, D.C.

237 "the head of a great army": Louisa Rodgers Meigs to Charles Meigs, November 5, 1863, Montgomery C. Meigs Papers, Manuscript Division, Library of Congress, Washington, D.C.

237 "still held the reins of power": Louisa Rodgers Meigs to Montgomery C. Meigs, October 25, 1863, Montgomery C. Meigs Papers, Manuscript Division, Library of Congress, Washington, D.C.

237 "your good health & spirits": Louisa Rodgers Meigs to Montgomery C. Meigs, November 23, 1863, Montgomery C. Meigs Papers, Manuscript Division, Library of Congress, Washington, D.C.

238 "We live very quietly": Louisa Rodgers Meigs to Montgomery C. Meigs, December 6, 1863, Montgomery C. Meigs Papers, Manuscript Division, Library of Congress, Washington, D.C.

238 "something I can give everybody": Glenna Schroeder-Lein, *Lincoln and Medicine* (Carbondale: Southern Illinois University Press, 2012), 30.

239 "now all subscribe to the message": Lee to Samuel Phillips Lee, December 8, 1863, in Laas, ed., *Wartime Washington*, 325.

239 "I bought a toy for Blair": Lee to Samuel Phillips Lee, December 21, 1863, in ibid., 332.

CHAPTER 7: ANNA SPEAKS, JESSIE CAMPAIGNS (AGAIN), SOJOURNER VISITS

241 "the help of the suffering freedmen": "Words for the Hour," *National Republican*, January 14, 1864, http://www.newspapers.com.

242 "services in the campaigns": Ibid.

243 the fiery young woman: Lois Leveen, "The Civil War's Oratorical Wunder-kind," *New York Times*, May 21, 2013, http://www.nytimes.com.

243 "a pitch of enthusiasm": "Complimentary to Miss Dickinson," *Liberator*, Boston, MA, May 8, 1863, http://www.newspapers.com.

244 "the dirty puddle of party politics": "Miss Dickinson, Mr. Beecher, and the Directors of the Academy of Music," *Brooklyn Daily Eagle*, May 1, 1863, http://www.newspapers.com.

244 shot off a lock of her hair: Judith E. Harper, *Women During the Civil War: An Encyclopedia* (New York: Routledge, 2004), 111.

244 "a splendid burst of applause": Noah Brooks, *Mr. Lincoln's Washington: Selections from the Writings of Noah Brooks, Civil War Correspondent*, ed. P. J. Staudenraus (South Brunswick, NJ: Thomas Yoseloff, 1967), 280.

244 "thunders of applause": Ibid., 281.

244 "her brief and splendid career": Ibid., 282.

245 "her long and picturesque career": Noah Brooks, *Washington in Lincoln's Time* (New York: Century, 1895), Google e-book, 74.

245 "disrespectful to the minority of this House": *National Republican*, January 19 1864, http://www.newspapers.com.

245 "an immense train flowed out behind": Brooks, *Mr. Lincoln's Washington*, 274–75.

246 "a blue brocade gown": Ibid., 275.

246 "affectedly call our 'Republican Court'": "Inklings of Idleness," *National Republican*, January 13, 1864, http://www.newspapers.com.

246 "such a rampage": Doris Kearns Goodwin, *Team of Rivals: The Political Genius of Abraham Lincoln* (New York: Simon & Schuster, 2006), 600.

247 "Abe has the inside of the track": Lee to Samuel Phillips Lee, January 13, 1864, in *Wartime Washington: The Civil War Letters of Elizabeth Blair Lee*, ed. Virginia Jeans Laas (Urbana and Chicago: University of Illinois Press, 1999), 340.

247 "The Radicals will throttle him": Lee to Samuel Phillips Lee, January 24, 1864, in ibid., 340n.

247 "the wishes of our friends in Ohio": Salmon P. Chase to Nettie Chase, March 15, 1864, in *"Spur Up Your Pegasus": Family Letters of Salmon, Kate and Nettie Chase, 1844–1873*, ed. James P. McClure, Peg A. Lamphier, and Erika M. Kreger (Kent, OH: Kent State University Press, 2009), 255.

248 "the field in the spring": Lee to Samuel Phillips Lee, January 12, 1864, in Laas, ed., *Wartime Washington*, 336.

248 "think how much easier said than done": Lee to Samuel Phillips Lee, December 13, 1863, in ibid., 332n.

248 "where there are no ladies": Lee to Samuel Phillips Lee, January 26, 1864, in ibid., 340n.

248 "the deep crimson shade of the silk": William O. Stoddard, *Inside Lincoln's White House in War Times* (1892; reprint, Big Byte Books, 2014), e-book, loc. 2076.

249 "far more of refinement in manner and appearance": Lee to Samuel Phillips Lee, January 28, 1864, in Laas, ed., *Wartime Washington*, 343.

249 "in virtuous black": "Heavy Raid Upon the Fancy, The Big Establishments Attended to, Mary Ann Hall and Others of the Elite Marched up to the City Hall," *Washington Evening Star*, January 15, 1864, quoted at Historic Congressional Cemetery website, accessed January 25, 2015, http://www.congressionalcemetery.org.

249 "for the last quarter century": "Criminal Court—Trial of Mary Ann Hall on Charge of Keeping a Bawdy House," *Evening Star*, February 22, 1864, at ibid.

249 "first class furniture, very showy": "Bawdy House Case—Trial of Mary Ann Hall, Criminal Court, Judge Olin," *Evening Star*, February 19, 1864, at ibid.

250 "more than twice the population of the District": Constance McLaughlin Green, *Washington Village and Capital, 1800–1878* (Princeton, NJ: Princeton University Press, 1962), 251.

250 "George Riggs has given in cash $25000": Lee to Samuel Phillips Lee, September 10, 1863, in Laas, ed., *Wartime Washington*, 309.

250 "every available nook and corner": Lois Bryan Adams, *Letter from Washington, 1863–1865*, ed. Evelyn Leasher (Detroit: Wayne State University Press, 1999), 34.

250 "$57,200 in government and railroad bonds": "The Estate of Mary A. Hall," *Evening Star*, February 11, 1886, quoted at Historic Congressional Cemetery website, accessed January 25, 2015, http://www.congressionalcemetery.org.

251 "many who knew her sterling worth": "Hall," *Evening Star*, at ibid.

251 "Piper-Heidsieck champagne corks and wire bales": T. Rees Shapiro, "Washington's Civil War Madam Could Keep a Secret," *Washington Post*, April 27, 2013, http://www.washingtonpost.com.

251 "the most extensive Whorehouse in the nation": Ernest B. Furgurson, *Freedom Rising: Washington in the Civil War* (New York: Vintage, 2005), 292.

251 "nor common decencies of life": Dr. John B. Ellis, *The Sights and Secrets of the National Capital* (1869; reprint, Lexington, KY: ULAN Press, 2013), 384.

252 "her first step in the road to ruin": Ibid., 386.

252 "devils in the form of men": Ibid., 387.

252 "whirled into the torrent": Brooks, *Mr. Lincoln's Washington*, 290.

253 " 'He is a butcher' ": Elizabeth Keckley, *Behind the Scenes, or Thirty Years a Slave and Four Years in the White House* (New York: G. W. Carleton, 1868), 117.

253 "All honor to our fair Jewesses!": *Jewish Messenger*, vol. 15, no. 17 (May 6, 1864): 134, quoted in Robert Shosteck, "The Jewish Community of Washington, D.C., During the Civil War," *American Jewish Historical Quarterly* 56 (March 1967): 319–47, accessed January 25, 2015, http://www.jhsgw.org/exhibitions/online/lincolns-city/exhibits/show/mr-lincolns-city/essays/jewish-community-of-washington.

254 " 'God bless the women of America!' ": *Soldiers' Journal*, Alexandria, Virginia, April 6, 1864, www.newspapers.com.

254 "we ask you to use it now to the utmost": "To the Women of the Republic, January 25, 1864," Center for Legislative Archives, National Records and Archives Administration, quoted at Slavery and the Making of America, The Slave Experience: Men, Women & Gender, Public Broadcasting Service, accessed January 25, 2015, http://www.pbs.org/wnet/slavery/experience/gender/docs2.html.

255 "the history of our second revolution": Stanton to Charles Sumner, February 1, 1864, in *Elizabeth Cady Stanton as Revealed in her Letters, Diary and Reminiscences*, vol. 2, ed. Theodore Stanton and Harriot Stanton Blatch (New York: Harper & Brothers, 1922), Google e-book, 96–97.

255 "the suppression of the rebellion": "Susan B. Anthony, Celebrating A 'Heroic Life,' " Department of Rare Books and Special Collections, University of Rochester Libraries, accessed January 25, 2015, http://www.lib.rochester.edu/index.cfm?PAGE=4113.

255 "she has grown huge": Lee to Samuel Phillips Lee, March 27, 1864, in Laas, ed., *Wartime Washington*, 360.

256 "a careless and imperfect one": Pamela Herr, *Jessie Benton Frémont: American Woman of the 19th Century* (New York: Franklin Watts, 1987), 366.

256 "the most charming evidences of sympathy": Frémont to James T. Fields, January 5, 1863, in *The Letters of Jessie Frémont*, ed. Pamela Herr and Mary Lee Spence (Urbana and Chicago: University of Illinois Press, 1993), 337.

256 "The restraints of ordinary times": Jessie Benton Frémont, *The Story of the Guard: The Chronicle of the War* (Boston: Ticknor & Fields, 1863), Kindle e-book, loc. 1618.

256 "unfaithful watchmen at Washington": Frémont to George Julian, March 3, 1863, in Herr and Spence, eds., *Letters*, 349.

257 "Thank Heaven & the Constitution": Frémont to John T. Fiala, July 19, 1863, in ibid., 354.

257 "sly slimy nature": Frémont to Thomas Starr King, October 16, 1863, in ibid., 356.

257 "the suffering caused by the war": Frémont to George Julian, January 16, 1864, in ibid., 361–62.

257 "preside at your meeting": Frémont to Elizabeth Cady Stanton, May 4, 1863, in ibid., 351.

257 "Mrs. Frémont is next door to us": Herr, *Jessie Benton Frémont*, 369.

258 "bound in uniform style": Ibid., 370n.

258 "make a growing fund": Frémont to Elizabeth Palmer Peabody, January 27, 1864, in Herr and Spence, eds., *Letters*, 365.

258 "We get on very civilly": Frémont to Elizabeth Palmer Peabody, March 20, 1864, in ibid., 374–75.

258 "Pontius Pilate of the slaves": Frémont to Elizabeth Palmer Peabody, February 14, 1864, in ibid., 369.

258 "The number of tickets taken at the door": *New York Times*, April 9, 1864, http://www.nytimes.com.

258 his own locks for the head, eyes, and backbone: Herr, *Jessie Benton Frémont*, 371.

258–59 "To the Editor of the New-York Times . . . (Signed) CATHARINE C. HUNT": *New York Times*, May 18, 1864, http://www.nytimes.com.

259 "renounce our laces, silks, velvets and diamonds": "The Ladies National Covenant; A Movement to Reduce the Consumption of Foreign Luxuries," *New York Times*, May 5, 1864, http://www.nytimes.com.

259 "the grand work of retrenchment and reform": Adams, May 9, 1864, *Letter from Washington*, 138.

260 "just as pretty in homespun": Herr and Spence, eds., *Letters*, 381n.

260 "inasmuch as they chose their leader first": Stanton to Jessie Benton Frémont, May 4, 1864, in Stanton and Blatch, eds., *Letters, Diary and Reminiscences*, 98.

261 "what a precious piece of foolery it all is": "The Cleveland Convention," *New York Times*, June 2, 1864, http://www.nytimes.com.

264 "A large concourse of citizens": "Local News, The Arsenal Catastrophe," *National Republican*, June 20, 1864, http://www.newspapers.com.

264 "sufferers by the recent explosion": *National Republican*, June 24, 1864, http://www.newspapers.com.

264 "Erected By Public Contributions": Brian Bergin, *The Washington Arsenal Explosion: Civil War Disaster in the Capital*, ed. Erin Bergin Voorhees (Charleston, SC: History Press, 2012), e-book, loc. 1629.

265 "overcome by the burning of Silver Spring": Lee to Samuel Phillips Lee, July 13, 1864, in Laas, ed., *Wartime Washington*, 402.

265 "cleaned out the larder & poultry": Lee to Samuel Phillips Lee, July 16, 1864, in ibid., 405.

265 "occupied by rebel troops that night": Jane Swisshelm, *Half a Century* (Chicago: Jansen, McClurg, 1880), Gutenberg project e-book, 242.

266 "an old age in poverty, homeless & etc.": Lee to Samuel Phillips Lee, July 14, 1864, in Laas, ed., *Wartime Washington*, 403.

266 "the advent of the enemy": Louisa Rodgers Meigs to Montgomery C. Meigs, July 1864, Montgomery C. Meigs Papers, Manuscript Division, Library of Congress, Washington, D.C.

266 "All the crops were left": Lee to Samuel Phillips Lee, July 16, 1864, in Laas, ed., *Wartime Washington*, 404.

266 "the bravest Union people": Lee to Samuel Phillips Lee, August 18, 1864, in ibid., 422n.

266 "the shot & shell fell thick": Lee to Samuel Phillips Lee, July 16, 1864, in ibid., 404–5.

267 "refugees come flying in from the country": Brooks, *Mr. Lincoln's Washington*, 353.

268 "make a penny outside of his salary'": Keckley, *Behind the Scenes . . .*

268 "Mrs. Lincoln ransacked the treasures": *New York Herald*, May 2, 1864, quoted in Catherine Clinton, *Mrs. Lincoln: A Life* (New York: Harper Perennial, 2010), 219.

268 "patriotic duty": Katherine Helm, *The True Story of Mary, Wife of Lincoln: Containing the Recollections of Mary Lincoln's Sister Emilie (Mrs. Ben Hardin Helm), Extracts of Her War-Time Diary, Numerous Letters and Other Documents* (New York: Harper & Brothers, 1928), 177.

268 "no hope of the re-election": Keckley, *Behind the Scenes*, 68, 136.

269 "a point of mutual embarrassment": Goodwin, *Team of Rivals*, 633.

269 "ablest of all the Republican Senators": Lee to Samuel Phillips Lee, July 2, 1864, in Laas, ed., *Wartime Washington*, 398.

269 "This looks like a true picture to me": Lee to Samuel Phillips Lee, February 10, 1864, in ibid., 346.

269 "a desperate effort made": Lee to Samuel Phillips Lee, July 3, 1864, in ibid., 399.

269 "they were mostly Democrats": Lee to Samuel Phillips Lee, April 23, 1864, in ibid., 369.

270 "heartily glad to be disconnected": Salmon P. Chase to Nettie, July 5, 1864, in McClure, Lamphier, and Kreger, eds., *Family Letters*, 258.

270 "People never sympathize with such feelings": Salmon P. Chase to Kate, July 11, 1864, in ibid., 260.

270 "a difference which cannot be healed": John Oller, *American Queen: The Rise and Fall of Kate Chase Sprague, Civil War "Belle of the North" and Gilded Age Woman of Scandal* (Boston: Da Capo Press, 2014), e-book, locs. 1851–64.

270 "deader than dead": McPherson, *Battle Cry of Freedom*, 758.

270 "the General will thankfully retire": Frémont to John Greenleaf Whittier, August 22, 1864, in Herr and Spence, eds., *Letters*, 382.

271 "Lincoln's stock is running down rapidly": Stanton to Susan B. Anthony, August 22, 1864, in Stanton and Blatch, eds., *Letters, Diary and Reminiscences*, 100.

271 "the nonsense she talks": Lee to Samuel Phillips Lee, July 2, 1864, in Laas, ed., *Wartime Washington*, 399.

273 "the merest twaddle": Elizabeth Cady Stanton to Susan B. Anthony, September 25, 1864., in Theodore Stanton and Harriot Stanton Blach, ed., Elizabeth Cady Stanton As Revealed in Her Letters, Diary and Reminiscences, Vol. II, Harper & Brothers, New York, 1922, p. 102.

273 "utterly refused any appointments, patronage or retaliation": Frémont to Rutherford B. Hayes, July 7, 1881, in Herr, *Jessie Benton Frémont*, 488.

273 "he was going to Europe": Lee to Samuel Phillips Lee, September 16, 1864, in Laas, ed., *Wartime Washington*, 429.

274 "They seem to depend upon your aid": Kate Chase Sprague to Salmon P. Chase, July 26, 1864, in McClure, Lamphier, and Kreger, eds., *Family Letters*, 261.

274 "terminate and forever prohibit the existence of Slavery": "Republican Party Platform, 1864," John C. Willis, University of the South, Sewanee, Tennessee, accessed January 26, 2015, http://static.sewanee.edu/faculty/willis/Civil_War/documents/republican.html.

275 When she learned about the abolitionist movement she quickly signed up. . . . And then she learned about the women's rights movement and added that cause to her quiver: Much of this biographical information comes from *Notable American Women 1607–1950: A Biographical Directory*, vol. 3, P–Z, ed. Edward T. James, Janet Wilson James, and assoc. ed. Paul S. Boyer (Cambridge, MA: Belknap Press of Harvard University Press, 1971), 47–81.

276 "the great and good man Abraham Lincoln": "Sojourner Truth Calls Upon the President: An 1864 Letter," *Massachusetts Review* 13, no. 1/2 (Winter–Spring 1972): 297–99, http://www.jstor.org/stable/25088237.

277 "the old slave-holding spirit": Barbara A. White, *Visits with Lincoln: Abolitionists Meet the President at the White House* (Lanham, MD: Lexington Books, 2011), Google e-book, 149.

277 "all excitement here over the election": Rebecca R. Pomroy, *Echoes from*

Hospital and White House: A Record of Mrs. Rebecca R. Pomroy's Experience in War-Times, ed. Anna L. Boyden (Boston: D. Lothrop, 1884), e-book, 227.

278 "'We can Vote as well as Fight'": Brooks, *Mr. Lincoln's Washington*, 379–80.

278 "I would like to give my vote": Pomroy, *Echoes*, 227.

278 "gone home on furloughs": Ibid., 228.

278 "as fearlessly at the ballot-box": Adams, October 31, 1864, in *Letter from Washington*, 205.

278 "she is more anxious than I": Goodwin, *Team of Rivals*, 665.

279 "in the midst of a great civil war": Ibid., 667.

279 "the beauty of its proportions": "The Capitol," *National Republican*, November 16, 1864, http://www.newspapers.com.

280 "I ought not to blame Chase": Col. William H. Crook, *Through Five Administrations: Reminiscences of Colonel William H. Crook, Body-Guard to President Lincoln*, ed. Margarita Spalding Gerry (New York: Harper & Brothers, 1907), Kindle e-book, locs. 358–73.

280 "cure him and he will be satisfied": Goodwin, *Team of Rivals*, 680.

280 "gorgeous in millinery": Brooks, *Mr. Lincoln's Washington*, 401.

281 "And as it is to so go at all events": Abraham Lincoln, "State of the Union Address, December 6, 1864," accessed January 25, 2015, http://www.infoplease.com/t/hist/state-of-the-union/76.html#ixzz3P1lDt0Hd.

281 "as a Christmas gift, the city of Savannah": "General Sherman to President Lincoln, December 22nd, 1864," Civil War Trust: Saving America's Civil War Battlefields, accessed January 25, 2015, http://www.civilwar.org/education/history/primarysources/general-sherman-to-president.html.

282 "I now look to the end of the War": Lee to Samuel Phillips Lee, December 26, 1864, in Laas, ed., *Wartime Washington*, 453.

CHAPTER 8: ONE MARY LEAVES, ONE MARY HANGS, AND LOIS WRITES ABOUT IT ALL

283 "a better talker than ever": Lee to Samuel Phillips Lee, January 16, 1865, in *Wartime Washington: The Civil War Letters of Elizabeth Blair Lee*, ed. Virginia Jeans Laas (Urbana and Chicago: University of Illinois Press, 1999), 463.

284 "for her good & ours I hope": Lee to Samuel Phillips Lee, December 27, 1864, in ibid., 455n.

284 "the story about his papers": January 12, 1865, in ibid., 461.

284 "his arrival in Richmond": January 14, 1865, in ibid., 462.

284 "no small sense of joy": Lee to Samuel Phillips Lee, January 16, 1865, in ibid., 464.

285 "our one common country": Doris Kearns Goodwin, *Team of Rivals: The Political Genius of Abraham Lincoln* (New York: Simon & Schuster, 2006), 691.

285 "her tone, her wit & etc.": Lee to Samuel Phillips Lee, January 18, 1865, in ibid., 466.

286 "'I did steal'": Lois Bryan Adams, January 17, 1865, in Lois Bryan Adams, *Letter from Washington, 1863–1865*, ed. Evelyn Leasher (Detroit: Wayne State University Press, 1999), 226.

286 "he will have the arsenal work restored": *Daily Dispatch*, February 6, 1865, www.perseus.tufts.edu/hopper/text?doc=Perseus%3Atext%3A2006.05 .1291%3Aarticle%3Dpos%3D11.

287 "without interfering with the public interest": Don E. Fehrenbacher and Virginia Fehrenbacher, eds., *Recollected Words of Abraham Lincoln* (Redwood City, CA: Stanford University Press, 1996), 15.

287 "most of the valuable instruments": "DESTRUCTIVE FIRE.; Burning of the Smithsonian Institute at Washington. Serious Loss of Valuable Documents, Records, &c.THE LIBRARY AND MUSEUM SAVED," *New York Times*, January 25, 1865, http://www.nytimes.com.

287 "one seething mass of flames": Adams, January 24, 1865, in *Letter from Washington*, 227.

287 "the most miserable imbecility": Lee to Samuel Phillips Lee, January 24, 1865, in Laas, ed., *Wartime Washington*, 468.

287 "thrown from the windows by excited individuals": *Washington Evening Star*, January 24, 1865, quoted in Laas, ed., *Wartime Washington*, 468n.

289 "graceful in her manners; naturally intelligent": *Daily Dispatch*, February 6, 1865, http://www.perseus.tufts.edu/hopper/text?doc=Perseus%3Atext%3A 2006.05.1291%3Aarticle%3Dpos%3D11..

290 "settle that question for all time": Lee to Samuel Phillips Lee, November 10, 1864, in Laas, ed., *Wartime Washington*, 454n.

290 "Our people are working hard for it": Elizabeth Blair Lee to Samuel Phillips Lee, December 26, 1864, in ibid., 453.

290 "immense power": Goodwin, *Team of Rivals*, 687.

290 "no peace commissioners in the City": Ibid., 688.

291 "the rumor that the mission was a failure": Lee to Samuel Phillips Lee, January 31, 1865, in Laas, ed., *Wartime Washington*, 469.

291 "NO desk was unattended, no aisle unfilled": "Passage—Abraham Lincoln," Mr. Lincoln and Freedom, the Lincoln Institute and the Lehrman Institute, accessed February 1, 2015, http://www.mrlincolnandfreedom.org/inside. asp?ID=59&subjectID=3.

292 "the friends of the measure jubilant": "Congressional," *Cleveland Daily Leader*, February 1, 1865, http://www.newspapers.com.

294 "the dusky race": Adams, February 13, 1865, in *Letter from Washington*, 233.

294 "Emancipate, Enfranchise and Educate": "The First African American to Speak in the House Chamber," History, Art & Archives, U.S. House of Representatives, accessed February 1, 2015, http://history.house.gov/HistoricalHighlight/Detail/35139.

294 "After an event like this": Adams, *Letter from Washington*...

294 "SUMTER 1861.UNION.SUMTER 1865": Adams, February 23, 1865, in ibid., 236–237.

294 Confederate deserters appeared daily: Margaret Leech, *Reveille in Washington 1860–1865* (New York: Harper, 1941), 440–41.

295 "He shall be hanged!": John C. Waugh, *Surviving the Confederacy: Rebellion, Ruin, and Recovery—Roger and Sara Pryor During the Civil War* (New York: Harcourt, 2002), 268.

296 "Mrs. L was kind & confidential": Lee to Samuel Phillips Lee, 4 March 1865, in Laas, ed., *Wartime Washington*, 479.

296 "in the bar-room of a country tavern": Adams, March 2, 1865, in *Letter from Washington*, 240.

297 "'who is secretary of the navy?'": "The Inauguration," *Vermont Transcript*, March 10, 1865, http://www.newspapers.com.

297 "a just and lasting peace": "Primary Documents in American History—Abraham Lincoln's Second Inaugural Address," Library of Congress Web Guides: Civil War and Reconstruction, accessed February 1, 2015, http://www.loc.gov/rr/program/bib/ourdocs/Lincoln2nd.html.

298 "the Inauguration day passes in peace": Adams, March 4, 1865, in *Letter from Washington*, 242–44.

298 "great jam": "The Inauguration," *Appleton Motor*, Appleton, Wisconsin, March 16, 1865, http://www.newspapers.com.

298 "the disgraceful business": Col. William H. Crook, *Through Five Administrations: Reminiscences of Colonel William H. Crook, Body-Guard to President Lincoln* ed. Margarita Spalding Gerry (New York: Harper & Brothers, 1907), Kindle e-book, loc. 316.

299 "as had everyone else in Washington": Ibid., 77–92.

300 "powdered with silver and golden dust": "The Inauguration Ball," *Cleveland Daily Leader*, March 10, 1865, http://www.newspapers.com.

300 President Lincoln's glove: Elizabeth Keckley, *Behind the Scenes, or Thirty*

Years a Slave and Four Years in the White House (New York: G. W. Carleton, 1868), 68.

301 "to see anything of the Army life": Louisa Rodgers Meigs to Nannie, March 1865, Rodgers Family Papers, Naval Historical Foundation Collection, Manuscript Division, Library of Congress, Washington, D.C.

301 "an increase of agony": Louisa Rodgers Meigs to Nannie, in *A Civil War Soldier of Christ and Country: The Selected Correspondence of John Rodgers Meigs, 1859–1864*, ed. Mary A. Giunta (Urbana and Chicago: University of Illinois Press, 2006), 244.

301 "bore him and have lost him": Louisa Rodgers Meigs to Nannie, November 27, 1864, in ibid., 246.

301 "I petitioned the General": Julia Dent Grant, *The Personal Memoirs of Julia Dent Grant (Mrs. Ulysses Grant)*, ed. John Y. Simon (New York: G. P. Putnam's Sons, 1975), 141.

302 "a regiment of deserters": Lee to Samuel Phillips Lee, March 24, 1864, in Laas, ed., *Wartime Washington*, 487.

303 "in fresh business": Lee to Samuel Phillips Lee, March 27, 1865, in ibid., 488.

303 "events are now so portentous": Lee to Samuel Phillips Lee, March 28, 1865, in ibid., 489n.

304 "a bunch of wild flowers for the President": Crook, *Through Five Administrations*, 550.

304 "Richmond Ours!!!": Leech, *Reveille in Washington*, 465.

305 "surrendered to colored troops": Keckley, *Behind the Scenes*, 72.

305 "some sympathy with the National feeling": Louisa Rodgers Meigs to Mary Meigs, April 4, 1865, Montgomery C. Meigs Papers, Manuscript Division, Library of Congress, Washington, D.C.

305 "put up the Flags": Montgomery C. Meigs to Louisa Rodgers Meigs, April 9, 1865, Montgomery C. Meigs Papers, Manuscript Division, Library of Congress, Washington, D.C.

305 "the Rebels had escaped": Lee to Samuel Phillips Lee, April 4, 1865, in Laas, ed., *Wartime Washington*, 489.

306 "a wanderer without a home": Crook, *Through Five Administrations*, 595–610.

306 "a mounted escort clattering after": Mrs. Burton Harrison (Constance Cary), *Recollections Grave and Gray* (New York: C. Scribner's Sons, 1911), 199.

306 "scowled darkly upon our party": Keckley, *Behind the Scenes*, 73.

307 "incurred Mrs. Lincoln's displeasure": Ibid., 74.

307 "Now You'll Remember Me": Grant, *Personal Memoirs*, 150–51.

307 "so disfigured by bruises": Diary of Fanny Seward, April 5, 1865, from Patricia Carley Johnson, "Sensitivity and Civil War: The Selected Diaries and Papers, 1858–1866, of Frances Adeline [Fanny] Seward" (Ph.D. diss., University of Rochester, 1963), 868.

308 "decked with flags and screaming desperately": Adams, April 11, 1865, in *Letter from Washington*, 254.

308 "a good plan for you to play *Dixie*": Crook, *Through Five Administrations*, 704.

308 "The great rebellion is crushed": "PEACE!; The Surrender of Gen. Lee The End of the Great Rebellion. Harmony Among the Generals of the Army," *New York Times*, April 10, 1865, http://www.nytimes.com.

309 "Hang 'em": Leech, *Reveille in Washington*, 472.

309 "Shouting the battle cry of freedom!": "Civil War Lyrics, Battle Cry of Freedom by George F. Root—Civil War Music," Civil War Heritage Trails in Georgia, Alabama, and South Carolina, accessed February 1, 2015, http://civilwarheritagetrails.org/civil-war-music/battle-cry-of-freedom.html.

309 "the last speech he will ever make": Goodwin, *Team of Rivals*, 728.

310 "a sudden and violent end": Keckley, *Behind the Scenes*, 79.

310 "literally swathed in flags and bunting": Grant, *Personal Memoirs*, 153.

310 "it was this I coveted": Ibid., 154.

311 "we have both been very miserable": Goodwin, *Team of Rivals*, 733.

311 "I did not want to go to the theater": Grant, *Personal Memoirs*, 155.

312 "glared in a disagreeable manner": Ibid., 156.

312 "They have shot the President!": Goodwin, *Team of Rivals*, 739.

313 "'the spirit fled to God who gave it'": Dr. Charles Leale, "Report on Death of President Lincoln," L.262.S.G.O. 1865, courtesy of the National Archives and Records Administration.

314 "My dress was stained with it": Diary of Fanny Seward, April 14, 1865, in Johnson, "Sensitivity and Civil War," 875–892. Fanny actually wrote her account of the assassination three weeks later.

314 "if the terrible news was true": Grant, *Personal Memoirs*, 156.

314–15 "'thus you escaped me'": Ibid., 157.

315 "a guard of 6 men to protect this house": Lee to Samuel Phillips Lee, April 14, 1865, in Laas, ed., *Wartime Washington*, 494.

315 "but not mortally wounded": Keckley, *Behind the Scenes*, 81.

315 "the hours drag so slowly": Ibid., 82.

315–16 "fallen in the hour of his triumph": Ibid., 84.

316 "the President himself was dead": Ibid., 83.

316 "some contradiction which we long for": Adams, April 15, 1865, in *Letter from Washington*, 256.

316 "the grief of the people here is sincere & intense": Lee to Samuel Phillips Lee, April 15, 1865, in Laas, ed., *Wartime Washington*, 495.

317 "absolute quiet . . . & a low diet": Lee to Samuel Phillips Lee, March 7, 1865, in ibid., 481.

317 "enjoys his food hugely": Lee to Samuel Phillips Lee, March 18, 1865, in ibid., 483.

317 "improves daily in health & cheerfulness": Lee to Samuel Phillips Lee, March 21, 1865, in ibid., 484–85.

318 "troubled about it": Lee to Samuel Phillips Lee, March 22, 1865, in ibid., 486.

318 "The strap which holds my skirts": Lee to Samuel Phillips Lee, March 27, 1865, in ibid., 489. ·

318 "entirely disappeared from sight": Lee to Samuel Phillips Lee, April 14, 1865, in ibid., 493–494.

318 "these last months of our long separation": Lee to Samuel Phillips Lee, April 15, 1865, in ibid., 495.

318 "outburst of grief from the soul": Keckley, *Behind the Scenes*, 84.

318 "dear heart-broken Mrs. Lincoln": Grant, *Personal Memoirs*, 157.

319 "She begs me not to smile": Lee to Samuel Phillips Lee, April 19, 1865, in Laas, ed., *Wartime Washington*, 497.

319 "by beauty's presence": *Cleveland Morning Leader*, April 22, 1865, quoted in John Oller, *American Queen: The Rise and Fall of Kate Chase Sprague, Civil War "Belle of the North" and Gilded Age Woman of Scandal* (Boston: Da Capo Press, 2014), e-book, 1932.

319 "unspeakable sorrow and affection": Rebecca R. Pomroy, *Echoes from Hospital and White House: A Record of Mrs. Rebecca R. Pomroy's Experience in War-Times*, ed. Anna L. Boyden (Boston: D. Lothrop, 1884), e-book, 247.

320 leading the other mourners: Leech, *Reveille in Washington*, 496.

320 "24 hours of unflagging watching": Lee to Samuel Phillips Lee, April 20, 1865, in Laas, ed., *Wartime Washington*, 498.

320 "constantly refers to his religious faith": Lee to Samuel Phillips Lee, April 22, 1865, in ibid., 499.

321 "no earthly power can prevent it": Nettie Coburn Maynard, *Séances in Washington: Abraham Lincoln and Spiritualism during the Civil War*, ed. with commentary Irene McGarvie (1891 as "Was Abraham Lincoln a Spiritualist?" reprint, Toronto: Ancient Wisdom, 2011), Kindle e-book, loc. 1505.

321 "branded all over with infamy": Adams, May 6, 1865, in *Letter from Washington*, 261.

322 "I do dread it more & more": Lee to Samuel Phillips Lee, May 4, 1865, in ibid., 500n.

322 "It was plundered": Mary Clemmer Ames, *Ten Years in Washington: Life and Scenes in the National Capital, as a Woman Sees Them* (1874; reprint, Ann Arbor: University of Michigan Library, The Michigan Historical Reprint Series, 2005), 240.

322 "The silence was almost painful": Keckley, *Behind the Scenes*, 92.

324 "She ranks me": L. P. Brockett, M.D. and Mrs. Mary C. Vaughn, *Woman's Work in the Civil War: A Record of Heroism, Patriotism and Patience* (Philadelphia: Zeigler, McCurdy, 1867), e-book, loc. 2305.

325 "what little money I had": *Janesville Weekly Gazette*, May 25, 1865, http://www.newspapers.com.

326 "the whole party": Varina Howell Davis to Montgomery Blair, June 6, 1865, in *Women's Letters: America from the Revolutionary War to the Present*, ed. Lisa Grunwald and Stephen J. Adler (New York: Dial Press, 2005), 331. Original document also can be found, "Letter (pages 13–20), Varina Davis to Montgomery Blair describing the capture of her husband, Jefferson Davis, 6 June 1865," Words and Deeds in American History, accessed February 1, 2015, http://memory.loc.gov/cgi-bin/query/r?ammem/mcc:@field(DOCID+@lit(mcc/005)).

326 "gifts of flowers and fruit": Virginia Clay Clopton, *A Belle of the Fifties: Memoirs of Mrs. Clay of Alabama, covering social and political life in Washington and the South, 1853–66, put into narrative form by Ada Sterling* (New York: Doubleday, Page, 1905), 274.

326 "first Class Nurse & attendant": Leech, *Reveille in Washington*, 519.

326 "My heart's sympathy is with her": Keckley, *Behind the Scenes*, 92.

328 "breaking up old associations": Ibid., 30.

328 "inclined to treat you harshly": Ibid., 31.

328 "remarkable woman": Catherine Clinton, *Mrs. Lincoln: A Life* (New York: Harper Perennial, 2010), 162.

328 "Mrs. Lincoln made frequent contributions": Ibid., 51.

329 four years of continuous migration to the capital: Constance McLaughlin Green, *Washington Village and Capital, 1800–1878* (Princeton, NJ: Princeton University Press, 1962), 277.

330 "the employment it affords them": J. S. Griffing to C. H. Howard, October 4, 1867, report on the operations of her industrial school, from Bureau Records, quoted in Keith E. Melder, "Angel of Mercy in Washington: Josephine Griffing and the Freedmen, 1864–1872," *Records of the Columbia Historical Society of Washington, D.C. 1963–1965*, ed. Francis Coleman Rosenberger (Washington, DC: Historical Society of Washington D.C., 1967), 254.

331 "a chartered car full of these freed people": Ibid., 257.

331 three to five thousand destitute freed people: Ibid., 259.

331 "no home, family, friendship or subsistence": J. S. Griffing, letter to Horace Greeley, September 12, 1870, in ibid., 267.

333 "Judges, counsel, prisoners, witnesses, and spectators, men, women, and children": Adams, June 23, 1865, in *Letter from Washington*, 274.

333 "'She made no scenes'": Elizabeth Steger Trindal, *Mary Surratt: An American Tragedy* (Gretna, LA: Pelican, 1996), 169.

334 "backed with certain political strength": "END OF THE ASSASSINS; Execution of Mrs. Surratt, Payne, Herrold[*sic*] and Atzeroth,[*sic*]" *New York Times*, July 7, 1865, http://www.nytimes.com.

335 "submit to the supreme physical power": Kate Clifford Larson, *The Assassin's Accomplice: Mary Surratt and the Plot to Kill Abraham Lincoln* (New York: Basic Books, 2008), 207.

335 "'women enough hanged in this war'": Ibid., 199.

336 "what will be ANNA's fate?": "END OF THE ASSASSINS; Execution of Mrs. Surratt, Payne, Herrold and Atzeroth," *New York Times*, July 7, 1865, http://www.nytimes.com.

336 "the testimony of an important witness": "The Assassination," *Daily Times*, New Berne, N.C., July 12, 1865, http://www.newspapers.com.

337 "unreasoning and dangerous enemies": Adams, July 18, 1865, in *Letter from Washington*, 280–81.

338 "the acquitted lady fainted": "The News," *Daily Progress*, Raleigh, North Carolina, July 25, 1865, http://www.newspapers.com.

338 "most unfortunately notorious": Adams, August 1, 1865, in *Letter from Washington*, 283–85.

339 "handsome blocks and dwellings": Adams, October 2, 1865, in ibid., 328–29.

342 "run up the old flag": Stephen B. Oates, *A Woman of Valor: Clara Barton and the Civil War* (New York: Free Press, 1994), 335.

342 responded to more than 63,000 letters: "Clara Barton's Missing Soldiers Office," Civil War Museum, National Museum of Civil War Medicine, accessed February 1, 2015, http://www.civilwarmed.org/clara-barton-museum /about-clara-bartons-missing-soldiers-office/.

342 "admires and criticizes itself": Adams, July 8, 1865, in *Letter from Washington*, 277.

343 "She was the stepping stone": "Eliza Johnson Biography," National First Ladies' Library and Historic Site, accessed February 1, 2015, http://www. firstladies.org/biographies/firstladies.aspx?biography=18.

343 "always dressed elegantly and appropriately": Grant, *Personal Memoirs*, 164.

344 "the utter impossibility of living another day": Mary Todd Lincoln to Elizabeth Blair Lee, August 25, 1865, quoted in Goodwin, *Team of Rivals*, 753.

344 "a needle in her hand": Keckley, *Behind the Scenes*, 99.

344 "gala days": Grant, *Personal Memoirs*, 161.

CHAPTER 9: VIRGINIA AND VARINA RETURN, SARA SURVIVES,
MARY IS HUMILIATED, KATE LOSES

348 "the talk of the whole country": Virginia Clay Clopton, *A Belle of the Fifties: Memoirs of Mrs. Clay of Alabama, Covering Social and Political Life in Washington and the South, 1853–66, Put into Narrative Form by Ada Sterling* (New York: Doubleday, Page, 1905), 301.

349 "no moment alone": Ibid., 307.

349 "an interview with the president": *Cleveland Daily Leader*, November 23, 1865, http://www.newspapers.com.

349 "one of the first familiar faces I saw": Clopton, *Belle of the Fifties*, 310–11.

349 "The amnesty was granted": *Staunton Spectator* (Staunton, Va.), August 15, 1865, Chronicling America: Historic American Newspapers, Library of Congress, http://chroniclingamerica.loc.gov/lccn/sn84024718/1865-08-15/ed-1/seq-2/.

350 "my heart was full of indignant protest": Clopton, *Belle of the Fifties*, 310–11.

350 "Your husband's manly surrender": Ibid., 316.

350 "Our next President": Ibid., 315.

351 "our treasury was terribly depleted": Ibid., 193.

351 "a prodigious amount of sewing": Ibid., 195.

352 "an outward indifference to Paris fashions": Ibid., 225.

352 "it will do us harm to let it get abroad": Ibid., 194.

352 "peanut chocolate": Ibid., 224.

352 "pins were the rarest of luxuries": Ibid., 227.

353 "God in mercy help us now!": November 20,1864, Virginia Clay diary, 1859–66, C. C. Clay Papers, David M. Rubenstein Rare Book & Manuscript Library, Duke University.

353 "No letters, no telegrams!": December 1864, ibid.

353 "no letter or intelligence from my husband": December 8, 1864, ibid.

353 "great loss of officers & men": December 16, 1864, ibid.

353 "*Savannah has fallen!*": December 22, 1864, ibid.

353 "homeless, husbandless, childless": Clopton, *Belle of the Fifties*, 237.

354 "the water deeply, darkly, beautifully blue": May 18, 1865, Virginia Clay diary, 1859–66, C. C. Clay Papers, David M. Rubenstein Rare Book & Manuscript Library, Duke University.

354 "land my darling at this fort": May 20, 1865, ibid.

354 "Mrs. Davis bore the parting remarkably well": *Raftsman's Journal* (Clearfield, Pa.), May 31, 1865, http://www.newspapers.com.

354 "weeping of children and the wailing of women": Clopton, *Belle of the Fifties*, 262.

354 "a regiment of Negroes in full dress!": Ibid., 275.

355 "rest passively under conditions so alarming": Ibid., 289.

355 "Some will offend you with malice": Ibid., 299.

355 "respectfully recommend the release of Mr. C. C. Clay": Ibid., 317.

355 "furnished with copies of the charges against him": Ibid., 318.

356 "hobnobbing with that old Abolitionist!": Ibid., 330.

357 *"My life depends upon it"*: Ibid., 337.

357 "the President's good offices": Ibid., 339.

358 " 'I do not fear Mr. Stanton or anyone else' ": Ibid., 341.

358 "the marriage was quite private": *Norfolk Post* (Norfolk, Va.), January 26, 1866, Chronicling America: Historic American Newspapers, Library of Congress, http://chroniclingamerica.loc.gov/lccn/sn85038624/1866-01-26/ed-1/seq-1/.

358 "one of the finest looking and most fascinating men in the country": *Evening Star* (Washington, D.C.), January 16, 1866, Chronicling America: Historic American Newspapers, Library of Congress, http://chroniclingamerica.loc.gov/lccn/sn83045462/1866-01-16/ed-1/seq-2/.

359 "reported and believed in the City": Lee to Samuel Phillips Lee, December 30, 1862, in *Wartime Washington: The Civil War Letters of Elizabeth Blair Lee*, ed. Virginia Jeans Laas (Urbana and Chicago: University of Illinois Press, 1999), 222.

359 "Mother's comment was witty": Lee to Samuel Phillips Lee, February 21, 1863, in ibid., 261.

359 "both granted special interviews": *Evening Star* (Washington, D.C.), October 11, 1865, Chronicling America: Historic American Newspapers, Library of Congress, http://chroniclingamerica.loc.gov/lccn/sn83045462/1865-10-11/ed-1/seq-2/.

359 "Was kind & I melted": February 14, 1866 Virginia Clay diary, 1859–66, C. C. Clay Papers, David M. Rubenstein Rare Book & Manuscript Library, Duke University.

360 "recommendations for her husband's release": "Probably Speedy Release of Clement C. Clay," *Progress Index* (Petersburg, Va.,) April 18, 1866, http://www.newspapers.com.

361 "he was not allowed to take leave of me": Davis to Varina Howell Davis,

April 21, 1866, in *Jefferson Davis, Private Letters 1823–1889*, ed. Hudson Strode (1966; reprint, Boston: Da Capo Press, 1995), 247.

361 "tied to a stake and burned a little bit at a time": Varina Howell Davis to Dr. John J. Craven, October 10, 1865, in John J. Craven, *Prison Life of Jefferson Davis: Embracing Details and Incidents in his Captivity, Particulars Concerning His Health and Habits, Together with Many Conversations on Topics of Great Public Interest* (New York: Carleton, 1866), Internet Archive e-book, loc. 2884.

361 "the most terrible newspaper extras": Varina Howell Davis to John J. Craven, June 1, 1865, in ibid., 756.

362 "He will surely visit upon such sin": Varina Howell Davis to Francis Preston Blair, June 6, 1865, quoted in Ishbel Ross, *First Lady of the South: The Life of Mrs. Jefferson Davis* (New York: Harper & Brothers, 1958), 261.

362 "the rebels take care of their own widows": David W. Miller, *Second Only to Grant: Quartermaster General Montgomery C. Meigs* (Shippensburg, PA: White Mane Books, 2000), 264.

363 releasing her mail to "newsmongers": Varina Howell Davis to William H. Seward, July 10, 1865, quoted in Ross, *First Lady of the South*, 264.

363 "I may bear all the insults, and agonies": Varina Howell Davis to Armistead Burt, October 20, 1865, in ibid., 273–74.

363 "tawny," according to a hostile Richmond editor: Joan E. Cashin, *First Lady of the Confederacy: Varina Davis's Civil War* (Cambridge, MA: The Belknap Press of Harvard University Press, 2006), 112.

363 "free, brown, & 64": Ibid., 269.

364 "coarse Western woman": Ibid., 113.

364 "all which might be offensive to anyone": Varina Howell Davis to Davis, October 23, 1865, in Strode, ed., *Private Letters*, 191–93.

364 "probably meet wounding repulse": Davis to Varina Howell Davis, March 22, 1866, in ibid., 242.

365 "keep me from my dying husband": Ross, *First Lady of the South*, 279.

365 "highly cultivated mind and admirable power of conversation": "Montreal Correspondent," *Toronto Globe*, in *Cleveland Daily Leader*, May 5, 1866, http://www.newspapers.com.

366 "She made no stoppage on the way": *Charleston Daily News*, May 8, 1866, http://www.newspapers.com.

366 "many distinguished personages": *New York Tribune*, May 28, 1866, in Ross, *First Lady of the South*, 281.

367 "my first and last experience as a supplicant": Varina Davis, *Jefferson Davis, Ex-President of the Confederate States of America: A Memoir by His Wife* (1890;

reprinted, Baltimore: Nautical and Aviation Publishing Company of America, 1990), 768–69.

367 "a man whose code of morals I could not understand": Ibid., 770–71.

367 "I congratulate you upon it": Minna Blair to Varina Howell Davis, September 9, 1866, quoted in Ross, *First Lady of the South*, 289.

369 Lee's take of the booty from confiscated ships: Dudley Taylor Cornish and Virginia Jeans Laas, *Lincoln's Lee: The Life of Samuel Phillips Lee, United States Navy 1812–1897* (Lawrence: University Press of Kansas, 1986), 123.

369 "bury this feud before you bury your parents": Francis Preston Blair to Montgomery Blair, May 26, 1866, in Elbert B. Smith, *Francis Preston Blair* (New York: Free Press, 1980), 408.

369 "Mrs. Lee could remain": Ibid., 408.

370 "her benevolent and diligent labors": Penny Colman, *Breaking the Chains: The Crusade of Dorothea Lynde Dix* (Lincoln, NE: ASJA Press, 1992, 2007), e-book, loc. 1427.

371 "at least fifty years in advance": Mary Elizabeth Massey, *Women in the Civil War* (Lincoln: University of Nebraska Press, 1966), 339.

371 "only hold our tongues and pray": Elizabeth Blair Lee to Francis Preston Blair, September 12, 1866, Papers of Elizabeth Blair Lee; 1818–1906; Blair and Lee Family Papers, Manuscripts Division, Department of Rare Books and Special Collections, Princeton University Library.

372 "he is endeavoring to ignore all the good": Mary Todd Lincoln to Charles Sumner, April 2, 1866, quoted in Jennifer L. Bach, "Acts of Remembrance: Mary Todd Lincoln and Her Husband's Memory," *Journal of the Abraham Lincoln Association* 25, no. 2 (Summer 2004), http://quod.lib.umich.edu/j/jala/2629860.0025.204?view=text;rgn=main#top.

374 "secure the re-election of her husband": Dr. John B. Ellis, *The Sights and Secrets of the National Capital* (Chicago: Jones, Junkin, 1869), 184–86.

374 "calls the blush to any true, loyal heart": Bach, "Acts of Remembrance."

375 "I am passing through a very painful ordeal": This is both cited in Elizabeth Keckley, *Behind the Scenes, or Thirty Years a Slave and Four Years in the White House* (New York: G. W. Carleton, 1868), 129–30, and the newspaper articles cited below.

375 "a round of newspaper abuse": Mary Todd Lincoln to Elizabeth Keckley, October 9, 1867, in Keckley, *Behind the Scenes*, 147.

376 "so loaded with shawls, laces, furs, diamonds, rings & etc": "Mrs. Lincoln's Wardrobe for Sale," *Hillsdale Standard* (Hillsdale, Mich.), October 15, 1867, from the *New York World*, October 3, 1867, http://www.newspapers.com.

376 "If I had committed murder in every city": Mary Todd Lincoln to Elizabeth Keckley, quoted in Keckley, *Behind the Scenes*, October 9, 1867, 148.

376–77 "she accepted costly presents from corrupt contractors": *Nashville Union and American*, October 9, 1867, http://www.newspapers.com.

377 "Mrs. Lincoln's peculiar wardrobe": *Brooklyn Eagle*, October 12, 1867, http://www.newspapers.com.

377 "I am feeling so *friendless* in the world": Mary Todd Lincoln to Elizabeth Keckley, October 13, 1867, quoted in Keckley, *Behind the Scenes*, 149.

378 "its peace and happiness destroyed": Jennifer Fleischner, *Mrs. Lincoln and Mrs. Keckly: The Remarkable Story of the Friendship Between a First Lady and a Former Slave* (New York: Random House, 2007), 316–17.

378 "a genius for making women look pretty": Ibid., 236.

378 "we were going to be happy young people": Mrs. Roger A. Pryor, *Reminiscences of Peace and War* (New York: Grosset & Dunlap, 1904), 42.

379 "It takes so little to make a woman happy!": Ibid., 109.

379 "Nothing is ridiculous that helps anxious women": Ibid., 133.

379 "blood would not be shed": Ibid., 142.

379 "the wounded men within their doors": Ibid., 171.

380 "no stores laid up for such an emergency": Ibid., 184.

380 "did not create a ripple of excitement": Ibid., 228.

380 "reprinted by a Charleston firm on the best paper": Ibid., 226.

380–81 "A sort of court is still kept up here": Ibid., 235.

381 "Doesn't it all seem so long ago": Ibid., 228.

381 "if we can win a battle or two": Ibid., 239.

381 "the coil was tightening around us": Ibid., 250.

381 "the sick, the wounded, or the women and children": Ibid., 279.

382 "Somebody, somewhere, is mightily to blame for all this business": Ibid., 293–94.

382 "dressed alike in gowns of tulle": Ibid., 312.

382 "These were my materials": Ibid., 313.

383 "a dainty vine of forget-me-knots on bodice and sleeves": Ibid., 316.

383 "one of the nicest ladies I ever saw": John C. Waugh, *Surviving the Confederacy: Rebellion, Ruin, and Recovery: Roger and Sara Pryor During the Civil War* (New York: Harcourt, 2002), 260.

383 " 'I am too busy keeping the wolf from my door": Pryor, *Reminiscences*, 330–31.

384 "Beg his release from Mr. Lincoln": Ibid., 328.

384 "she has left the city with her family": Ibid., 342.

384 "the firing had all ceased": Ibid., 350.

384 "no hope now of our ultimate success": Ibid., 356–57.

384 "the *entourage* of a lady is taken from me": Ibid., 376.

385 "rations designated for the poor of the city": *Evening Star* (Washington, D.C.), June 3, 1865, Chronicling America: Historic American Newspapers, Library of Congress, http://chroniclingamerica.loc.gov/lccn/sn83045462/1865-06-03/ed-1/seq-1/.

385 "no better means of settling a family quarrel": Pryor, *Reminiscences*, 410.

386 "dissatisfaction resulting from your administration": Clopton, *Belle of the Fifties*, 366.

386 "inquire into the official conduct of Andrew Johnson": "Impeachment Efforts Against President Andrew Johnson," History, Art & Archives, U.S. House of Representatives, accessed February 7, 2015, http://history.house.gov/Historical-Highlights/1851-1900/Impeachment-efforts-against-President-Andrew-Johnson/.

386 "'we intend to have it & pretty quickly too'": Elizabeth Blair Lee to Samuel Phillips Lee, January 14, 1867, Papers of Elizabeth Blair Lee; 1818–1906; Blair and Lee Family Papers, Manuscripts Division, Department of Rare Books and Special Collections, Princeton University Library.

387 "private hates or gusts of caprice": Salmon P. Chase to Nettie, October 18, 1866, in *"Spur Up Your Pegasus": Family Letters of Salmon, Kate and Nettie Chase, 1844–1873*, ed. James P. McClure, Peg A. Lamphier, and Erika M. Kreger (Kent, OH: Kent State University Press, 2009), 329.

387 "she is very bitter on this point": Elizabeth Blair Lee to Samuel Phillips Lee, January 9, 1867, Papers of Elizabeth Blair Lee; 1818–1906; Blair and Lee Family Papers, Manuscripts Division, Department of Rare Books and Special Collections, Princeton University Library.

388 "to save the Constitution": John Oller, *American Queen: The Rise and Fall of Kate Chase Sprague, Civil War "Belle of the North" and Gilded Age Woman of Scandal* (Boston: Da Capo Press, 2014), e-book, locs. 2216–28.

388 "that is the queen of fashion": April 14, 1868, in Emily Edson Briggs, *The Olivia Letters: Being Some History of Washington City for Forty Years as Told by the Letters of a Newspaper Correspondent* (New York: Neale, 1906), 49–51.

389 "the wretched hut, the sick, and the afflicted": April 23, 1868, in ibid., 70.

389 "no room for dispute as to who is 'First Lady'": "Who Is the First American Lady—Curious Gossip from Washington," *Brooklyn Daily Eagle*, March 21, 1868, from the *Pittsburg Gazette*, http:// www.newspapers.com.

389–90 "no insinuation, no charge against them": Mary Clemmer Ames, *Ten Years in Washington: Life and Scenes in the National Capital, as a Woman Sees Them* (1874; reprint, Ann Arbor: University of Michigan Library, Michigan Historical Reprint Series, 2005), 252.

390 "give us our poverty and our peace again": Ellis, *Sights and Secrets*, 427.

390 "she lives happily with her husband": "From Washington," *Montana Post*,
     May 16, 1868, http://www.newspapers.com.

391 "My own judgment & feeling favors acquittal": Salmon P. Chase to Kate
     Chase Sprague, May 10, 1868, in McClure, Lamphier, and Kreger, eds.,
     Family Letters, 367.

391 "it was a dangerous precedent": Julia Dent Grant, *The Personal Memoirs of
     Julia Dent Grant (Mrs. Ulysses Grant)*, ed. John Y. Simon (New York: G. P.
     Putnam's Sons, 1975), 170.

391 " 'I suppose if I am nominated, I will be elected' ": Ibid., 171.

392 "Affectionately & ambitiously for Country": Kate Chase Sprague to Salmon
     P. Chase, July 7, 1868, in McClure, Lamphier, and Kreger, eds., *Family Let-
     ters*, 372.

392 "notoriously managed the political affairs of her father": "Democratic Na-
     tional Convention, second day," *Semi-Weekly* (Milwaukee, Wis.), June 11,
     1868, http://www.newspapers.com.

393 "Does Mrs. Sprague know?": Oller, *American Queen*, loc. 2375.

393 "burst into tears": *Hawaiian Gazette* (Honolulu, Hawaii), September 2, 1868,
     http://www.newspapers.com.

393 "the first inaugural address of my husband": Grant, *Personal Memoirs*, 172.

EPILOGUE

Unless otherwise noted, all quotations in this epilogue come from newspapers
     found on http://www.newspapers.com.

398 "played Mrs. Partington for United Charities": Diary of Virginia Clopton-
     Clay, January 1903, C. C. Clay Papers, David M. Rubenstein Rare Book &
     Manuscript Library, Duke University.

407 "to put the sea between you & your work": Louisa Rodgers Meigs to Mont-
     gomery C. Meigs, March 3, 1867, Meigs Family Papers, Library of Congress.

409 "for we all were Americans": Sara A. Pryor, *Reminiscences of Peace and War*
     (London: Macmillan, 1905), 417.

410 "with the Monument *as its symbol*": Frederick L. Harvey, *History of the Wash-
     ington National Monument and of the Washington National Monument Society*
     (Washington, DC: U.S. Government Printing Office, 1903), kindle ebook
     reprint, loc. 1173).

Bibliography

Abbott, Karen. *Liar, Temptress, Soldier, Spy: Four Women Undercover in the Civil War*. New York: HarperCollins, 2014.

Adams, Charles Francis, and Henry Cabot Lodge. *Charles Francis Adams, 1835–1915: An Autobiography*. Boston: Houghton Mifflin, 1916.

Adams, Lois Bryan. *Letter from Washington, 1863–1865*. Detroit: Wayne State University Press, 1999.

Alcott, Louisa May. *Hospital Sketches*. Bedford, MA: Applewood Books, 1986.

———. *The Journals of Louisa May Alcott*. Athens: University of Georgia Press, 1997, ed., Joel Myerson, Daniel Shealy, Madeleine B. Stern.

Alef, Daniel. *James C. Frémont: Pathfinder, Provocateur and Presidential Candidate*. Santa Barbara, CA: Meta4, 2008.

———. *Jessie Benton Frémont: General "Jessie" and the "Pathfinder."* Santa Barbara, CA: Titans of Fortune, 2008.

Angelo, Bonnie. *First Families*. New York: Harper Collins e-books, 2007.

———. *First Mothers: The Women Who Shaped the Presidents*. New York: Thorndike Press, 2001.

Associated Press. "This Week in the Civil War." *Washington Post*, October 10, 2012.

Ayers, Edward L., ed. *America's War: Talking About the Civil War and Emancipation on Their 150th Anniversaries*. Chicago: American Library Association, 2012.

Baker, Jean H. *Mary Todd Lincoln: A Biography*. New York: Norton, 1989.

Barrett, Joseph Hartwell. *Abraham Lincoln and His Presidency*. Cincinnati: Robert Clarke, 1904.

Barstow, Charles Lester, ed. *The Civil War*. New York: Century, 1915.

Bayne, Julia Taft. *Tad Lincoln's Father*. Lincoln: University of Nebraska Press, 2001, first published 1924.

Bergin, Brian. *The Washington Arsenal Explosion: Civil War Disaster in the Capital*. Charleston, SC: History Press, 2012.

Berkin, Carol. *Civil War Wives: The Lives and Times of Angelina Grimké Weld, Varina Howell Davis, and Julia Dent Grant*. New York: Random House, 2010.

Blackman, Ann. *Wild Rose: Rose O'Neale Greenhow, Civil War Spy*. New York: Random House, 2005.

Blackwell, Sarah Ellen. *A Military Genius: Life of Anna Ella Carroll of Maryland*. Washington, D.C.: Judd & Detweiler, 1891.

Boller, Paul F. *Presidential Wives*. Oxford: Oxford University Press, 1998.

Bradford, Gamaliel. *Wives*. New York: Harper & Brothers, 1925.

Brewster, Todd. *Lincoln's Gamble: The Tumultuous Six Months That Gave America the Emancipation Proclamation and Changed the Course of the Civil War*. New York: Simon & Schuster, 2014.

Briggs, Emily Edson. *The Olivia Letters: Being Some History of Washington City for Forty Years as Told by the Letters of a Newspaper Correspondent*. New York: Neale, 1906.

Brockett, Linus Pierpont, and Mary C. Vaughan. *Woman's Work in the Civil War*. Philadelphia: Zeigler, McCurdy, 1867.

Brooks, Noah. *Abraham Lincoln and the Downfall of American Slavery*. New York: G. P. Putnam's Sons, 1894.

———. *Washington in Lincoln's Time*. New York: Century, 1895.

Browne, Francis F. *The Everyday Life of Abraham Lincoln*. New York: G. P. Putnam's Sons, 2008.

Carpenter, Frances, ed. *Carp's Washington*. New York: McGraw-Hill, 1960.

Carroll, Anna Ella. *The War Powers of the General Government*. Washington, D.C.: H. Polkinhorn, 1861.

Cashin, Joan E. *First Lady of the Confederacy: Varina Davis's Civil War*. Cambridge, MA: Belknap Press, 2006.

Chesnut, Mary Boykin Miller. *The Private Mary Chesnut: The Unpublished Civil War Diaries*. Oxford: Oxford University Press, 1984.

Chesnut, Mary Boykin Miller, and Comer Vann Woodward, eds. *Mary Chesnut's Civil War*. New Haven, CT: Yale University Press, 1981.

Chiaverini, Jennifer. *Mrs. Lincoln's Dressmaker.* New York: Dutton, 2013.

Clay-Clopton, Virginia. *A Belle of the Fifties: Memoirs of Mrs. Clay of Alabama, Covering Social and Political Life in Washington and the South, 1853–66.* New York: Heinemann, 1905.

Clemmer, Mary. *Ten Years in Washington: Life and Scenes in the National Capital, as a Woman Sees Them.* Hartford, CT: A. D. Worthington, 1873.

Clinton, Catherine. *Mrs. Lincoln: A Life.* New York: Harper, 2009.

Colbun Maynard, Nettie. *Séances in Washington: Abraham Lincoln and Spiritualism During the Civil War.* Toronto: Ancient Wisdom, 2011, first published in 1891 as *Was Abraham Lincoln a Spiritualist?*

Coleman, Penny. *Breaking the Chains: The Crusade of Dorothea Lynde Dix.* New York: ASJA Press, 1992.

Conderacci, Jacqueline. *Seward House Museum.* Auburn, NY: Trillum Graphics, 2012.

Cornish, Dudley Taylor, and Virginia Jeans Laas. *Lincoln's Lee: The Life of Samuel Phillips Lee, United States Navy, 1812–1897.* Lawrence: University Press of Kansas, 1986.

Coryell, Janet L. *Neither Heroine nor Fool: Anna Ella Carroll of Maryland.* Kent, OH: Kent State University Press, 1990.

Croffert, William A. *The Leisure Class in America.* New York: Arno Press, 1975.

Dana, Charles Anderson. *Recollections of the Civil War.* New York: Collier Books, 1963, first published 1902.

Davidson, James Wood. *The Living Writers of the South.* New York: Carleton, 1869.

Davis, Varina. *Christmas in the Confederate Whitehouse.* Cherry Lane EBooks, 2011, from the New York World, Sunday, December 13, 1896.

———. *Jefferson Davis.* Baltimore: Nautical and Aviation Publishing Company of America, 1890.

———. *A Romance of Summer Seas.* New York: Harper & Brothers, 1898.

———. *The Veiled Doctor.* New York: Harper & Brothers, 1895.

Dawson, Sarah Morgan. *A Confederate Girl's Diary.* Boston: Houghton Mifflin, 1913.

De Leon, Thomas Cooper. *Belles, Beaux and Brains of the 60's.* New York: G. W. Dillingham, 1909.

DeFerrari, John. *Historic Restaurants of Washington, D.C.: Capital Eats.* Charleston, SC: History Press, 2013.

Dickens, Charles. *American Notes for General Circulation.* London: Chapman & Hall, 1842.

Donald, David Herbert. *Lincoln.* New York: Simon & Schuster, 2011.

————. *We Are Lincoln Men: Abraham Lincoln and His Friends*. New York: Simon & Schuster, 2004.

Douglass, Frederick. *Narrative of the Life of Frederick Douglass, an American Slave*. New York: Random House Digital, 2000.

Edmonds, S. Emma E. *Nurse and Spy in the Union Army: The Adventures and Experiences of a Woman in the Hospitals, Camps and Battlefields*. Hartford, CT: Digital Scanning, 2000, first published 1865.

Ellis, Dr. John B. *The Sights and Secrets of the National Capital*. Chicago: Jones, Junkin, 1869.

Elson, Henry William. *The Civil War Through the Camera*. New York: McKinlay, Stone & Mackenzie, 1912.

Emert, Phyllis Raybin, ed. *Women in the Civil War: Warriors, Patriots, Nurses, and Spies*. Boston: History Compass, 2007.

Entrikin, Isabelle Webb. *Sarah Josepha Hale and* Godey's Lady's Book. Philadelphia: University of Pennsylvania Press, 1946.

Faulkner, Carol. *Women's Radical Reconstruction: The Freedmen's Aid Movement*. Philadelphia: University of Pennsylvania Press, 2007.

Faust, Drew Gilpin. *This Republic of Suffering*. New York: Random House, 2008.

Field, Maunsell B. *Memories of Many Men, and of Some Women*. New York: Harper & Brothers, 1874.

Fleischner, Jennifer. *Mrs. Lincoln and Mrs. Keckly: The Remarkable Story of the Friendship Between a First Lady and a Former Slave*. New York: Random House, 2007.

Flood, Charles Bracelen. *1864: Lincoln at the Gates of History*. New York: Simon & Schuster, 2009.

Flower, Frank Anial. *Edwin McMasters Stanton: The Autocrat of Rebellion, Emancipation, and Reconstruction*. Akron, OH: Saalfield, 1905.

Foner, Eric. *Reconstruction: America's Unfinished Revolution*. New York: HarperCollins, 1988.

Frémont, Jessie Benton. *Souvenirs of My Time*. Boston: D. Lothrop, 1887.

————. *The Story of the Guard: A Chronicle of the War*. Boston: Ticknor & Fields, 1863.

————. *A Year of American Travel*. New York: Harper & Brothers, 1878.

Frémont, Jessie Benton, Pamela Herr, and Mary Lee Spence, eds. *The Letters of Jessie Benton Frémont*. Urbana: University of Illinois Press, 1993.

Furgurson, Ernest B. *Freedom Rising: Washington in the Civil War*. New York: Random House, 2007.

Gage, Matilda Joslyn. "Who Planned the Tennessee Campaign of 1862." *National Citizen Tract* 1 (1880): 1600–1730.

Garrison, Nancy Scripture. *With Courage and Delicacy: Civil War on the Peninsula: Women and the U.S. Sanitary Commission.* Cambridge, MA: Da Capo Press, 2009.

Garrison, Webb. *Amazing Women of the Civil War: Fascinating True Stories of Women Who Made a Difference.* Nashville, TN: Thomas Nelson, 1999.

Gerry, Margarita Spalding. *Through Five Administrations: Reminiscences of Colonel William H. Crook, Body Guard to President Lincoln.* New York: Kessinger, 2004.

Giesberg, Judith Ann. *Civil War Sisterhood: The U.S. Sanitary Commission and Women's Politics in Transition.* Boston: Northeastern University Press, 2006.

Goodheart, Adam. *1861: The Civil War Awakening.* New York: Random House, 2011.

Goodwin, Doris Kearns. *Team of Rivals: The Political Genius of Abraham Lincoln.* London: Penguin, 2009.

Gordon-Reed, Annette, *Andrew Johnson.* New York: Times Books, 2011. Arthur M. Schlesinger Jr., and Sean Wilentz, ed.

Gould, Lewis L., ed. *American First Ladies: Their Lives and Their Legacy.* New York: Routledge, 1996.

Grant, Julia Dent. *The Personal Memoirs of Julia Dent Grant (Mrs. Ulysses S. Grant).* Carbondale: Southern Illinois University Press, 1988.

Grant, Ulysses S. *Personal Memoirs of Ulysses S. Grant.* New York: Cosimo, 2006, first published 1885.

Green, Constance McLaughlin. *Washington; village and capital, 1800–1878.* Princeton, NJ: Princeton University Press, 1962.

Greenhow, Rose O'Neal. *My Imprisonment and the First Year of Abolition Rule at Washington.* London: R. Bentley, 1863.

———. *Rose's War: Memoirs of a Confederate Spy.* N.p.: Parsons, 2012.

Greenwood, Grace. *Records of Five Years.* Boston: Ticknor & Fields, 1867.

———. *Stories of Many Lands.* New York: John B. Alden, 1885.

Guelzo, Allen C. *Lincoln and Douglas: The Debates That Defined America.* New York: Simon & Schuster, 2008.

Gugliotta, Guy. *Freedom's Cap: The United States Capitol and the Coming of the Civil War.* New York: Macmillan, 2012.

Gurko, Miriam. *The Ladies of Seneca Falls.* New York: Schocken Books, 1974.

Gwynne, S. C. *Rebel Yell: The Violence, Passion, and Redemption of Stonewall Jackson.* New York: Scribner, 2014.

Hanaford, Phebe. *Daughters of America, or Women of the Century*. Boston: Cosimo, 2005, first published 1883.

Harrison, Mrs Burton. *Recollections Grave and Gay*. New York: Charles Scribner's Sons, 1911.

Harvey, Frederick, L., *History of the Washington National Monument and Washington National Monument Society*. Washington, D.C.: U.S. Government Printing Office, 1988. First published 1898.

Henderson, George Francis Robert. *Stonewall Jackson and the American Civil War*. New York: Da Capo Press, 1943.

Herold, David E. *The Trial of the Alleged Assassins and Conspirators at Washington*. Philadelphia: T. B. Peterson & Brothers, 1865.

Herr, Pamela. *Jessie Benton Frémont: American Woman of the 19th Century*. New York: Franklin Watts, 1987.

Hoehling, Adolph A. *Vicksburg: 47 Days of Siege*. New York: Stackpole Books, 1991.

Holloway, Laura Carter. *The Ladies of the White House*. Philadelphia: United States Publishing, 1870.

Holzer, Harold. *Lincoln and the Power of the Press: The War for Public Opinion*. New York: Simon & Schuster, 2014.

———. *The Lincoln Anthology: Great Writers on His Life and Legacy from 1860 to Now*. New York: Penguin Putnam, 2009.

Horn, Jonathan. *The Man Who Would Not Be Washington: Robert E. Lee's Civil War and His Decision That Changed American History*. New York: Simon & Schuster, 2015.

Howe, Julia Ward. *Reminiscences, 1819–1899*. Boston: Houghton Mifflin, 1900.

Jacob, Kathryn Allamong. *Capital Elites: High Society in Washington, D.C., after the Civil War*. Washington, D.C.: Smithsonian Institution Press, 1995.

———. *King of the Lobby*. Baltimore: Johns Hopkins University Press, 2010.

James, Edward T., Janet Wilson James, and Paul S. Boyer, eds. *Notable American Women, 1607–1950: A Biographical Dictionary*. Cambridge, MA: Harvard University Press, 1971.

Jernigan, Adam, ed. *A View of Lincoln. Abraham Lincoln and Elizabeth Keckley*, compiled by Amy Gary. Watermark.Publishing,

Johannsen, Robert W. ed *The Letters of Stephen A. Douglas*. Urbana: University of Illinois Press, 1961.

Jolly, Ellen Ryan. *Nuns of the Battlefield*. Providence, RI: Kessinger, 2006.

Katz, William Loren, ed. *The American Negro: His History and Literature*. New York: Arno Press, 1969.

Keckley, Elizabeth. *Behind the Scenes: Formerly a Slave, but More Recently Modiste, and a Friend to Mrs. Lincoln, or, Thirty Years a Slave and Four Years in the White House.* New York: G.W. Carleton & Co., 1868.

Keneally, Thomas. *American Scoundrel: The Life of the Notorious Civil War General Dan Sickles.* New York: Random House, 2003.

Kennicott, Philip. "The Freedom Conundrum." *Washington Post*, September 12, 2012.

———. "A War of All Heroes and No Villain." *Washington Post*, September 10, 2012.

Kimmel, Stanley Preston. *Mr. Lincoln's Washington.* New York: Coward-McCann, 1957.

Kingsland, Florence. *Etiquette for All Occasions.* New York: Doubleday, 1901.

Korda, Michael. *Ulysses S. Grant.* New York: HarperCollins, 2009.

Langguth, A. J. *After Lincoln: How the North Won the Civil War and Lost the Peace.* New York: Simon & Schuster, 2014.

———. *Driven West: Andrew Jackson and the Trail of Tears to the Civil War.* New York: Simon & Schuster, 2010.

Larson, Kate Clifford. *The Assassin's Accomplice: Mary Surratt and the Plot to Kill Abraham Lincoln.* New York: Basic Books, 2011.

Leale, Charles A. *Lincoln's Last Hours.* New York: Start Classics, 2014, first published 1909.

Lee, Captain Robert E. *Recollections and Letters of General Robert E. Lee.* digireads.com publication, 2004.

Lee, Elizabeth Blair, and Virginia Jeans Laas, ed. *Wartime Washington: The Civil War Letters of Elizabeth Blair Lee.* Urbana: University of Illinois Press, 1991.

Leech, Margaret. *Reveille in Washington: 1860–1865.* New York: Harper, 1941.

Leepson, Marc. *Desperate Engagement.* New York: St. Martin's Press: 2007.

Lincoln, Abraham, *The Writings of Abraham Lincoln*, New Haven, CT: Yale University Press, 2012.

Livermore, Mary Ashton Rice. *My Story of the War: A Woman's Narrative of Four Years Personal Experience as Nurse in the Union Army, and in Relief Work at Home, in Hospitals, Camps, and at the Front, During the War of the Rebellion.* Hartford, CT: A. D. Worthington, 1890.

Lockwood, John, and Charles Lockwood. *The Siege of Washington: The Untold Story of the Twelve Days That Shook the Union.* Oxford: Oxford University Press, 2011.

Logan, Mrs. John A. *Thirty Years in Washington: Or, Life and Scenes in Our National Capital.* Hartford, CT: A. D. Worthington, 1901.

Lomax, Elizabeth Lindsay. *Leaves from an Old Washington Diary, 1854–1863.* Mount Vernon, NY: EP Dutton, 1943.

London Anderson, Lucy. *North Carolina Women of the Confederacy*. Wilmington, NC: Winoca Press, 2006.

Massey, Mary Elizabeth. *Women in the Civil War*. Lincoln: University of Nebraska Press, 1966.

McAllister, Anna Shannon. *Ellen Ewing: Wife of General Sherman*. New York: Benziger Brothers, 1936.

McClure, James P., ed., Peg A. Lamphier and Erika Kreger, *"Spur Up Your Pegasus": Family Letters of Salmon, Kate, and Nettie Chase, 1844–1873*. Kent, OH: Kent State University Press, 2009.

McPherson, James M. *Battle Cry of Freedom: The Civil War Era*. Oxford: Oxford University Press, 1988.

———. *Embattled Rebel: Jefferson Davis as Commander in Chief*. New York: Penguin, 2014.

Meacham, Jon. *American Lion: Andrew Jackson in the White House*. New York: Random House, 2009.

Meigs, John Rodgers. *A Civil War Soldier of Christ and Country: The Selected Correspondence of John Rodgers Meigs, 1859–64*. Urbana.: University of Illinois Press, 2006.

Miller, David W. *Second Only to Grant: Quartermaster General Montgomery C. Meigs: a Biography*. Shippensburg, PA: White Mane, 2000.

Milton, George Fort. *The Eve of Conflict: Stephen A. Douglas and the Needless War*. New York: Octagon Books, 1963.

Mitchell, Mary. *Divided Town: A Study of Georgetown, D.C. During the Civil War*. Barre, MA: Barre Publishers, [1968].

Muhlenfeld, Elisabeth S. *Mary Boykin Chesnut: A Biography*. Baton Rouge: Louisiana State University Press, 1992.

Nagel, Paul C. *The Adams Women: Abigail and Louisa Adams, Their Sisters and Daughters*. Cambridge, MA: Harvard University Press, 1999.

———. *Descent from Glory: Four Generations of the John Adams Family*. Cambridge, MA: Harvard University Press, 1999.

Nicolay, John G. *A Short Life of Abraham Lincoln*. New York: Century, 1904.

Norgren, Jill. *Belva Lockwood: The Woman Who Would Be President*. New York: New York University Press, 2007.

Oates, Stephen B. *A Woman of Valor: Clara Barton and the Civil War*. New York: Free Press, 1994.

Oller, John. *American Queen: The Rise and Fall of Kate Chase Sprague—Civil War "Belle of the North" and Gilded Age Woman of Scandal*. Boston: Da Capo Press, 2014.

Parton, James, and Horace Greeley. *Eminent Women of the Age: Being Narratives of the Lives and Deeds of the Most Prominent Women of the Present Generation.* Hartford, CT: S. M. Betts, 1869.

Peacock, Virginia Tatnall. *Famous American Belles of the Nineteenth Century.* Philadelphia: J. B. Lippincott Company, 1901.

Pember, Phoebe Yates. *A Southern Woman's Story.* Columbia, SC: G. W. Carleton, 1879.

Peraino, Kevin. *Lincoln in the World: The Making of a Statesman and the Dawn of American Power.* New York: Random House, 2013.

Philipson, Rabbi David. *Letters of Rebecca Gratz.* Philadelphia: Jewish Publication Society of America, 1929.

Phillips, Catherine Coffin. *Jessie Benton Frémont: A Woman Who Made History.* Lincoln: University of Nebraska Press, 1935.

Pierson, Michael D. *Free Hearts and Free Homes: Gender and American Antislavery Politics.* Chapel Hill: University of North Carolina Press, 2003.

Poore, Benjamin Perley. *Perley's Reminiscences of Sixty Years in the national Metropolis.* Philadelphia: Hubbard Brothers, 1885.

Prout Janke, Lucinda. *A Guide to Civil War Washington, D.C.: The Capital of the Union.* Charleston, SC: The History Press, 2013.

Pryor, Elizabeth Brown. *Clara Barton: Professional Angel.* Philadelphia: University of Pennsylvania Press, 1987.

Pryor, Alton. *The Real Story of John C. Fremont.* Roseville, CA: Stagecoach, 2011.

Pryor, Sara Agnes Rice. *The Birth of the Nation: Jamestown, 1607.* New York: Macmillan, 1907.

———. *The Colonel's Story.* New York: Macmillan, 1911.

———. *The Mother of Washington and Her Times.* New York: Grosset & Dunlap, 1903.

———. *My Day: Reminiscences of a Long Life.* New York: Macmillan, 1909.

———. *Reminiscences of Peace and War.* London: Macmillan, 1905.

Randolph, Mary. *The Virginia Housewife, Or, Methodical Cook.* New York: Dover, 1993. First published 1824.

Rankin, Henry Bascom. *Personal Recollections of Abraham Lincoln.* New York: Putnam, 1916.

Remini, Robert V. *At the Edge of the Precipice: Henry Clay and the Compromise That Saved the Union.* New York: Basic Books, 2011.

Reynolds, Patrick M. *Strange but True Facts About the Civil War.* Lanham, MD: Taylor Trade, 2007.

Rhodes, James Ford. *History of the Civil War, 1861–1865.* New York: Courier, 2012. First published 1917.

Richards, Laura Elizabeth Howe, Maud Howe Elliott, and Florence Howe Hall. *Julia Ward Howe, 1819–1910*. Boston: Houghton Mifflin, 1915.

Ritchie, Donald A. *Press Gallery: Congress and the Washington Correspondents*. Cambridge, MA: Harvard University Press, 2009.

Roberts, Cokie. *Ladies of Liberty*. New York: Thorndike Press, 2008.

———. *We Are Our Mothers' Daughters*. Revised and expanded edition. New York: HarperCollins, 2009.

Roberts, Rebecca Boggs, and Sandra K. Schmidt. *Images of America: Historic Congressional Cemetery*. Charleston, SC: Arcadia, 2012.

Ropes, Hannah Anderson. *Civil War Nurse: The Diary and Letters of Hannah Ropes*. John R. Baumgardt, ed. Knoxville: University of Tennessee Press, 1993.

Ross, Ishbel. *First Lady of the South: The Life of Mrs. Jefferson Davis*. New York: Harper, 1958.

———. *The General's Wife: The Life of Mrs. Ulysses S. Grant*. New York: Dodd, Mead, 1959.

———. *The President's Wife: Mary Todd Lincoln, A Biography*. New York: Putnam, 1973.

———. *Proud Kate: Portrait of an Ambitious Woman*. New York: Harper, 1953.

———. *Rebel Rose: Life of Rose O'Neal Greenhow, Confederate Spy*. New York: Harper and Bros., 1954.

Sarmiento, F. L. *Life of Pauline Cushman, the Celebrated Union Spy and Scout*. Philadelphia: John E. Potter, 1865.

Scott, Anne Firor. *Natural Allies: Women's Associations in American History*. Urbana: University of Illinois Press, 1993.

Scott, Frances, and Anne Cipriani Webb. *Who is Markie? The Life of Martha Curtis Williams Carter, Cousin and Confidante of Robert E. Lee*. Westminster, MD: Heritage Books, 2007.

Seward, Janet W. *Personal Experiences of the Civil War*. Worcester, MA: F. S. Blanchard, 1899.

Shaw, John. *Crete and James: Personal letters of Lucretia and James Garfield*. East Lansing: Michigan State University Press, 1994.

Sherman, William Tecumseh. *Memoirs of General William T. Sherman*. New York: D. Appleton, 1889; ebook for Kindle by Charles River Editors.

Smith, Elbert B. *Francis Preston Blair*. New York: Free Press, 1980.

Smith, William Ernest. *The Francis Preston Blair Family in Politics*. Vol. 2. New York: Macmillan, 1933.

Somervill, Barbara A. *Clara Barton: Founder of the American Red Cross*. Minneapolis: Capstone, 2007.

Southworth, Emma Dorothy Eliza Nevitte. *Capitola's Peril.* Originally serialized in the *New York Ledger,* 1859; ebook by Kindle.

Soyer, Alexis. *The Modern Housewife: Or, Ménagère. Comprising Nearly One Thousand Receipts, for the Economic and Judicious Preparation of Every Meal of the Day, and Those for the Nursery and Sick Room; and Minute Directions for Family Management in All Its Branches. Illustrated with Engravings Including the Modern Housewife's Unique Kitchen, and Magic Stove.* New York: Simpkin, Marshall, 1851.

Spivack, Miranda S. "The Not-Quite-Free State: Maryland Dragged its feet on Emancipation During Civil War." *Washington Post,* September 13, 2013.

Stahr, Walter. *Seward: Lincoln's Indispensable Man.* New York: Simon & Schuster, 2013.

Staudenraus, P. J., ed. *Mr. Lincoln's Washington, Selections from the Writings of Noah Brooks, Civil War Correspondent.* South Brunswick, NJ: Thomas Yoseloff, 1967.

Stanton, Elizabeth Cady. *Elizabeth Cady Stanton as Revealed in Her Letters, Diary, and Reminiscences, Vol. II,* ed. Theodore Stanton and Harriet Stanton Blatch. New York: Harper & Brothers, 1922.

Stanton, Elizabeth Cady, Susan B. Anthony, and Matilda Joslyn Gage, eds. *History of Woman Suffrage.* Rochester, NY: Charles Mann, 1886.

Sterling, Ada. *A Belle of the Fifties: Memoirs of Mrs Clay, of Alabama, Covering Social and Political Life in Washington and the South, 1853–66, Put Into Narrative Form.* New York: Doubleday, 1904.

Stern, Milton. *Harriet Lane: America's First Lady.* Lulu.com, 2005.

Stoddard, William Osborn. *Inside the White House in War Times.* New York: C. L. Webster, 1890.

Strode, Hudson, ed. *Jefferson Davis: Private Letters, 1823–1889.* New York: Harcourt, Brace, 1966.

Sullivan, Eleanore C. *Georgetown Visitation Since 1799.* Washington, D.C.: Sullivan, 1975.

Sweetser, Kate Dickinson. *Famous Girls of the White House.* New York: Thomas Y. Crowell, 1930.

Swisshelm, Jane Grey Cannon. *Half a Century.* Chicago: Jansen, McClurg, 1880.

Swortzell, Lowell, and Tom Taylor. *Our American Cousin.* Bedford, MA: Dramatic, 1962. First published 1858.

Taliaferro, John. *All the Great Prizes: The Life of John Hay, from Lincoln to Roosevelt.* New York: Simon & Schuster, 2014.

Thomson, Mrs. A. T., and Philip Wharton. *The Queens of Society.* Philadelphia: Harper & Brothers, 1860.

Trindal, Elizabeth Steger. *Mary Surratt: An American Tragedy.* Gretna, LA: Pelican, 1996.

Tripler, Eunice, and Louis Augustus Arthur. *Eunice Tripler: Some Notes of Her Personal Recollections.* New York: Grafton Press, 1910.

Trollope, Anthony. *North America.* 3 vols. Leipzig: Tauchnitz, 1862.

Trollope, Frances. *Domestic Manners of the Americans.* London: Whitaker, Treacher, 1832.

Truth, Sojourner. *Narrative of Sojourner Truth.* Toronto: Penguin, 1998, first published 1850

Venet, Wendy Hamand. *A Strong-Minded Woman: The Life of Mary Livermore.* Amherst: University of Massachusetts Press, 2005.

Wakeman, Sarah Rosetta. *An Uncommon Soldier: The Civil War Letters of Sarah Rosetta Wakeman, Alias Private Lyons Wakeman, 153rd Regiment, New York State Volunteers.* Oxford: Oxford University Press, 1994.

Waugh, John C. *Surviving the Confederacy: Rebellion, Ruin, and Recovery; Roger and Sara Pryor During the Civil War.* New York: Houghton Mifflin Harcourt, 2002.

Weinstein, Allen, and David Rubel. *The Story of America: Freedom and Crisis from Settlement to Superpower.* London: Pearson Prentice Hall, 2002.

Wharton, Anne Hollingsworth. *Social Life in the early Republic.* Philadelphia: J. B. Lippincott, 1902.

White, Annie Randall. *Twentieth Century Etiquette: An Up-to-Date Book for Polite Society.* [N.p.: n.pub.], 1901.

White, Barbara A. *Visits with Lincoln: Abolitionists Meet the President at the White House.* Lanham, MD: Lexington Books, 2011.

Whyte, James H. *The Uncivil War: Washington During the Reconstruction, 1865–1878.* New York: Twayne, 1958.

Windle, Mary Jane. *Life in Washington: And Life Here and There.* Philadelphia: J. B. Lippincott, 1859.

Winik, Jay. *April 1865: The Month That Saved America.* New York: Harper-Collins, 2002.

Winkle, Kenneth J. *Lincoln's Citadel: The Civil War in Washington, DC.* New York: Norton, 2013.

Illustration Credits

Illustration Credits in Order of Appearance

Introduction: Library of Congress, Prints & Photographs Division, Civil War Photographs, [LC-DIG-ppmsca-07302].

Chapter One: National Portrait Gallery, Smithsonian Institution / Art Resource, NY.

Chapter Two: Granger, NYC—All rights reserved; Granger, NYC—All rights reserved.

Chapter Three: Picture History; National Portrait Gallery, Smithsonian Institution / Art Resource, NY.

Chapter Four: Granger, NYC—All rights reserved; Library of Congress, Prints & Photographs Division, [LC_USZ62_108564].

Chapter Five: Library of Congress, Prints & Photographs Division, [LC_USZ62_108564]; Courtesy of Blair House, The President's Guest House, U.S. Department of State.

Chapter Six: Picture History; © Medford Historical Society Collection/CORBIS

Chapter Seven: © CORBIS; Granger, NYC—All rights reserved.

Chapter Eight: Library of Congress, Prints & Photographs Division, [LC-DIG-ppmsca-19221]; Apic / Hulton Archive / Getty Images.

Chapter Nine: Library of Congress, Prints & Photographs Division, [LC_USZC4_7988]; strph480020010, William Emerson Strong Photograph

Album, David M. Rubenstein Rare Book & Manuscript Library, Duke University.

Epilogue: Library of Congress, Prints & Photographs Division, Brady-Handy Photograph Collection, [LC_DIG_cwpbh_03248].

Index

About the author

About the book

Read on

Insights,
Interviews
& More . . .

Meet Cokie Roberts

COKIE ROBERTS is a political commentator for ABC News and NPR. She has won countless awards and in 2008 was named a "Living Legend" by the Library of Congress. She is the author of the *New York Times* bestsellers *We Are Our Mothers' Daughters, Founding Mothers, Ladies of Liberty,* and, with her husband, journalist Steven V. Roberts, *From This Day Forward* and *Our Haggadah*. She lives just outside Washington, D.C.

Cokie Roberts
The Unexpected Revelations of *Capital Dames*

HERE'S WHAT'S WONDERFUL about delving into history from the female perspective: one woman writes about another that she was "perfectly happy." Why? "My first marriage was for love, and it was mine as fully as I could wish; my second for money, and Heaven was as good to me in this instance; my third was for position, and that too is mine. What more could I ask?" Now that would give me a good giggle in any era, but it's so completely unexpected from a mid-nineteenth century woman that it makes me laugh out loud. And in researching *Capital Dames* I continually came upon the unexpected.

In my day job as a journalist covering Washington, D.C., and politics, I tell the current American story. But to do that well, I need to know what came before, to know our history. For too long that history has been written about only half of the human race, so it's by definition an incomplete portrayal of the events and ideas shaping the nation. I set about trying to remedy that several years ago with the publication in 2004 of *Founding Mothers* and then in 2008 with *Ladies of Liberty*. In writing those books I learned that the valiant women during our country's fight for independence in the eight long years of the Revolutionary War—familiar women like Martha ▶

3

The Unexpected Revelations of *Capital Dames* (continued)

Washington and less well known patriots like Sarah Livingston Jay—made it possible for the men to do what they did, to become the heroes we call the Founding Fathers. And then, when the fledgling government was threatened almost instantly by the kind of partisanship and polarization we see today, it took women like Dolley Madison to hold the country together. And a woman like Sacajawea to explore the expanding territory. And other women, like Rebecca Gratz and Mother Elizabeth Seton, to establish the schools and social-service agencies in order to make the American promise accessible to more and more people, including girls.

But of course it took the great horror of the Civil War, with its more than six hundred thousand deaths, to rid the nation of the sin of slavery, as Abigail Adams defined it, and extend the rights fought for by the Founders to African-Americans. And as the country embarked on the sesquicentennial commemoration of that war, I started thinking about what it might also have meant for women. Had it affected the place of women in society the way I knew World War II had done? Was there some Victorian version of Rosie the Riveter? I found that, in fact, there was. Dangerous jobs in the arsenals were considered women's work. And what about the "government girls" who poured into Washington during WWII?

Did they have a counterpart? Yes, it turned out, women came to the Capital City to toil at the Treasury Department cutting banknotes, and by the end of the war a contemporary journalist reported, "Women of education and the finest intellectual gifts are to be found in every department." Later in the century, reflecting on the conflict's impact on women, Clara Barton, an intrepid battlefield nurse during that war and later the founder of the American Red Cross, concluded, "Woman was at least fifty years in advance of the normal position which continued peace . . . would have assigned her."

To get a handle on the women's shifting roles, I concentrated on the place I know best—Washington, D.C. And I started with the wives, sisters, and friends of politicians, the women who described themselves as the "belles" of society. I learned how deeply political they were, how engaged in the questions of the day, but engaged mainly through the men. The war changed that. Women came to Washington to affect policy themselves, and the belles blossomed into purposeful suffragists, journalists, reformers, and writers. The wit and wisdom of their writing, much of it never before published, intrigued and delighted me. These dames were indeed "capital," in all senses of the word. ᘒ

Have You Read?
More by Cokie Roberts

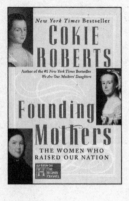

FOUNDING MOTHERS

A *New York Times* bestseller, *Founding Mothers* provides an intimate and illuminating look at the fervently patriotic and passionate women whose tireless pursuits on behalf of their families—and their country—proved just as crucial to the forging of a new nation as the rebellion that established it.

While much has been written about the men who signed the Declaration of Independence, battled the British, and framed the Constitution, the wives, mothers, sisters, and daughters they left behind have been little noticed by history. Number-one *New York Times* bestselling author Cokie Roberts brings us women who fought in the Revolutionary War as valiantly as the men did, often defending their very doorsteps. Drawing upon personal correspondence, private journals, and even favored recipes, Roberts reveals the often surprising stories of these fascinating women, bringing to life the everyday trials and extraordinary triumphs of individuals like Abigail Adams, Mercy Otis Warren, Deborah Read Franklin, Eliza Pinckney, Catherine Littlefield Green, Esther DeBerdt Reed, and Martha Washington—proving that without our exemplary women, the new country might have never survived.

LADIES OF LIBERTY

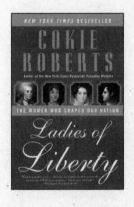

In this eye-opening companion volume to her acclaimed history *Founding Mothers*, number-one *New York Times* bestselling author and renowned political commentator Cokie Roberts brings to life the extraordinary accomplishments of women who laid the groundwork for a better society. Recounted with insight and humor, and drawing on personal correspondence, private journals, and other primary sources, many of them previously unpublished, here are the fascinating and inspiring true stories of first ladies and freethinkers, educators and explorers. Featuring an exceptional group of women—including Abigail Adams, Dolley Madison, Rebecca Gratz, Louise Livingston, Sacagawea, and others—*Ladies of Liberty* sheds new light on the generation of heroines, reformers, and visionaries who helped shape our nation, finally giving these extraordinary ladies the recognition they so greatly deserve.

WE ARE OUR MOTHERS' DAUGHTERS

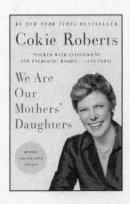

Renowned political commentator Cokie Roberts examines the nature of women's roles through the revealing lens of her personal experience. From mother to mechanic, sister to soldier, Roberts reveals how much progress has now been made—and how much further we have to go. An updated and expanded tenth-anniversary edition of this essay collection includes a diverse new cast of women, offering tremendous insight into the opportunities and challenges that women encounter today.

In a series of new profiles and revealing updates, Roberts reflects upon the number of female achievers who have graced the public stage in the past decade. In addition to the illuminating and sometimes surprising history of women in a variety of fields, several chapters also introduce us to some of the fascinating women she has encountered during the course of her reporting career—including Hillary Rodham Clinton, Nancy Pelosi, Laura Bush, Billie Jean King, Michelle Rhee, and Dorothy Height. Looking to the future, Roberts focuses on the question of "What next?," exploring how several women—including herself—have begun to define themselves in the next stages of their lives. She also relates moving anecdotes about the women in her personal life, including her mother, former congresswoman Lindy Boggs.

Sensitive, straightforward, and perceptive, *We Are Our Mothers' Daughters* celebrates the new diversity of choices and perspectives available to women today, and affirms the bonds of sisterhood over the centuries— a vital, powerful interconnection among all women, regardless of background.

FROM THIS DAY FORWARD,
with Steven V. Roberts

After fifty years together, Cokie and Steve Roberts know something about marriage, and after fifty distinguished years in journalism they know how to write about it. In *From This Day Forward*, Cokie and Steve weave their personal stories of matrimony into a wider reflection on the state of marriage in American today.

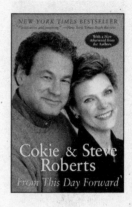

Here they write with the same conversational style that catapulted Cokie's *We Are Our Mother's Daughters* to the top of the *New York Times* bestseller list. They ruminate on their early worries about their different faiths—she's Catholic, he's Jewish— and describe their wedding day at Cokie's childhood home. They discuss the struggle to balance careers and parenthood, and how they compromise when they disagree. They also tell the stories of other American marriages: that of John and Abigail Adams, and those of pioneers, slaves, and immigrants. They offer stories of broken marriages as well, of contemporary families living through the "divorce revolution." Taken together, these tales reveal the special nature of the wedding bond in America. Wise and funny, this book is more than an endearing chronicle of a loving marriage—it is a story of all husbands and wives, and how they support and strengthen each other.

OUR HAGGADAH, with Steven V. Roberts

New York Times bestsellers Cokie Roberts and Steven V. Roberts offer a unique, personalized vision of the traditional Passover Haggadah, combining their own family traditions with favorites from other families in a fun, intimate guide written especially for couples of mixed faiths. A fresh and informative tour through the rituals of the Pesach Seder as well as a compelling rendition of the Exodus story, *Our Haggadah* is the perfect book for any interfaith family celebrating Passover. Readers of the couple's compelling account of their marriage, *From This Day Forward* ("Instructive and inspiring."—*New York Times Book Review*), as well as Cokie Roberts' *We Are Our Mothers' Daughters* and Steven V. Roberts' *My Father's Houses*, will be enthralled by this glimpse into the couple's inclusive Passover rituals.

Discover great authors, exclusive offers, and more at hc.com.